Sharing the Sacred

Sharing the Sacred

Practicing Pluralism in Muslim North India

Anna Bigelow

OXFORD

UNIVERSITY PRESS

2010

OXFORD
UNIVERSITY PRESS

Oxford University Press, Inc., publishes works that further
Oxford University's objective of excellence
in research, scholarship, and education.

Oxford   New York
Auckland   Cape Town   Dar es Salaam   Hong Kong   Karachi
Kuala Lumpur   Madrid   Melbourne   Mexico City   Nairobi
New Delhi   Shanghai   Taipei   Toronto

With offices in
Argentina   Austria   Brazil   Chile   Czech Republic   France   Greece
Guatemala   Hungary   Italy   Japan   Poland   Portugal   Singapore
South Korea   Switzerland   Thailand   Turkey   Ukraine   Vietnam

Published by Oxford University Press, Inc.
198 Madison Avenue, New York, New York 10016

www.oup.com

Library of Congress Cataloging-in-Publication Data
Bigelow, Anna.
Sharing the sacred : practicing pluralism in Muslim North India / Anna Bigelow.
p. cm.
Includes bibliographical references.
ISBN 978-0-19-536823-9
1. Religious pluralism—India—Maler Kotla—History. 2. Maler Kotla (India)—History.
3. Maler Kotla (India)—Religion. 4. Sadruddin, Sheikh, fl. 1449-1508. I. Title.
BL2015.R44B55 2009
201'.50954552—dc22   2009018035

1 3 5 7 9 8 6 4 2
Printed in the United States of America
on acid-free paper

Dedicated to the memory and inspiration of my grandmother, Alice Whiting Ellis (Ph.D. Classics, Harvard, 1936)

Though much is taken, much abides

Preface

My first visit to India was in 1992, a watershed year for communal relations in India. On December 6, Hindu militants, believing that the sixteenth-century Babri Masjid was built on the birthplace of the god Rama, tore down the mosque. India seemed to explode. At the time, I was in Bihar, a state neighboring Uttar Pradesh where Ayodhya is located. In the pilgrimage town of Bodh Gaya, the mixed population of Hindus, Buddhists, and Muslims remained largely unscathed by the violence that wracked India for months. There was no curfew, and people went about their business unimpeded. There were rumors of things happening in Gaya, the large town to the west, and of course the news from elsewhere in India was chilling as thousands died in riots. In January 1993—a full month after the triggering events—I and many other arriving passengers had to spend a night in the railway station in Ahmedabad, Gujarat, because curfews and ongoing clashes there prevented our leaving. These experiences led me to wonder about many things. Of course I wondered how it was that neighbors could "turn on each other," as the description is commonly given. But I was also curious why some places were calm while others were troubled. How did Ayodhya go from being a sleepy pilgrimage town where intrareligious competition was a bigger problem than interreligious strife to one of the most hotly contested pieces of earth in India? What was the role of the shared sacred site itself (the mosque/divine birthplace) in the conflict? Most of all, I wanted to understand why, given that there are far more peacefully shared religious sites in India than conflicted ones, some work while others explode? These questions remained with me throughout graduate school and eventually led me to Malerkotla, Punjab—a place where certain conditions for conflict exist, but harmony by and large prevails. This book explores the ways in which residents and pilgrims to the tomb shrine of the Sufi saint who founded the town explain the situation in Malerkotla. It is my hope that we can learn something from finely grained studies such as this one about specific places where people have learned how to live together with all of their differences and similarities, their agreements and disagreements, and their cooperative efforts as well as their competitive interests.

After fixing on my interest in studying Muslims in India and shared religious spaces, I did not intend to do research in Punjab. Like many others, I was under the impression there were few Muslims in Punjab since Partition in 1947. So I was very fortunate that one of my advisors, Gurinder Singh Mann, took me to Malerkotla in the summer of 1999. His introduction to the town and to the Ghazanfar Ali Khan family made my study possible. On that first visit to Malerkotla, with the UCSB Punjab Studies Program, we went to several places: the tomb of the Sufi saint, popularly known as Haider Shaykh, the 'Id prayer grounds, the Namdhari memorial, and one of the disintegrating palaces of the former rulers. Each place provided some insight into what people from Malerkotla think is important to show visitors about their town. The visit to the tomb shrine, or *dargah*, of the founder Haider Shaykh established the miraculous, blessed foundations of the community. The presence of Muslims and non-Muslims at the tomb was not unusual, but in post-Partition Punjab, the fact that Muslims who descended from the saint still existed in large numbers set the site apart from the many other tomb shrines in Indian Punjab, some of which are now managed by non-Muslims. The 'Id Gah prayer grounds mark the town as one of Punjab's most substantial Muslim communities, requiring a large space and needing to expand. The Namdhari memorial is a testimony to the complicated history of the British Raj and the martyrdom of sixty-nine members of this Sikh sect at the order of the British. The site also hinted, though I didn't know it at the time, of the more complicated history of interreligious relations in Malerkotla than that presented to outsiders. The palace, in its fading glory, and the audience given to us by the last nawab's youngest wife, Sajjida Begum, evoked the powerful legacy of Malerkotla's ruling family and the kingdom that lasted from the time of the Shaykh in the fifteenth century until the 1948 dissolution of the princely states following the independence of India from British rule in 1947. The palace spoke simultaneously of ancient power and a declining way of life, as the last nawab had no children, and the political ground was shifting.

All in all, that first visit introduced me to certain aspects of the complicated web of Malerkotla's history and its idealized identity, but it was not until I came back in the summer of 2000 to stay for seventeen months that I began to glimpse this complexity in detail. It was an interesting time to be doing field research on a Muslim community in India. Politically, the central Indian government at the time was dominated by a coalition led by the Bharatiya Janata Party (BJP), a Hindu nationalist party. A Sikh nationalist party, the Shiromani Akali Dal (SAD-Badal) controlled the state government of Punjab in coalition with the BJP. The member of the Legislative Assembly (MLA) from Malerkotla was a Muslim partisan of the SAD and a descendent of Haider Shaykh, the saintly founder. Relations with Pakistan remained on edge since the Kargil conflict in 1999 and the nuclear tests of 1998, and there were sporadic anti-Muslim incidents throughout my time there. Whenever tensions flared domestically or internationally, the eyes of Punjab turned toward Malerkotla—the only major Muslim majority community in the state.

For many months I lived in Malerkotla, going about daily life as a participant-observer. I lived with a locally prominent family who had connections to the tomb of Shaykh Sadruddin Sadri Jahan but who were not directly involved with its management and operations. Over time I got to know people in all neighborhoods and all communities, following leads to meet new people and revisiting people I had met before. I would go to the various holy places in town, attend all the festivals and holidays I could, and follow up with those whom I encountered. After a while, as the only foreigner in the town, I was asked to come to weddings and other events, which were both educational and heartwarming. I had many amazing experiences that did not make it into my study. I stayed up much of the night with some Namdharis at the *mela* observing the 1872 martyrdom of many Namdharis by the British. I played cards in the courtyard with the quite elderly "Tonk-walli Begum," another of the last nawab's five wives, while peacocks strolled around and paint and bricks sheered off the mansion around us. I was at the closing of a reading of the *Ramcaritmanas* at a small, very old temple when the smoke from the *havan* (a blessing ceremony involving a sacred fire) drove a swarm of bees out of a tree and created a panic among the people assembled. I ate guavas fresh from the trees and tried to make Punjab's famous corn flatbread *makki roti* without its falling apart (I failed). All of these and many more amazing experiences are due to the *mehman niwazi*, the incredible hospitality of Malerkotla's citizens. I feel enormously fortunate to have been welcomed into this community.

Indeed, my debts of gratitude in this project are many. My field research was funded by an International Dissertation Research Fellowship from the Social Science Research Council and a Junior Fellowship from the American Institute of Indian Studies. Both institutions held fellows conferences that were enormously helpful. I received a Kline International Studies grant from the University of California and writing fellowships from the Interdisciplinary Humanities Center and the Graduate Division at UC, Santa Barbara. The Religious Studies Department at UCSB was also supportive of my research and work in countless ways, personal and financial. In this regard I thank first my primary advisor, Dwight Reynolds, and my committee: Juan Campo, Roger Friedland, R. Stephen Humphreys, Gurinder Singh Mann, and David White. I would also like to thank Catherine L. Albanese, Magda Campo, Richard Hecht, Victoria Kline, Charles Li, and Sally Lombrozo. Versions of some of the material in this book have appeared as "Saved by the Saint: Refusing and Reversing Partition in Muslim North India," *Journal of Asian Studies* 68, 2 (2009) and "Muslim Punjab: The History and Significance of Malerkotla," *International Journal of Punjab Studies* 12, 1 (2005).

In India I am indebted to the offices and staff people at the Punjab State Archives, Patiala; the Archaeological Survey of India Office, Chandigarh; the National

Archives, Delhi; the Oriental and India Office Collection at the British Library; the Punjabi University; Punjab University; and Guru Nanak Dev University Libraries. I also thank Dr. Muhammad Rizwan al-Haque of the Central Waqf Board. Roopinder Singh and his office at the *Tribune* in Chandigarh were helpful and unfailingly kind. At Punjabi University I especially thank Dr. Darshan Singh, Dr. Shivani Sharma, and Akhil Sharma for their friendship and support. In Chandigarh I thank Dr. Indu Banga, Dr. J. S. Grewal, and, above all, Dr. Khalid Mohammad and his family. A million thanks to Gurmeet Rai and everyone at the Cultural Resources Conservation Initiative in New Delhi, especially Savyasaachi. In Malerkotla I am grateful to many, including Dr. Mahmud Alam, Amjad Ali, Anwar Ali, Shaykh Azadar Hussain, Mr. Chamanlal Jain, Azmat Ali Khan, Ikhlaq Ahmad Khan, Dr. Mohammad Hayat Khan, Khalid Kifayatullah, Dr. Jamil, Dr. Zeenatullah Javed, Dr. Indu Malhotra, Anwar Mehboob, Satnam Singh Sodhi, Dr. Muhammad Rafi, Hafiz Ghulam Rasul, the late Maulana Muhammad Abdul Rauf, Chaudhry Ahmad Shah, Afsha Sheikh, Sardar Gurlovleen Singh Sidhu, Dr. Anila Sultana, Mufti Fazlur Rehman Hilal Usmani, and Khalid Zubaidy. My greatest debt in Malerkotla is to the Ghazanfar Ali Khan family who fed, housed, and accepted me as a member of the family: Khan Sahib, Nusrat Begum, Saulat Jahan, Shalu, Neelu, Bushra, Sonia, Muzammil, Zaid, and the extended Khan clan. I am especially grateful to Dr. Neelam Sherwani for her invaluable assistance and friendship.

At Oxford University Press, I especially would like to thank Cynthia Read for her faith in adopting this project and seeing it through to publication. I am also enormously appreciative of the professionalism and patience of Paul Hobson, Mariana Templin, and Norma McLemore. The feedback from the anonymous reviewers was extremely perceptive and helpful. Many others worked behind the scenes to bring the book to print, and I am grateful for their efforts as well. In spite of their help and that of many other readers and interlocutors, all errors, mistakes, and shortcomings are mine alone.

I am very grateful to many friends and colleagues. In particular, I must thank Rob Rozehnal for his thoughtful and helpful reading of an early draft. I also thank William Adler, Tariq al-Jamil, Andrew Mullen Bidwell, Charles Bidwell, Jason Bivins, Allison Busch, Chip Callahan, Julia Clarke, Mary Kathleen Cunningham, Dana Damico, Esme Damico-Lassman, Mark and Florie Elmore, Amy Boiselle FitzGerald, Sandy Frietag, David Gilmartin, Karey Harwood, Elizabeth Howie, the Kapila family, Jeff Kasser, Ann Marie Kennedy, Akram Khater, Karen Kletter, Scott Kugle, Kent Lassmann, Katie McShane, Farina Mir, Rob Mitchell, Libby Kleine Modern, John Lardas Modern, Lee Moore, Rebecca Mullen, Devin and Marsha Orgeron, Michael Pendlebury, Ellen Posman, Rob Rozehnal, Omid Safi, Neil Schmid, Tony Stewart, Wendy Wiseman, and Pete Yancey. Thanks to my family: Isabel Bigelow, Luis Castro, Lucia Alice Castro Bigelow, Isabel Kurzon, Charles Kurzon, Nick Kurzon, Prill Ellis, Bob Crabtree, Ben Crabtree, Sam Crabtree, and Zoe Valentine. Finally, I am eternally grateful to my parents, Deborah Ellis Bigelow and Llewellyn Bigelow, for everything.

Contents

TAJIKISTAN

AFGHANISTAN

CHINA

PAKISTAN

PUNJAB

CHINA
(Tibet)

NEPAL

BHUTAN

BANGLADESH

INDIA

MYANMAR

Arabian
Sea

Bay
of
Bengal

Andaman
Sea

SRI LANKA

INDIAN OCEAN

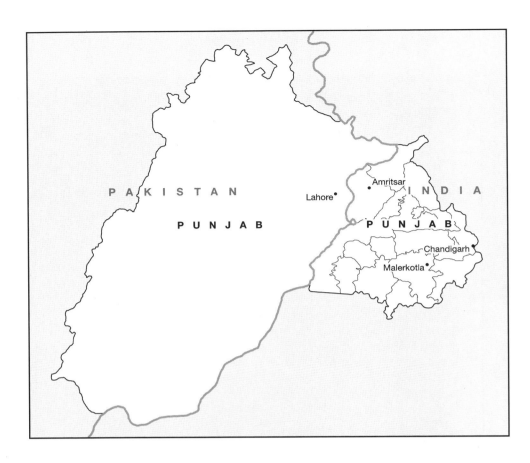

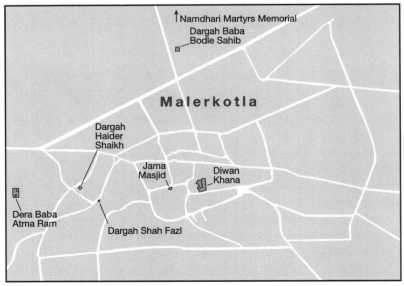

Sharing the Sacred

Introduction

> The nature of Malerkotla is such that the people easily move towards peace.
>
> —Abdullah, retired schoolteacher

MALERKOTLA is not a utopia. But when this town in North India appears in the media, it is usually labeled with headlines such as "Where Peace Reigns Supreme" or "Oasis of Tolerance" or "Cradle of Love and Friendship," from which a reader might assume that this is some kind of earthly paradise.[1] Many residents, including the retired schoolteacher Abdullah, quoted above, reinforce this idealized image, asserting that the fundamental nature of the town is inclined towards peace.[2] As the only Muslim-majority town in Indian Punjab, Malerkotla has a high profile, and projecting a positive and nonthreatening image is necessary to maintain its exemplary status as a zone of peace. The production and proliferation of ethically emblematic stories about Malerkotla's past imparts togetherness and connects the Muslim-majority town to the wider region and the state, projecting a value structure that exemplifies the secular ideal promoted by the Indian state. It turns out that a great deal of work goes into producing and maintaining this stable multireligious community. This book tells the story of the day to day peace workers of Malerkotla, the histories that enable and complicate their efforts, and the strategies they employ to achieve a dynamic equilibrium of peaceful pluralism.

Malerkotla experiences all the normal trials of life for an industrial town in central Punjab. It is a former princely state in a region deeply divided by Partition in 1947 and scarred by Sikh separatism in the 1980s and 1990s. Although India and Punjab both struggle with religious tensions, discrimination, and violence, Malerkotla inspires residents and visitors alike to speak of the *bhaichara* (brotherhood) that characterizes the collective identity of the town. As in many other places around the world, the residents of the town have achieved what sociologist James Aho termed "tension-wisdom," the ability to manage stress when it arises.[3] Tension-wisdom and an ethos of brotherhood have sustained Malerkotla through the challenges that inevitably arise, providing precedents and motivating ideals to the community.

Depending on whom you ask, the reasons for Malerkotla's peace and brotherhood vary. Over the course of research there in 1999, 2000–2001, and 2004 I heard a wide range of explanations, sometimes several from the same person, but I rarely found dissenting voices. Many residents and visitors asserted that Malerkotla is peaceful because it is blessed by its fifteenth-century founder, the Suhrawardi Sufi saint Shaykh Sadruddin Sadri Jahan, popularly known as Haider Shaykh. Others claimed that the tenth Sikh guru Gobind Singh blessed Malerkotla in the eighteenth century after the nawab (ruler) of Malerkotla spoke up in defense of his captive sons before they were executed. Some asserted that it was the will of God that no trouble between religions occurs here. Others said that since everyone here is a minority in some way, there is an enlightened self-interest in maintaining the peace. Still others credited the pacific nature of the citizens and their core values of justice and harmony, the good governance of the rulers of the erstwhile princely state, or their collective interest in political and economic stability. These local theories all point to more elaborate theories of causation, running the gamut from the political to the spiritual to the moral to the material. Taken together, these ideas illuminate how Malerkotla's current harmony is constructed and made sense of by both residents and visitors. This network of causation itself promotes peaceful pluralism by allowing individuals and groups to produce or locate themselves within autochthonous theories; the availability of multiple explanations allows Malerkotla's residents and interested visitors to become stakeholders in the production of peace.

The facts that the town's pacific reputation is newsworthy and that it appears regularly in local and national media speak to a deep desire on the part of many Indians for a place like Malerkotla to exist, a place that exemplifies the promise of India to embrace its multireligious, multiethnic society. Independent India's first prime minister, Jawaharlal Nehru, envisioned this promise as a unity born of diversity. "Some kind of a dream of unity has occupied the mind of India since the dawn of civilization," Nehru said. "That unity was not conceived as something imposed from outside, a standardization of externals or even of beliefs. It was something deeper and, within its fold, the widest tolerance of belief and custom was practiced and every variety acknowledged and even encouraged."[4] The embrace of diversity is in many ways integral to the national identity, even as it is imperfectly realized.

With the establishment of its constitution in 1950, India proclaimed itself a secular republic.[5] It is important to recognize that secularism is a contested concept in contemporary social theory. In particular, Talal Asad and others have raised compelling critiques of the notion, highlighting its Western colonial genealogy and suggesting that religious discourses cannot be separated from other personal and social identity constructing processes.[6] However, in general usage in India, *secularism* usually refers not to the separation of religion and state based on a post-Enlightenment model of the relations between state and citizen, public and private, but to the equality of distribution of state services to all religious communities and equal representation and respect in the public sphere. Indeed, the mythology of secularism is a core element in the building of India's national identity. Ashis Nandy sees secularism as "modern India's way of 'understanding' the religious tolerance that survives outside modern India" and indicates a "loss of confidence in the traditional codes of religious tolerance."[7] For those who adopt secularism as an ideology, religion is seen as the enemy, the source of backward thinking and communalized social action that threatens to undermine an Indian polity that no longer recognizes its own heritage of tolerance. Communalism in the South Asian sense refers to a politicized religious chauvinism and is often contrasted with secularism by social scientists as a way to identify political actors who organize around and for the interests of particular religious groups. However, somewhat more subtly, Nandy argues that secularism is actually the "disowned double" of communalism, inasmuch as it sets up an opposition and antagonism toward people whose lifeways are profoundly shaped by belief and tradition. As an activist and a scholar, Nandy tries to get past the opposition and find resources within traditional Indian values that promote an authentic tolerance. Although such values do exist (and one often reads articles extolling, for example, the shared devotional religious culture of *bhakti* and Sufism) certain aspects of India's version of secularism are in fact institutionalized by the state. And as Partha Chatterjee points out, the problem of secularism vis-à-vis India's minorities is that it is structurally contradictory. There is deep conflict in the fact that India's ruling elites have historically been involved in supporting and regulating religious institutions even as they, and the Indian Constitution, assert the importance of separating religion and politics as a fundamental principle.[8] The ambivalent simultaneity of separation and regulation is evidenced by the fact that India's Constitution enshrines many more rights for religious minorities in India than does the U.S. Constitution, prohibiting religious discrimination and guaranteeing freedom of practice, propagation, management of institutions, preservation of language and culture, and the establishment of educational institutions, which must be given equal state support.[9] The failure of the supposedly secular state to remain neutral toward all religious entities and institutions resulted in its being "seen as hopelessly compromised by its legal protection of the differential and allegedly backward practices of the minority communities."[10] Hindu communalists see secularism at the state level as appeasing minorities and question whether Muslims and Christians in particular, as members of faiths that originated outside South Asia, can be truly Indian. Sikh communalists see secularism as another word for Hindu majoritarianism and seek a homeland of their own separate from both India and Pakistan. Muslim communalists see secularism as a screen behind which India's Hindu majority determines national policy.

The Moral Past and the Frame of Peace

As a Muslim-majority town, Malerkotla's well-publicized reputation for inter-religious harmony makes it a useful example of the multireligious Indian polity at its best. Thus it becomes a kind of leitmotif in certain discourses about Islam in India, the legacy of Partition, and the possibility of true secularism. In addition to the proliferation of news stories proclaiming Malerkotla to be an "oasis of tolerance" in which "brotherhood is handed down as tradition," in 1999 AIM Television produced a documentary called "The Legend of Malerkotla."[11] The film portrayed the town as mythically harmonious and as potentially wielding an influence far greater than what one might expect from a place seven hours from Delhi and three from Punjab's capital, Chandigarh. In film and in print, then, Malerkotla appears as the poster child of communal harmony. The following chapters elucidate how, in a certain sense, this ideal is fulfilled. Residents and visitors collectively produce a romanticized version of the past by selectively mining the town's history for figures and events whose exemplary qualities provide useful models for people today. This is a deliberate process that produces a *moral past*—a particular version of historic actors and events that serves the ethical interests of actors in the present. The moral past is articulated in the present in conversations, anecdotes, testimonials, public addresses, media accounts, and historical writings. These articulations of the moral past take place in the shared civic and sacred spaces of Malerkotla such as the local Peace Committee, the Rotary Club, and the integrated neighborhoods, and at the tomb of the town's Sufi founder. This study exposes the choreography behind the subtle dance of collective life in a town that is in some ways unique in present-day Punjab but in other ways is unremarkable.

Malerkotla is unique because it is the only significant Muslim majority center in Indian Punjab.[12] Not only did most Muslims stay during the Partition of India and Pakistan in 1947, but also during that violent division and migration no one was killed in the borders of what was then a Muslim-ruled princely state. This is quite unusual in Punjab, the state that experienced the most intense violence of Partition, during which hundreds of thousands of people died.[13] In the six decades since Partition there have been conflicts between religious groups in Malerkotla. But by and large the residents managed those tensions extremely well, avoiding serious violence and making speedy reparations and remediation when necessary. Though post-Partition communal relations are generally positive, in the turbulent 1920s and 1930s there were several clashes between Hindus and Muslims in Malerkotla, as there were all over India as the Independence movement gained ground and the British lost it. The town today is an agricultural and industrial center in its district, Sangrur. And like many former princely states, the erstwhile ruling family has remained politically powerful, dominating post-Partition electoral politics. So in these regards the town is like anywhere else, both unique and similar, neither incomparable nor identical. Precisely because Malerkotla is not altogether an anomaly, its success is worth understanding, both as a corrective to the prejudice held by many within India and without that Muslim culture is violent, antidemocratic, and fundamentalist, and as a crucial insight into how stable multireligious communities function on a daily basis.

Three events in Malerkotla's history stand out as constitutive and representative of the town's peaceful nature: the fifteenth-century foundation of the settlement by the Sufi saint Haider Shaykh, the eighteenth-century blessing from the Sikh guru, and the peace during Partition in 1947. These three watershed moments are the most frequently cited reasons for the town's general peace and as such take on a rich and varied patina through many tellings by residents and visitors from all backgrounds. Examining these three key events clarifies how residents and observers of Malerkotla interpret their history and experience in light of their reputation as a communal oasis. First, like many places in India and elsewhere, Malerkotla has a myth of its origins that connects the character of the town today to its sacred beginnings. Public ritual and collective identification often involves Haider Shaykh and his tomb shrine (see fig. I.1). This tomb complex, or *dargah,* is owned and managed by descendants of the shaykh but is visited and patronized by non-Muslims as well as Muslims. Though the mere existence of this site neither explains Malerkotla's overall harmony nor sets it apart from countless other places where such shrines exist throughout South Asia, the *dargah* of Haider Shaykh is a key signifying site in the construction of Malerkotla's shared moral past, ethical framework, and collective identity. As an important conceptual and physical zone of interreligious encounter, the tomb shrine provides a window into how such interactions unfold. In particular, locals and visitors credit the saint with the preservation of the town during Partition and the ethos of harmony that prevails. As one elderly woman in the lineage of the saint said, "A lot of Muslims stayed here. Though there were wars in '47, '65, '71 elsewhere, still nothing happened here. Muslims meet Sikhs with equanimity. Sikhs meet Muslims in the same way because of [Haider Shaykh]. Nothing happened in '47, '65, and '71."[14] Residents and pilgrims frequently speak of Haider Shaykh in similar terms, and this is one of many ways they connect to the saint and, through him, to one another. Such testimonials make explicit the association of the present peace with this foundational figure and his ethical worldview.

Second, the blessing from the tenth and last Sikh guru Gobind Singh is so commonly credited for preserving Malerkotla during all periods of strife that it is without doubt the best known event in the history of the territory. In 1705 the guru was at war with the forces loyal to the Mughal emperor Aurangzeb.[15] The

FIGURE I.1. The *dargah* (tomb shrine) of Haider Shaikh.

nawab of Malerkotla at the time, Sher Muhammad Khan, fought against the Sikhs but then distinguished himself when the two younger sons of the guru were captured and sentenced to death. There is a strong historical tradition that Sher Muhammad Khan spoke up against this execution and petitioned Aurangzeb himself to prevent the execution, claiming that it was against Islam to harm children, as they are de facto noncombatants.[16] Though his sons were ultimately killed, Guru Gobind Singh is said to have heard of the nawab's protest and blessed the kingdom. In the post-Partition era this blessing has come to be the rationale of first resort as to why Malerkotla was spared the violence that devastated much of Punjab in 1946 and 1947. For example, writing in a Pakistani newspaper in January of 2008, the political scientist Ishtiaq Ahmed claimed,

> The Sikh hordes did not touch Muslims who crossed into Malerkotla State, but those just a few feet away from its borders were cut down without any mercy. Thanks to Guru Gobind Singh's

instructions, the Muslims of Malerkotla were not to be harmed
come what may in the future because the Nawab had not complied
with the demands of the Mughals to arrest the Guru's minor sons
who were passing through his State.[17]

Although most versions of this story place the nawab's protest after the arrest of
the guru's sons in Sirhind, the perception of the power of the guru's blessing
remains the same. Interlocutors of all sorts attribute Malerkotla's security at that
time to the guru's blessing.[18] The ubiquity and symbolic significance of this
moment is such that almost no public gathering in Malerkotla takes place without
mention of the nawab's protest, known as the *haah da naara* or cry for justice.

The third feature of Malerkotla's history that stands out in most sources is
the peace at Partition itself, whether credited to the blessings of Haider Shaykh
or the Sikh guru or to the kingdom's army or the moral fiber of the community.
The peace at Partition is nearly always brought up in press accounts and personal narratives about the town. The nonevent of violence in Malerkotla is
remarkable since estimates of the number of deaths in Partition range from
200,000 to one million. The plurality of these casualties occurred in Punjab
where the violence was most severe. Malerkotla weathered that crisis, though
strained to the limits by the influx of Muslim refugees who stopped off in the
territory as they fled to Pakistan. Indeed, just as Ishtiaq Ahmed claims, the
border of the state is remembered as an almost magical shield for those in flight.
Local memories about this time recount moments of fear, solidarity, and some
desperation in terms of the condition of the refugees in the monsoons. Maulana
Abdul Rauf, a longtime community leader who was a young boy during Partition, described Malerkotla as stressed but secure. "We see in Malerkotla that
people have stood by the other communities of people. The Muslims, Hindus
and Sikhs—they have helped each other. When there was Partition of India and
Pakistan, at that time Malerkotla was like an island. There was no facility for
food, so the Sikhs brought food from outside to Malerkotla."[19] Not only was the
communal tension kept in control, but Hindu, Muslim, and Sikh residents alike
praised the ruler of the kingdom for his evenhandedness in protecting the
security of the lives and property of all citizens, no matter what their religion.
While British records from the time express frustration with other regional
rulers for their incitement, support, and even organization of the communal
violence of the period, Malerkotla stood out as the "island of peace" the popular
press later declared it to be. Indeed there are comparatively few files about
Malerkotla among the volumes of Partition-related documents in the British
and Indian archives. Occasionally mentioned as a stopping-off point for evac-
uees, neither the state leadership nor the territory is part of the detailed reporting on violence, abduction of women, refugees, property issues, borders, and
other issues relating to the complicated process of dividing one country
into two.[20]

The pervasive and persistent civic harmony in Malerkotla is also sometimes explained by its unusual demography. Malerkotla today is made up of a wide range of religious and ethnic groups. According to the most recent census of India (2001), India as a whole is 80 percent Hindu, 13 percent Muslim, and just under 2 percent Sikh, whereas Punjab is 37 percent Hindu, 1 percent Muslim, and 60 percent Sikh (see table I.1).[21] This demographic is entirely reversed in Malerkotla. In 2001, the town's population was 69 percent Muslim, 21 percent Hindu, and 8 percent Sikh[22] (see Table I.1). It is interesting that in 1881 undivided Punjab was 51 percent Muslim, 41 percent Hindu, and 7.6 percent Sikh, whereas Malerkotla at that time was actually a Sikh majority region, with an urban population 35 percent Muslim, 23 percent Hindu, and 41 percent Sikh. In 1904, the urban population of Malerkotla was relatively evenly divided among the three major religions. In 1951, the first (though notoriously problematic) census taken after Partition, the numbers are quite different. In Punjab as a whole, Hindus were 42 percent, Sikhs 56 percent, and Muslims 0.8 percent. However, in the city of Malerkotla itself in 1951 the population became 66 percent Muslim, 22 percent Hindu, 6 percent Jain, and 5 percent Sikh. This distribution of the urban population continues to this day, with only a slight increase in Sikh representation. In the remainder of Punjab, as shown in the 2001 census data, the Hindu population has decreased, whereas the Sikh and Muslim populations have grown, reflecting emigration of Hindus, immigration of Sikhs, and the alterations in Punjab's borders to create Haryana and Himachal Pradesh in primarily Hindu eastern regions.[23]

This unusual demographic profile is a mixed blessing for Malerkotla's population. Indeed there are residents who claim that their unique demography is one of the reasons the town has maintained relative peace and harmony over the years. Some Muslims in town assert that because Islam itself is a religion of equality, peace, and justice, this Muslim-majority town resists the sectarian violence that plagued the neighboring regions during and after Partition. Others say that, as the only Muslim-majority region, Malerkotla has a heightened importance and is a key constituency for Punjab's politicians. The ability to carry this electorate is proof of a nonsectarian appeal. Residents' consciousness of their token status generates a sociopolitical dynamic conducive to coalition building and community harmony. Or, as one young Muslim woman put it, "everyone here is a minority." As a Muslim majority town, in a Sikh majority state, in a Hindu majority nation, no group is able to definitively establish dominance. All religious groups are in some regard vulnerable and cognizant that their well-being depends on their positive relations with others. Thus under certain conditions the lack of clear hegemony actually promotes peace rather than undermines it. The principle of mutual protection or the solidarity of minorities has force and appeal because the residents have experienced the benefits of shared civic life.

Table I.1 Malerkotla Population
It is important to note that pre-independence figures reflect population of the entire kingdom, which measured 167 square miles at the time, whereas more current data reflect only the town's concentrated urban area.

1876: 91,560
1881: 71,051
1901: 77,506
1991: 88,600
2001: 106,802

Year	Malerkotla	Punjab	India
1881	35% Muslim	51% Muslim	19.97% Muslim
	23% Hindu	41% Hindu	78.09% Hindu
	41% Sikh	7.6% Sikh	
1941	70.27% Muslim (20,605)	53% Muslim	24.28% Muslim
	20.8% Hindu (6,098)	31% Hindu	69.46% Hindu
	5.81% Jain (1,705)	15% Sikh	
	2.64% Sikh (823)		
	.48% Christian (90)		
1951	66% Muslim (21,502)	62% Hindu	9.9% Muslim
	22.1% Hindu (7,200)	35% Sikh	85% Hindu
	5.84% Jain (1,780)	0.8% Muslim	
	5.09% Sikh (1,902)		
	.97% Christian (191)		
1961	61.47% Muslim (24,307)	64% Hindu	83.5% Hindu
	23.75% Hindu (9,390)	33% Sikh	10.7% Muslim
	5.02% Jain (2,080)	0.8% Muslim	1.8% Sikh
	8.78% Sikh (3,473)		
	.98% Christian (293)		
1971	64.96% Muslim (31,740)	38% Hindu	82.7% Hindu
	24.81% Hindu (12,124)	60% Sikh	11.2% Muslim
	2.58% Jain (1,263)	1% Muslim	1.9% Sikh
	7.53% Sikh (3,683)		
	.0001% Christian (48)		
1981	67.3% Muslim	36% Hindu	82.6% Hindu
	20.2% Hindu	62% Sikh	11.4% Muslim
	10.7% Sikh.	1% Muslim	2% Sikh
1991	No Data Available[1]	34.5% Hindu	82.41% Hindu
		1.18% Muslim	11.67% Muslim
		62.95% Sikh	1.99% Sikh
2001	69.11% Muslim (73,813)	36.8% Hindu	80.4% Hindu
	20.88% Hindu (22,304)	1.5% Muslim	13.4% Muslim
	1.61% Jain (1,717)	59.9% Sikh	1.86% Sikh
	8.37% Sikh (8.937)		
	0.001% Christian (169)		

1. According to the Census of India, religion data is not kept for towns with population below 100,000. The population of Malerkotla was 88,600 in 1991, so there is no data for this year.

One of the central features of Malerkotla's civic culture is the collective memory that highlights episodes of peace, justice, and cooperation among religious groups. The cultural memories that support the ethical ideals of the present are remarkably consistent across social, religious, gender, and class categories. As Jan Assmann describes it, cultural memory "comprises that body of reusable texts, images and rituals specific to each society in each epoch, whose 'cultivation' serves to stabilize and convey that society's self-image."[24] Stories about Haider Shaykh and his cult, the guru's blessing, and the peace at Partition stabilize and convey Malerkotla's self-image. Creating such coherent accounts of the past is a critical means of cultural production. These histories not only represent the events of the past but also make those events meaningful for the present, giving historical narratives a great deal of power.

Historian Hayden White emphasizes the importance of the narrative process in generating historical accounts. In White's view, an event is unavailable to history unless it is narrativized. Both factual and mythic events are rendered meaningful within a particular context only through their narration. Thus, he writes, "the very distinction between real and imaginary events that is basic to modern discussions of both history and fiction presupposes a notion of reality in which 'the true' is identified with 'the real' only insofar as it can be shown to possess the character of narrativity."[25] That is to say that a particular version of events must become part of the story that a person, group, or community tells about himself or itself to be recognizable as reality. Such histories that are remembered actively by the group constitute what Jan Assmann calls connective memories. Even when replete with counterfactual material, the repetition of a story in multiple communicative genres (conversations, narratives, journalism, histories, hagiographies, testimonials) and its localization through commemorative practices binds the community together. In Malerkotla these connective memories depict the town as harmonious and selectively mine the past to fit that narrative.[26]

These historic events and present realities are creatively brought together by residents and other interlocutors to generate a frame of peace through which Malerkotla's identity is interpreted. A frame is a mental structure that shapes our understanding of our experiences.[27] And as the linguist George Lakoff argues, there is nothing given or natural about frames: they are social, psychological constructs and are subject to change. Frames are known primarily "by their consequences: the way we reason and what counts as common sense."[28] They are in some part unconscious, but they work best when they resonate with experience and come to have the force of common sense. A frame is produced and reinforced in large part through repetition and resonance. The frame that has developed over time about Malerkotla, but especially since Partition, is one of peace and *bhaichara* (brotherhood). We shall see how this frame is produced and perpetuated through social, political, and ritual practices that have become deeply embedded in the collective consciousness as well as unconscious. The stability of the peace frame in Malerkotla helps the community regain equilibrium quickly when there are internal or external shocks to the system.

Communalism as Context

Such shocks are not uncommon in India, where interreligious relations are often fraught. Therefore it is important to understand Malerkotla in the broader context of Indian communalism and the challenges for the large Muslim minority there. In South Asia, Hindus, Muslims, and Sikhs have complicated relations ranging from familial ties to deep antipathies. These latter manifest most particularly as the chauvinistic sectarianism called "communalism." Historian Romila Thapar defines communalism as an ideology that "perceives Indian society as constituted of a number of religious communities and the identity of Indian society is seen essentially in these terms."[29] Communalism, religious violence, and politicized religion have long been important topics of research in South Asian studies, but especially since December 6, 1992.[30] On that day Hindu extremists tore down a sixteenth-century mosque in the North Indian town of Ayodhya that they believed to occupy the site of the god Rama's birthplace; the subsequent riots killed thousands.[31] Many of the organizers of the movement to "liberate" the temple were also prominent members of a political party, the BJP, which a few years later came to power in the central government and in a number of states. Communal politics were no longer the province of marginal groups or fringe actors, but were overtly shaping the agenda of the nation.

Communalism is a challenge to the constitutional secularism of the state and to interreligious dialogue. Religious organizations and religiously based political parties are extremely active in the Indian political sphere, and the influence of religio-ethnic identity on politics is not new. During the colonial era, competition between religions was exacerbated by the British system, which sometimes distributed authority, autonomy, and benefits such as voting rights and employment on the basis of religion. This system essentially guaranteed that the population would have to organize and agitate for increased rights on the same basis by which those rights were distributed—that is, religion.[32] This fissiparous logic was intensified by the tendency of the British to regard instances of unrest, agitation, or violence as evidence of deep-rooted religious hatreds that required their mediating authority to keep in check.[33] In reality, most riots and other conflicts between religious communities or sects within a religion were multi-causal, with religious sentiment only one of many factors.[34] The struggle for independence, though engendering solidarity in some cases among India's many ethnic and religious groups, also pushed them apart. In particular, the division between the Hindu majority seeking a strong central government and Muslims desirous of a federated system in which Muslim-majority regions would have relative autonomy combined with British desire to speed their departure, precipitating the 1947 Partition of India and Pakistan.[35] The Muslim population of India was reduced to about 10 percent from 25 percent in a matter of months. The remaining Muslims, now a sizable minority of almost 14 percent, have struggled ever since to establish their place in Indian society.

The continuing difficulties faced by Muslim Indians were made vividly clear in a recent report commissioned by the government of India. Released in November 2006, "Social, Economic, and Educational Status of the Muslim Community of India," known as the Sachar Report, was authored by a blue-ribbon panel led by Rajinder Sachar, a Supreme Court justice.[36] The report found systemic and widespread inequality, discrimination, and underdevelopment among the Muslim population, which in 2001 was estimated at more than 138 million. Muslims are disproportionately excluded from civil service jobs, police and military ranks, and political office. They have disproportionately high rates of incarceration, illiteracy, poverty, and health problems. The Sachar Report further describes Muslim Indians as carrying the "double burden of being labeled as 'anti-national' and as being 'appeased' at the same time. While Muslims need to prove on a daily basis that they are not 'anti-national' and 'terrorists,' it is not recognized that the alleged 'appeasement' has not resulted in the desired level of socio-economic development."[37] Blamed by some for Partition, the ongoing dispute in Kashmir, and the terrorism that occasionally occurs, Muslim Indians remain caught between suspicion and exceptionalism—an uncomfortable position.

Among the chief purveyors of the canard that Muslims cannot truly be Indians are the powerful groups known collectively as the "Sangh Parivar," or family of the Sangh. The Sangh refers to the principle group fronting the Hindu right, the Rashtriya Swayamsevak Sangh (RSS–National Volunteer Corps). Its two principle offshoots are a coalition of religious leaders called the Vishwa Hindu Parishad (VHP–World Hindu Council) and a political wing, the Bharatiya Janata Party (BJP—Indian Popular Party).[38] There are numerous other groups affiliated with these Hindu nationalist groups having agendas advocating everything from the expulsion of Muslims to Pakistan as terrorists (or at least terrorist sympathizers) to majoritarians who oppose policies designed to correct systemic discrimination against Muslims, claiming such programs are coddling or appeasing a minority rather than working toward justice and equality.[39] This attitude was forcefully articulated on March 17, 2002, when K. S. Sudarshan, the head of the RSS (which has an estimated membership of more than a million) drafted the so-called Bangalore Resolution. Issued at a time when communal violence was engulfing the western state of Gujarat, this statement declared, in part, "Let the Muslims understand that their real safety lies in the goodwill of the majority."[40] Such stark reminders of their vulnerability complicate the process of identity formation for Muslim Indians. The implication is that for Muslims to be considered fully Indian by this vocal minority of Hindus, Islam must be given up. Being Hindu, on the other hand, is seen as synonymous with being Indian and requires no accommodation or adjustment. Therefore, in order for Muslims to be successful in public life they are expected by some to curtail their Muslim-ness. Indeed, it is the stated goal of the RSS and its affiliate organizations, including the BJP political party, that all Indians worthy of the name should also accept the label of Hindu as referring to a cultural rather than a religious identity. Put this way, no true Indian should object to being called Hindu.

Muslims know, even without being reminded by people like the RSS's Sudarshan, that their continued survival depends upon the goodwill of the majority Hindu population. They are painfully confronted with proof of their vulnerability by events such as those that took place in Gujarat in the spring of 2002 when Muslims were killed and displaced in enormous numbers. News reports and human rights investigations estimated that two thousand people were killed in violence following the burning of a train car containing Hindus returning from the flashpoint city of Ayodhya just outside a station in a Muslim neighborhood. Although reports of the cause of the violence vary, in the aftermath there were systematic attacks on Muslims, their neighborhoods, and their businesses. After two months of disturbances, more than a hundred thousand people were displaced, again mostly Muslim. The Gujarat government in power during the violence called for early elections, which they won handily, and Chief Minister Narendra Modi remains one of the rising stars of the BJP today. As yet no major case against the perpetrators has been brought successfully. Furthermore, in the summer of 2003 several of the few cases brought against the perpetrators of the Gujarat violence were initially dismissed because of witness intimidation and a lack of institutional will to prosecute the criminals.[41] In 2003 and 2004 the U.S. Commission on International Religious Freedom (USCIRF), an agency of the U.S. State Department, listed India as a "Country of Particular Concern," in no small part because of the atmosphere of impunity for the perpetrators of the Gujarat riots.[42] In 2004 the USCIRF wrote, "Despite India's democratic traditions, religious minorities in India have periodically been subject to severe violence, including mass killings," and further noted that "those responsible for the violence are rarely ever held to account." Significantly, the report implicated the Hindu nationalist BJP government, which ruled the central government from 1999 to 2004 and has been reelected twice in Gujarat since the riots, most recently in December 2007. The USCIRF report noted "an increase in such violence has coincided with the rise in political influence of groups associated with the Sangh Parivar." The empowerment of the Parivar has resulted in a growing "climate of immunity for the perpetrators of attacks on minorities."[43] In this atmosphere of fear, amid clear evidence that pogroms against Muslims will not only go unpunished but also provide substantial electoral gains, the nature of daily interactions between Hindus, Muslims, Sikhs, and others throughout India becomes a matter of urgent concern. Though not in power in the central government since 2004, the BJP remains the most powerful opposition party with the most disciplined and organized cadres of supporters. Such reports confirm Gyan Pandey's argument in his article "Can a Muslim Be an Indian?" in which he described how Muslim Indians are not only constantly reminded of their vulnerability, but also are required to actively manifest their identities as loyal and legitimate citizens.[44]

Several revealing incidents relating to Malerkotla bear out Pandey's contention and the Sachar Report's claim that Muslim Indians must constantly provide evidence of their allegiance to India over and above their sectarian loyalty. For example, in 1999 the Pakistani and Indian armies clashed in the Kashmiri region of Kargil. The Pakistani forces were routed in the skirmish, and an all-out war between the nuclear-armed neighbors was averted. Yet during the tensions, a Punjab newspaper, the *Tribune*, thought it newsworthy that in Malerkotla, Muslims had burned an effigy of Nawaz Sharif, who then was the prime minister of Pakistan.[45] This public demonstration of the Muslim-majority town's loyalty to India during the conflict is not as remarkable as the fact that a newspaper article was devoted to such an event. Doubtless many effigies went up in flames during that time without headlines identifying the religions of those who lit the fires. In another example, in the summer of 2006 there were celebrations in India to mark the hundredth anniversary of the composition of the patriotic song "Vande Mataram," the lyrics of which are strongly Hindu. This song is one of the favorite anthems of Hindu nationalist groups, but some Muslim Indians have objected to it due to its sectarian sensibility. Perhaps unsurprisingly, a September 6, 2006, story in the *Tribune* bore the headline "Malerkotla Muslims Sing Vande Mataram."[46] The fact that this event was reported at all indicates a climate in which the anthem was seen as a litmus test for India's Muslims.[47]

In part because of the efforts of the Sangh Parivar and other such groups and partly because of the legacy of Partition, it is difficult for Muslim Indians to organize nationally as Muslims. Such efforts are seen in certain quarters as highly suspicious and leading to questions concerning Muslim loyalty to the Indian nation. As a substantial minority of about fourteen percent or 140 million, Muslims experience numerous challenges. In 2008 only two of the 545 members of Parliament were from explicitly Muslim parties.[48] Muslim coherence is also challenged from within because Muslim Indians are ethnically, linguistically, geographically, and culturally diverse. In fact, there are few Muslim organizations with a national presence, and there is little agreement among Muslims on whether those groups represent Muslim interests as a whole.

The challenge of communalism in India is that it feeds and is fed by numerous politico-religious groups and movements. Every religious group has an extremist minority within it that is actively mobilizing to defend what it sees as its community's interests. Key to the mind-set of communal organizations of this sort is the view that rights, services, and the very essence of the Indian polity are a zero-sum game: if one religious group feels that it has lost ground or is discriminated against, it is because another group has gained. Since Partition, such organizations have had little success in Malerkotla. Though Hindu nationalist groups are present in Malerkotla, they are small and not confrontational. They also tend to work with organizations representing other religions to foster dialogue, in addition to their efforts to lift up local Hindus. As Dharamvir Gupta, the head of the RSS in Malerkotla put it, "We are not against any community. One should support one's own community."[49] The RSS was banned briefly in 1948 in Malerkotla as it was throughout India after a former member of the group, Nathuram Godse, assassinated Mahatma Gandhi. Prior to independence, the Hindu Mahasabha was active in Malerkotla, agitating for Hindu causes and playing a key role in several communal clashes in the 1930s, which will be explored in chapter 3. Before independence, Muslim groups too would appeal to the nawabs and protest against them, complaining of bias and a lack of religious freedom. The Muslim groups Jama'at-i Islami and the Tablighi Jama'at, both conservative religious organizations, are active in Malerkotla, but, like their Hindu counterparts, they focus on concerns relating to their religious group's uplift: the establishment of schools, mosques, and health clinics. Although they are in certain ways "communal," the leaders of sectarian groups participate in local peace initiatives and in the more formal peace committees that are occasionally convened in response to communal stress locally or regionally. In Malerkotla, the heads of the RSS and the Jama'at-i Islami claim that they have "family relations" with one another, meaning that they exchange visits and consider each other friends.

Peace Triggers: Institutionalizing Harmony

These personal relationships bolster initiatives such as peace committees, giving credibility to their responses to crises. The efficacy of such groups is critical to mitigating conflict and restoring equilibrium since a frequently cited exacerbating factor for negative communal relations is a past history of interreligious conflict or violence. Areas plagued by hostility or repeated acts of violence are vulnerable to new contestations. In such places, what Paul Brass termed an "institutionalized riot system" takes root, expediting the transition from a triggering incident to a conflagration through well-worn channels of communication and alert cadres of activists.[50] In some places old grievances never seem fully buried but resurface with each new incident, generating a well of resentment that is easily mobilized by the elites who stand to gain from civil discord. In this regard, Malerkotla initially appears to fit the profile of a "riot-prone" area. The town's history is replete with periods of conflict between the local Muslim majority and the Hindu and Sikh populations. But, especially since Partition, the conflicts of the past have not carried into the present and are rarely discussed by locals from any community. Not only do they not fit the frame of *bhaichara* (brotherhood) and the values established through representations of the moral past, but they do not serve the collective interest of the majority in Malerkotla. The critical issue, therefore, is not the existence or nonexistence of violent histories, but how histories conducive to coalition building and civic harmony come to dominate the public and private spheres. In Malerkotla active efforts by locals and visitors maintain openness and multivocality, and dissenting and divisive elements are suppressed. This has strengthened the peace frame and prevented a conflict frame or institutionalized riot system from gaining ground.

It is also common for riots to be triggered or accompanied by rumors accusing members of other religious groups of all kinds of malfeasance, particularly sexual or sacred violence.[51] When reports of kidnappings and rape or desecrations of shrines and religious symbols circulate unchecked and are perpetuated by interest groups, a critical mass of ambient frustration becomes focused on a particular community, producing a conflict frame. This process of identifying a culpable party and attaching negative experiences and emotions to it is termed "transvaluation and focalization" by Stanley Tambiah.[52] Transvaluation and focalization connect anger over a rumor's implications to dissatisfaction over any number of other issues. This is a dangerous conjunction, creating a fertile ground for violence. In Malerkotla in recent years a number of rumors have circulated that might elsewhere have led to conflict among Muslims, Sikhs, and Hindus. However, as we shall see in chapter 6, these rumors were effectively managed by local leaders and community members, minimizing the deleterious impact on interreligious relations and feeding the peace frame.

One factor that scholars of interreligious and ethnic relations in India have focused on recently is the role of civil society in promoting or undermining peaceful relations between communities in a given locale. Paul Brass and Stanley Tambiah, for example, have both studied the networks of "riot specialists" who instigate, organize, and perpetuate violent conflicts—often mobilized and motivated by political parties or labor groups.[53] Though their analyses emphasize the role of elites rather than that of ordinary actors, their studies help to undermine the notion that riots and other forms of collective violence result from an upwelling of primordial animosity or are examples of a so-called "crowd psychology" that Gustave Le Bon and others believed was prone to mass irrationality and potential violence.[54] More recently, political scientist Ashutosh Varshney focused on civil society as the key factor in building and maintaining stable societies.[55] In areas that have long records of interethnic peace, Varshney identified, following Brass, an "institutionalized peace system," the processes of which he sees operating chiefly at the level of civil society. Within civil society, Varshney identified two levels: the associational and the everyday. He asserted that formal associational interethnic links substantially exceed the importance of *everyday* interethnic links as the crucial element in sustaining peace in a region. According to Varshney, "though valuable in itself," the warmth generated by daily interactions "does not necessarily constitute the bedrock for strong civic organizations."[56]

The presence or absence of positive everyday relations is indeed an essential contributing factor in establishing and maintaining the stable, integrated civil societal associations upon which Varshney places such a premium. Such relations also help achieve "balanced sociation," in which a society develops structures through which conflict and cooperation are in productive tension.[57] Balanced sociation provides opportunities for grievances to be managed and social change to occur through institutions and relationships that sustain the social fabric rather than undermine it. As Varshney puts it, "ethnic peace should, for all practical purposes, be conceptualized as an institutionalized channeling and resolution of ethnic conflicts. It should be visualized as an absence of *violence*, not as an absence of *conflict*."[58] His point that conflict is always present in society in some form is key. Conflict is inevitable, but its impact on society is variable. Nonetheless, by privileging the associational over the everyday Varshney obscures the cumulative impact on particular communities of successes and failures in handling internal and external stresses.[59] Without observing closely how people within a community make sense of conflicts when they happen and how they communicate their meaning to one another and to subsequent generations, the actual operations of the institutionalized peace system remain unaccounted for, and the microstrategies of peacemaking disappear.

For example, the most common local explanations for the ambient peace in Malerkotla present challenges to quantitative analyses. As discussed previously, residents and visitors almost universally attribute Malerkotla's present idealized harmony and the safety during Partition to one of several divine interventions: the founding of the settlement by a Sufi saint and his ongoing protection of it, the legacy of a ruler who spoke out against the execution of Guru Gobind Singh's sons, or simply protection by God for reasons that God alone knows. What is the combined effect of these metaphysical justifications? By providing explanatory narratives, the sacralization of Malerkotla's peace by residents and visitors generates a shared moral frame that connects and sustains the community. Pragmatically, the shared religious traditions and the shared moral frame are grounded in social and political institutions. But these institutions are sustained by the collective life of the community. Among all of the factors that contribute to or militate against communal harmony, the sharing of sacred space and pietistic traditions has been relatively unexplored by scholars and activists concerned with social conflict.

Shared Sacred Space

While it is not uncommon for shared sacred sites to be treated as powder kegs waiting to ignite primordial tensions between religious groups historically and elementally at odds with one another, the reality of life in India belies such treatment. In fact, shared sacred sites hide in plain sight throughout the sub-continent and enjoy vibrant and enthusiastic patronage and devotion from all sectors of society. Still it is undeniable that shared sacred sites have been and continue to be the flashpoints for antagonism and violence. The death toll related to the movement to establish a temple at Ayodhya on the site of the destroyed mosque is above five thousand human lives to date.[60]

It is important to understand the tomb of Haider Shaykh because multi-confessional sacred sites are not always peacefully shared in India or anywhere else. As in the case of Ayodhya, shared sites are sometimes disputed and destroyed. Places where shared shrines proliferate experience violence between religions just as places without them do. However, such sites, their lore, and management are crucial indices of the quality of civil societal integration, thereby providing an important locus for understanding the workings of multi-religious communities. The dynamics of exchange at shared shrines on the ritual, social, and mundane levels have not been well explored and sustained comparative work has yet to be done.[61] Some of the best work on interreligious exchange in India has focused on the literary productions of shared religious traditions, for example, the studies of Farina Mir, Sufia Uddin, and Tony Stewart.[62] This work has done much to complicate stereotypes of Muslims and Hindus in particular as being in perpetual opposition, harboring primordial hatreds. Recent studies by Jackie Assayag and Peter Gottschalk seek to under-stand how people live these religious identities and how they blur in practice. Much remains to be done to understand such religious cultures in India and elsewhere, but there is a growing body of literature from which to draw.[63]

A key place to observe and understand the degree of integration between religious groups in Malerkotla is the *dargah* of Haider Shaykh. Here the simul-taneous presence of Sikhs, Hindus, and Muslims challenges notions of definite and definable boundaries between religions, countering the expectation of inter-religious communal conflict in South Asia. Pilgrims often call Haider Shaykh *hamare sanjhe pir*—our shared or common holy man. This moniker is both possessive (our, *hamare*) and inclusive (shared or common, *sanjhe*). The per-sonal connection evoked with the possessive pronoun is expanded to the col-lectivity, all of whom may, if they choose, appeal to the founding father for blessings, healing, or simply to acknowledge his role as founder. Hindus, Sikhs, Muslims, Christians, and Jains attend the *dargah* for a variety of purposes both sacred and mundane—to offer a prayer, make or fulfill a vow, obtain a blessing from the saint, ward off evil, seek relief from mental and physical suffering, or any number of other personal motivations. Residents and visitors alike perceive the tomb and the town as spaces of communal peace and harmony, made possible by several interlocking factors—the power of the saint upon whose body the city rests, the history of the region, and the will of the community. This ethos of harmony both reflects past success in managing internal and external challenges to the harmonious status quo and organizes the community's ongoing struggles to live up to the ideal. Furthermore, the workings of the microstrategies of attunement through which members of a diverse population adjust to and accommodate one another is especially apparent in such enclosed arenas of engagement. The perception of Haider Shaykh and Malerkotla as zones of peace is not merely passively transmitted but is actively maintained through collective discourses and practices that guide and structure social, political, religious, and economic exchanges among Muslims, Sikhs, and Hindus in Malerkotla.

Shared sites are important to understand in the context of peace building because of the everyday interactions that occur there and the implications of such relations for the daily workings of microlevel communal relations. As Roger Friedland and Richard Hecht have argued, disputes over sacred space are also necessarily struggles over the choreography of daily life.[64] Conversely, the mundane harmony at shared sacred sites is indicative of another sort of choreography in which potential conflict and commonplace competition may be harmonized or attuned. To co-opt a term used in linguistics and musicology, much of what happens practically in a shared sacred space is a kind of *spatial attunement* in which pilgrims consciously and unconsciously adjust to and accommodate one another. Some of these attuning practices are overt and explicit, such as conversations and mimicry, others are implicit as people make room for one another, avoid others, and generally seek to internalize their pilgrimage experience for maximum transformative effect.[65] An examination of effective interactive practices at shared sites, therefore, will illuminate modes, systems, and strategies of exchange that substantively contribute to the production and perpetuation of peace. The quality of these interactions is a key contributing factor in generating conflict or cooperation at such places, and it inevitably influences the communities in which each shrine is situated.

At root in the question of how shared sites both reflect and engender a particular mode of interreligious relations is the issue of sacred space itself— what makes it sacred and under what conditions is its sharing possible. In the classic formulation of one of the founders of the discipline of comparative religion, Mircea Eliade, sacred spaces are the loci of *hierophanies*. A hierophany is the breaking through from the divine realm into the mundane. In the Abrahamic faiths, a place such as Jerusalem, where God communicated directly with his prophet, is understood as an *axis mundi,* a pivot around which the world turns. These places become the spiritual and physical centers of their constituent communities, providing orientation in both a literal and a metaphysical sense for the believers. For Eliade, these sacred centers are seen as microcosms of a divine perfection, as near on earth as it is possible to find an approximation of a higher reality. But this approach excessively separates sacred places from their sociopolitical contexts. Friedland and Hecht rightly challenge the tendency to interpret sacred space as the imprint of heaven on earth, a semiotic, spatialized

FIGURE I.2. Muslim and Sikh women praying at Haider Shaikh's *dargah* (tomb).

representation of a divine reality. Simultaneously they critique the social scientific reversal of this formulation in which earth imprints heaven, projecting the terrestrial social order into the celestial. Both views erase the politics of the center, and it is this very politics, they argue, that both centers sacrality and sacralizes centers. The sharing of a sacred center by multiple religious traditions necessitates politics, negotiation, strategy, and compromise. These are "signifying sites" at which and through which various identities are projected and received between and within religious and social groups. As such, they are "intertextual" and subject to potentially "conflictual readings."[66] The daily use of the site and the choreography of its use create at least partially observable traces of interweaving, overlapping discourses of bodies, practices, and imaginations. Thus, it is no longer a matter of reading the imprints of earth on heaven or vice versa. In order to comprehend the various significations of the narratives and behaviors that transmit the meaning of place into a message, a hermeneutic capable of rendering this mutual imprimatur is required. This hermeneutic engages the ritual and narrative transactional idioms and repertoires of multivocal constituent communities and evaluates the modes in which the administrative regimes at multi-confessional sites enable or frustrate the simultaneity of plural and potentially contradictory beliefs and practices.

Thus, in addition to the transactions between the mundane and the divine occurring at sacred sites, these places also mediate transactions between multiple actors and the divine agencies in whom they believe through a diverse repertoire of rituals, narratives, and authoritative schemes. In some cases this multiplicity and simultaneity occurs uneventfully and without a formal scheme to coordinate its functioning. Other situations require highly elaborate systems—such as the time-share arrangement at the Church of the Nativity—or even regulatory personnel—such as the police or the military.[67] However, as phenomenologist of space Edward Casey asserts, one of the unique qualities of place in general is its ability to incorporate without conflict the most diverse elements that constitute its being. He writes: "There is a peculiar power to place and its ability to contain multiple meanings, diverse intentions, contradictory interactions. Surpassing the capacity of humans to sustain such a *gathering,* place permits a simultaneity and a filtering of experience, history, imagination, action." Casey states that, "places also gather experiences and histories, even languages and thoughts." Further, the power of place "consists in gathering these lives and things, each with its own space and time, into one arena of common engagement."[68] In this way we see that the containment of multiple meanings, interests, and intentions is not merely a function of sacred places, it is the very nature of place. Although by no means inevitably free of conflict, the capacity of place to contain and represent such multiplicity is certainly possible and is sometimes explicitly celebrated. Conflict and competition, though potentially destructive, also contribute to and assure the continuing significance of the site in question. Far from undermining the sacred power of a site, conflict increases it. The multiplicity gathered in a single space—the suspended tensions of contradictory beliefs and practices—help to constitute the significance of shared sacred sites. In other words, by physically and discursively connecting people and their practices at a single site, by gathering and then maintaining that gathering, place is animated, enlivened, and made meaningful.

However, the frustration of phenomenological studies such as Casey's is that in spite of seductive language and sentiment, they lack grounding in the sociopolitical context. This is a critique articulated in a provocative article titled "Antagonistic Tolerance" by Robert Hayden. Hayden reminds us of the importance of attending to the politics as well as the poetry as he questions the possibility of non-contentious sharing of sacred space. In Hayden's view, the sites that scholars portray as uncontested are instead exemplary of a "negative definition of tolerance as passive noninterference."[69] He claims that in some cases a radical imbalance of power is necessary for peace to be maintained, merely suppressing hostility and competition rather than eliminating it. For Hayden, depictions of "uncontested" or peaceful shrines require a false erasure of time from the theoretical analysis that obscures a socially enforced political stasis. Synthesis of traditions, he writes, is a "temporal manifestation of relations between social groups, which continue to differentiate themselves from each other."[70]

Hayden's points are valid as it would be absurd to claim that shared sites are devoid of competition or the possibility of antagonism. After all, as Georg Simmel famously argued, competition is an indirect form of conflict.[71] Indeed some conflict studies scholars, such as Anthony Gill, view the activation of conflicts as the strategic action of rationally motivated actors taking advantage of perceived opportunities to advance their interests.[72] However, sociologist

John Hall also reminds us that, "Much competition between religious groups is peaceful, and it unfolds within a larger frame of mutual respect and sometime cooperation."[73] Competition at shared sites may be episodic and contextual. For example, the ownership of a site may be clear, but ritual authority less so or vice versa. Still, even situations with multiple owners or ritual authorities are inevitably neither antagonistic nor harmonious. We must examine specific situations of sharing to determine patterns of both conflict and cooperation. In his work on conflict over shared sacred space, Ron Hassner identified several key variables that may determine which shared spaces are prone to conflict. He asserts that the centrality and exclusivity of sacred sites results in an "indivisibility conundrum."[74] A site is indivisible to the extent that its identity is constituted both existentially and socially as coherent, nonfungible, and bounded. Depending upon factors of division or inclusion operative in a given instance, a sacred site may become contested. The conditions for nonconflictual sharing are more restrictive, Hassner argues, but not impossible and depend in no small part upon the role of religious leaders and constituent communities as well as political authorities in facilitating the process.

It is important to understand how shared sites function within their constituent communities on a daily basis. In particular, *dargah*s are spaces in which the religious identities that obtain absolutely in certain arenas (such as marriage, commensality, or burial) may recede in favor of something less absolute or exclusive. In India, shared sacred sites frequently thwart spatial and iconographic categorization. Indeed in some cases, constituents of these shrines do not identify themselves with an institutional religion (say, Hinduism or Islam), indicating how misguided notions of fixed religious identity may be. As Joyce Flueckiger points out in her study of a Muslim healer in Hyderabad India, in relation to some issues or concerns (marriage, employment, admissions, elections) "differences between Hindus and Muslims matter very much." But in such places as the healing room she describes, "these differences are overridden by what is shared."[75] Flueckiger's study further demonstrates that it is not merely the need for healing that is shared, but also the "ritual grammar" that bespeaks efficacy. The rejection of sectarian religious identity within the confines or environs of a shared sanctuary does not therefore mean that religious identity has no meaning. Religious identities *do* matter to people, and understanding how, when, and why is essential to our understanding of the broader phenomenon of interreligious relations in India.[76] This is particularly important in relation to minority religious communities, such as those in Malerkotla, which are caught between national and local identity politics. The former requires minority populations to project a defensive image that emphasizes their nonthreatening, pacific identity, whereas the latter demands that interreligious friction be suppressed and denied to maintain the dominant ethic of harmony.

The contingent and contextual nature of religious identities is born out in Jackie Assayag's study of Muslim-Hindu relations in Karnataka. He argues that "when all is said and done, it is possible that the relationship between Hinduism and Islam has been, and still is in some regions, a cultural system, i.e. a codification of the differences between neighbouring groups, a set of changing interrelations within configurations that are constantly adapting themselves to changing circumstances."[77] In particular, in his finely grained study Assayag alerts us to the minutiae of the relations among religions, rather than the macrolevel theological debates and comparisons that are more readily accessible. He sees that religious identity can be asserted or withdrawn depending on the needs of the moment and that this is accomplished "not by enunciating basic spiritual truths but through seemingly insignificant though decisive signs."[78] In Malerkotla, religious labels matter at some times and not others, and they often become evident in small actions and omissions. Observation of the spatial attunement practiced by pilgrims and ritual specialists illuminates the pragmatics of coexistence as physical as well as conceptual room is made for the Other.

Those devotees at shared sacred sites who do claim a single religious label may also assert that religious identity is a matter of ethnic background or personal preference rather than inherent superiority or exclusivity. A reluctance to claim a single identity for self or space may indicate several things simultaneously. First, it could be a challenge to the pervasive religious politics in India, the position of the influential Hindu right, whose rhetoric tends to subsume all legitimate Indian religion under the label "Hindu." The BJP and its affiliates have actively sought not to share sacred space with non-Hindus but to "liberate" them. "Liberation," in Hindutva jargon, means the elimination of Muslim shrines identified as previously Hindu. In this context, by refusing to accept religious labels of any sort, devotees at shared shrines thwart the Hindutva ideologues who seek to subsume all religions into one Hindu identity. The refusal to deal in the common currency of sectarianism is as an act of everyday resistance against majority-minority politics that rewards exclusive religious affiliation and seeks to homogenize the nation.

Second, the rejection of religious labels by devotees at *dargah*s reveals awareness of the agendas potentially implicit in such queries from outsiders and demonstrates an instinctive refusal to further fuel an already well fed fire. Indians are painfully aware of the ways in which religion is used by politicians, journalists, and scholars to define every dispute and conflict. Most Indians live in a much more complicated world in which religious identities alone are not satisfactory explanations for animosity or violence. Some devotees whom I met at Haider Shaykh's tomb and other such places confounded easy categorization. The clothing, language, and even devotional practices of pilgrims were such that they betrayed no particular affiliation. Some claimed a non-denominational identity, and others asserted the normalcy of so many religions being co-present at the shrine. Pilgrims frequently explain that they love this ostensibly Muslim saint for the very reason that he is a shared holy man, a saint who did not believe in *jat-path,* meaning caste and sectarian religious division.

Third, this refusal reveals a genuine concern to maintain the shared sense of community at the shrine, which is predicated on the simultaneous and uncontested presence of multiple religious groups. At the sites I studied in India this quality of openness and universal welcome was among the most commonly given reasons for the appeal of the shrine and why visitors enjoyed coming there. The combination of reasons for sharing sacred and civic spaces creates an interesting conundrum. No single factor can or should be isolated as the key element of a stable society without which the delicate balance of exchange would collapse. Indeed, the combination of social and political institutional will, integrated civil societal institutions, everyday interaction and integration, religious tradition, and powerful motivating ideals are all activated by the existence and maintenance of a dominant symbolic identity and ideology at Haider Shaykh's tomb and in Malerkotla. This identity and ideology is one of peace, communal harmony, and interreligious exchange.

Malerkotla's Shared Sacred Spaces

Malerkotla, like the rest of India, is home to numerous saint's shrines, places where Muslim, Sikh, and Hindu residents alike seek comfort, assistance, contemplation, and conviviality.[79] The tomb of Haider Shaykh is unquestionably the most popular *dargah* (tomb shrine) in the region, not just the town.[80] Festivals for the saint draw over a hundred thousand people to the hewn stone structure on the top of a low hill, surrounded by houses and narrow lanes (see fig. I.3). Due to the post-Partition demographics of Punjab, most visitors to the tomb are Sikhs and Hindus. Although the caretakers are Muslim descendants of the saint, and many local Muslims also attend the shrine. This multi-confessional appeal is not new. Nineteenth-century British accounts report an equal or greater number of non-Muslims at the shrine. The 1883 ethnography *Glossary of the Tribes and Castes of the Punjab* and several texts on the folklore of the Punjab all make reference to the large number of Hindus and others who come to the shrine to pray for children and for relief from possession. The authors of the *Glossary* write "the attendance at the fair of Hazrat Shaykh is very large, people of all creeds and ages and of both sexes being attracted to it from long distances."[81] The *Maler Kotla State Gazetteer* from 1904 remarks that every Thursday people gather at the shrine—in the thousands on the first Thursday of the lunar month—and that several large fairs are held there during the month of Jeth (a Hindu month falling in May–June).[82] The *Gazetteer* further notes, "It is strange that these fairs are mostly attended by Hindus, though Sadr-ud-Din was a Muhammadan Saint."[83] Why the authors considered this strange is unclear, since other gazetteers and ethnographies of the period remarked upon similar circumstances with some frequency.

FIGURE I.3. A *mela* (festival) at Haider Shaikh's *dargah.*

The situation of peaceful exchange in Malerkotla is not exclusive to Punjab or to India. Research by Glenn Bowman at prophetic sites attended by Christians and Muslims in Palestine bears this out. Bowman describes these shared shrines as "semantically multivocal." Semantic multivocality allows multiple users to maintain relations with a site that is central to their local or religious identity without overdetermining the site and rendering it fixed and unavailable to contradictory uses and interpretations. In Bowman's study in Palestine, as in my study in Punjab, the openness of the shrine is deliberately maintained through actions and interactions among the constituents that allow for a lack of uniformity of belief and practice. Indeed, the communities in which such places are situated often value shared sites precisely for their quality of openness. As Bowman puts it, "While the miraculous power seen to be resident there served as a general pretext for the gathering of local persons of Muslim and various Christian persuasions, the specific reasons people gave for attending ranged from the need for cures through the demands of religion, to the pleasures of conviviality."[84] A common primary motivator for allegiance to such shrines, their miraculous power, enables and perhaps even draws from another powerful factor in the site's appeal: their multireligious constituency. Furthermore, Bowman found that part of the appeal of the shrines shared by Muslims and Christians was the opportunity to demonstrate nonconfrontational solidarity against the Israeli occupation.[85] At least within the confines of the shrines, normally disempowered minorities exercise a degree of autonomy. United in their resistance to Israeli authority, the symbolic value of public exchange at the shrines demonstrates an unforeseen impact of the usually divisive religious politics in Israel-Palestine to intensify the bonds between the disempowered. Similarly, in the communally charged politics of present-day India, mundane interactions at shared shrines must be understood within the broader context of communal politics.

At most shared shrines, although distinctions between religions are made, these discrepancies are rarely seen as antagonistic or threatening. On the contrary, the multivocality of the shared ritual, narrative, and administrative life of the shrines and the town is not only part of the appeal but is also a source of their effective power. In this way, shared sacred places serve as powerful resources for community building and the promotion of harmonious civil society and the peace frame. As interactive nodes between individuals, religions, genders, classes, age groups, and so on, the bodily and discursive practices and experiences at the site are opportunities for the public performance of a community and individual identity characterized by openness and inclusiveness rather than exclusivity and hostility. Furthermore, not only does harmonious interreligious exchange occur, but the exchange itself is part of the appeal *and* part of the power of these places.[86]

Outline of the Book

This book is arranged both chronologically and thematically. Each chapter explores one of the building blocks of the stories that Malerkotla tells about itself and that are told by others about Malerkotla. These narratives correspond to the autochthonous theories of coexistence produced over generations. Each explanation is built upon histories carefully mined by interested actors both inside and outside Malerkotla. Through repetition and ritualization these theories are naturalized to become part of Malerkotla's essential self-perception—the frame of brotherhood, the ethos of harmony, the moral past, and the collective identity of a peaceful plural community. Once established, this interpretive frame of peace sustains Malerkotla during times of trial. It is important to understand that the frame is not merely a narrative construct but is realized through collective and individual action in the form of the institutionalized peace system. This situation is an ongoing process. It is contested and emergent and is by no means guaranteed to persist. Its strength lies in its multiple sources and sustainers, without which the myth of Malerkotla's future is beyond our capacity to predict.

Beginning with the founder of Malerkotla, the Sufi saint Shaykh Sadruddin Sadri Jahan, or Haider Shaykh, chapter 1 explores historiographical and hagiographical materials that tell the story of the saint and recount his spiritual qualities and miracles. These written and oral accounts of his life illustrate the rhetorical techniques through which different people remember the saint and establish the moral past from which present values are drawn. Drawing on insights about cultural memory and the construction of history, this chapter explores how the saint's life in its many versions generates a shared idiom of piety through which Malerkotla residents as well as pilgrims from outside the town are able to imagine and articulate Haider Shaykh's legacy. In particular the shift in emphasis in the narratives from before and after Partition that shows the saint's depiction changing from being the genealogical progenitor of the ruling lineage to the progenitor of the town's collective ethos of harmony.

Chapter 2 investigates Haider Shaykh's lineage. There are two main branches of Haider Shaykh's descendants: the nawabs who ruled the kingdom, and the *khalifah*s who take care of the saint's tomb shrine. Of the ruling lineage prior to the twentieth century, one nawab stands out in particular: Sher Muhammad Khan, who spoke up in defense of the tenth Sikh guru Gobind Singh's young sons when they were about to be executed in Sirhind in 1705 and was subsequently blessed by the guru. The nawab's protest, known as the *haah da naara* or "cry for justice," features prominently in political rituals, personal narratives, and regional histories, profoundly shaping the public perception of Malerkotla through the frame of justice and antisectarianism. Chapter 3 explores pre-Partition religious conflicts that challenge the popular image of Malerkotla as an island of peace. Yet these troubles—including a Hindu-Muslim riot in which a Hindu was killed—were defused in such a way that Malerkotla navigated the tumult of Partition without loss of life or communal conflict. Furthermore, the management of the crises added to the tension-wisdom that helps Malerkotlans maintain equilibrium during subsequent trials and laid the groundwork for what would become the institutionalized peace system of Malerkotla.

The greatest of these trials was surely the Partition of India and Pakistan in 1947. The fact that no one died in Malerkotla due to interreligious violence during Partition and that most of the Muslim population remained is an extremely important element in the myth of Malerkotla as an island of peace. Chapter 4 focuses on contemporary histories and perceptions of Partition, both written and oral, illustrating the many ways in which locals and visitors explain the peace. This chapter brings together the explanatory elements from the preceding chapters as Haider Shaykh, the governance practices of the nawabs, the *haah da naara*, and the pacific nature of the citizenry are all used today as reasons for Malerkotla's comparatively positive experience of Partition. Here we see Malerkotla's frame of peace solidifying into an enduring narrative as interlocutors from various social and temporal locations affirm that Malerkotla was a haven, miraculously preserved from Partition's worst aspects.

One of the key venues in which Malerkotla's peaceful identity is realized and enacted is the tomb, or *dargah,* of Haider Shaykh. Chapter 5 explores the devotional practices at the tomb and the spatial attunement of the multireligious constituency at the shrine. The interactions and exchanges between residents and pilgrims facilitated by devotion at the *dargah* are a key element in the production and perpetuation of a stable multireligious community because they contribute to the ritualized peace system and provide daily visible testimony to the perceived character of Malerkotla. This peaceful, pluralistic community comes into focus in chapter 6, which explores the ritualized and institutionalized peace system produced and perpetuated by local actors. Through a wide range of activities and interactions, grass-roots techniques of conflict management and reconciliation take root and bear fruit. Often through reference to the moral past as imagined through the core narratives about the town's history and historical figures, Malerkotlans reaffirm the defining values of their society. In this way, they manage the inevitable stresses of group life and the challenges of internal and external conflicts through the institutionalized peace system constructed by citizens and sustained by internal and external actors. Through personal narratives and observations, these microstrategies of peace building become clear.

Conclusion

The importance of understanding a community like Malerkotla at this historical juncture cannot be overemphasized. Questions about clashes of civilizations and the ocean of literature seeking to explain Islam and Muslims to Western audiences speak to a real need for more nuanced and subtle analyses of Muslim cultures. This study provides just such a corrective by exploring the inner workings of a peaceful, pluralistic community that also happens to be majority Muslim. By interrogating all of these concepts—peace, pluralism, and community—none emerges as merely given. Rather, each is constructed and produced through memories, practices, stories, and the concerted efforts of the interested parties. Narratives are disciplined, activities are circumscribed, and acceptable speech and behavior are constrained by the institutions and ideologies that dominate in Malerkotla. Produced at the shrine and in the streets, a hegemonic identity of peace is authenticated and perpetuated in the interest of sustaining this Muslim majority locale and maximizing its regional influence.

Peace, pluralism, and a unified conception of community, therefore, are the products of the intersection of spiritual, political, and cultural interest. It is important to understand the situation in Malerkotla because India is a secular democracy in which conflicts between religious groups can be violent. Furthermore, that violence frequently serves the political, social, economic, and cultural goals of the antagonists. As recently as 2008, a small group of Muslims led a shooting campaign over several days in Mumbai, terrorizing thousands and killing 173. In 2007, Christian villages in the state of Orissa were attacked, and churches were burned by Hindu nationalists, displacing hundreds and killing at least twenty. Several bombs in Mumbai trains in July 2006 killed about two hundred and were blamed on Muslim militants. There are reports almost weekly of incidents such as these and their aftermath. While the deaths and displacement of Partition were on a scale that has thankfully not been repeated, clashes between Hindu, Muslim, and Sikh groups arise periodically, and in some cases national, state, and local governments have been complicit in or even perpetrated the violence. Thus the overall harmonious relationships between religions in Malerkotla are worth comprehending. It is important to analyze this town and its effective management of interreligious stress because if we only understand how communities fall apart and only study extremist militants, we cannot hope to work toward more sustainable pluralistic societies. By studying functioning multireligious communities and their strategies of cohabitation, we can learn how to help develop such societies in a variety of circumstances. It is particularly important therefore, to explore nonviolent communities located in regions where there is a history of interreligious conflict. By tracing the history and mythology of Malerkotla, its founding saint and his cult, its heroic nawabs, its Partition experience, and its idealistic yet pragmatic citizens, we discover the inner workings of a peaceful, plural community.

The Saint: Shaykh Sadruddin Sadri Jahan

Baba Haider Shaykh is the head [*sadr*] of all [the saints].
Shaykh Sadruddin Sadri Jahan. The head of religion [*din*]
and head of the world [*jahan*] also. We are his children.
                    —Ibrahim, spiritual guide, Malerkotla

W HEN I first arrived at the *dargah* of Shaykh Sadruddin Sadri Jahan
in 1999, I was told that the wall surrounding the Sufi saint's tomb was built in a
single night by jinn, the beings of fire that were created by God along with
humans and angels. Not only did this substantial, fortress-like wall appear over-
night, but it is also a unique structure in Malerkotla. There is no mortar holding
the large, hewn gray stones together, and no other buildings in town use this
stone or method of construction. The uniqueness of the building and its materials were presented to me as clear evidence of the miraculous nature of the
dargah and, by extension, of the main inhabitant of the precincts, Haider
Shaykh. My host that day, Zulfikar, told me the story. A former head of the
Punjab Wakf Board, which oversees Muslim religious endowments, he ran an
ice factory and was related to the saint through the lineage of Malerkotla's ruling
family. His wife, Nur, also a prolific teller of tales about Haider Shaykh, was
from one of the principle families of *khalifah*s, the hereditary custodians of the
shrine. They have six children and live in the literal as well as the spiritual
shadow of the saint.

Zulfikar's story about the wall touches on several aspects of Haider Shaykh's
hagiographic personality as founder, protector, integrator, and moral exemplar
for Malerkotla's community. The wall's origins point to the origins of Malerkotla itself as a settlement founded by the saint and symbolize the protective
role that he plays in local and regional lore about Malerkotla. Like the wall,
variant views about him and his legacy balance and even sustain one another,

drawing together disparate voices into a coherent whole. Finally, the miraculous wall is a divine acknowledgment of Haider Shaykh's saintly perfection and therefore authorizes his admirable qualities, such as his personal integrity, compassion, protectiveness, and acceptance of his true devotees regardless of their religious or ethnic origin. His descendants, the pilgrims to his tomb, residents of Malerkotla, professional and amateur historians, journalists, and others all relate to the Sufi saint with different interests and agendas that are then reflected in their stories. Taken together, it is clear that distinctive narratives emerge from various religious affiliations and that shifts in emphasis and information take place over time in accordance with changing contexts, demographics, and concerns.

Most histories of Malerkotla begin with the arrival of Shaykh Sadruddin Sadri Jahan and his encounter with Sultan Bahlol Lodhi (r. 1451–1489). The shaykh is described in a history of the dynasty written by one of his descendants, the last nawab of Malerkotla, as a Sherwani Afghan from Khurasan, "a very pious man of much celebrity in his time."[1] Haider Shaykh came to the area from Kabul via Multan where he studied and became adept in the spiritual path under the guidance of a *murshid,* or spiritual guide, of the Suhrawardi Sufi lineage.[2] This *murshid* is variously, and anachronistically, identified as Baha ul-Din Zakariyya (d. 1262) or his grandson Shaykh Rukn ud-Din Abu'l Fath (d. 1335).[3] At the behest of his *murshid* (whoever he was) Haider Shaykh settled on the banks of the Bhumsi, a tributary of the Sutlej River, which used to run through Malerkotla. It was there that Bahlol Lodhi encountered him where he had set up a hut in which to perform devotions. In the night a great storm arose, creating havoc throughout the army's camp, but Haider Shaykh's shelter was undisturbed. Impressed by the pious power of the saint who remained peacefully reading the Qur'an during the chaos, Lodhi asked for a blessing so that he would conquer Delhi.[4] After his victory, the sultan pressed a gift upon the *faqir,* a beautiful horse fit for an emperor. But Haider Shaykh had no need for a horse, so it was slaughtered to feed the *faqir*s and other people drawn to live in his holy presence. Hearing of the treatment of his gift, the sultan was insulted and demanded that the horse be returned. The saint miraculously produced multiple horses of equal beauty. Humbled, the sultan repented and vowed to marry his daughter Taj Murassa Begum to Haider Shaykh.[5] The sultan gave a large land grant, or *jagir,* as a dowry, and the *faqir* became a *jagirdar* (the holder of a *jagir*).[6] The date most often given for these events is 1454.

The shaykh and the sultan's daughter had two children, Hassan and Bibi Mangi. As Haider Shaykh rose in the world from a humble *faqir* to a major *jagirdar* with close ties to the sultan, the ruler of a nearby kingdom sought an alliance and offered his daughter in marriage. Two sons, 'Isa and Musa, were born from Haider Shaykh's second marriage.[7] Eventually the shaykh's daughter, Bibi Mangi, was married. However, she was widowed shortly afterward, and when her in-laws suggested that she marry her dead husband's younger brother,

FIGURE 1.1. The *dargah* of Haider Shaykh's daughter, Bibi Mangi.

she demurred. Her father ordered her brother, Hassan, to retrieve her from her marital home, but he refused. So her half-brothers, 'Isa and Musa, came to her rescue. On the return journey, Bibi Mangi implored the earth to open and receive her, which it did.[8] Though her motivation in seeking interment in this way is unspecified, the assumption is that she was driven by the tendency to blame widows for their husbands' deaths and to regard them as bad omens. As a pious woman and devoted daughter, she did not wish to bring shame on her father's household. There is a memorial shrine to her at the spot where she is believed to have entered the ground (fig. 1.1). The shaykh disinherited Hassan for refusing to help his sister. Shaykh Sadruddin Sadri Jahan died on 14 Ramadan, 922 hijri/1515 CE[9] Hassan was denied the bulk of the *jagir*, though he did receive some property, and his descendants eventually became the caretakers of the shaykh's tomb (fig. 1.2).[10] Musa became a *faqir* like his father, but he lived as a renunciant and had no children. 'Isa (d. 1538) and his descendants inherited the *jagir*. Not until 1657, under the Mughal ruler Aurangzeb, did the region became a quasi-independent principality, when Bayzid Khan was granted the title of nawab, and the *jagir* became a *riyasat* (kingdom).

"Proper Knowledge": Searching for the Shaykh

Clearly this is an oversimplified version of Haider Shaykh's life, though it does reflect current conventional wisdom. In fact, little authenticated information about the Shaykh exists. However, all is not lost. As Sufi Muhammad Ismail, one of the saint's modern-day hagiographers, explains, "It is well known that

FIGURE 1.2. *Khalifahs* sitting at the tomb.

through the illuminating light of many histories, readers and listeners can obtain proper knowledge."[11] Seeking proper knowledge about Shaykh Sadruddin Sadri Jahan brought me to many doorsteps in Malerkotla, to official archives, and to the edge of the saint's tomb. In each of these places his life and legacy appeared in more and more illuminating light, until it began to disappear into an over-exposed, blinding blur. Facts and fictions bled into one another, leaving a story with a deceptive coherence. This coherence represents the common knowledge about the saint and how the majority of the residents of his *wilayat* (spiritual territory) remember him. As Haider Shaykh's *wilayat,* Malerkotla is under his custodianship in both spiritual and temporal terms. *Wilayat* refers to the ability and the authority to protect a particular region.[12] Understood as *wilayat,* Malerkotla's protectors–known as *auliya'* (sg. *wali*)–are those figures whose shadows lie over the town's history and landscape.

There are historical sources that reference Haider Shaykh, though few pre-date the late nineteenth century, and so most of the stories are the stuff of memory and legend. Unlike some Sufi saints, Haider Shaykh did not have a lineage of disciples who recorded his life during his time. He also does not appear in any of the major collections of Sufi biographies.[13] These memories and legends appear in documents, gazetteers, newspapers, and personal testimonials that combine to provide a shared hagiographical reservoir from which Haider Shaykh's legacy flows. The testimonials of pilgrims and residents bolster Haider Shaykh's reputation for working miracles and express the moral values of egalitarianism, pluralism, and tolerance that are most central to the saint's cult and his territory.

Sufi Muhammad Ismail, the hagiographer cited above, believes that these multiple historical sources, rather than demonstrate the impossibility of discovering the "true" shaykh, in fact reveal "proper knowledge" in their "illuminating light." Although this multiplicity of histories can as easily obscure the past as illuminate it, a great deal of proper knowledge of moral personhood in the present emerges into an illuminating light by tracing which version of history is brought forth from the real or imagined past, and by whom and to what end. In other words, the ethical values of the present are made sense of and made authoritative through historicizing practices that are evident in the histories and hagiographies produced at particular junctures. By paying attention to the transitions in these accounts from the actual past, in so far as it can be established, to the moral past as it is constructed by historiographers, hagiographers, and others, we see the way in which collective memory takes on normative power through the stories a society tells about itself and its central historical figures. By observing these shifts in relation to Haider Shaykh's roles as founder, protector, integrator, and moral exemplar, it is possible to grasp how a complex tapestry retains its integrity and provides a shared discursive context for the past and present interlocutors of the saint.

For example, a profound shift in the intent and content of the stories about Haider Shaykh occurs after Partition. Tracing the available stories illustrates this shift from a narrative focused on legitimating the saint's lineage and the settlement he founded to legitimating interreligious cohabitation. Pre-Partition accounts, written mostly by dynastic chroniclers or descendants, are concerned with genealogy and the existence of Malerkotla as a principality, whereas post-Partition narratives are preoccupied with justifying the continued presence of Muslims in Indian Punjab and proving their ability to coexist with non-Muslim compatriots. After Partition, Malerkotla becomes the one place in Indian Punjab where a majority Muslim population remained and a place where no interreligious violence occurred. And so the imperative shifts from establishing and sanctifying the kingdom of Malerkotla to authenticating and excavating the primordial character of the town as a place of interreligious harmony both before and after the great division. Malerkotla is thenceforth depicted in the press as an "island of peace," an "oasis of tolerance," and so on.[14] Furthermore, this pacific character is extended temporally to become essential to Malerkotla and its inhabitants from the beginnings of recorded history. In particular, as we shall see, the person of Haider Shaykh emerges as the embodiment of the very ethical values that are said to characterize the town in the present. The fact that Malerkotla's history contains numerous episodes of conflict is rarely mentioned. The mythic status and near beatification of Malerkotla seem to be effective tools in generating an aspirational identity that is for the most part realized on the ground. Interestingly, this idealized identity is articulated not only by devotees of the saint, but also by residents, local historians, regional and national journalists, and seemingly anyone with Internet access who chooses to write about

Malerkotla in an online forum. So stories about the past establish a bank of collective memories from which various interlocutors may draw to further their agendas and interests. These written and oral narratives give Malerkotla's aspirational identity a genealogy.

The mobilization of memories preserved by a community carries the identity of the community forward, allowing old values and truths to metamorphose into shapes that are appropriate in a new context. In the construction of a moral past, an ethical present is also imagined. And, as folklorist Charles Briggs puts it, "the present can stand alone no more, bearing a false self-sufficiency and limiting the imagination to seeing what is present to the senses."[15] The present *needs* the past, to give it depth and meaning. The narrators who do the memory work of bringing the past into the present "use their historical force to confront the present with a value-laden interpretation of itself."[16] Briggs describes such memory work in his study of Mexicano use of "speech of the elders of bygone days" in conversations and narratives. Introducing an account of bygone days— such as the stories of the saint, or references to past practice, the "way things used to be"—into the discourse of the present expands the context of a speech event from a temporally discrete moment. What Briggs terms "historical discourse," therefore, serves several purposes: to validate a cultural action, transmit particular values associated with the past, and provide a source of collective identity. The past "stands as a communicative resource, providing a setting and an expressive pattern for discussions that transform both past and present."[17]

The collective memory work involved in passing on accounts of the past is an inherently interpretive process, requiring the communicator and the audience to engage the communicated events and determine their personal and social meanings. A hagiographer, the biographer of saints, is a "professional remembrancer commissioned by the community to preserve its knowledge of the saint."[18] This knowledge is purposeful and may "be considered socially useful too—to be stored within the community for its edification."[19] In relating events of moral exemplars from the past, whether prophetic, divine, or saintly, a narrator grounds his or her recommendations for ideal action in the present, effectively extending their significance and opening up a new field of meaning. Thus, oft-repeated tales, their tellers, and the contexts in which the tales are told reveal a great deal about how the popular narratives about Haider Shaykh shape the identity and culture of the *dargah* and the town. Variations, anomalies, and unique features of the narratives indicate how narratives of Haider Shaykh serve as vehicles for the representation of multiple personal and group identities. The formation of social order based on shared social knowledge about past practice hinges upon the coherence of collective memory.[20] When collective memories are narrated, orally and in writing, and come to possess a normative force, they represent what literary theorist Steven Knapp calls "collective authority."[21] Without knowing what collective memory is omitting, it is impossible to understand the workings and the intentions of collective authority.

In Malerkotla, the collective authority that upholds the ongoing social order is frequently grounded in the stories that residents and observers tell about the place and its founder. Pre-Partition stories tell of the saint, his lineage, and the founding of Malerkotla. These were elite narratives for elite audiences. The moral character of Malerkotla's populace was not important. The characters of the rulers and the territorial boundaries were central. By contrast, post-Partition stories, some anecdotal and some archival, naturalize and generalize the ethos of harmony that allowed Malerkotla's comparatively peaceful Partition experience, depicting it as part of the foundational fiber and ongoing reality of social life in the territory. After 1947, both histories and hagiographies tend to constellate around the shared project of authenticating a collective identity based on peaceful pluralism.

Founder: The Dark and Stormy Night

The accounts of the actual past of Malerkotla from before Partition are found in either chronicles of Afghan lineages or British colonial accounts. The Urdu and English histories written by the shaykh's descendants tend, unsurprisingly, to be mostly concerned with indexing the ruling lineage of the kingdom. They all mention Haider Shaykh's coming to central Punjab, his pious character, and the encounter with Bahlol Lodhi that led to his marriage to the sultan's daughter. These accounts are generally consistent with the historical genre of *tazkira*, the biographical dictionaries that record lineages of saints or rulers. As Marcia Hermansen points out, typically the purpose of such works is not only to memorialize individuals, but also to sanctify the soil of a new land. She writes, "The inscription of memory as a cultural activity involved both an appropriation of power over a space and the creation of an emotional investment in it."[22] Hermansen particularly emphasizes the centrality of place in the biographical dictionary, hinting at the way in which saints became identified with territory. The available accounts of Malerkotla generate precisely this link between the arrival of Haider Shaykh, the establishment of the kingdom, and the eventual Islamicization of the region.

Clan Histories

Two members of the ruling family of Malerkotla wrote histories of their clan, both in English. Inayat Ali Khan, the brother of Nawab Ibrahim Ali Khan (r. 1871–1908), wrote a chronicle of the ruling clan in 1882, *A Description of the Principal Kotla Afghans*. Sometime around the time of Partition the last nawab, Iftikhar Ali Khan, produced a manuscript history that was not available publicly until historian R. K. Ghai put out an edited edition titled the *History of the Ruling Family of Sheikh Sadruddin* in 2000. The two are very different in tone and intention. Whereas Iftikhar extols the virtues of his ancestor, Inayat criticizes the saint for failing to divide his property clearly at the time of his death. In Inayat's view, this set an unfortunate precedent resulting in generations of internecine disputes in which he was deeply involved.[23] Inayat's book has two clear audiences: his own family, with whom he was in dispute, and the British government, which could (and eventually would) intervene to resolve some thorny inheritance issues.[24] Inayat gives a great deal of information about the ruling lineage and also highlights the connection with Bahlol Lodhi. However, in his estimation Lodhi is not a great ruler, pious Muslim, or particularly praiseworthy character. Nor is Inayat particularly interested in his progenitor Haider Shaykh's saintly qualifications. Rather, he is critical of Lodhi's superstitious faith in saints:

> About the year 1450 when Bahlol Lodi, at the suggestion of Vazier Hamid Khan, was on his way down to Delhi to assume the direction of the Government of India, a country too extended to remain long under one head, he happened to halt near the hut of the Seikh [*sic*], whose devoted piety so much impressed him that he asked for an interview, which was granted to him by the Saint. Accordingly, Bahlol visited the Seikh, and implored him to invoke the aid of the Supreme Being for his success; and of this, in reply, he was assured by the Saint, *whose words were taken as those of God, under the prevailing belief of his possessing miraculous power.* Though to all appearance this agreeable assurance seems to have been framed on the past triumphs of Afghan invaders over the weak Princes of India whenever the former took up arms against them, yet, at any rate, Bahlol departed quite rejoiced, and positive of winning the prize of the Empire—after the wont of Afghans, *who rely more upon the prayer of a Saint than upon their own energy and action*; and at the same time avowed in his heart that should he succeed in his enterprise he would marry one of his daughters to the Seikh. Bahlol did not forget his vow. No sooner had he declared himself the King of Delhi, than he duly fulfilled it, and gave twelve large and fifty-six small villages by way of dowry into the bargain.[25] (emphasis added)

Although Inayat Ali Khan depicts Haider Shaykh as a pious saint and worthy of respect, he also dismisses Bahlol Lodhi's faith in him as typical of Afghans, who fail to show initiative and depend on miracles and saintly intervention instead. He gives little attention to the notion that saintly persons have miraculous powers. His concern in this narrative is to establish how the land grant of the sultan to his ancestor came about, no matter how misguided that *jagir* might have been.

Overall, Inayat Ali Khan's tone indicates enormous suspicion and a rather patronizing attitude toward the shaykh. The reason for this emerges as he arrives at his main reason for writing the book and takes the saint to task for failing to clarify the rules of inheritance at the time of his death.

> The Seikh died at the mature age of seventy-one, leaving three sons—Hassan, Isa, and Musa, the former of whom was born of the first marriage and the two latter of the second. The death of Sadr-ud-deen gave rise to a series of dissensions amongst his sons regarding the succession to the patrimony, as may easily be understood from the character of the age, when the people were indifferent to a testamentary disposition of property, either by nature or *through being over-occupied in religious matters* or forays, an occupation generally followed in and characteristic of the state of India under the Mahommedan rule even when it was at its highest pitch.[26] (emphasis added)

Preoccupation with religion clearly contributes to a disastrous neglect of worldly affairs, in Inayat Ali Khan's estimation, though religion was not the cause of his particular grievances about property disposition. So a precedent for messy succession and inheritance was set from the beginning and would remain an issue in Malerkotla, plaguing the ruling family throughout its history, taking up the latter third of the *Description* and a substantial file in the British India Office archives. In establishing the ontogeny of irregular inheritance practices in his clan, Inayat Ali Khan builds his case that his brother's personal property should have been made over to him after Ibrahim was named successor to the throne. He is not particularly concerned with Haider Shaykh's spiritual prowess or the reception of his charismatic power by the local community.

In contrast, the manuscript written by the last nawab, Iftikhar Ali Khan (d. 1982), is deeply concerned with the shaykh's spiritual prowess.[27] Iftikhar chronicled the lineage of his ancestor Haider Shaykh, including a lengthy discussion of the Sherwani and Lodhi clans, tracing them back to a twelfth-century Afghan chief, Shaykh Hussain Ghori. The encounter with Bahlol Lodhi, and Haider Shaykh's subsequent marriage to the sultan's daughter, are recounted in great detail. The episode of Bibi Mangi's doomed marriage is also described at length as part of a larger explanation as to why the descendants of Bahlol Lodhi's daughter were not the rulers of the state. Iftikhar Ali Khan is writing just after Partition and the dissolution of the princely states in democratic India. He is therefore at some pains to establish his credentials as a just leader in the new political order. Indeed he is elected repeatedly to the Punjab Legislative Assembly as the representative from the region. No longer able to claim birthright alone as justification of his rule, Iftikhar Ali Khan looks back at his ancestors as a politician, criticizing some points and praising others as indicative of good judgment and ethical behavior. For example, in contrast to Inayat's grievances regarding inheritance practices, Iftikhar defends Haider Shaykh's decision to bypass his eldest son's claim to the throne. "Some historians criticise him for not recognizing the claim of his eldest son to the *gaddi* of the State. They probably lose sight of the fact that he had lost the goodwill of his father and incurred his displeasure by refusing to go to the help of his sister."[28] This emphasis on the shaykh's ethics and the principled manner of his rule sets a strong precedent for his descendants and is repeatedly referenced throughout the text.

Iftikhar details the piety of the saint and the continuing power of his *dargah*. He especially highlights what for him would be a central issue: the possibility of being both a worldly and spiritual leader. In this regard, he does not see the shaykh's decision to accept the daughter of a sultan in marriage as requiring justification. Since he was a renunciant holy man who had come to India to spread Islam and perform religious devotions, marrying royalty would require a substantial change of lifestyle. Accepting the *jagir* entailed responsibilities as a landlord, judge, and military leader.[29] Although stories are often told of Sufi saints who shunned temporal authority as evidence of their moral superiority, Iftikhar counters that notion by asserting the possibility of being both a worldly and spiritual leader.[30] After the marriage, the "hut life was renounced and in consonance with his dignity and position proper buildings were erected."[31] But this adoption of a kingly standard of living ultimately in no way compromises his saintliness. He writes, the "career of this remarkable man serves to remind us of the old adage 'that it is possible to be engaged in worldly pursuits and yet remain Godly.'"[32] Indeed historically, Suhrawardi Sufis were more comfortable with temporal power than some their Sufi brethren from other orders, such as the popular South Asian Chishti lineage. Though no records confirm this, it is easy to imagine that Haider Shaykh's descendant Iftikhar, as a former ruler establishing his political credibility in a fledgling democracy, would be eager to demonstrate the compatibility of piety and moral righteousness with worldly authority.

Another point Iftikhar raises is the nature of the tomb itself as a site where the prayers of pilgrims are answered. He describes the shrine in his *History*:

> It was his piety that gave him a distinguished position even after his death. He was buried in Malerkotla and his grave promptly became a shrine to the glory of the sophisticate. But although the Eastern mind is by nature inclined to be impressed by supernatural manifestations and raises many happenings to the pedestal of miracles, yet the faith of the people to regard Sadar-i-Jahan's tomb as holding curative properties was in a way justified. That certain cures have been affected is not a wild story. Even in the light of new experience of spiritual thinkers a certain section admits that spirits have decidedly an influence on the human mind.[33]

In this rendering by his descendant, Haider Shaykh is no hut-dwelling *faqir*, but a "sophisticate" whose source of spiritual power was his piety, not his austerity.

Iftikhar goes on to describe the tomb as a center for healing. Perhaps filtered through his own British-style education, the nawab asserts that claims of miracles are not merely the inventions of the impressionable "Eastern mind" but are documentable and potentially scientifically verifiable. Iftikhar strikes an interesting balance between emphasizing the regal nature of Haider Shaykh and his saintly power. He cites historical works such as the *Ain-i Akbari* and Lepel Griffin's *Chiefs of Punjab*, but he incorporates elements of hagiographical writing as he reports the saint's miraculous powers both past and present. He also dwells on the nature of Malerkotla society and its special role in Punjab history. In his view Malerkotla as Haider Shaykh's *wilayat* is a pluralistic utopia, and these utopian values can be documented from the earliest period of the territory's existence.

In addition to these two histories by members of the ruling family, a 1907 Urdu work *Hayat-e Lodhi* (Lives of the Lodhis) by Israr Afghani gives brief biographical notes on each of the rulers of Malerkotla. Though I have been unable to trace the author, he is primarily concerned with chronicling the Pathan Lodhi clan's rule and is not particularly interested in the spiritual heritage of Haider Shaykh.[34] An entire section of the Malerkotla entry considers the admittedly puzzling issue of how Malerkotla got its name. One theory espoused in some British records and among some residents is that the town was founded by a previous ruler named Malher Singh, whose lineage is mythologically linked to Raja Bhim Sen, a figure in the epic *Mahabharata*. In *Hayat-e Lodhi*, however, Afghani dismisses this as absurd, arguing that no ruler would name his territory after the previous authority. This is a fair point, but hardly definitive proof of anything. Afghani raises other possibilities involving potential etymologies of the term Maler, such as devotees of the saint who were gardeners, or *malis*.[35] Returning to his discussion of Haider Shaykh, Afghani describes his second marriage to a Rajput woman and the continuation of the lineage, one line becoming the rulers, another becoming caretakers of Haider Shaykh's tomb shrine, *khalifah*s.

Afghani was writing during the colonial period, when Malerkotla was under British protection. Although he mentions Haider Shaykh's piety, he says nothing about his ongoing cult. The history does highlight the encounter with Lodhi but discusses Haider Shaykh's family heritage at greater length. The section on Malerkotla begins by detailing the route taken by Haider Shaykh to get to the area where he settled, thereby firmly establishing his Pathan Afghan heritage and connection to the Lodhis. Then he encountered Lodhi, and the marriage with Lodhi's daughter took place. Afghani writes:

> Lamih Qatal's great grandson [Haider Shaykh] was Ahmad Zinda
> Pir's son. He arrived in Hindustan on a voyage from Daraban and
> then arrived there at that settlement called Maler that was on the
> bank of a branch of the Sutlej. And on the bank a village Bhumsi was

settled (this village was here from when Raja Bhim Sen was living here). He made his dwelling place in the open and remained absorbed in remembering Allah. One day in about 1450 Hamid Khan Wazir had summoned Bahlol Lodhi to come to Delhi from Sirhind, and his encampment was near the dwelling place of the saint. Having heard about the piety of the saint, he came before him to pray for victory and when he went to leave he made the vow that if he became the Badshah of Delhi he would marry his daughter to him. Arriving in Delhi his desire was fulfilled. The Sultan in his satisfaction married his daughter to the saint; by way of a wedding gift he gave her fifty-six small and twelve large villages. After the wedding he [Haider Shaykh] went to one of the villages and settled it and named it Maler.[36]

This is consistent with the standard account of the meeting between Haider Shaykh and Bahlol Lodhi. But in this version no storms come up, no horses are given, and the only miracle performed (and it is not clear Afghani considers this a miracle) was the fulfilled prayer for Lodhi's victory at Delhi. Haider Shaykh is described as "absorbed in remembering Allah" and having an impressive degree of piety, which in addition to his Pathan Afghan heritage make him a suitable marriage partner. Afghani's reference to the commonly held view that this region was once connected to Bhim Sen, a hero of the Hindu epic *Mahabharata*, helps establish the powerful and important pedigree of the territory. The wording gives no indication of Afghani trying either to establish Muslim domination over a Hindu hero or to demonstrate the ecumenical history of the region. He simply remarks upon the connection as a point of distinction worthy of mention and draws it out no further. The biographical entries on each subsequent ruler mostly describe the villages and settlements that each establishes in the region. This interest in territory and lineage supports Hermansen's view that such historical works focus on place to legitimate authority.

British Colonial Accounts

Like the descendants of the shaykh, the British chroniclers of Malerkotla history from the late nineteenth through the mid-twentieth century are interested in both the saint's lineage and his piety. Every *Gazetteer*—the historical, economic, and cultural almanacs kept by the British in India—from 1881, 1883, 1891, and 1904 commences with the remark that the ruling family are Sherwani Afghans whose founding ancestor came from Daraban to settle in Punjab. In these brief accounts, Haider Shaykh encounters Bahlol Lodhi, who gives his daughter in marriage and several villages as a wedding present. There are some discrepancies regarding which of Haider Shaykh's children was born to which wife or the number of villages given in dowry, but generally the historical notes are nearly identical. In addition to addressing issues of lineage, property, and authority, the British histories almost universally remark upon Bahlol Lodhi's reasons for marrying his daughter to Haider Shaykh. Rarely mentioned is their shared Pathan ethnicity. Instead, the anonymous British *Gazetteer* authors attribute the marriage solely to religious sentiment. They claim that Bahlol Lodhi was "greatly impressed by his piety and sagacity"[37] or that Haider Shaykh was "a very learned and pious man"[38] or "a very pious man of much celebrity in his time."[39]

A similar preoccupation with religious belief is evident in an 1883 British ethnography *A Glossary of the Tribes and Castes of the Punjab*, which was written by British civil servants Denzil Ibbetson, H. A. Rose, and E. D. MacLagan. This study describes the cultural practices of the "tribes and castes of the Punjab" and briefly mentions the cult that develops around Haider Shaykh. Indeed, there is little interest in the personality of the saint or the history of Malerkotla. The *Glossary* reports the saint's lineage, origins, and marriage to Lodhi's daughter, but the bulk of the material focuses on the customs and practices associated with the cult comprised of "Hindus and Muhammadans from the State as well as from distant places." In particular the ethnographers describe the tradition of spirit possession associated with the tomb. They take care to note that Haider Shaykh's "fair, held on the first Thursday of every lunar month, is largely attended by Hindus and Muhammadans from the State as well as from distant places."[40] This observation is also supported by the 1904 *Maler Kotla State Gazetteer*, which reports, "It is strange that these fairs are mostly attended by Hindus, though Sadr-ud-Din was a Muhammadan Saint."[41]

These remarks are certainly consistent with the present-day reality at the shrine, but the concern with religious sentiment in the British accounts of the late nineteenth century should not be divorced from their political agenda. In fact, this period saw a number of colonial governing practices introduced, such as the census project that began in 1881 and sought, among other things, to identify every subject of the Raj by religious affiliation. These efforts required the enumeration of religious and ethnic communities to bring unprecedented order to the perceived chaos of Indian religious life. It also required a specificity and singularity of identity that had hitherto not been part of the mind-set of most South Asians, which certainly contributed to the development of the religious chauvinism known in this region as communalism. As Indian subjects of British colonialism began to organize to advocate for their interests, they were often constrained to do so as members of a particular religious or ethnic group. This imperial enumerative project of the census exemplifies, almost more than any other bureaucratic effort, the morality of order often used to ethically justify British rule.[42] Their spectacular organization and scientific bureaucracy provided the evidence that they deserved the authority they exercised so efficiently.

British archival records demonstrate a strong interest in stabilizing the rule of client states such as Malerkotla and establishing orderly bureaucracies. The

Malerkotla files tell of debt and inheritance disputes. There is even a fair amount of material on communal conflicts in the state, in spite of the currently popular portrayals of Malerkotla as an "island of peace."[43] British intervention in these matters reveals an imperial power desirous of maintaining the status quo. In particular, the presence of a Muslim principality surrounded by Sikh and Hindu states served British interests. The Sikh states had been among the last to submit to protectorate status in the mid-nineteenth century after the death of Maharaja Ranjit Singh (d. 1839). Malerkotla was under British protection since 1809 largely as a defense against the growing Sikh powers. Though small, the state was not without strategic and symbolic value. And so, while the archival records describe occasional incompetence—another justification for British intervention—they also document British efforts to shore up the ruling family by managing its debt, resolving inheritance disputes, and attempting to mediate communal conflicts. The ethnography's depiction of the multireligious worship of Malerkotla's founder intensified the impression that Indians are primarily, if indiscriminately, religiously motivated in their behavior. This helped validate the enumerative and other rationalizing governance practices introduced into the state. And, perhaps not coincidentally, this affirmation of the power of the saint and his lineage also supported the morality of order upon which the Raj placed a great premium.

Khalifah Tales

In contrast to the written histories of Inayat, Iftikhar, and the British, in the stories told by the descendants of Haider Shaykh who manage his tomb shrine, the *khalifah*s, the many miracles of the shaykh come to the fore. They describe the encounter with the sultan, the ruler's amazement at the saint's holiness, his subsequent gifts, and his eventual marriage with Taj Murassa Begum. These miracles not only justify the connection with Bahlol Lodhi but also affirm the saint's role as a moral exemplar. For example, the eldest son of the current chief caretaker of the *dargah*, known as the *gaddi nishin*, gave the following rendition of the basic tale when I inquired about what pilgrims tended to ask the *khalifah*s when they arrived at the tomb:

> People ask about his history. He came from Kabul. He was a Sufi saint, a big *buzurg* [pious man]. He came from Kabul to Punjab, Malerkotla. Once at night Babaji [Haider Shaykh] was inside his hut. From that direction [gestures north] Bahlol Lodhi Badshah was going for war; he also put his tents there. Suddenly a storm came, and his tents were destroyed, but in Babaji's hut, the lamp was still burning. The rest of the people were really surprised that in spite of such a storm, the lamp is still burning. They were impressed by him. The king asked Babaji to pray for him so that he should be

victorious in the war. Babaji prayed for him, and he won the battle. The Badshah out of happiness gave Babaji a horse, but Babaji was a Sufi, what was he to do with the horse? Babaji then gave the horse to somebody else. Somebody complained to the Badshah that Babaji has not accepted his gift. When the Badshah asked, Babaji with his miraculous power lined up a thousand horses just like that one in front of Babaji. Then the sultan married his daughter to Babaji.[44]

This account is quite similar to the outline of the shaykh's story we have already encountered. The meeting with Lodhi in the storm is the key event, followed by his marriage to the sultan's daughter. Added into this version is the well-known story of the saint's refusal of the gift of a horse. This episode serves to demonstrate Haider Shaykh's lack of worldly attachments and also his miraculous powers as he first rejects the horse and then conjures a thousand more. The brief rendering of all these details reveals an efficiency born of repetition. In a few brief words, the *khalifah* situated Haider Shaykh historically, validated his spiritual and temporal authority, established his moral character, and explained what he thinks the devotees need to know about the saint when they ask.

Several other members of the *khalifah* family command large repertories of stories related to their progenitor, and from them I heard accounts that were not commonly told by others in the community. These tales tended to emphasize the shaykh's miraculous powers and the superiority of spiritual power over worldly authority. I heard many stories from Ahmad, a *khalifah* who worked as a *numbardar* (revenue collector), that I never heard elsewhere. He was particularly interested in the lore of the shaykh and in Sufi practice. Ahmad's father and grandfather were well-known local Sufis. He did not sit at the tomb or collect money from it. He kept horses and mused that this perhaps revealed an affinity with his royal Afghan forefathers and the gift of Bahlol Lodhi to the shaykh. Ahmad had a reputation for knowing a great deal about Haider Shaykh, and many local people referred me to him as a source of knowledge.

One of Ahmad's stories offered an explanation of Haider Shaykh's motivation in coming to the region. In this rendition the shaykh was not just a religious adept but also a military man, a general in the army who had become increasingly absorbed in his religious practices and was neglecting his military duties. Completely lost in *zikr* (repetition of the names of God), Haider Shaykh ignored the marching orders sent to him by the ruler. However, his negligence of his worldly duties led to the revelation of his high spiritual attainment when the battle was miraculously won, in spite of his failure to lead the troops to war. Here is Ahmad's tale:

Baba Hazrat Shaykh Sadruddin Sadri Jahan (may God have mercy upon him) is his full name. He was a general in the army before, but he was a *faqir* also. Once, the king asked him to go somewhere because at that place a revolt was going on. But when the command came to him he took it and threw it on one side—because he was doing *zikr* at that time, in the Lord's name. So his followers who were jinn, they picked it up.[45] Those jinn who obeyed his command picked it up. And therefore they understood that they were given this command, and they went to that place, and they conquered it. And they got the booty from the people there, and the king asked, "My army didn't go there, [so] how were they conquered?" And he inquired [of Haider Shaykh], "If my general was here, and my army was also here, who went to conquer that place?" He answered, "Your command came, but I was praying and threw it to one side, and my followers thought the command was for them, so they went there and conquered." So the king ordered that he should not be given any work; he should only rest. But he left [the king's service]. Because his secret was exposed before everyone, which is not good. So his *pir* [spiritual guide] ordered him to go to Malerkotla and spread Islam there and pray to God. On all sides there was water here, except the place where the *dargah* is now. That was dry, so he sat there.[46]

Ahmad's tale has multiple levels, and it taps into several themes commonly associated with the foundation of Malerkotla and the advent of Sufism in South Asia more broadly. First, Haider Shaykh is depicted as a saint capable of anything, including commanding jinn and winning battles without moving. He is completely unconcerned with his worldly duties; commands from his overlord and ruler do not disturb his devotions, and he remains lost in prayer. But significantly, this great shaykh who ignores temporal authority and has armies of jinn at his command humbly obeys his *pir*, and he goes to work as a simple man of faith, spreading Islam and praying in a place previously uninhabited and apparently uninhabitable because it was submerged in water. This demonstrates his capacity to wield power in both the temporal and spiritual worlds.

Second, Ahmad's narrative evokes a common trope in the hagiographies of Sufi saints in which the holy man goes to a wild and uncultivated land and establishes himself. In Ahmad's story, Haider Shaykh arrives at a place that was isolated and surrounded by water. In other oral accounts, the area was described as a jungle. In either case, the region is portrayed as uninhabited and uncivilized prior to the saint's arrival. This contrasts sharply with the elite histories of the British and the ruling clan that claim there was a preexisting, prestigious kingdom. Through the saint's spiritual discipline, charisma, and *barakat* or spiritual power, the region is simultaneously civilized and Islamicized as people are drawn to the saint's teachings and settle around him. Richard Eaton's study of Bengal points out the "association of Muslim holy men (*pir*), or charismatic persons popularly identified as such, with forest clearing and land reclamation." These holy men come to symbolize the very process of Islamicizing a region. Eaton continues, asserting that the popularity of such figures has "endured precisely because, in the collective folk memory, their careers captured and telescoped a complex historical socioreligious process whereby a land originally forested and non-Muslim became arable and predominantly Muslim."[47] A common theme in such narratives is that the area was wild and unsettled. This cycle of stories about the saint's coming thus represents his arrival as the first significant human settlement of the region and credits him with making the place habitable.[48]

Third, Ahmad credits Haider Shaykh with the conversion of the local population who gathered around him and helped to establish the settlement. Although this places Haider Shaykh right on the cusp of the wave of spiritual and temporal power that was rolling into Punjab in the fifteenth century, Islam had been present in the Punjab since the eleventh century. Significant conversion seems to have begun in the fifteenth and sixteenth centuries.[49] Though Haider Shaykh may have had a military past, that is erased from most active memories. Residents and visitors tend to attribute the success of Haider Shaykh's cult, and by extension the success of Islam, to the saint's charisma and the egalitarian values he embodied.

Residents unrelated to the saint also tell stories about Haider Shaykh and the foundation of Malerkotla. Even those who do not attend the shrine seem to take pride in this legacy. For example, around the Jama Masjid, or Friday congregational mosque, there are numerous stalls and shops that sell Islamic books and paraphernalia—prayer beads, Qur'ans, recordings of Qur'anic recitation, and prayer rugs. This neighborhood is the bastion of Islamic conservatism in town; the mosque is the base of operations for activists from the Tablighi Jama at, a reformist and revivalist movement critical of saint cults. Stopping into one of these bookshops early during my time in Malerkotla, I was looking over the merchandise when the proprietor asked me what brought me to town. I said I was interested in the history of Malerkotla. Then the bookseller told me his version of that history, crediting the foundation of the town to the saint, Haider Shaykh, whose tomb lay across town. He said,

> The Lodhi army was resting near the 'Id prayer grounds. There was a big storm in the night. And this Babaji [Haider Shaykh], he was staying near the old fort. On that particular night the Badshah [Bahlol Lodhi] was surveying his army. He saw that in spite of such a big storm, a lamp was burning in Babaji's house. When he went there and saw, he found Babaji there. Babaji was very beautiful. "I want to marry my daughter with you." Babaji said, "I am a *faqir*; I can't do that." But after a long dialogue he said yes. Bahlol Lodhi was the emperor at that time.[50]

This story deftly illustrates the binding power of the story of Haider Shaykh. Most residents of Malerkotla know this account of the Sufi saint's encounter with the Afghan warlord Bahlol Lodhi, and they tell it as one of the primary myths of the origins of their hometown. In other examples, a local Jain merchant explained that the Jains came to the area with the daughter of Bahlol Lodhi to make the area more cosmopolitan. A Hindu craftsman told the same core story, then recounted at length the various ways in which Haider Shaykh demonstrated his moral and spiritual superiority to the emperor. Descendants of the saint call him *dada* (grandfather) and explain how the shaykh's lineage still keeps his tomb and his protective legacy alive. This multiplicity of voices and perspectives demonstrates how integrated Haider Shaykh is into the collective consciousness about Malerkotla's origins. The stories focus on the shaykh's miraculous powers and his connection with the imperial family, through which Malerkotla came into being through a land grant that was part of Lodhi's daughter's dowry. Malerkotla is thus founded with divine and imperial sanction, allowing interlocutors to emphasize whichever aspect they choose.

Protection: Saved by the Saint

Haider Shaykh's role as the founder of Malerkotla places him and his *dargah* at the spiritual center of the town. But, like the wall that encircles his tomb, the saint protects his *wilayat*, the zone of his spiritual authority.[51] Through his charismatic, sacred power (called *baraka* in the Islamic tradition), Haider Shaykh preserves and protects the area and its inhabitants from all kinds of dangers. For many pilgrims, and not just Muslims, the *baraka* of Haider Shaykh explains the anomalous peace and security of Malerkotla during times of strife elsewhere. Most of the Shaykh's descendants attribute Malerkotla's state of peace to their ancestor. But, as with the bookseller above, even those who do not participate in the cult of the saint still identify Haider Shaykh as one of Malerkotla's most important historical figures. Among this group are residents who recognize that their livelihoods are improved because his tomb shrine draws thousands of visitors every year who patronize their shops and services. Still others perceive the social rather than spiritual importance of attending the shrine, recognizing the *dargah* as a key gathering place for a variety of purposes from gossiping to politicking. Taken together, these multiple perspectives on Haider Shaykh justify the continued presence of this Muslim town, explain the peace at Partition, and validate the multireligious cult that centers on the Shaykh's tomb, or *dargah*.

The *dargah*'s popularity, according to locals, has grown in recent years. Pilgrims from outside of town are also invested in the claims of the saint's protective power. For example, Mahesh, a Hindu pilgrim from Sirsa in the neighboring state of Haryana, expressed the view that Haider Shaykh alone preserved Malerkotla. Mahesh is a *chela*—a person who is possessed by the spirit of the saint and communicates Haider Shaykh's counsel and wishes to his devotees. I asked Mahesh if he had heard the story that Malerkotla was a zone of peace where no one was killed in Partition.

> MAHESH: Yes. No Sikh was killed, and no Muslim was killed. In its boundary no one was killed.
>
> AB: Why?
>
> MAHESH: Because of the power of Babaji [Haider Shaykh], and I can't explain that.
>
> AB: No other reason?
>
> MAHESH: No, if there had been some other reason then this would have been the case in other places as well. Other places men and women were murdered.[52]

For Mahesh, not only was Malerkotla's reputation as a peaceful place true, but the very fact of the peace is proof of Haider Shaykh's power. Recalling that hundreds of thousands of people died during the transfer of population, Malerkotla stands out as one of very few places in Punjab that was able to prevent the violence from entering its borders.

Oral testimonies such as these also demonstrate an interest in explaining the anomalous presence of Muslims in Punjab. Many residents and pilgrims attribute both the demographics and the harmony to the spiritual power of Haider Shaykh. For example, Ibrahim, a local Muslim who worked as a kind of *murshid*, spiritual guide, to a largely non-Muslim clientele, insisted that the preservation of Malerkotla was ascribable to the presence of Haider Shaykh and the many other saints buried in the area. "Yes, it is special, all the other places here or there, they have some kind of problem or trouble, but there is nothing in Malerkotla. This is because of these *pirs* who are in such a big number in Malerkotla. The other places don't have this, this is the problem."[53] In Ibrahim's view, it is the spiritual power of the saints that protected Malerkotla when all other places were caught up in the conflagration of Partition. Although towns with buried saints all over South Asia have experienced violence, for Ibrahim that fact only supported his theory that the *pirs* of Malerkotla were exceptionally powerful.

Other residents and visitors also link the present character and condition of Malerkotla to the saint's protective power. It is not surprising, perhaps, that many Muslims connected the peace in Malerkotla to Haider Shaykh. But it is not only local Muslims who claim these powers for the founding saint. As Mahesh explained:

> Whatever I have in this life, I have from Baba. Baba got God in his life because he worshiped him so much. He was a *faqir*, and the

other children were nawabs. The nawabs are finished, but the *faqirs* still go on. That is why people from different religions believe in him. Earlier they used to believe, and now they believe still.[54]

Exemplification: The Morals of the Saint's Stories

The stories about Haider Shaykh all describe the moral qualities of the saint. He is depicted as a pious man who valued justice, equality, and honesty. His lack of mercenary motivations is clear in his initial refusal of the horse and his reluctance to marry the sultan's daughter. His piety (and his Pathan ethnicity) made him an acceptable son-in-law for a sultan. His benevolence results in his ongoing care for the people in the territory he founded. Evidence of his compassion and mercy appears in all of the children born through his blessings. All of these qualities, verified through testimonials and texts, add to his appeal and give evidence of his saintly character. In a hagiographical pamphlet written by the current chief custodian of Haider Shaykh's *dargah*, Anwar Ahmad Khan recounts other stories that flesh out the moral character of the shaykh. In one story, the saint refuses to accept an offering of money from a soldier, throwing the coins into a vessel of water. "After some time passed, what did he see? In place of the currency, spots of blood were floating in the water and bubbles were being made. He gave the judgment that these earnings were from forbidden sources."[55]

Haider Shaykh possessed a charismatic authority that drew people to him in his own time and ever since. The qualities that come to the fore in the stories depend on the concerns of each interlocutor. For example, a visiting *faqir* from Uttar Pradesh called Maulani Baba described the shaykh as a peaceful apostle of the faith. This *faqir* travels continuously from one *dargah* to another, and the tomb shrine in Malerkotla is one of his semi-regular haunts. Coming from outside Punjab, Maulani Baba is one of the rare nonresidents with a large repertoire of tales about Haider Shaykh whom I encountered. Although he did not cite the sources of his lore, he does stay during his visits with a family connected to the shrine. The family showed him great respect and affection during their interactions. In his narratives, the *faqir* depicted Haider Shaykh as a warrior, but in this case, he used the military career of the saint as a classic conversion story in which the past ungodly life is forsaken and a life dedicated to God is taken up. The military life becomes a foil for the life of God, and this dedication results in sufficient charismatic power to produce conversions to Islam.

At that time he was a major in the military, and he came to see that the world's law was *jutha* (untrue) and that the Lord's law was true. To adopt the rules of God, he did whatever Allah, Ishvar, Prabhu, Bhagwan, Paramatma, he did whatever pleased Allah Most High, and when God was happy then he was God's and God was his. And from then on he resigned from the army and came to Malerkotla, which was a princely state, and this was a region where a lot of other saints were preaching. And when he stopped in this region, after seeing his personality, the people were drawn to pray through him to Allah.[56]

Maulani Baba's tale emphasized Haider Shaykh's abandonment of his worldly and military life to take up the pursuit of God's will, a choice mirrored in the *faqir*'s own life.[57] As the shaykh grew in knowledge and devotion to the one true God (who has many names), he came to prefer the company of other saints to material or military rewards. Furthermore, the force of his personality drew people to him, and through him they came to Islam. In this way a wandering *faqir* from Uttar Pradesh, who had also given up his daily life, work, and family to seek God forged a connection with Haider Shaykh, an Afghan whose royal lineage and saintly tradition are deeply rooted at the tomb and in Malerkotla.

Maulani Baba also generalized the identity of God in such a way as to include all religious believers in the saint's devotional community. He carefully enumerated a wide variety of appellations for God in order to include all religious faiths within his knowledge. This incorporation and identification of the many names of God also incorporates the multi-confessional community of Haider Shaykh into a single group devoted to a single all-encompassing, all-inclusive God. These multiple communities may know God by different names, but all are able to reach him through Haider Shaykh. Thus Maulani Baba affirmed the unity of God and the variety of his names, and simultaneously asserted the preeminence of Haider Shaykh and his magnetic power.

From all of these historiographical materials and personal testimonials it becomes clear that it is impossible to establish the veracity of the events described—particularly those with miraculous dimensions. But in many ways, verification is secondary to understanding the significance of Haider Shaykh. To his devotees and the residents of the settlement that he founded, the significance of the shaykh is communicated through which stories they tell, and their choices illuminate the ways in which Haider Shaykh and his lore permeate the social space of Malerkotla. He is a touchstone, providing an easy referent in conversation to exemplify certain qualities or events most associated with him. Oft-repeated stories are condensed and recycled. As Catherine Cubitt points out in her study of Anglo-Saxon saints, "Remembering is an inherently social activity. Individual memory is structured through language and ideas shared by society."[58] People learn what is important about the saint by what they hear about him from others. Many residents who attend the shrine know quite a few stories about Haider Shaykh, the site's miraculous construction, and numerous accounts of healing or fulfilled desires. Pilgrims from outside Malerkotla often do not know the historic accounts of the shaykh. Indeed many are unaware that his full name is Shaykh Sadruddin Sadri Jahan.[59] Whether or not they know any of the lore of the saint and the town, devotees from outside tend to be more concerned with experiencing and communicating the living presence and power of the saint than with extolling his past deeds. Given the multiple possible orientations toward the saint, it is natural that different features and variant narratives come to the fore with different tellers and in various contexts. These nuances, emphases, deviations, and contradictions reveal how the stories become several identity markers for the interlocutors, shaping the personal and public meaning of the shaykh.

As identity-shaping narratives, such stories integrate the ideology of peace into the community's past and present. They also provide important ideals and models of positive interreligious relations. The selection of key moments in the past and their subsequent reemergence, sometimes in altered or variant forms, allows the past to conform to an ethical or strategic need of a later time, constructing a moral past that grounds a present reality. Alessandro Portelli describes a similar process in his article "The Death of Luigi Trastulli," which outlines the mechanisms of memory in relation to identity in an Italian town in the twentieth century. In his study, a community remembers the facts of a certain past event inaccurately, but these factual inaccuracies are enormously revealing of the culture, conditions, and needs of the community in the present. The situation is also telling of how collective memory works and how "the memory of this brief episode has exerted a shaping influence on the town's identity and culture."[60] This "shaping influence" is an important process to observe as it reveals the ways in which particular events take on such a heightened degree of symbolic importance for personal or collective identities that they become identity markers. An identity marker provides a reference point, a semantically and symbolically rich instrument for conveying meaning. In certain contexts the mere mention of a particular event may be laden with significance that far exceeds the moment of a story's telling. Thus emerges the shaping influence of the saint and certain events in the town's history on the identity of Malerkotla. Identity-shaping stories must resonate with the experience of those who hear and tell them in order to function as effective transmitters of a collective identity.

Some narrators connect the saint to their personal circumstances by committing what some would call an historical "error," displacing Haider Shaykh in time to generate a hereditary or sentimental link. This is also consistent with the oral narratives collected by Portelli in relation to the misplacement of a symbolic event in community memories to associate the event with the ideological concerns of the present. Similarly, temporal displacement of the saint is a common technique employed to connect him in some way to the narrator's own history. Thus many local Hindus place Haider Shaykh as a contemporary of Baba Atma Ram, a Hindu saint whose shrine lies about a kilometer from Haider Shaykh's tomb. Although the best estimate places Baba Atma Ram in the early eighteenth century rather than the fifteenth, in these oral accounts there is a deep friendship between the two. Some people even describe them as playing games together. For Hindus, this temporal shift reduces the dominant shadow cast by Haider Shaykh over the town, presenting the Hindu saint as a contemporary and peer with his own repertoire of miracle stories and entourage of devotees.

Portelli also points out that such shifts in the temporal or material structure of a narrative are interpretive acts. Changing the place or time of an event determines the meaning of the event by defining the parameters of its occurrence and its relations to previous and subsequent events. An example of this interpretive process is the extremely common practice among nonresident devotees of displacing Haider Shaykh from the fifteenth to the eighteenth century and attributing to him the protest of his descendant, Nawab Sher Muhammad Khan, against the execution of Guru Gobind Singh's sons in 1705. Although historically in "error," as Portelli argues, this act of displacement and condensation of Haider Shaykh with Sher Muhammad Khan reveals a great deal about the interests of those who make this assertion. The Muslim saint is connected to the Sikh guru, authorizing Sikh devotion and drawing together two spiritual adepts whose power to protect, heal, and bless is desired by Muslims and Sikhs alike.

Integration: Pluralism in History and Story

Earlier in this chapter we saw how British colonial accounts took particular note of the presence of non-Muslims at Haider Shaykh's *dargah*. In a similar vein, the last Nawab, Iftikhar Ali Khan, writes in his *History of the Ruling Family of Malerkotla* that "men of all shades of opinion, of all religions, cults and denominations flocked from all parts of India to the hut of the Sheikh."[61] Whether this was true in the fifteenth century or not, it certainly is true today. Thus it is clear that both before and after Partition in 1947 the saint has enjoyed multireligious devotion and respect. As a founder, protector, and moral exemplar, Haider Shaykh's personality also makes space for non-Muslims in his cult and community. Jains in Malerkotla tell stories that link their presence to the time of the Shaykh's marriage to the sultan's daughter, and other non-Muslims also express gratitude for the saint's protection of all the residents of Malerkotla at Partition. One of Haider Shaykh's key moral qualities is the perception of his egalitarianism. He is portrayed in modern discourses as unconcerned with status and unmoved by wealth. This egalitarian ethos also contributes to Haider Shaykh's persona as an integrator of the people living in and visiting his *wilayat*. As noted above, he is identified as a *sanjha*, or common, saint who does not believe in *jat-path* (caste and sect). Many non-Muslim pilgrims value the saint for this nonsectarian outlook. This is another aspect of the local lore about his friendship with Baba Atma Ram. For these Hindus, displacing Haider Shaykh in time and condensing his cult with that of Baba Atma Ram strategically incorporates

Haider Shaykh's symbolic meaning: he remains a key symbol of interreligious harmony, but on terms that generate a powerful precedent for non-Muslims. This association sets a precedent for his devotees to supercede religious boundaries in the present as he himself did in earlier times.

Hindus in the past and present patronize Haider Shaykh's *dargah* and many other such places. Furthermore, Hindus both figure in the stories told about Haider Shaykh, and Hindus tell their own stories about Haider Shaykh. These narratives establish direct links between the saint and the non-Muslim community in Malerkotla. The stories may also provide vehicles to make social commentaries on the quality of Muslim authority. For example, Balram, an elderly Hindu *mistri* (craftsman) recounted one of the most detailed oral renditions of the tale of Haider Shaykh's meeting with Bahlol Lodhi I ever heard.[62] Balram was also the president of the committee that manages the Vishvakarma Mandir in the Bhumsi neighborhood, very close to Haider Shaykh's *dargah*. Vishvakarma is the deity worshiped particularly by carpenters, ironworkers, builders, and others who do skilled manual labor. In Malerkotla, as in most areas in India, devotees of Vishvakarma are among the lower strata of society. I encountered Balram during an interview originally meant to be with a local Jain scholar of Jainism. He was among the small group (about five) of Hindus and Jains present. He was the oldest member of the gathering but was also the lowest caste, the remainder being Aggarwals, a mostly merchant caste. Those assembled had shown an impatient deference as the elderly Balram frequently interrupted the published Jain historian to interject his own commentary. The initial discussion focused on the first Jain presence in the area and then turned to an event in which the last nawab of Malerkotla came to meet a famous Jain *muni*, or ascetic. This meeting clearly stood out for the Jains as a significant moment when the Muslim authority of the town publicly acknowledged the importance of the Jain community and indeed deferred to him by visiting him, rather than being visited, a gesture of respect. At this point, in what initially seemed to be a non sequitur, Balram interrupted the historian's account and launched into an extended narrative of the arrival of the most famous local resident, Haider Shaykh. He began with the story of the saint's encounter with Sultan Bahlol Lodhi in a standard fashion:

> When Bahlol Lodhi's army came there, they were on the march, and at once a storm came and all the tents blew up. The king saw that all the tents had blown up except one a long distance away, and in it a light was burning. He stopped and went to him and said, "Give me a blessing that I should conquer Delhi." As the saint's work is to give blessings, he gave it, but the king put him in a fix as he gave him a horse. Baba said, "I am a saint, I do not need a horse." But he [Lodhi] said, "I have come to a saint, so I should give something," and he forcibly gave the horse.

Before giving the entire narrative, which continued at some length, it is worth pointing out several distinctive features of Balram's version. First, Haider Shaykh is portrayed as not particularly interested in whether Lodhi conquers Delhi. He gives the blessing as a matter of course, because "the saint's work is to give blessings." This places Haider Shaykh at some distance from the military exploits of the Lodhi clan. Second, Balram emphasized the resistance of the *faqir* to such an ostentatious and useless gift as a horse, emphasizing Haider Shaykh's poverty and nonattachment to worldly things. Finally, Balram placed the blame for what he clearly considered an inappropriate gift firmly upon the king who refused to take no for an answer. This suggests, and he later asserts, a negative opinion of the sultan. Rather than establishing a personal link with a powerful lineage, as we saw in the accounts of the lineage historians, the meeting of Haider Shaykh and Bahlol Lodhi provided Balram with an opportunity to demonstrate the profligacy and obstinacy of the Afghan ruler and the more genuine authority of those who renounce the world. He continued this theme with a protracted parable explaining that it is in fact the nature of most rulers to be so obstinate:

> We [people] have three kinds of stubbornness or rigidness. One is the king's stubbornness or rigidness, one is the woman's stubbornness, and the third is the child's stubbornness, and in front of these even God has to bow. No one can speak in front of the king's stubbornness. We have a lot of examples of the stubbornness of women. Ram Chandra went into exile because of his [step]mother's stubbornness.[63] The example of a child's rigidness occurs [in a tale] from Babur[64] and Birbal, who were sitting, and Babur said, "I have seen the king's and the woman's stubbornness. The king's example is me, the woman's in the *Ramayana*, but what is the stubbornness of a child?" Birbal said, "I will show you just now." He brought a child from somewhere, and soon the child started crying. The king asked, "What do you want?" The child said a small pot. He was given it. He became quiet, but again started crying. The king again asked, "What do you want?" He said an elephant. He was given it, then again he started crying and said, "I want to put this elephant into the pot," which was impossible, so the king has to bow. So the king [Lodhi] because of that nature, tied the horse there and went.

This digression into the parable of the king was loaded with Balram's opinion of rulers in general. Clearly unimpressed by royalty, he depicted Lodhi's behavior as inappropriate in foisting a horse on a *faqir*. He expressed his displeasure through his morality tale about stubbornness. The tale contrasts sharply the king's obstinacy with the extraordinary patience of the saint. Balram continued:

He [Lodhi] won in Delhi. In the meantime Haider Shaykh gave the
horse to one of his disciples. Somebody complained to the king that
he [Haider Shaykh] did not accept your offer and gave it to somebody. So the king came and asked, "Where is the horse?" So he said,
"I told you before that I do not need it, so I gave it to somebody." So
Haider Shaykh made [miraculously] a horse and gave it to the king,
but the king said, "I want my horse." So Haider Shaykh said, "You
are arrogant, but I will give you your horse. You just close your
eyes." Bahlol Lodhi blinked his eyes and saw there were thousands
of horses more beautiful than his standing there, and his horse was
standing behind them all and was eating the [excrement] of all the
other horses. He saw the miracle and cooled down. He apologized
and said, "I will marry my daughter to you." His daughter was
thirty-five years old. She gave birth to two children. [Lodhi] gave
them fifty-five villages in dowry. Faith in [Haider Shaykh] was
endless. When he expired he had two sons. His younger son took
the offering. This is the nawab family. They are first Pathans and
later Mughals. In Malerkotla there was never a Mughal rule, there
was not even the rule of Aurangzeb. Malerkotla's nawab was called
jagirdar, he was not called nawab earlier. Aurangzeb gave Sher Shah
[Sher Mohammad Khan] this status for the first time three hundred
years back.[65]

In one sense, the Hindu *mistri*'s account of Haider Shaykh's meeting with Sultan
Bahlol Lodhi followed the standard structure for this tale: the sultan's army
caught in a storm, the undisturbed saint, the request for a blessing, victory in
battle, miracle of the horse, marriage to the ruler's daughter. However, Balram
also inserted a number of narrative elements that vary from the dominant
structure. By embedding his variations in the standard framing tale of the meeting of the sultan and the shaykh, Balram demonstrates his proficiency in the lore
of the saint and renders the tale meaningful in his own idiom. Highlighting these
variations clarifies his particular perspective on Haider Shaykh, the Muslim
ruler Bahlol Lodhi, and the moral significance of the foundational narrative
of Malerkotla. Rather than emphasizing the link between the royal and spiritual
lineages, as is done by the *khalifah*s and many Muslim residents, this low-caste
Hindu narrator highlights the superiority of spiritual over temporal authority.
He uses the story of Haider Shaykh's arrival to critique autocratic and imperious
rulers who insist on having their own way.

By demonstrating his familiarity with the core elements of the tale and of
other narrative traditions such as the *Mahabharata* and the tales of Birbal,
Balram gives voice to a complex morality tale. He established his authority by
interrupting the conversation and shifting his language from a conversational
and fragmentary style to a declamatory mode employing lengthy sentences that

allowed for the growth and development of a narrative arc and discouraged interruption. He also used a richer and symbolically denser narrative style that incorporated didactic fables and local hagiographical tales to illustrate his point. Commencing his account in the middle of a discussion about the origins and contributions of Jain society in Malerkotla, Balram represented the figure of Haider Shaykh in such a way as to demonstrate the general superiority of religious renunciants over worldly authorities, and the particular superiority of the hometown saint Haider Shaykh over the Delhi sultan Bahlol Lodhi. Balram's tale established the moral and temporal independence of Haider Shaykh and Malerkotla from the Lodhis and the subsequent Muslim rulers. He saw this distance from central Muslim authority as a point of pride.

By signaling his approbation of the saint's behavior over that of Bahlol Lodhi, Balram argues for a shared value structure that favors spiritual poverty over material wealth. The telling of the story seems less random when one considers that Balram broke in immediately after the local Jains had spoken with pride and pleasure of the respect the nawab had shown by visiting the Jain mendicant rather than requiring him to attend his court. The nawab demonstrated proper etiquette and seemingly acknowledged the superiority of spiritual over temporal authority. As Cubitt points out, these remembered narratives are not an exact science. On the contrary, "the process of recollection is not an exact one of information retrieval but rather one in which memories are put together from fragmented sources, often in a simplified form, according to pre-existing patterns."[66] Thus the narrative tradition of Haider Shaykh provides a structure through which a wide range of opinions, ethical values, and personal agendas are expressed with authority and enormous creativity.

The Post-Partition Shift

Having seen in the previous four sections the four aspects of Haider Shaykh's hagiographic personality—founder, protector, integrator, and moral exemplar—we are now in a position to observe how the accounts written after Partition shift in emphasis from those from before 1947. In these accounts the enormous piety and power of the saint, his multireligious appeal, and the importance of Malerkotla as his spiritual and temporal territory come to the fore. In this section we will explore post-Partition writings by two descendants of the saint and one by a local religious leader.

Anwar Ahmad Khan is the current *gaddi nishin* or head of the *dargah* of Haider Shaykh. At some shrines this role also entails a spiritual component, and the *gaddi nishin* is a spiritual guide to a number of disciples. In Malerkotla the role is largely symbolic and managerial. Anwar is elderly and no longer spends much time at the *dargah* himself, and in December of 2000 he did not attend the shaykh's *'urs*, or death day memorial ceremony. Some time ago he wrote a small chapbook (undated) that was printed but not widely distributed locally.[67] It is

available in Hindi and Punjabi. The chapbook includes the two most commonly
known stories about Haider Shaykh–the story of the storm and the gift of the
horse, both of which establish Haider Shaykh's privileged relationship with
Bahlol Lodhi.[68] Yet the focus of the chapbook is mostly on demonstrating
Haider Shaykh's pious character and miraculous powers and on providing a
guide to the proper etiquette for his followers. Anwar Ahmad Khan clearly
understands the followers to be Sikh and Hindu as well as Muslim, as reflected
in his word choice and address. The chapbook makes clear that the real index of
their right to participate in the tomb cult is the purity of their hearts in
approaching the shaykh. The etiquette that is laid out in the text is defined
through descriptions of Haider Shaykh's temperament. Anwar Ahmad Khan
portrays the shaykh as easily angered. The very first paragraph of the text ends
with the observation that the Hindus, Muslims, and Sikhs of the region come in
the hundreds of thousands to Haider Shaykh's *mela* (festival) because "it is their
belief that if Baba Haider Shaykh became angry [*naraz ho gaye*], then they will
fall into trouble."[69] Then in the following paragraph the crowds of devotional
groups, called *chaunki*, are described as coming to *dargah* to pay respects and
then taking leave to return to their gatherings. They must observe the proper
procedure, or else they will suffer serious consequences. "The belief is that unless
they observe every prescribed rule, then Babaji will become angry at them [*un
par naraz ho jayenge to unki murad bhar na hon ayenge*] so their desire will not be
fulfilled."[70] This view of Haider Shaykh as a *jalali* (terrifying and awe-inspiring)
pir is common among the visitors to the *dargah* and the *khalifah*s, though many
also emphasize his compassionate and just nature (see fig. 1.3). For example, one
of Anwar Ahmad Khan's sons pointed out that Haider Shaykh is usually gentle,
but he may become angry with devotees who fail to observe the proper etiquette
at his tomb. He said, "If somebody does not keep his dress properly, then Babaji
gets annoyed. Otherwise he is a gentle [*naram*] natured *buzurg*. But if somebody
makes a mistake, then he shows his power, he gets annoyed."[71]

The chapbook stresses the connection with Bahlol Lodhi and the saint's
miraculous powers. The first supports the saint's role as the founder, and the
second demonstrates Haider Shaykh's protective power for his devotees—if they
behave properly. This proper behavior is delineated through stories exemplify-
ing moral behavior and some specific directions about performing prayer and
being generous that are given as a kind of appendix. Anwar Ahmad Khan only
briefly discusses the shaykh's childhood, primarily to establish the saint's pious
character. Several tropes typical of hagiographies appear here. For example,
before his birth his mother is said to have had a dream in which a wondrously
strange light burned throughout the house and then flew away to another place.
A wise man (*mahanpurush*) interpreted the dream as signifying that a child
would be born in whose name lamps would be lit in other countries.

Anwar Ahmad Khan gives several reasons for Haider Shaykh's coming to
India. First, he asserts that the saint's fame had proliferated, and so the residents,

FIGURE 1.3. A family returns to thank Haider Shaykh for the birth of a child.

who longed for his spiritual guidance, summoned him. Another possibility Anwar puts forward evokes the theory that Islam spread in South Asia primarily through state support of Sufis. He writes, "In those days with the foreign Muslim rulers came a great number of pious people of the new religion. They continued to come and they spread the religion of Islam."[72] As with the *numbardar* Ahmad and Maulani Baba's stories of Haider Shaykh given above, Sufi saints are commonly portrayed as the agents who spread Islam.[73] In the *gaddi nishin's* account, there is no reference to specific conversions attributable to Haider Shaykh's presence, but he is said to have come to *tabligh karne* (to spread the faith).

Anwar's vocabulary choices also demonstrate the milieu of his writing. He interchanges synonymous terms derived from various languages, each associated with a different religious community. For example, the common terms in Punjabi for desires and wishes presented at a shrine are *mang* (from the Hindi, Punjabi *mangna*—to beg, demand, request) or *iccha* (Hindi—desire) or sometimes *kam* (Hindi, Punjabi—work). In this text the Arabic term *murad* (desire) is also employed. In another example, "to offer" is alternately signified by the terms *cadhana* (Hindi) and *pesh karna* (Persian-derived Urdu). The variations in usage demonstrate Anwar Ahmad Khan's familiarity with the wide range of terms and establish what Tony Stewart termed equivalences, if not exact correspondence, between conceptually and ritually dense ideas.[74] In so doing, the *gaddi nishin* presents Haider Shaykh's miracles and lineage in language accessible to non-Muslims and Muslims alike.

In contrast to the chapbook, Sufi Muhammad Ismail's hagiography is written in Urdu and clearly directed toward a primarily if not exclusively Muslim audience. In Ismail's *tazkira, Bagh anbiya' punjab* or *The Garden of the Prophets of Punjab*, the entry on Haider Shaykh focuses on his role in bringing Islam to the region and establishing both the religion of Islam and the kingdom of Malerkotla. Malerkotla's continued existence as a zone of Islam is explained through the life story of Haider Shaykh and his descendants. As an anomaly in modern Indian Punjab, Malerkotla's Muslim majority is as noteworthy as the peace at Partition. The shaykh was sent by his Sufi master

> far away from Multan to the town of Maler so that the people here could be called to God's way and receive the blessings of His power and essence.
>
> Thus, from his having lived in this place of Maler, the whole region today has been unified. And he called the forgetful and lost people back to the path of righteousness. In this way it is clear that the people here accepted Islam at his hands. From his service and example Islam spread in the region and the kingdom of Islam arrived within these boundaries, and God knows everything.[75]

This explains both Haider Shaykh's role and purpose in founding the settlement.

This text bears resemblance to classic South Asian *tazkira* texts, such as the *Akhbar al-akhyar* (Tales of the Great Ones) of Shaykh 'Abd al-Haqq Muhaddith Dihlawi (d. 1642) and the *Siyar al'Arifin* of Shaykh Jamali (d. 1536), in terms of structure, language, and thematic choices. The entry on Haider Shaykh opens with the saint's parentage and his taking of *bay'a* (Sufi initiation) from Shaykh Baha'ul Haq Zakariyya at Multan. As previously mentioned, the dates make this meeting impossible, as Haider Shaykh died in 1515 and Baha-ud Din Zakariyya in 1262. Still, it is not uncommon to draw links to a more famous *pir* for the purpose of increasing the prestige of another. The discussion, though brief, of the shaykh's time in Multan contrasts sharply with the account of Anwar Ahmad Khan, who did not even name Haider Shaykh's *murshid* or describe his training in his chapbook. Another marked difference between the accounts is that, unlike the *gaddi nishin*, Sufi Ismail does not emphasize miracles or Haider Shaykh's encounter with Bahlol Lodhi. The meeting with the sultan is given as evidence of the ruler's piety and interest in seeking out and supporting men of religion. His description of Bahlol Lodhi also contrasts sharply with that of Inayat Ali Khan, who berates him for being superstitious. Sufi Ismail, on the other hand, highlights Lodhi's piety: "Sultan Bahlol Shah Lodhi had a very pious heart, he greatly respected the *'auliya' Allah* (friends of God) the saints (*buzurganedin*), the noble men of learning (*'ulama'*), and pious people and he was constantly desirous [*arzomand*] of their prayers."[76] This account of Bahlol Lodhi leads to a brief rundown of the Lodhi dynasty and their ultimate defeat by the first Mughal emperor Babur. The mention of Babur opens the way for Sufi Ismail to discuss Mir Baqi's building the Babri Masjid in Ayodhya in his master's name.[77] As the *tazkira* was published shortly after the destruction of that mosque by Hindu militants, the mention is significant and resonates far beyond Haider Shaykh and Punjab.

Ismail repeatedly declares Haider Shaykh's character as a perfected saint (*wali kamil*) and describes Haider Shaykh's praying for Bahlol Lodhi's victory in battle in a way very different from the *gaddi nishin*'s account: "And he implored [*darkhwast*] a prayer for his victory in battle. He [Hazrat Shaykh] gave the request that he be victorious, issued a prayer that was accepted by Allah most High was granted, and the Badshah was successful [*kamiyan*]. Because of this the Badshah believed from his heart."[78] In Ismail's rendition, Lodhi's victory is attributed to the grace of God through the mediating endeavors of Haider Shaykh. The saint's prayer merely brought the matter to God's attention, but it was God who fulfilled the entreaty. Haider Shaykh is described as an unveiler of miracles (*kashf o karamat*) and a victory giving holy man (*buland paye buzurg*). Nonetheless, the supremacy and omnipotence of Allah is constantly reaffirmed through Qur'anic passages or formulas and the constant invocation of blessings on the saints and the Prophet. This contrasts notably with Anwar's account, in which Allah is mentioned rarely, and no verse of the Qur'an, not a single Hadith or even the simplest *du'a* (prayer), is given as means of relating Haider Shaykh's tradition to orthodox Islam. For Anwar Ahmad Khan, who is descended from the saint, Haider Shaykh was and is capable of performing miracles, and his blood descendants likewise possess the charisma of this royal connection and the power to bestow the saint's miracle-working blessings on all pilgrims, regardless of their religious affiliation. Sufi Ismail, perhaps unsurprisingly, makes no mention of the multireligious appeal of the tomb cult.

The Partition and independence of 1947 changed the status of the state and the saint. Haider Shaykh's role as a uniter of a devotional community made up of multiple religious adherents grows increasingly prominent in oral narratives and written accounts. Interreligious conflicts that occurred prior to 1947 fade into the background. The recent book *Malerkotla itihas ke darpan me* (Malerkotla in the Mirror of History) by local historian Muhammad Khalid Zubairy is a perfect example of this.[79] Zubairy extols the many virtues of the town and the high points of its history without any complicating black spots. Local industry, educational institutions, architectural features, and other attributes are all described. Haider Shaykh's life story is given in detail, but this detail is an almost verbatim restatement of the devotional pamphlet about the saint written by Anwar Ahmad Khan. No mention is made of the several communal conflagrations in the early twentieth century, including at least two riots, one involving a fatality. These events do not fit into the story Zubairy wants to tell about the place and its people.

The hagiographical material shared by Zubairy and Anwar Ahmad Khan is also presented in language and terms designed to be accessible to non-Muslims as well as Muslims. Writing in Hindi and Punjabi respectively, both Zubairy and Khan describe miracles associated with Haider Shaykh including the horse story, the meeting with Bahlol Lodhi, and an incident in which a rivulet that had run through Malerkotla moved after the saint's shoe fell in while he performed ablutions before prayer. Zubairy also includes anecdotes of non-Muslim pilgrims who have come to the tomb shrine. One devotee says that his family comes to the tomb whenever there is a marriage or a birth to thank Haider Shaykh and prevent the saint from being enraged by ingratitude. In a similar effort to appeal to a multireligious audience, Khan mixes Hindu and Sikh terms for certain devotional practices and even for God (*bhagwan*), creating a semantic space for non-Muslims at this shrine. Both authors demonstrate a concern with documenting the multireligious nature of the saint's cult and in presenting the saint's life story in terms that are familiar to non-Muslims. These two depictions of Haider Shaykh portray a saint for all people—Hindu, Muslim, and Sikh—and a tradition that is open to all comers. The omission of interreligious strife from Zubairy's history is therefore not surprising. This history situates Malerkotla's ruling lineage, who remain politically powerful to this day, as powerful but just heirs to their founder's ethos of peaceful pluralism.

This link is made absolutely explicit in the brief history written by local historian Nur Faruqi for a felicitation volume published locally in Malerkotla in 2000. He also omits violent interreligious incidents in the town's past, but he goes further in attributing the present situation to the moral fiber of Haider Shaykh. He writes, "Maler Kotla is a place of communal harmony. It was founded on these principles by Sheikh Sadruddin and these values are still found today."[80] Faruqi clearly links the current reputation and peaceful status quo of Malerkotla to its origins as a territory, rooting the currently harmonious relations between religions to the charismatic force of the founding saint. This interweaving of the actual past (the foundation by Haider Shaykh) with the ideal present (pacific interreligious relations) is held together by the imagined moral past in which Haider Shaykh is made to embody and charismatically perpetuate the ethos of harmony that is most strongly associated with Malerkotla today.

An additional example of the imagined moral past comes from an online historian of Pathan communities, Safia Haleem, who, in describing the atmosphere in Malerkotla, writes, "Muslims and Sikhs live peacefully at present and there was never any ethnic violence since the partition."[81] This description is given in a section describing Haider Shaykh's descendants, both the nawabs and the caretakers of the saint's shrine. The situation of her commentary on Malerkotla's character in the midst of her discussion of these Pathan lineages strongly suggests (and helps to create) a connection between the political and spiritual authority of the shaykh's descendants and the pacific situation in Malerkotla.

Conclusion

These narratives about Haider Shaykh demonstrate the role the saint plays in giving shape to Malerkotla's primary symbolic identity as a zone of peace. In this chapter we have seen how oral and written narratives about Haider Shaykh create space for all the local religious communities to identify with him and his tradition. These narratives establish the four functions of Haider Shaykh's persona as a founder, protector, integrator, and exemplar. This generates a powerful resource in the forging of a local identity grounded in an ecumenical ethos. The narratives from the *khalifah* family emphasize the aspects of Haider Shaykh's history that maximize his stature such as his relationship with Bahlol Lodhi and his miracle working. The last nawab in particular emphasizes the compatibility of spiritual and worldly power. By contrast Balram's tale clearly places the saint above the sultan. Not content to merely express the supremacy of spiritual authority, he goes much further to undermine the power of the worldly ruler in his account, depicting him as arrogant and stubborn. Balram also embedded his narrative about Haider Shaykh's coming to the region into a broader context that encompassed relations between the local Muslim rulers and the non-Muslim population. This narrative strategy maximized the links between the past and the present, exalting the saint for his spiritual prowess, praising the nawab for his ecumenical attitude in visiting the Jain *muni*, and challenging the character of the sultan and by extension the institution of Muslim rule.

The didactic aspect of the stories told about Haider Shaykh and Malerkotla is wholly consistent with the genres of prescriptive literature in Islam that model appropriate behavior in the present on the perfect model of the prophet and his companions. In relating events of moral exemplars from the past, a narrator grounds his or her recommendations for ideal action in the present, effectively extending its significance and opening up a new field of meaning. The narrative technique of evoking the past to interpret the present is therefore quite consistent with the use of didactic exemplars in the transmission of Islamic principles. Thus, oft-repeated tales, their tellers, and the contexts in which the tales are told reveal a great deal about how the popular narratives about Haider Shaykh shape the identity and culture of the *dargah* and the town. Variations, anomalies, and unique features of the narratives indicate how narratives of Haider Shaykh serve as vehicles for the representation of multiple personal and group identities.

The moral force of the imagined past is generated through repetition in these writings and narratives, adding weight to the ethical imperative to maintain peaceful interreligious relations. The impulse to link the present situation to the past helps to authenticate current conditions. We were always like this; this is fundamentally *who we are*, and it cannot be otherwise. Through the force of repeated assertions of the eternal, foundational, and essential quality of Malerkotla, the town's collective authority generates an aspirational ideal that takes on some quality of the real. As residents and visitors continually assert Malerkotla's uniquely peaceful past and present, they counter any dissenting or challenging individuals and events. Thus when tension occurs, as of course it does, the gravitational pull of the story that Malerkotla residents and visitors tell about themselves is extremely difficult to destabilize. It does not take long for such contradictory and inconvenient occurrences to be reconciled with the dominant narrative.

The next chapter continues the historical narrative of Malerkotla, focusing on several key moments in the territory's past when interreligious relations were challenged by wars and conflicts. Above all, the protest (the *haah da naara*) of Nawab Sher Muhammad Khan to the execution of Guru Gobind Singh's sons emerges as the single most significant event in the history of the principality. This protest, through a variety of interlocutors and perspectives, comes to be a condensed symbol of Malerkotla itself and its ethos of justice, brotherhood, and harmony. Through strategic narrative links between the present and the imagined moral past, the collective memory project of Malerkotla's interlocutors naturalizes a particular notion of Malerkotla's essential identity as a zone of peace.

The Nawabs: Good, Bad, and Ugly

When the children of Guru Gobind Singh were walled up alive, nobody else said anything, but only this king, he gave the *haah da naara* [cry for justice]. He was a kindhearted and generous person. Some people are very hardhearted, but this king was kindhearted.

—Fatima, Malerkotla resident

SOME say that Malerkotla's peaceful experience during Partition must have been the result of good governance. Others, such as the historian Ian Copland, claim that there was less violence in the princely states in general because of the authoritarian nature of such states.[1] Yet in the case of Malerkotla, both of these theories come up short; the story is much more complicated. Malerkotla was not always well governed, and for much of its history was a rather weak state. The hereditary ruling family was often internally riven by strife over property, money, authority, and religion. The state was dwarfed militarily and territorially by much larger neighboring kingdoms—Patiala, Nabha, and Jind. These states were ruled by Sikh and Hindu clans with whom the Malerkotla Khans fought and allied by turns. Attacked several times by other outside forces, Malerkotla eventually accepted British protection in 1809—as did its immediate neighbors. British archives document financial mismanagement, succession disputes, and religious conflict. Not all rulers were incompetent, of course; several were quite distinguished. In particular, Nawab Sher Muhammad Khan (r. 1672–1712) stands out as an exemplar of moral rectitude and ethical leadership under duress, and he is celebrated and remembered for it to this day. Few other rulers between Haider Shaykh, Sher Muhammad Khan, and the last two nawabs who ruled in the twentieth century are remembered at all. This chapter explores the failures and successes of leadership and governance in the making of Malerkotla.

A Short History of Malerkotla's Rulers

From its founding in 1454 to the present day, Malerkotla's borders and population have fluctuated widely, from eight thousand square miles in the late seventeenth century to only three square miles in the early eighteenth. At the time of its dissolution, Malerkotla was 167 miles square with a population of eighty-five thousand. The original settlement was known as Maler. This still exists as the neighborhood that surrounds the tomb of the founding shaykh. Kotla came into being in 1657 when a descendant of Haider Shaykh, Bayzid Khan, received permission from the Mughal ruler Aurangzeb (r. 1658–1707) to build a fortified city. After this period the *jagir* or land grant originally endowed by Bahlol Lodhi was confirmed as a hereditary state, and the ruler was given the title of nawab. As the Mughal Empire declined after the death of Aurangzeb, Malerkotla increasingly sought independence from Delhi and allied with tribes of Afghan invaders, most notably Ahmad Shah Abdali (d. 1773), whose Rohilla forces dominated the region of Punjab in the mid-eighteenth century.[2] In the late eighteenth century Malerkotla alternated between alliances and battles with the larger Sikh states surrounding the small kingdom such as Patiala, Nabha, and Jind. As Sikh power in the Punjab consolidated under Maharaja Ranjit Singh in the early nineteenth century, Malerkotla and several neighboring states acceded to the British in 1809 to preserve their territorial integrity and retain a degree of autonomy. After independence from Britain in 1947 the kingdom acceded to the republic of India in 1948, and the last nawab, Iftikhar Ali Khan (d. 1982), transitioned into a role as the elected representative from the area. From 1948 until his death in 1982, with one brief exception, either Iftikhar (who had no children) or one of his wives held that position.[3] With the death of Sajida Begum, his last politically inclined wife, in 2006, the era of the nawabs' rule essentially came to a close, though the descendants of the shaykh remain involved in politics and are very influential locally. (See appendix A.)

As indicated in the previous chapter, inheritance and succession have often been thorny issues in Malerkotla. Criticized by his descendant Inayat Ali Khan in the latter's 1882 book about the family, *A Description of the Principle Kotla Afghans*, for his failure to establish a clear procedure for succession, Haider Shaykh left his second son, 'Isa, the bulk of the estate, with a smaller portion going to Hassan and his heirs. This set a precedent of dividing the *jagir* among the male heirs that resulted in disputes that persist to this day.[4] Under the Mughal Emperor Akbar (r. 1556–1605), Maler (as Malerkotla was known at that time) was a part of the Delhi Suba, subsidiary to the Sarkar of Sirhind.[5] Six generations after Haider Shaykh, Bayzid Khan became the first true ruler of the territory, after the Mughal emperor Shah Jahan awarded him the title of nawab.

Under Bayzid the estate was enlarged, and he received permission to build a fortified city in 1657, which came to be called Kotla, meaning fortress.[6] Bayzid supported Aurangzeb in his campaign against his eldest brother Dara Shikoh for the throne at Delhi. Having thus gained favor with the court, he was allowed to build the walled city, and he was given permission to mint coins in his own name. According to the history authored by the last nawab of the kingdom, Iftikhar Ali Khan, written shortly after Partition, Bayzid was responsible for the building of the tomb shrine for his progenitor Haider Shaykh. Yet of all Malerkotla's rulers, without question the most celebrated is Bayzid's grandson, Nawab Sher Muhammad Khan, who ruled from 1672 until his death in 1712.

Sher Muhammad Khan was in power during a particularly critical period in the history of Punjab as the growing popularity and authority of the Sikh gurus brought increasing conflict with the Mughals. Beginning as a spiritual and social movement with Guru Nanak (1469–1539) in the fifteenth century, the Sikhs became, increasingly, a political as well as religious force. As their community grew in number and territory, they drew the attention of the Mughal emperors based at Delhi and the other regional rulers. Relations with the Mughals were not always antagonistic, but following the death of the fifth guru, Arjan Dev, at the order of the Emperor Jahangir in 1606, hostilities between the Sikhs and the Mughals grew. Periodic battles increased from the time of the sixth guru, Hargobind (d. 1644), until the effective demise of Mughal authority in 1757.[7] During these wars Nawab Sher Muhammad Khan and the Malerkotla forces played prominent roles. He was an able general and served in the Mughal campaign against the Marathas, after which service he received an additional *jagir* of seventy villages. According to Inayat Ali Khan's 1882 history of the ruling clan, the borders of the kingdom at that time extended nearly eight thousand square miles to Ludhiana and Ropar. Sher Mohammad Khan also supported the Mughals against the Rohilla Afghans in the eighteenth century. The wars with the Sikhs heated up as Mughal power waned in the region, and Nawab Sher Mohammad Khan himself fought against three great Sikh leaders: Guru Tegh Bahadur, Guru Gobind Singh, and Banda Bahadur.[8]

Interestingly, in spite of this support for Aurangzeb and the Mughal regime in battles against the Sikhs, most available sources, including numerous Sikh histories from the nineteenth century onward, emphasize only one event in Malerkotla's history: the *haah da naara* or cry for justice.[9] Sher Muhammad Khan gave the *haah da naara* after a pivotal battle between the Mughals and their allies and Guru Gobind Singh at Anandpur. The guru and his forces were besieged by the Mughals and their allies in this stronghold. During the siege the guru's mother, Mata Gujri, and his two younger sons, Zorawar and Fateh, escaped. However, they were betrayed, captured, and imprisoned at Sirhind (approximately fifty kilometers northeast of Malerkotla). Refusing to convert to Islam, the *sahibzadas* (children of the guru) were condemned to be bricked into a wall while still alive. Of all the assembled allies of Wazir Khan, the Mughal governor of Sirhind, Sher Muhammad Khan was the only one who spoke up in the children's defense. He declared that the fight was with the father, not the sons, and that their lives should be preserved. According to a popular version of these events he went so far as to declare the death sentence to be un-Islamic, violating the acceptable rules of combat. Hearing of his efforts on their behalf after his sons' death, Guru Gobind Singh blessed the nawab and his lineage. Although the appeal was unsuccessful and the Guru's sons were ultimately executed, this is by far the single most famous moment in Malerkotla's history. This chapter explores the enduring legacy of this moment and other significant events in the history of Malerkotla as a Muslim princely state.

The incident with the guru's sons would not be the last encounter between Muslim-ruled Malerkotla and the Sikhs. Not long before his death in 1708, the last Sikh guru Gobind Singh met and converted a Hindu Bairagi yogi, Madho Das, to Sikhism.[10] Adopting the name Gurbaksh Singh, the former yogi became more widely known as Banda Bahadur (the Brave Servant); he gave up the path of renunciation and took up arms for the guru. Following Guru Gobind Singh's death, Banda and a large army of Sikhs conquered vast areas of Punjab, but it appears that he did not attack Malerkotla. Whereas other Muslim principalities such as Sirhind—the scene of the guru's sons' death—were razed to the ground, Malerkotla was spared. Although historians such as J. S. Grewal attribute this to Banda's route, which took him elsewhere, Iftikhar Ali Khan, the last nawab of Malerkotla, declares in his history of the kingdom (as do many Sikh residents and visitors) that Banda did not attack the otherwise rather vulnerable state out of respect for Nawab Sher Mohammad Khan's defense of the two *sahibzadas*. Though the historical record is silent on this point, the nawab's version is unquestionably reflective of the popular wisdom on Banda's avoidance of Malerkotla.

Despite such moments of peace, wars between Malerkotla and the Sikh powers in Punjab were common. Malerkotla consistently fought on the side of the Mughals until their power dissipated, at which point the rulers supported Ahmad Shah Abdali and the Rohilla Afghans, who repeatedly raided from the northwest in the middle of the eighteenth century. Punjab in the eighteenth century was characterized by frequent battles and skirmishes between various princely states and tribal leaders. These rulers formed alliances and attacked each other by turns, depending on to whom they owed money, whether they judged victory likely, or whether they were at the behest of a more powerful leader such as the Mughal ruler at Delhi, Muslim chieftains such as Ahmad Shah Abdali or Adina Beg, Hindu forces such as the Marathas, or Sikh leaders such as Banda Bahadur or Maharaja Ranjit Singh.[11] Most memorably, not far from Malerkotla in February of 1762, thirty thousand Sikhs died in a battle against Ahmad Shah and his allies, including the ruler of Malerkotla. This event has gone down in Sikh history as "the Great Holocaust," or *Wadda Ghalughara*.

The mid-eighteenth century was a period of turmoil in Malerkotla. Nawab Jamal Khan (r. 1717–1755) succeeded his brother Sher Muhammad Khan's son

Ghulam Hussain (r. 1712–1717), who abdicated, apparently because he was unsuited to the throne. As the latter's son, Wazir Khan, was a minor, Jamal Khan ascended to the *gaddi* (throne). Jamal Khan fought more or less constantly against various Rajas of Patiala, the large Sikh state to the east of Malerkotla, as did his brothers who succeeded him. This fraternal succession was unusual as the kingdom's land was divided between Jamal Khan and his brothers. One brother at a time, beginning with Bhikam (r. 1755–1763), came to power, further dividing property and authority within the family. Relations with the Sikh neighbors also fluctuated wildly during this period. For example, in 1766 Amar Singh of Patiala captured two villages from Bahadur Khan (r. 1763–66) and then in 1768 seized another from Bahadur's brother and successor, Ataullah Khan (r. 1784–1810). Between Bahadur and Ataullah were two other ruling brothers, 'Umar (r. 1766–1780) and Asadullah (r. 1780–1784).[12] At one point, under Bahadur Khan, the principality was reduced essentially to the boundary walls of Kotla, a mere three miles in circumference. There were, however, bright spots. In 1769 Nawab 'Umar Khan signed a treaty with Raja Amar Singh of Patiala guaranteeing mutual protection and respect. Patiala's rulers occasionally came to the aid of the much smaller and more vulnerable Malerkotla against extra-local Sikh invaders such as the Sahib Singh Bedi, who attacked in 1795.

In his *History of the Family of Shaykh Sadruddin Sadri Jahan*, the last nawab, Iftikhar Ali Khan, is critical of the leadership qualities of some of his progenitors and predecessors. Bahadur Khan was "overbearing and presumptuous," and Ataullah was "fickle." On the other hand, Bhikam Khan inherited almost all the noble qualities of his ancestors.

> He was kind hearted and benevolent and extended sympathy not only to his own relations but to strangers also and did not allow any friction to prevail amongst his kinsmen. He followed a policy of toleration and was above fanaticism so common at that time. He spared no pains in making his people happy and prosperous and made lavish and generous gifts of lands without any distinction of caste and creed. His rule was one of great prosperity and contentment in the history of the state.[13]

Writing shortly after Partition, Iftikhar Ali Khan carefully highlights the praise-worthy tolerance and lack of zealotry in Bhikam Khan's character. This no doubt reflects the experience and interests of his own time as much as his estimation of his ancestor's effective governance two centuries earlier. The characterization also reveals Iftikhar's assessment of what qualities a leader should ideally possess—benevolence, peace making, toleration, and egalitarianism.

The period after the death of Guru Gobind Singh and his disciple Banda Bahadur was also a period in which political and religious authority among the Sikhs was diffuse. Called the *missal* period, the mid-eighteenth century saw the rise of clan- and family-based power centers called *missals*, which functioned within a kind of confederacy.[14] They were unified, or unifiable, only inasmuch as collective Sikh interests superceded local or individual agendas. External challenges from Mughal authorities, Afghan invaders, and the increasing presence of the British East India Company could consolidate the Sikh rulers, but when these dangers ebbed, they were as likely to skirmish with each other over territory. The rise of Maharaja Ranjit Singh (d. 1839) in the early eighteenth century saw a long period of consolidation, ultimately uniting much of Punjab, Kashmir, and Himachal Pradesh under his authority. Though this unprecedented solidarity did not outlast Ranjit Singh's lifetime, it represents the highwater mark of Sikh power.

Yet even during Ranjit Singh's time there were other Sikh leaders, such as Sahib Singh Bedi, who wielded both spiritual authority and considerable charisma and were periodically able to amass armies of their own. Sahib Singh Bedi (1756–1834) was a direct descendant of Guru Nanak. Since the time of the first guru his family commanded great respect and authority within the Sikh religion and the sociopolitical power networks of Sikhs throughout Punjab. Indeed some Sikhs never acknowledged that authority shifted from Nanak's bloodline. Bedi and his family had many loyal supporters who believed that the first guru's power descended through his lineage.[15] In 1795, Bedi attacked Malerkotla, ostensibly over the perennial issue of cow killing. Sikhs and Hindus both traditionally abstain from killing cows, holding the cow to be sacred as a source of life and sustenance. Muslim consumption and ritual sacrifice of cows has often been a stated provocation for interreligious conflict, a precipitating incident. However, in this case, as in most others, there were other motivations. Bedi's men had attacked a number of other places prior to their arrival at Malerkotla, including Sikh regions. At Malerkotla, Sahib Singh Bedi's forces were stopped at the village of Amargarh, just east of the capital city, and were repelled with assistance from Patiala.

Malerkotla joined the British in fighting the Marathas in the early part of the nineteenth century. During this time Maharaja Ranjit Singh was in the process of expanding his territory, which at its greatest extent included much of present-day Punjab, Kashmir, Himachal Pradesh, and the northwestern regions of Pakistan. Pushing into the southern Malwa region in which Malerkotla is located, Ranjit Singh arrived at the town in 1808. There the Maharaja demanded such an enormous amount in tribute that the state was forced to borrow heavily from its wealthier neighbors—Nabha, Jind, and Patiala. The nawab at the time, Ataullah Khan, offered an elephant, but Singh demanded a million rupees.[16] Summoning all his resources, he drummed up 566,391 rupees. Maharaja Ranjit Singh attacked on October 22, and the nawab threw himself at the mercy of his wealthier Sikh neighbors who assisted with loans. He then appealed to the British Viceroy Lord Metcalfe, who was also concerned by Maharaja Ranjit Singh's expanding territory and power.[17]

Shortly after this, in 1809 the British and the Maharaja signed a treaty ceding the Cis-Sutlej region in which Malerkotla is located to British suzerainty. This marked another milestone in the growth of British dominance of the subcontinent. After the Battle of Plassey in 1757 the British East India Company began to shift from being primarily a trading company forging alliances with local rulers to pursuing its own military and sovereign interests. This process culminated in the assumption of direct rule by the British crown in 1857. In that year the British famously crushed the rebellion of Indian army regiments, and India officially became a colony of the British Empire. Since 1803 the Mughals had been subordinate to the British, although nominally the dynasty did not end until 1857. From 1809 until independence in 1947 Malerkotla supported the British and assisted in a number of key battles such as the Gurkha wars (1814–1816) and also the 1857 Rebellion.[18] Family disputes over the right to succession continued and were now arbitrated by the British government.[19] Relations with the British appear typical of British dealings with other kingdoms. The Malerkotla chiefs were given nominal respect, listed in attendance at various courts, or *darbars*, of the viceroys; ranked ninth among the Punjab states; and given an eleven-gun salute.[20] Exhaustive lists of exchanged gifts and other formalities are detailed in the nawab's history. The male royal family members were generally educated in England or in British-run schools in India.

A resident British official assisted in state government from 1809 onward, exercising varying degrees of control, depending upon the age and competence of the native ruler and, of course, upon British interests. According to the British records the royal family was deeply in debt and so was constantly on the verge of ruin.[21] Apart from brokering loans for the nawab, the British also used this weakness to justify greater exercise of control in state affairs. In a letter to the political agent at Ambala, Sir George Russell Clerk, dated May 16, 1831, a British officer named Captain Murray observed, "I believe it to be impossible to extract any generally beneficial measure from the collected members of this turbulent and distracted family because their conflicting interests, ceaseless intrigues and mutual jealousy are too opposed to system and inimical to order, to be regulated on just and fundamental principles."[22] In an 1836 letter Clerk himself reiterated this pessimistic impression, describing a visit to the state to settle a question of succession and inheritance. This case concerned the fact that, because of the minority of Wazir Khan and his father Ghulam Hussain's abdication in 1717, his four uncles succeeded to the throne prior to his eventual ascension in 1810. Following the controversy a precedent in British India was set concerning the rights of primogeniture.[23] In the process of the investigation, Clerk observed the fractious quality of family relations.

> What Captain Murray anticipated, my own experience has confirmed. It is vain to effect unanimity among the members of this

family on this point. Some of the most influential are interested in subjecting inheritance to the Shurreh *[sic]*, claiming its laws as applicable to all of their religious persuasion. Others discard the Shurreh, deny that its rules have hitherto been the guidance of the family ... , which is the fact, ... and prefer to adhere to their ancient usages. Unfortunately their family customs in respect to inheritance have not hitherto been uniform.[24]

Internecine disputes continued throughout the nineteenth and twentieth centuries. As we saw in the previous chapter, Inayat Ali Khan himself devotes approximately one-third of his 1882 manuscript to his claim to the estate of his brother Ibrahim Ali Khan who, as the adopted son of Nawab Sikandar Ali Khan, inherited the lands and properties of the throne. Although neither the accession of Ahmad Ali Khan (Ibrahim's son) nor the leadership of Ahmad's son Iftikhar was disputed, family disputations over property continue to this day.[25]

The Namdhari Massacre

Ten years before Inayat Ali Khan published *A Description of the Principal Kotla Afghans* as a record of his property grievances and their genesis, one of the most notorious incidents in British colonial history occurred. In 1872 Malerkotla was governed by a British agent, Mr. Heath, under the jurisdiction of the deputy commissioner at Ludhiana, J. C. Cowan. The nawab, Ibrahim Ali Khan, was a minor when he succeeded his uncle and adoptive father, Sikander Ali Khan, in 1871.[26] In January of 1872 Malerkotla was attacked by a group of Namdhari Sikhs, a sect widely and onomatopoetically known as the Kukas because of the ecstatic cries they utter during prayer. The Namdharis believe in the continuation of the living personal guru after the death of Gobind Singh, and so they were and are seen as beyond the pale of the majority of Sikhs. However, Namdharis see themselves not only as custodians of the true Sikh tradition but also as the first freedom fighters against British colonialism. They called for a boycott of British goods in the late nineteenth century, established their own postal system, refused to serve in the army, and waged active struggles against cow slaughter. According to Namdhari sources, the attack on Malerkotla was prompted by their opposition to the British presence there, the killing of cows by the British and the Muslims, and the worship of saints.[27] Namdhari literature today emphasizes British imperialism and intransigent discriminatory policies as the provocation for their attack. Mainstream Punjab historians claim that the group wanted guns and that Malerkotla at the time was weak and an easy target. Perhaps unsurprisingly the British records portray the Namdharis not as freedom fighters but fanatics. According to the 1904 British-authored *Maler Kotla State Gazetteer*, "the fanatic Kukas attacked Kotla, killing some townspeople and plundering houses."[28] Nawab Iftikhar Ali Khan's history, on the other hand, tells the story altogether differently. He describes the leader of the movement, Bhai Ram Singh, as a "sensible man" who was opposed to the attack on the grounds that Malerkotla had been blessed by the guru. Indeed he claimed that the attack occurred without Bhai Ram Singh's wishes and was undertaken by a rogue follower. Furthermore, Iftikhar Ali Khan supplies yet another motive: the rumor that a Namdhari woman was raped while in custody at Malerkotla. Whatever the cause, the assault on the state was limited, resulting in few deaths and the theft of some guns. In spite of the relatively minor damage, the punishment visited upon the Kukas by the British was grim indeed. After hunting down and capturing the perpetrators at Patiala, they were brought back to Malerkotla and executed without trial. Sixty-nine Namdharis, including women and children, were placed in front of cannons and blown away over the course of three bloody days. Iftikhar Ali Khan recounts that the British official who commanded this action was subsequently declared insane and removed. This incident stands out both in Malerkotla and Namdhari histories for its brutality. A large monument built by the Namdharis in the early 1990s towers over the town and is well advertised with road signs. An annual festival marking the executions draws thousands of Namdharis and many mainstream Sikhs.[29]

The *haah da naara*: The Cry for Justice

Of all the events that took place in Malerkotla between the time of Haider Shaykh and Partition, without question the *haah da naara* stands out as the most iconic and actively remembered. Indeed, this event has become emblematic of the moral character and secular spirit of the town itself. Few public assemblies in Malerkotla go by without mention of Nawab Sher Muhammad Khan's heroic defense of the sons of Guru Gobind Singh in 1705. As mentioned in the previous chapter, some of Haider Shaykh's devotees falsely attribute the *haah da naara* to the saint, thereby condensing all of the idealistic power of this righteous act into one central figure in the town. Every Malerkotla resident, many Punjabis, and most Sikhs know the story of the guru's sons, and most know of the small but important role that Sher Muhammad Khan played in the events leading up to their martyrdom. Written accounts of the *haah da naara* are numerous, ranging from nineteenth-century Sikh histories such as Rattan Singh Bhangu's *Panth Prakash* (1841) and Giani Gian Singh's *Tawarikh Guru Khalsa* (1892), to Puran Singh's 1908 chapbook *The Victory of Faith*, to renditions given in biographies of Guru Gobind Singh, to martyrologies on the Web and even children's books.[30] These events clearly captured the imagination of many Sikh writers and Malerkotla residents in particular, revealing the interests and concerns of their narrators and their historical contexts.

The haah da naara *in Sikh Sources*

Guru Gobind Singh founded the Sikh *khalsa*, the army of the pure, in 1699 at Anandpur, the city founded by his father, Guru Tegh Bahadur. Driven from other Sikh centers at Kartarpur, Goindwal, and Amritsar, Gobind Singh retreated into the hills of present-day Himachal Pradesh to regain strength.[31] According to Sikh tradition, on the day of the spring festival of Baisakhi the guru summoned his followers and asked them to commit fully to the path established by Guru Nanak by adhering to a special code of dress and behavior. This was the moment in which the famous five *k*'s of the Sikh faith were inaugurated—the five outward signs that indicate adherence to the Sikh faith: *kesh* (uncut hair), *kirpan* (knife), *kachera* (short undergarments), *kanga* (comb), and *kada* (steel bracelet).[32] Furthermore, the *amrit pahul,* or nectar ceremony, was established as a ritual of commitment to the Sikh faith performed by drinking blessed water and promising to adhere to the code of conduct set forth by the gurus.[33]

The inauguration of these ceremonies contributed to the consolidation of the Sikh community, already perceived as a threat by the Mughal Emperor Aurangzeb and the regional chieftains. To curtail this growing threat, Aurangzeb instructed his commander at Sirhind, Wazir Khan, to "admonish" the guru.[34] As the Mughal forces were heavily committed to expansionist campaigns in the southern region of the Deccan, it was imperative that the north should remain a stable, revenue-enhancing region. The growing power of the Sikh Khalsa also disturbed the neighboring kingdoms, and thus in December of 1704 a coalition of Mughal forces and regional chiefs attacked Anandpur and laid siege to the guru's fortress. As food and water became scarce, Gobind Singh and his army agreed to evacuate the town and shift elsewhere, but they were attacked upon their departure. Gobind Singh and a small band including his two elder sons managed to fight their way clear, but his two younger sons and his mother were captured. Their servant, a Hindu named Gangu Brahmin, helped them escape from the Anandpur battle and then turned them over to the Mughal authorities. They were brought to Sirhind where they were imprisoned in the Thanda Burj (the Cold Tower).[35]

Fateh and Zorawar, the two youngest sons of Guru Gobind Singh, were only seven and nine years old at the time of their capture. Their grandmother Mata Gujri had already lost her husband, Guru Tegh Bahadur, who was executed by Shah Jahan in 1675. Sikh martyrologies portray the three as facing their situation with enormous courage, in spite of the frightening conditions and their vulnerable ages. The two *sahibzadas* (sons of the guru) were brought to the court repeatedly and pressured to accept Islam. Sikh accounts depict a full court of witnesses: Wazir Khan, his Hindu advisor Sucha Nand, and a number of regional allies including the nawab of Malerkotla, Sher Muhammad Khan. As the young boys were tested, they continued to profess their faith in the teachings of their father and to refuse Islam. According to nearly every version of these events, at some point in the proceedings, Sher Muhammad Khan rose up and protested their execution. His plea went unheeded, and Zorawar and Fateh were executed. Upon hearing of the death of his sons, the guru reportedly inquired if anyone had spoken up on their behalf. Told of Sher Muhammad Khan's defense of the boys, Gobind Singh is said to have blessed him and his descendants, declaring that his "roots shall remain forever green," which is to say that his lineage will never fail.[36] In Malerkotla many believe that the guru sent a sword to Sher Muhammad Khan in acknowledgment of his gratitude and the blessing.[37]

Several elements of this basic narrative must be highlighted. First, although this story becomes exemplary of Malerkotla's characteristic of rising above sectarian chauvanism, Sher Muhammad Khan was by no means an ally of the Sikhs. He was present and active in the attack against the guru. Indeed the nawab's commitment to the fight was such that his brother Khizr Khan and nephew Nahir Khan were killed in action during this campaign.[38] Second, in this Sikh story, there are both Hindu and Muslim villains. Mata Gujri, Zorawar, and Fateh are betrayed by their Hindu servant and guide Gangu Brahmin. Later in the court of Wazir Khan, his Hindu advisor, Sucha Nand, is described in several versions as the strongest advocate for executing the children. Nonetheless, Wazir Khan is generally given the harshest treatment in Sikh accounts. Third, some versions of these events claim that the "honor" of killing them was first offered to Sher Muhammad Khan because he had suffered such personal losses in the battle. This heightens the tension of the moment and adds to the righteous forbearance of Sher Muhammad Khan when he not only refuses to kill the children himself but objects to their execution altogether. Fourth, in some accounts the nawab's refusal is based on his religious convictions as a pious Muslim and the principle that children are noncombatants. His opposition is couched in moral and ethical terms rooted in his interpretation of sharia.

Finally, one of the most important aspects of this event is that the nawab was unable to save Zorawar and Fateh Singh. This is, in certain sense, a story of failure. Yet in that failure there are roots of future success as the nawab's protest becomes a meaningful resource and a motivating ideal in maintaining the integrity of the multireligious community in Malerkotla. Indeed, the hopelessness of the cause seems to render the nawab's opposition and the *sahibzadas*' bravery all the more poignant and morally revealing. This also intensifies the martyrdom aspect of the events, and martyrdom is a powerful, central trope in the Sikh tradition.[39] Overall, the enduring appeal of this moment is evident in the name given to Sher Muhammad Khan's protest, which is known throughout Malerkotla, the Punjab, and the entire Sikh community as the *haah da naara*, "the cry for justice."

Although certain details vary, most Sikh narrators emphasize the futile bravery of Sher Muhammad Khan and especially the innocence and courage of Zorawar and Fateh Singh. There are no contemporary accounts, but two nineteenth-century Sikh texts, Rattan Singh Bhangu's *Panth Prakash* (1841) and Giani Gian Singh's *Tawarikh Guru Khalsa* (1892), report the guru's response to the news of his sons' deaths. The proliferation of historical texts in the late nineteenth century in particular reflects the dynamics of Punjabi society during this period. In the late-nineteenth-century Sikh reform movements such as the Singh Sabha had a profound influence on Sikh identity politics. The Singh Sabha, founded in 1872 in Amritsar, sought to purify and revitalize Sikhism, counter the encroachments of Christian missionizing, and become a representative institution for the Sikh community.[40] They published tract literature, formed many branches in local communities, and established gurdwaras to disseminate their version of Sikh orthodoxy. During this same period numerous organizations arose in all three of the major religious traditions seeking to define the faiths in a rapidly changing sociopolitical context. Muslim *anjuman*s (organizations) appeared throughout Punjab in the late nineteenth century with varying purposes, but generally to purify the faith and solidify Islam socially and politically. Their goals included "imparting and popularization of religious and modern education, reform and welfare of the community, acquainting the Government with the problems and desires of the community, and taking up other matters in the interests of the community."[41] Such groups also formed in Malerkotla at least as early as 1894 with the establishment of the Anjuman Musleh-ul-Akhwan.[42] The Hindu "revival" was also extremely influential. The work of Swami Dayanand, the founder of the Arya Samaj, was particularly well received in Punjab. The Arya Samaj, the Punjabi Hindu Sabha, and the Hindu Mahasabha were all active in the region during this period and in Malerkotla as well.[43] Although their methods and motivations were diverse, all of these Sikh, Muslim, and Hindu groups shared several goals: to curtail the inroads of Christian missionaries, to educate and uplift their communities, and to work on behalf of their community. In so doing, these communities had to define themselves more clearly in terms of belief, practice, and social organization. These movements drove and were driven by the ongoing hardening of boundaries between religions and a rise in communal politics. In short, all three major religions went through a period of intensive identity formation in the late nineteenth century.

During this critical period Giani Gian Singh (1822–1921) was one of the most productive scholars of Sikh historical works, and his writings were an important part of the identity formation process. His comprehensive history of the Sikh faith and religion, *Tawarikh Guru Khalsa* (Histories of the Gurus and the Khalsa) spanned the lifetimes of the gurus and all subsequent Sikh history, thereby defining the parameters of what he viewed as the normative tradition. In his account of Guru Gobind Singh, he described the martyrdom of the *sahibzadas*, the guru's sons. He focused his narrative on the reaction of the guru, who was sitting with his Sikhs after the battle in which his two elder sons were killed, when an emissary from Sirhind approached. It is worth quoting this source at some length.

> The next day a messenger came and gave everyone the news, and it became known that first Mata [Gujri] was brought with the *sahibzadas* to the village Kheri to Ganga Ram Brahman's kitchen. Then all their wealth was taken, and Mata said how can it be stolen, no one has come? Then having been rebuked, [Ganga Ram] called a Ranghera from Morinda and he caught Mataji and the *sahibzadas* together and brought them to Sirhind. Bazid [Wazir] Khan the administrator tempted them and threatened them greatly to leave their religion, but they did not believe anything. They did not give up their religion. They gave their bodies. Hearing the cruel death sentence of the *sahibzadas,* then Nawab Sher Muhammad Khan of Malerkotla said, "It is a great sin to kill these very young and sinless children. Furthermore the killing of these innocents will not enhance your reputation. Honor would come from killing the lion Gobind Singh. If you are able to kill him then God does not consider this wrong." Hearing this all the people became silent but Nand Khatri Diwan [the minister Sucha Nand] spoke, "It is not good to save the children of a serpent." Hearing this the stonehearted Bazid Khan had the innocent children, as innocent as rosebuds, bricked up in a wall. Then the wall was opened, and they were killed but it is a great thing that these children never forsook their religion, they offered up their bodies. Hearing of their murder, Mata Gujri fainted and fell from the tower in which she was imprisoned and gave up her breath. Tears filled the eyes of everyone as they heard this tale and the wailing and crying went on for such a long time that the Guruji's neck drooped and he began digging at the seedling plants of a reed. Having heard the entire account, the Guru pledged, "Having given this call for justice, their roots will be preserved. In no other place will the roots of Muslim men be continued. Those Turks' lineages will be uprooted." Having said this, he pulled up the sprigs of grass and threw them away and with them the roots of Sirhind were uprooted and the order was given that that city should not dwell in peace. "From such a great sin, my Sikhs will plunder and loot and devastate the place and every Sikh will take its bricks and throw into the Sutlej [River]."[44]

Clearly, Giani Gian Singh places great emphasis on the innocence and courage of the *sahibzadas,* "innocent as rosebuds." The youth and purity of the two children contrasts with the strength of their convictions as they face the Sirhindi chieftain determined to give up their bodies rather than their faith. Indeed, even the words placed in the mouth of Sher Muhammad Khan highlight their youth and lack of sin. He describes them as very young, *shirkhor*, meaning breastfed, implying that they are so young as to be barely weaned. He also refers to them as *beguna*, without sin, and *masum*, an Arabic derived term meaning innocent. Yet Sher Muhammad Khan's defense does not advocate giving up the conflict or retreating from what he perceives as an unjust fight. Rather, he argues that glory and honor derive only from killing their father, "the lion Gobind Singh," on the field of battle. That would be a fair and righteous fight, worthy of a true soldier. Sher Muhammad Khan is made to observe that it would be very sinful (*vadha bhari gunah*) to kill the *sahibzadas*, though killing their father in a fair fight would be honorable. Giani Gian Singh does not depict the Nawab as grounding his objection in Islam explicitly, but his objections are based on an ethos of justice and religiously informed understandings of sin and innocence.

As the reform movements of the late nineteenth century expanded and the Indian independence movement began in earnest, Sikh identity politics become more apparent in narratives about the *haah da naara*. In this period, the producers of great quantities of tract literature sought to acquaint people with the fundamental tenets and histories of their faiths were produced.[45] One example is the 1908 English chapbook by Puran Singh (1881–1931), a prolific writer and scientist. Puran Singh's poetic compositions and other writings include highly romanticized visions of the Sikh faith. His collection of poetry *Sisters of the Spinning Wheel* is a paean to the glory of Punjabi culture and the gurus. The 51-page booklet called *The Victory of Faith or the Story of the Martyrdom of the Four Sons of Shri Guru Gobind Singh* is the story of the deaths of Guru Gobind Singh's four sons. Puran Singh portrays the episode involving Sher Muhammad Khan in a more minimal fashion than the earlier Sikh historians. In fact, this text almost glosses over the nawab's protest. No religious objection or moral motivation is attached to Sher Muhammad Khan's objection to the killing of the *sahibzadas*. Instead Puran Singh describes the nawab's demand that they be freed with extreme brevity: "At this juncture the Nawab of Malerkotla boldly proposed to the Nawab of Sirhind for the release of the innocent boys." This is the totality of Sher Muhammad Khan's appearance in this version. His proposal for the *sahibzadas'* release was unsuccessful, though it did move the nawab of Sirhind, whose "face blushed with the shame of cowardice which he had shown and he felt half inclined to set them free when Suchanand, a Khatri minister, put in a remark that the young one of a snake grows to be a dangerous snake and hence it was not politic to show any mercy towards the sons of a dangerous rebel."[46] This remark strengthened Wazir Khan's resolve, and the grisly execution proceeded.

By the time this short book was published, the reformist agenda of the Singh Sabha dominated Sikh institution building. The Chief Khalsa Diwan, founded in 1902, formalized the goals of the Singh Sabha and established a central body based at Amritsar to oversee and implement a cohesive identity for the Sikh community. Puran Singh's chapbook also appeared just after the British government's first attempt to partition India internally along communal lines. The failed partition of Bengal in 1905 was a turning point in terms of religious politics and the independence movement. The formation of the Muslim League in 1906 and the Indian National Congress's debates over *swaraj* or self-rule followed shortly after the debacle in Bengal.[47] The Morley-Minto reforms instituted by the British in 1909 to expand the electorate were also based on communally divided representation with reservations for Muslims, a move deeply resented by many Hindus. Thus this was an important period in which India's religious communities were striving for self-determination and for independence from the British but were simultaneously growing more self-conscious and divided. Puran Singh's focus on the guru's sons and his minimization of the nawab's role are perhaps unsurprising in such an atmosphere.

Partition, of course, changed everything. After 1947, Sikhs in Indian Punjab became a majority of the population for the first time ever (55 percent, according to the 1951 census). Muslims constituted less than 1 percent as most migrated to Pakistan. Post-Partition, the *sahibzadas'* martyrdom story remains prominent in Sikh lore, but the flavor of the tale alters somewhat. In a 1957 version of the incident written by Ganda Singh, an eminent historian of Punjab, Sher Muhammad Khan takes a more central position, but his objections are not presented in explicitly Islamic terms. As in Giani Gian Singh's rendition, a more generalized ethos of justice is invoked. Ganda Singh's account appeared in the *Sikh Review,* a well-regarded journal that was largely directed at a Sikh audience. In this version, Sher Muhammad Khan was offered the "privilege" of executing the *sahibzadas* out of revenge for the deaths of his brother Khizr Khan and nephew Nabhi Khan at the siege of Anandpur. But according to Ganda Singh the Malerkotla nawab did not advocate avenging these deaths by killing the guru's sons. On the contrary, he protested vehemently, declaring that the boys were innocent and that the Mughal forces were at war with their father, not them. Ganda Singh described the event thus:

> But the brave Afghan refused to kill the innocent children, one of whom was six years old, and the other eight. "Both I and my followers are soldiers and whoever opposes us in open war, we either kill him or are killed ourselves, but what you propose," said Sher Muhammad Khan, "is the business of an executioner." Saying this he left the Darbar [court] and went away.[48]

This version emphasized the nawab's particular objections to the method of killing the *sahibzadas,* which he dismisses as unsoldierly rather than un-Islamic. The nawab does not remain to plead his case, however, but leaves the scene and abandons the *sahibzadas* to their fate. This emphasized even further the bravery of the two young boys who are now wholly friendless as they face their fate. Ganda Singh stuck fairly closely to the outline of Giani Gian Singh's earlier version, but it does not elaborate upon the nawab's role in the events. Published just ten years after Partition, this short essay could not have been much concerned with the totally unnecessary task of differentiating Sikhs from the relatively nonexistent Muslims nor with building bridges with the Muslim population. The *Sikh Review* and its readership were being reminded (as they were nearly annually) of the great sacrifice the two boys made for their faith.

The *haah da naara* is imbued with religious motivation in an undated (but likely late-twentieth-century) Punjabi chapbook available in shops near the Fatehgarh Sahib Gurdwara in Sirhind, which commemorates the martyrdom. The pamphlet is by a writer named Bachan Singh, about whom we know nothing, and is about Fatehgarh Sahib (the name given to Sirhind after these events, meaning the place of victory). Titled *Divine Vision of Fatehgarh Sahib (Fatehgarh Sahib di Darshan),* the narrative resembles Ganda Singh's in its broad outlines, but is much more fully elaborated and quotes verses from Santokh Singh's *Sri Gurpratap Suraj Granth* (1843), a compendium of Sikh history and hagiography. Bachan Singh draws out the *sahibzadas'* plight in great detail, so when Sher Muhammad Khan rises to protest, the drama is at a fever pitch. Offered the opportunity to kill the boys himself to avenge the deaths of his brother and nephew, Sher Muhammad Khan refuses.

> But Sher Mohammad Khan was a tenderhearted man. He said, "My brother and nephew were killed in battle. I can take my revenge from Guru Gobind Singh on the battlefield. If there is any disagreement between us, then it is with Guru Gobind Singh, not with them. They are very young [unweaned] children, what sin could be theirs? Above and beyond this, it is against the sharia of Islam. Therefore I cannot do this."
>
> Saying this, Sher Mohammad Khan gave a call for justice (*haah da naara mariya*) and rising from the *darbar* he left. Bhai Santokh Singh gives the following opinion about the above mentioned:
>
> > Although you are the enemy of the Guru's people
> >   on behalf of these innocents you rebelled
> > Saying, do not kill these unweaned children
> >   The cruel order you neither justified nor fulfilled.[49]

Bachan Singh portrays Sher Muhammad Khan in a light quite different from that of the earlier Sikh texts. No longer merely a consummate soldier, willing to face the guru on the battlefield but unwilling to kill children, he is tenderhearted. Furthermore, he adds the objection that to execute the *sahibzadas* would violate sharia. The verse cited from Santokh Singh reinforces the power of Sher Muhammad Khan's objection. He is called the "enemy of the Guru's people," intensifying the power of his "rebellion" against his own community on behalf of the innocents. This separates the Muslims who conspire to kill the children from the Muslim who refuses to do so.

This differentiation between "good" Muslims and "bad" Muslims is an important one, bespeaking sensitivity to the peculiar tensions of minority religious politics and the complicated nature of Muslim-Sikh relations vis-à-vis the Hindu majority. With the rise of Hindutva influence in the late twentieth century, Sikhs and Muslims alike must walk a fine line. Hindutva ideology views Sikhism as part of Hinduism. Indeed the BJP party often refers to Sikhs as Hindus, and the VHP lists Sikhism as one of the religions it considers within the Hindu fold. Sikhs, for their part, have mostly attempted to distinguish themselves from Hinduism. Perhaps the most famous instance of this was the publication of Bhai Kahn Singh Nabha's tract *Ham Hindu Nahin* (We Are Not Hindu) in 1898.[50] Sikhs have also frequently pressed for greater autonomy from the central government. There were significant agitations in the 1910s for an independent Sikh state, a call that was revived during Partition and again in the 1980s. The first movement was brutally suppressed by the British, and the last was brutally suppressed by the Indian government under Indira Gandhi.[51]

The Sikh presence in cyberspace is extensive. There are official and unofficial sites devoted to Sikh doctrine and history, even a SikhiWiki. Many of these Web sites include the *haah da naara* in their description of the *sahibzadas* martyrdom, testifying to the ongoing popularity of these events. The continuity of the content is remarkable, testifying to the currency of the older Sikh sources for modern audiences. An unattributed *Sikh Review* article posted online in December of 2000 describes the *haah da naara* thus, "Amid this grilling, Nawab Sher Muhammad Khan of Malerkotla, who happened to be there, earnestly implored that the children were too young and innocent to be punished and pleaded that Islam did not sanction such conduct."[52] In this rendition the nawab is shown as objecting on the same grounds as in previous accounts, although the emphasis on his opposing the execution on religious grounds is greater. A few Web sites dramatize the scene further, such as this version at sikhworld.co.uk, which is repeated verbatim on several other sites, making its origin unclear but evidencing its popularity:

> Nawab Wazir Khan called Sher Mohammad Khan, the Nawab of Malerkotla, and conveyed the Qazi's orders to him, "Your brother lost his life at the hands of Guru Gobind Singh. Here is an opportunity for you to wreak your vengeance. The Qazi has sentenced these two sons of Guru Gobind Singh to death and has further ordered that they be bricked alive. We are handing them over to you for doing the needful" On hearing this Sher Mohammad Khan

was dumb founded. After some pause he said to the Nawab in a faltering voice, "This is cruelty! my brother was killed on the battle-field. These innocent boys are not responsible for his death. If we have to take revenge it shall be from the father. God save us from this sinful act." Saying this he got up and remarked in a mournful tone, "O God, how cruel!"[53]

Here Sher Muhammad Khan's motivation to object is the avoidance of sin and the protection of the innocent, just as in the versions of Giani Gian Singh and Ganda Singh. By placing an ethical, moral objection in the mouth of the person most likely to desire revenge, the author further accentuates the injustice of the eventual death of the *sahibzadas*.

Not all sources give a positive spin to Sher Muhammad Khan's role in these events. In one highly Islamophobic rendition, the case of the *sahibzadas'* execution was presented by one participant in an Internet discussion site devoted to Sikh issues as evidence of "how animal-like the Mohammedans are, have been and in every likelihood will be in the future." In another version, posted in April of 2000, Nawab Sher Muhammad Khan does protest. The person who posted the comment, using the name Sukha Singh, writes:

> The Nawab of Malerkotla, Sher Muhammad, stood up and argued that Islam forbids slaughter of innocent children. That these kids have done no wrong and they should not be punished for wrongs done by their father. There was a furore [*sic*] in the court. The Qazis, however, argued and expostulated with Sher Muhammad about the true meaning of Islam and said that Sher Muhammad did not know true Islam and so on. That the kids should die. And finally, the Nawab agreed with the Qazis.[54]

In Sukha Singh's account, the nawab caves under pressure from the Qazis (judges) and comes to agree with their death sentence. This also implies an agreement with their interpretation of "the true meaning of Islam." By present-ing the Muslim characters in this narrative as having a consensus view about the meaning of Islam, Sukha Singh claims that consensus represents true Islam. Interestingly, Sucha Nand, the Hindu minister who strengthens Wazir Khan's resolve in most renditions, disappears altogether in this version, and his role is taken up by the Qazis. This posting hardly represents a mainstream Sikh view of Islam, but is does speak to the existence of such extreme positions.

These accounts of the *haah da naara* from a variety of Sikh sources demon-strate the enduring appeal and power of this incident. Shifts in emphasis are evident, reflecting the concerns and values of the times in which the stories were generated. The core of the narratives remains generally consistent from the nine-teenth century to the present. In all of the accounts Sher Muhammad Khan's plea for the guru's sons goes unheeded. Their grandmother, Mata Gujri, also dies, and she too is regarded as a martyr to the faith.[55] Interestingly, of the key elements of the story, the one that varies most is the motivation of Sher Muhammad Khan in giving the *haah da naara*. Giani Gian Singh portrayed the nawab as viewing the proposed execution to be sinful as did the pamphlet author Bachan Singh. On the other hand, Puran Singh and Ganda Singh are more general in their descriptions, simply noting the event rather than attributing moral or religious motivations to the Muslim ruler. The religio-moral dimension seems to increase in the more recent sources, whether portraying Islam as fundamentally just (as on sikhworld.co.uk) or inherently bloodthirsty (as in Sukha Singh's posting).

The rhetoric of these later accounts of the *haah da naara* is more explicit in portraying Nawab Sher Muhammad Khan as a "good Muslim" who, to defend the *sahibzadas*, sets aside loyalty to his master, the Mughal emperor, and to any sense of religious solidarity. This understanding of the meaning of the *haah da naara* and the guru's blessing comes to dominate not only modern Sikh versions, but also most popular oral narratives that I heard and the Muslim oral and written accounts. In general, this moment is held up as evidence of the possibility of a society in which religious affiliation does not determine loyalty and enmity, reaffirming the central interpretive frame in Malerkotla. The symbolic power of Sher Muhammad Khan's action increases in the post-Partition period when Malerkotla becomes the only Muslim majority region in Indian Punjab. One exacerbating reason for the violence in Punjab was the national aspiration of many in the Sikh community. According to Ian Copland, the goal of these campaigners was to "clear a territorial space for the Sikh homeland—a space bereft of Muslims that the Sikhs could dominate by virtue of their military dominance and control over the agrarian economy."[56] Malerkotla, as the remaining Muslim region, must be reconciled and incorporated into the new Sikh-dominated polity. The depictions of the *haah da naara* laud past examples of interreligious cooperation, thereby providing both a motivating ideal for people from all communities and a security strategy for religious minorities. The fact of Malerkotla's survival of the Partition crisis, combined with the wholly new demographic and political dynamic in the Punjab, allows this narrative representation of Malerkotla's ethic of harmony to take on real force in generating the kind of ideal society it represents and increasing the profile of Malerkotla as a so-called zone of peace. As a result, the power of the guru's blessing to preserve Malerkotla from harm in all subsequent periods of tension with Sikh armies, rulers, and movements becomes quite real and ever more prominent in histories of the region.

The haah da naara *in Muslim Sources*

One of the most elaborate versions of the *haah da naara* by a Muslim author is in the *History of the Ruling Family of Sheikh Sadruddin* by Iftikhar Ali Khan, the last nawab of Malerkotla. Although undated, the *History* was likely written shortly after independence, as the last chapter is Iftikhar Ali Khan's speech on ascending to the throne in 1948.[57] For Iftikhar Ali Khan, writing in the immediate aftermath of the trauma and bloodshed of Partition that nearly eradicated Muslims from the surrounding region, it is not surprising that he would be at pains to emphasize the possibility of interreligious cooperation and loyalty. Many of his subjects were Sikhs, and the kingdom of Malerkotla was surrounded by two much larger Sikh-ruled states, Patiala and Nabha. Efforts to maintain positive relations with his own population as well as with his neighbors could not have been hurt by the way in which he depicts the *haah da naara* and its effects on Malerkotla history.

However, as a historical document, questions may certainly be raised. Iftikhar Ali Khan erroneously asserts that after the failure of the *haah da naara*, Sher Muhammad Khan returned to his kingdom and did not participate in any further campaigns against the guru.[58] He gives three reasons for Sher Muhammad Khan's decision not to rejoin the fight against the guru. First, Sher Muhammad Khan "was so much touched by the calamities and hardships that Guru Gobind Singh had to face that he had not the heart to add to his troubles and considered it a crime to participate in any struggle against him."[59] This description reinforces the representation of Sher Muhammad Khan, and by extension his descendants, as compassionate and tenderhearted. Second, lest this impression lead to his being thought weak or unmilitary, Iftikhar Ali Khan also points out that his decision was also pragmatic. Sher Muhammad Khan chose for military and strategic reasons not to subject his troops to the hardships of the continuing campaign. Third, Iftikhar Ali Khan argues that Sher Muhammad Khan wished to cultivate the goodwill of the guru. He writes, "on hearing that the Guru was pleased with him at the protest he had launched with the Chakladar [i.e., Wazir Khan of Sirhind] to spare the lives of his sons, he did not think it advisable to turn his blessings into curses."[60] Through his assessment, the modern nawab emphasizes his progenitor's pragmatism, political acumen, and moral rectitude in his handling of the delicate situation in which he was caught between his Mughal overlords, his conscience, and the rising tide of Sikhs. The fact that Sher Muhammad Khan did in fact subsequently fight the Sikhs makes this portrayal all the more revealing of the ethics of rulership that Iftikhar Ali Khan wishes to associate himself with.

Although Iftikhar Ali Khan does describe the valor of Nawab Sher Muhammad Khan in battle against the Sikhs, he devotes much more text to the *haah da naara*. He depicts the two boys brought before the court as tenaciously holding their ground and their faith. "Many temptations were placed before them, and they were persuaded in every possible way to become Muslims, but they refused to do so. They were offered the entire *jagir* of Anandpur, besides the high rank of an official which would eventually be bestowed upon them, but they spurned all temptations."[61] Wazir Khan eventually decides that the boys must die, as they are potential leaders and powerful symbols for the Sikh community, and it is determined that they should be walled up alive. At this point, Iftikhar Ali Khan writes, Nawab Sher Muhammad Khan strenuously objected: "He was bold enough to say that it was against all principles of equity and justice that the two children should be made to suffer for no fault of their own and should pay for the deeds of their father. Such tyranny was against the dictates of Shariat and Islam."[62] In his descendant's account, Sher Muhammad Khan's rationale is not based on general moral principles or a warrior ethic, but on core Islamic doctrines. The killing of the *sahibzadas* is unjust because it is against *sharia*, Islamic law. Although Iftikhar Ali Khan does not specify texts or laws that would contravene the execution, he does assert a general religious basis for pursuing justice even against one's co-religionists.[63]

Through Iftikhar Ali Khan's prose, Sher Muhammad Khan is made to insist repeatedly that, although he would gladly meet the guru on an open battlefield, the killing of captives has no honor, and "True Chivalry does not lie in tormenting helpless prisoners but lies in treating them with compassion."[64] According to Iftikhar Ali Khan, the nawab even offered himself as guardian for the boys, "so as to keep a check on their actions and movements and not to allow them to entertain any kind of ideas of sedition or disloyalty."[65] In this rendition, the *haah da naara* itself is much more fully fleshed out, as might be expected in an account by Sher Muhammad Khan's descendant. The nawab is portrayed as just, compassionate, and brave for standing up to his commander and, through him, to the Mughal emperor. When Wazir Khan decides to disregard the plea, no particular motivation for his refusal is given. The Hindu vizier does not figure in this account, nor does any other scapegoat.

In Iftikhar Ali Khan's *History,* the *haah da naara* takes the form of a letter purportedly written by the nawab to Aurangzeb on behalf of the boys. In the letter, Sher Muhammad Khan appeals to the emperor's sense of justice and his faith in Islam for mercy.[66] The claim that the nawab actually wrote a letter to Aurangzeb describing his objections is dubious at best. A verifiable copy of this letter is no longer extant. Although photocopies of a Persian letter and translations do exist, many scholars of Punjab history are skeptical of its authenticity. At the 1983 meeting of the Punjab Historical Society, an archivist from the National Archives in Delhi displayed a copy of the supposed letter, but the experts there were unconvinced. Nawab Iftikhar Ali Khan himself had presented the copy to Jawaharlal Nehru in the 1950s. However, "on the basis of a critical appraisal of the document . . . the Conference expressed its strong doubts about the authenticity of the petition."[67]

Still, in spite of its doubtful origins, the letter is very popular in Malerkotla and beyond. For example, a gurdwara known as the Haah Da Naara Gurdwara was built twenty years ago on property formerly belonging to the nawab. It has a Punjabi and English translation of the letter posted in its courtyard (see fig. 2.1). Also, several historians of Punjab have published translations of the letter in

FIGURE 2.1. The "text" of the *haah da naara* at the Haah Da Naara Gurdwara, Malerkotla.

the *Sikh Review*. In January of 1967 a reprint of the Persian original and a translation appeared without attribution. In December of 1968 M. L. Peace published a poetic rendition of the letter under the title "Historic Epistle." A history of Malerkotla, *Malerkotla: Itihas ke Darpan mein* (Malerkotla: In the Mirror of History), published by local historian Khalid Zubairy in 2000, includes a Hindi translation of the letter. Yet earlier accounts, including the nineteenth-century Sikh histories discussed previously, make no mention of a letter. It is difficult to determine when the belief that the *haah da naara* referred to a letter written to Aurangzeb came into currency.[68] Certainly it is a stretch to imagine that a letter posted in the midst of a battle to Aurangzeb, who was himself campaigning in the Deccan many hundreds of miles away, would have had any efficacy or purpose.

Iftikhar Ali Khan presents the entirety of the letter in his *History*. Whatever its origins, this letter version of the *haah da naara* contains the most fully articulated religious and moral justification for sparing the *sahibzadas* found in any of the accounts examined thus far.[69] Sher Muhammad Khan is made to declare in this epistle:

> . . . it would, in no way be consistent with the principles of sovereignty and supreme power to wreak the vengeance of the misdeeds of a whole nation on two innocent children who, on account of their tender age are quite innocent and unable to take a stand against the

all powerful Viceroy [of Sirhind]. This sort of action obviously
appears to be absolutely against the dictates of Islam and the laws
propounded by the founder of Islam (May God's blessings be showered on him) and your Majesty's humble servant is afraid that the
enactment of such an atrocious act would perpetually remain an
ugly blot on the face of your Majesty's renowned justice and
righteousness.[70]

In this version, Sher Muhammad Khan appears aware that his proposals and
his protests will likely go unheeded (though possibly not unpunished) as he
then asserts, "the fear of God and the urge of faith does not allow the undue
suppression of truths." He goes on to declare that if his plea "is deprived of
the honor of acceptance, still your Majesty's humble and devoted servant
shall have the consolation of having performed the sacred duty of expressing
what was right and just and not having allowed his pen to deviate in the
expression of truth."[71] By emphasizing Nawab Sher Muhammad Khan's
commitment to justice and basing this commitment in his strong faith in
Islam, the author of the letter places the past into the service of the present.
Including the text of the letter in his *History*, Iftikhar Ali Khan lays claim to
the values of humanitarianism and justice expressed therein. He not only
lauds these values in general, but also grounds them in Islamic principles.
The case of the nawab and the guru's sons comes to prove that true Islam is
based on principles of justice and righteousness that supersede battle lines
and religious boundaries.

Iftikhar Ali Khan also describes the moment when the guru hears of his sons'
deaths, reportedly asking if anyone at the trial spoke for them. On "hearing that
Nawab Sher Muhammad Khan had strongly protested and tried his best to save
his sons from their awful fate, the hands of the Guru were raised in prayer for
the Nawab's prosperity saying that 'His roots will ever remain green.' And that
from now onwards the Mughal Empire would decline."[72] Because of this
blessing, Iftikhar Ali Khan asserts, in subsequent battles and confrontations
with Sikh armies and movements Malerkotla was spared the full force of Sikh
violence.

By contrast, Inayat Ali Khan, also a descendant of Sher Muhammad Khan,
gave a much briefer account of the *haah da naara* in his 1882 book, *Description of
the Principal Kotla Afghans*. Although more text is devoted to the numbers of
villages acquired and the battles waged by Sher Muhammad Khan, Inayat does
portray the scene as a moment when his ancestor spoke courageously against an
injustice. Having been captured, the *sahibzadas*

> fell into the hands of the conquerors and were tortured to death,
> being buried alive under the walls of Sirhind by the order of the
> Subah. At the time of this horrible execution Sher Mahommed [*sic*]

was present: he[,] being disgusted at such a shameful and cowardly manner of taking revenge upon the innocent, remonstrated against it. The imperial officers did not pay heed to the remonstrance; they were resolutely determined to set a severe example, and to carry this into effect had decided upon the above mode of punishment. However, Sher Mahommed's efforts to do away with that cruel punishment were not altogether without result, seeing that they won the affection of Guru Govind Singh who, on hearing the sad news of his sons' death, enquired if there was any one who advocated mercy to the children, and being told that Sher Mahommed had used every endeavour to obtain their release, was so influenced by his feelings that he offered up his fervent prayers for Sher Mahommed despite the past troubles and defeat he had received at the Khan's hands.[73]

Inayat Ali Khan is largely uninterested in the scene of the *sahibzadas* questioning and ultimate execution. Sher Muhammad Khan is not depicted as having any religiously based objections, and the execution is described succinctly as "cruel" and "cowardly." Written long before Partition in a Muslim-ruled kingdom, Inayat Ali Khan does not present this incident as an example of interreligious solidarity or as a model for present or future behavior. In his view the significant aspects of the event are that Sher Muhammad Khan spoke against the killing and that Guru Gobind Singh blessed him for his mercy. It is interesting that no mention is made of a letter written by his ancestor to Aurangzeb or of any other "endeavour" to save Zorawar and Fateh Singh.

The episode with Sher Muhammad Khan and the guru appears briefly in the *tazkira* by Sufi Ismail, *Bagh al-Anbiya' Punjab* discussed in the previous chapter. A local imam and prolific author of books on religious subjects, Ismail crafts a description that seems to serve several purposes. First, he points out that the nearby town of Sherpur was founded in the name of the Sher Muhammad Khan. Second, he attributes the affection of the Sikhs for Sher Muhammad Khan to his mercy and justice in petitioning on their behalf. Finally, he remarks upon the subsequent neglect of the nawab's grave—perhaps a slight criticism of those who supposedly "believe strongly in him."[74] Sufi Ismail gives little detail about these events other than in the mark they left on the built environment of the region.

Unlike Inayat Ali Khan and Sufi Ismail, the last nawab, Iftikhar Ali Khan, emphasized both the Islamic aspects of Sher Muhammad Khan's defense and the enduring power of the *haah da naara* or the guru's blessing. He repeats the claim that because of the blessing, Banda Bahadur, the Sikh general who waged campaigns across Punjab after Guru Gobind Singh's death, never attacked Malerkotla. Although nawab Sher Muhammad Khan had materially assisted the ruler of Sirhind in the campaign against Guru Gobind Singh, Malerkotla was unscathed. On the other hand, Sirhind, where the execution of the guru's sons took place, was leveled. In the *History*, Iftikhar Ali Khan explains the apparent mystery of Bahadur's avoidance of Malerkotla:

> After the destruction of Sirhind the power of the Sikhs grew enormously and they were practically the paramount power in the Panjab. The small Muslim States of the Panjab were scenes of horror and bloodshed and Sikh atrocities were beyond description. On several occasions during these disturbances the Sikhs tried to persuade their leader to attack Malerkotla but he always pacified them by saying that as Nawab Sher Muhammad Khan was dear to Guru Gobind Singh he would never think of attacking the ruler of Malerkotla. During the course of these upheavals, the Sikh army had to pass through the State several times but no damage was done to anything belonging to its territory.[75]

Iftikhar Ali Khan clearly attributes Banda's avoidance of Malerkotla to the guru's blessing, but other histories say that Bahadur did come to Malerkotla. According to historian Sohan Singh's 2000 biography, Bahadur came to punish the kingdom for its role in the attack on the guru at Anandpur, just prior to the capture of his sons, and for the captivity by Sher Muhammad Khan of Anup Kaur, a woman of the guru's household.[76] She refused to accept Islam and took her own life. Her body was buried rather than burned, and according to some historians this incident has been used as a precipitating excuse for attack by a number of assailants, including Banda Bahadur and Sahib Singh Bedi.[77] Varinder Singh Bhatia, a history professor at Punjabi University, Patiala, claims that Banda Bahadur sought Anup Kaur's remains but spared Malerkotla because of the guru's blessing. In a brief article seeking to counter the common view that Banda Bahadur was anti-Muslim, Bhatia writes of this event as evidence of Banda's selective campaigning only against those who participated in anti-Sikh campaigning. To refute the claim that Banda desecrated the graves of Muslims, Bhatia rightly points out that the monumental tombs at Sirhind remain intact. He also claims that during Banda's campaign across Punjab, only one grave was dug up—Anup Kaur's in Malerkotla. But even as he references this dark rumor of Sher Muhammad Khan's less than honorable actions in battle with the guru, Bhatia quickly follows it with Sher Muhammad Khan's famous act of honor.

> As regards the digging of graves we may say that only at Malerkotla the grave of Bibi Anoop Kaur, was dug out and her remains were cremated according to Sikh rites, because she had been forcibly carried away by Sher Muhammad Khan from Sirsa rivulet in December 1704 and buried in a grave after she had committed suicide to save her honour. The town of Malerkotla was also spared

for Sher Muhammad Khan who had appealed for mercy for the sons of Guru Govind Singh at the time of their execution at Sirhind.[78]

Thus it is a widespread belief that the power of the guru's blessing prevented Banda from attacking Malerkotla. Ganda Singh also claims that "the Sikhs have always remembered this protest of the Nawab with gratitude, and throughout their troubled relations with the Muslim powers they have always spared the house of Malerkotla from their attacks."[79] The guru's blessing of Sher Muhammad Khan is believed by many Punjab historians, Malerkotla residents, and visitors to outweigh the nawab's participation with the Mughals in the campaigns against the guru, *and* the capture and death of Anup Kaur demonstrates the centrality of this narrative in forming Malerkotla's identity.[80]

Although some historians, such as J. S. Grewal, assert that Malerkotla was spared because Banda's campaign simply did not take him through the kingdom, popular wisdom generally attributes Malerkotla's safety at this and other moments to the guru's blessing. For example, this is the assessment of Ramesh Walia, a historian of the Praja Mandal movement, which was an effort to end princely states in India. He writes:

> The Phulkian rulers [i.e., Patiala and Jind] never tried to capture this small Muslim State because of an interesting fact of Sikh history. Nawab Sher Mohammad Khan who came to power in 1672 had remonstrated with the Sirhind Faujdar against the cold-blooded murder of the innocent younger children of Guru Gobind Singh who were butchered to death in December 1704. So even this Muslim State had a link with Sikh history and claimed blessings of the Gurus.[81]

Walia, like so many other Sikh historians, sees the blessing of the guru as a sufficient explanation for Malerkotla's relative security. As we have seen, Walia is incorrect in his view that the neighboring Sikh states never tried to capture Malerkotla, but his perspective on the power of the guru's blessing confirms that the social force of the belief in the blessing is widespread in academic as well as popular circles.

The haah da naara *in Popular Culture*

Indian Punjabis of all religions tell the story of the *haah da naara*, usually citing it as evidence of a shared history of interreligious cooperation, a precedent for secular practices, and a justification for continued exchange. The range and variety of occasions upon which the story of the *haah da naara* was and is told testify to its ongoing role in shaping the moral past from which the ethical standards of the present are derived. For many of the people with whom I discussed these events, it was a gripping tale of a moment that exemplifies an idealized view of Punjab's interreligious harmony and exchange. This pluralistic ideal is pervasive in Punjab, as is the story of the *haah da naara,* and both are integral to Punjabi identity.

The widespread force and appeal of the *haah da naara* became vividly apparent to me quite far away from both Malerkotla and Sirhind. I was at a festival for the great Chishti Sufi saint Baba Farid in Faridkot, a town named for him some 250 kilometers away from Malerkotla near the Pakistan border. My purpose there was to see how Sufi saints in Punjab are celebrated by non-Muslims in a largely non-Muslim environment. I was inquiring from the mostly Sikh pilgrims at two shrines to Baba Farid about their perceptions of the Muslim saint and their relationship to his tradition as non-Muslims. A small group gathered on the grass at Godhri Sahib Gurdwara where Baba Farid is said to have performed a *chilla,* or forty-day retreat. I asked several people to tell me stories about the saint. Although most knew some of the poetic compositions attributed to Baba Farid in the Guru Granth Sahib, only a few knew accounts of his life. Those who did know, however, were aware of his coming to the area and of several miracles he performed there. At one point I remarked that there were few Muslims in the area. An elderly man sitting across from me responded, "There are Muslims in Malerkotla." Then, a woman beside me, who had earlier recounted a number of tales about Baba Farid, chimed in, saying:

> Also in Malerkotla, which is a Muslim city, one Muslim rose up against the Muslims and said, "Do not put the sons of Guru Gobind Singh into the walls. If you want to fight, fight directly with Guru Gobind Singh. Why are you killing these innocent children?" So he gave the *haah da naara.* A gurdwara is built there in Malerkotla. And Guru Gobind Singh blessed the city, saying that the rule of Muslims will always remain. That is why [Muslims are there]. Only one man gave the *haah da naara,* and they [the *sahibzadas*] were later killed. That gurdwara is named *haah da naara.* So he was the man who stood against his own religion and said right is right, and wrong is wrong. Otherwise people say that they might be right if some Hindu has done something and we were also Hindu, or a Sikh might have said right to what a Sikh has done. So the guru gave his blessing because that man was against his own religion. Guru Gobind Singh not only uplifted the honor of the Sikhs, but also of the Hindus. At the age of nine years he gave his father for the help and security of the Hindus. He [the father] said you cannot forcibly ask anybody to change his religion.[82]

The Sikh woman applauded the righteousness of those who stand up for justice, even against their own religion, as in the case of the Muslim of Malerkotla.

Though she did not give the name of the Muslim who stood up for the sons of the guru, she knew very well of the event known as the *haah da naara,* the cry for justice. I had not mentioned Malerkotla and my research there. To make a point about the possibility of humanity superceding religious boundaries, this Sikh admirer of Baba Farid spontaneously recounted an incident in Malerkotla's past that is emblematic of such a gesture. She also connected it to the martyrdom of Gobind Singh's father, Guru Tegh Bahadur, who is understood to have been killed for advocating before the Mughal emperor Aurangzeb for the freedom of Hindus to worship as they please. Her perspective and depth of feeling about the event and its significance were by no means unique. By the end of my research it was apparent to me that the *haah da naara* is the single most famous and powerful episode in Malerkotla's history, providing an important narrative element in the construction of Malerkotla's peaceful present. Furthermore, this episode is a powerful rhetorical resource that gives history and credence to those seeking to establish the frame of interreligious harmony in the present.

Mistaking History, Revealing Values

In Malerkotla the *haah da naara* is such an important part of local lore that almost no public gathering goes by without mention of the nawab's protest, the guru's blessing, or both. For example, at a literary event in 2001, the president of the Sikh Students Federation in Malerkotla claimed that the electoral successes of the Pathan Muslims were ascribable to Sikh support. He said that the Sikhs vote for the Pathan nawabs because they are descendants of the ruler who gave the *haah da naara.* Because of this abiding respect and gratitude, the Sikhs vote in a bloc, whereas Hindus are divided between BJP and Congress. Because both Muslims and Sikhs vote for the Pathans, no matter what their political party, they win in the elections. A similar view was given in a conversation with the *granthi* (reciter of the Guru Granth Sahib) at the Haah da Naara Gurdwara. He claimed that because of the *haah da naara,* Muslims are elected as members of the Legislative Assembly and Parliament. "In our area in District Sangrur from here the MLA is always Muslim," he said. "Sikh people vote for them."[83]

Not only do people use the *haah da naara* to explain Sikh electoral support for Muslim candidates, but also to account for the enormous power and appeal of Haider Shaykh. As I described in the previous chapter, many devotees at Haider Shaykh's *dargah* conflate Sher Muhammad Khan and Haider Shaykh, believing that it was the shaykh, not the nawab, who defended Guru Gobind Singh's young sons. Yet this "error" does not reveal a false history. Rather, as Alessandro Portelli observes, citing Hans Magnus Enzenberger, history " 'is an invention which reality supplies with raw materials. It is not, however, an arbitrary invention, and the interest it arouses is rooted in the interests of the teller.' This is why 'wrong' tales ... are so very valuable. They allow us to recognize the interests of the tellers, and the dreams and desires beneath them."[84] Clearly, any telling of history reveals interest, and the nature of that interest becomes (more) apparent by studying how the memories of an event are organized. The meaning of the telling changes with alterations in the temporal location or sequence of events, revealing the interest of the interlocutor. One of the key narrative strategies employed in making these shifts is what Portelli terms displacement and condensation. Instead of merely hunting for the "truth" of an incorrectly reported event, "the causes of this collective error must be sought, rather than in the event itself, in the meaning which it derived from the actors' state of mind at the time; from its relation to subsequent historical developments; and from the activity of memory and imagination."[85] Thus the meaning of a historical narrative is most clearly discernible in the ways people use it, not solely in the accuracy of the events themselves.

The "error" of nonresident pilgrims' attribution of the *haah da naara* to the saint rather than to Sher Muhammad Khan reveals reasons why the Muslim town of Malerkotla and the Muslim saint Haider Shaykh have such significance among nonresident Punjabis, the vast majority of whom are non-Muslim. For example, a Sikh pilgrim from Hathoi explained that the power of Haider Shaykh derived from Guru Gobind Singh's blessing. In his view, the guru's blessing endowed Haider Shaykh with the power to grant the wishes of all those who come to pray with sincerity at his tomb. This claim introduces several possible interpretations and narrative intentions for the story of the shaykh and the *haah da naara*. First, the power of the Muslim saint is described as deriving from the Sikh guru, thus establishing a spiritual hierarchy of efficacy. This view may also provide theological cover for some non-Muslims to attend a Muslim shrine. This is potentially a sensitive point, however, for Muslim patrons. While it does justify non-Muslim presence, such a claim of derivative power also appropriates the saint, thereby minimizing or even erasing his Islamic identity. We will see in chapter 6 how such tensions are negotiated. Second, the shaykh is credited by extension with the impartial sense of justice that is often ascribed to Sher Muhammad Khan because of the protest. This elision is consistent with the prevailing view that Haider Shaykh does not discriminate between his devotees on the basis of religion. The Hathoi Sikh devotee also explained that Haider Shaykh's appeal is multireligious not only because the saint fulfills the desires of everyone regardless of religious affiliation, but also because he does not believe in *jat-path*, meaning caste and creed. Numerous pilgrims, especially those from lower castes, echoed this. In the hearts of these devotees, Haider Shaykh is *hamare sanjhe pir*, "our common *pir*." For the Sikh from Hathoi and many, many others who expressed similar views, the *haah da naara* is the local paradigm for the human capacity for justice and fairness and transcendence of sectarian affiliation. Third, by identifying Haider Shaykh with Sher Muhammad Khan, the saint is linked to an event in which the defenseless are defended and the tyrannical are confronted. In spite of the fact that in a certain sense the *haah da naara* was not successful—the *sahibzadas* were executed—the symbolic gesture alone carries enormous power for the constituents of Haider Shaykh's tradition, many of whom are from oppressed and disempowered communities themselves. These qualities of justice and courage are emphasized in most of the stories told about the saint, but this conflation of the shaykh and the nawab causes the most powerful symbolic action in Malerkotla's history to resonate with Malerkotla's founder.

The temporal and figural displacement of Sher Muhammad Khan and his conflation with Haider Shaykh increases the shaykh's importance for the non-Muslim population in particular. In part this is because the *haah da naara* placed religious divisions secondary to human rights. As one Hindu pilgrim said, "This *pir* of Malerkotla raised his voice against the walling up of the children. He rose above religious differences to the realm of humanity."[86] The identification of a realm beyond religious divisions as a "realm of humanity" is an important addition to our understanding of the significance of the *haah da naara* for locals and visitors to Malerkotla. Clearly one of the great appeals of the town and the shrine for those who are present there is its symbolic power as a model for such nonsectarian behavior. This sentiment was clearly expressed by a Sikh devotee who pulled me aside at one of the festivals for Haider Shaykh in May 2001 and said, "There is no Hindu, no Sikh, there is only the community of the saints (*piran da sanjha*). This *pir* gave the *haah da naara* when Guru Gobind Singh's son's were bricked up alive."[87]

Like the Sikh pilgrim from Hathoi, numerous other non-Muslim pilgrims report that Haider Shaykh is capable of fulfilling the desires of the faithful *because* of Guru Gobind Singh's blessing. Because Haider Shaykh is believed to have protested the *sahibzadas* execution, he was endowed with the power to perform miracles. For example, a Sikh visitor to Malerkotla gave a detailed, if factually incorrect, account of Haider Shaykh that expressed his belief that the source of the Shaykh's power was the guru.

> Baba Shaykh Sadruddin is from a Pathan family, Afghans who came to worship at Sirhind in the name of God. Two of his sons married; he had one other son and one daughter. When Aurangzeb was acting like a despot, then he was the only one to say, "Do not do this." The saint said, "Why are you doing this?" When Guru Gobind Singh came and asked who had protested his children's killing, then they said that Baba Haider Shaykh did, and he was blessed forever after. Because of this blessing, Haider Shaykh has power. He can clear the mixed-up mind and encourage concentration. He can heal diseases, give children, help studies, improve business. You can offer anything, but you must come with a clean heart, doing no wrong, harming no others, following God.[88]

This view of Haider Shaykh's personality and power in many ways encapsulates the reasons for his enormous appeal among non-Muslims. Whether he is placed in the fifteenth century or the eighteenth, Haider Shaykh represents a spirit of ecumenicism. After all, as the Hindu pilgrim above remarked, he rose above religion to humanity. For many of the pilgrims, confusing Haider Shaykh with Sher Muhammad Khan and attributing the *haah da naara* to the shaykh intensifies these qualities. Given that the elision is so common among visitors to the tomb, it is clear that the nonsectarian spirit of the saint is an important part of his appeal for pilgrims who wish to associate themselves with these values.

Conclusion

The peculiar power of the *haah da naara* is somewhat paradoxical. After all, Sher Muhammad Khan was unable to prevent the death of the *sahibzadas*. However, inasmuch as martyrdom for one's faith and values is celebrated by most religious communities, the nawab's protest has an important catalytic effect on this episode in Punjabi history. The *haah da naara* intensifies the drama and highlights the evil that humans do as being essentially human rather than attributable to any core religious tenets. Those who perpetrated the execution cannot hide behind a religious veil and are accountable for their own misdeeds. Sher Muhammad Khan clearly raised the possibility that Islamic values do not sanction such an action. The events surrounding the escape, betrayal, imprisonment, and execution of Zorawar and Fateh Singh are among the most poignant in Sikh history. Perhaps the nawab's popularity is in part ascribable to the stark contrast between him and Wazir Khan, the *faujdar* of Sirhind, and those who supported him and encouraged him in his decision to kill the children.[89] The event epitomizes the nadir of relations between the Mughals and the Sikhs, giving clear proof to the Sikhs of Mughal (and, by extension, Muslim) intolerance, injustice and cruelty. The Sikhs rallied around this outrage and cried out for retribution. Indeed, as discussed above, Sirhind was one of Banda Bahadur's first stops on his campaign through Punjab after Guru Gobind Singh's death. Sirhind was basically razed, though numerous monumental tombs remain standing in the area, all of which are emblems of Muslim authority, whether religious, worldly, or both. For many years it was a popular custom among Sikh pilgrims to take one of the tiny ancient bricks from the remaining walls and ruins away with them—thereby obtaining a relic and helping to further demolish the Mughal edifice.[90]

Why is this story of the nawab's protest on behalf of the guru's sons such a powerful narrative, known by most every Sikh in the world and every resident of Malerkotla? Had the protest been successful and the boys freed or given over to the nawab, would the story be as prevalent or as meaningful? I would argue not. It is the very futility of the attempt that gives the event such a compelling pathos.

The nawab tried to do what by most moral standards past or present was the right thing. After all, seven- and nine-year-old children did not present immediate threats to the vast Mughal Empire. However, as martyrs the *sahibzadas* become rallying points to mobilize and consolidate the Sikh community in their name. Thus in death they are far more symbolically powerful than they were in life. And so the nawab's effort on their behalf likewise increases in fame and in its effect on future generations. So although he failed to save the boys, he, like the martyred *sahibzadas*, succeeded on a much broader plane. He rose above sectarian divisions; he refused to submit to the pressure of his overlords and Mughal master. It was a simple act, a mere gesture of conscience, but the *haah da naara* remains as one of the most powerful symbols of the possibility that humanity may on occasion rise above sectarian chauvinism, religious prejudice, and the fear of reprisal. Part of the power of this narrative does in fact rely on the failure of the plea itself.

The argument that the nawab's failure is part of the drama and the appeal of the story is also strengthened by the fact that Muslims helped the guru at other times and in other places. They were likewise blessed, but with remarkably different results. For example, after escaping from the very battle in which his two older sons were killed, Guru Gobind Singh arrived at a town called Macchiwara. There Mughal forces surrounded him, and escape seemed impossible. However, Gobind Singh was saved by two Muslim brothers, Ghani and Nabhi Khan, who dressed him up in blue garments and, placing him on a palanquin, carried him out of town between the ranks of the soldiers, declaring he was Uch ka Pir—a Muslim holy man from a placed called Uch (now in Pakistan). The guru was freed, and he blessed the Khan brothers, much as he had blessed the nawab of Malerkotla. This event appears in Sikh art and histories but is not memorialized to the extent of the martyrdom of the *sahibzadas*. It is not unusual to see galleries of paintings housed next to many historic gurdwaras displaying a series of images depicting grotesque torture scenes of the Sikh faithful by various Muslim forces. Sandwiched between them will be a picture of the guru on the palanquin being carried out of Macchiwara by Ghani and Nabhi Khan. These galleries usually also display an image of Zorawar and Fateh Singh being bricked up alive. Sometimes the image includes a remonstrating figure—Sher Muhammad Khan objecting to the execution. Yet in the collective memory of the Punjab, especially among the Sikh population, the protest of Sher Muhammad Khan features much more prominently than the rescue of the guru. The trauma and drama of the boys' death increases exponentially the significance of the event. The *successful* rescue merits gratitude and a place in the gallery of important events in Gobind Singh's life. Not only does the event play a less prominent role in Sikh history, but also there was considerable violence in Macchiwara at Partition, and most of the Muslim population left. Belief in the Guru's goodwill had little effect there, and the bravery of Nabhi and Ghani Khan did not suffice to save the town's Muslims.

This suggests that the Malerkotla nawab's protest receives greater attention because of the subsequent peace in Malerkotla at Partition. The guru's blessing is without question the most common explanation among Sikhs, Hindus, and nonresidents for Malerkotla's having been spared the violence that happened elsewhere. Although many people—Sikh, Hindu, and Muslim—will also attribute peace to Haider Shaykh and the many saints in Malerkotla, even those who do not believe in the salvific power of the guru's blessing *do* acknowledge that what has been effective in protecting Malerkotla is the very strong belief of the Sikhs in the blessing. By this account, it is not necessary to judge whether the guru had any divine powers. The blessing works because the faithful, especially the Sikhs, respect its sentiment. The symbolic significance of Malerkotla as a place where religious divisions do not obtain is given even greater force when perceived as a directive from the guru himself.

In spite of this generalized belief that since the *haah da naara*, Malerkotla's Muslim and non-Muslim residents have enjoyed pacific relations, the early part of the twentieth century in particular was fraught with tensions. The next chapter investigates how these conflicts arose and how, by managing them effectively, Malerkotla's citizens gained the critical tension-wisdom needed to withstand the coming trials during Partition.

Before Partition: Challenges to the Plural Kingdom

As I told you earlier, it is like in a house: brothers fight momentarily if they have some problem. But with passage of time they think with cool heads and again become one. It is a similar situation here between Hindu and Muslim brothers. If something happens they fight, but as time passes they think with a cool head. Everybody realizes their mistakes easily, and things go back to normal.

—Mahmud, Malerkotla resident

T H E story of Haider Shaykh and his descendants, the rulers of Malerkotla from its founding in 1454 through the nineteenth century, has seen many twists and turns, but the early twentieth heralded an even more contentious and confusing period. British India during this time was in the throes of the independence movement. Led by the Indian National Congress, the Muslim League, and other groups, nationalist sentiment was on the rise. In India's more than six hundred princely states, such groups were strictly curtailed if not banned outright. Yet the suppression of formal organizations could not suppress the wave of nationalism and the call for democratic reform. Thus the early twentieth century also saw an increase in protests and agitations for citizens' rights within princely states as well as British India. Furthermore, as noted in the previous chapter, many movements and activists framed their resistance to colonial rule along communal or sectarian lines. Paralleling the British focus on religious communities as electoral blocs and establishment of the census, Indians increasingly organized along religious and ethnic lines, and they made their claims and grievances to the government based on these identities. In the previous chapter we saw how the public memory has interpreted the political and military relations between the Muslim-ruled kingdom of Malerkotla and the Sikh and Hindu chiefs with whom they periodically clashed through the dominant filter of interreligious harmony. In particular we saw that Malerkotlans today imagine and understand interreligious relations through the prism of symbolic events. The story of the *haah da naara* is exemplary of a moment of interreligious cooperation and a resource through which later Malerkotlans have imagined and understood the nature of interreligious relations. This chapter explores a period of interreligious and intersectarian tension within Malerkotla shortly before Partition. Given the watershed of Partition and the near-universal recollection of it as tense but peaceful, it is particularly important to understand what Malerkotla was like just prior to that challenging time. Indeed, since Malerkotla today is often characterized as primordially harmonious, the more complicated reality is illustrative of both the resilience of the community and the complex operations of collective memory.

Nowadays, if one did not know of Malerkotla's complex history, it would be possible to accept uncritically the common perception that it is a place where nothing bad has ever happened between Muslims, Sikhs, and Hindus. One could see the storefront names in the bazaars alternate—Narendra Singh Cloth, Jindal Glass, Hussain Sweets, Jain Books—and believe that such integration is the whole story. One could observe the variety of turbans, caps, beards, scarves, and veils in a tea, sweet, or snack shop and assume that people of all religions have always patronized each other's businesses regardless of sect or ethnic group. Membership in political parties, local businesses, and civic groups is quite integrated. Interreligious relations in town appear to be healthy from all observable indices. Likewise, media reports about Malerkotla present a remarkably homogeneous catalogue of stories about Malerkotla as a peaceful town. This is the "public transcript" of Malerkotla's history, to put it in James Scott's terms. The "hidden transcript," however, includes episodes of turbulence and counternarratives to the rosy glow shed by headlines like "An Oasis of Tolerance." I began to understand this hidden transcript and where and how it operated after I published a newspaper article on the declining condition of many of Malerkotla's heritage sites. I had seen files in the Punjab State Archives that spoke of past conflicts, and my friend Zulfikar had told me versions of these events, but for the most part they were either not discussed or were given a harmonious spin. After the article came out, people began to stop me to talk about Malerkotla's history, and in this way I began to hear the more complicated story of the town from a few residents.[1] One of the most determined and informed individuals was Abdullah, a retired schoolteacher and a Sunni Muslim from the weaver caste, who wrote me a letter after reading the article. We met, and he spent hours recounting some of these challenging times, most of which predated Partition. One issue he raised was widely known and is well chronicled in the state archives. This was a dispute about prayer timings between a temple and a mosque, called the *arati-namaz* dispute in the British records, which stretched from 1935 to 1940. (*Arati* is the regular evening worship of enshrined

Hindu deities, during which a priest performs rituals to the accompaniment of hymns, ringing bells, and sometimes other instrumentation; *namaz* is the five-time daily Islamic prayer.) But this saga took root in the context of two other conflicts in Malerkotla: the antiroyal, land-rights movement called Praja Mandal and a protracted Sunni-Shi'i dispute within the ruling clan over the conduct of the Muharram parades.

As we investigate these several conflicts and their relationships, it is important to remember how absent from the present collective memory all these events are. Only a handful of the hundreds of residents of Malerkotla with whom I spoke about my interest in the area's history felt that these were important stories to tell. Whether out of fear of reigniting the past problems, desire to whitewash the history for a foreign audience, or genuine lack of knowledge, stories about these disturbances (when told at all) are usually presented so as to reaffirm the present peace rather than to demonstrate its fragility or inauthenticity. They also reflect the interests of the tellers. For example, Zulfikar's version of the riots presented the nawab as the hero of the story. The British archives describe near incompetence on the part of the rulers. Abdallah highlighted the character of the citizenry in resolving the issues.

Whatever the causes and whatever the resolutions, the troubles of the early-to mid-twentieth century challenge the usual narrative of Malerkotla's eternally pacific nature. First, these events complicate the picture of Malerkotla as primordially harmonious, revealing important lessons about the operations of collective memory and forgetting. Indeed these stories represent potential cultural memories that never made it into the standard repertoire.[2] What interest is served by this collective amnesia? Second, the conflicts involve interreligious disputes as well as broader issues of class, caste, and ethnic struggles within a British-protected princely state where political organization was not possible. Third, the Hindu-Muslim clash and its eventual resolution provide important case studies both for studies of communal conflict and to the field of conflict resolution. Although the riot arose after an almost classic "triggering incident" in which the sound spaces of prayer were violated, the web of issues involved indicate that far more than religious sensitivities were in play. Furthermore, the resolution came about almost *in spite of* rather than through the leadership of the rulers or the British. The community itself forged a response that helped to create a trust between Hindus and Muslims that proved sufficient to surmount the challenge of Partition in 1947.

Of Kingdoms and Karbala: The Praja Mandal Movement and Sunni-Shi'i Tensions

During the period that Malerkotla was a British protectorate, from 1809 to 1947, the nawabs of Malerkotla in some ways followed a steady course with respect to the non-Muslim population. Land grants were given, temples and gurdwaras were built, and high-ranking officials were drawn from the elites of all religious communities. In 1907, Ahmad Ali Khan (r. 1908–1947) donated 52 *bighas* of land to support the building of the Singh Sabha Gurdwara. Given the increasing influence of the Singh Sabha movement, which sought to purify, regulate, and consolidate the Sikh community, this move was no doubt an important gesture toward the Sikh citizens of Malerkotla, who at that time accounted for the largest segment of the urban population (41 percent, according to the 1891 census). Ahmad Ali Khan had in effect been ruling for several years because of his father's deteriorating mental condition, and upon ascending to the throne he pursued numerous projects to maintain the loyalty of all his subjects. He supported the Dera of Baba Atma Ram, and during his rule several of the larger Hindu temples were built, including the Kali Mandir and the Gopal Bhavan. The latter temple was the local center for the Hindu Mahasabha and RSS.[3] It is also in the heart of the old city, which was mostly the property of members of the royal family. However, incidents of dissent, rebellion, and rioting did occur in this period.

In Malerkotla, as throughout the subcontinent, the 1920s and 1930s were full of unrest both in terms of communal relations and the independence movement. But as a princely state with an independent standing army, little agitation against the nawab or the British was tolerated. Under British protection since 1809, Malerkotla was not only loyal to the Crown, but also was deeply in its debt.[4] Malerkotla battalions fought with the British in the mid-nineteenth century Afghan wars, World War I, and World War II. Yet there was certainly opposition to both the British and the native princes. For example, during India's movement for freedom from the British in the first half of the twentieth century, a parallel movement known as Praja Mandal emerged in the princely states to oppose these indigenous monarchical regimes.[5] In Malerkotla this movement was present, particularly among the non-Muslim (Hindu and Sikh) cultivators seeking land-tenure rights. According to Ramesh Walia, a historian of the Praja Mandal movement in Punjab,

> In Malerkotla the Praja Mandal was very weak. The Muslims were predominantly on the side of the Nawab[,] and the peasantry sided with the Akalis and the Communists. This State was an exception to the mass slaughter and emigration of the Muslim population in the wake of the country's partition. In the towns of Malerkotla and Ahmedgarh where Hindus were in substantial numbers some activity of the Praja Mandal was witnessed[,] and the State promised to introduce constitutional reforms.[6]

However, there is little evidence that such reforms took place, and Walia's view contrasts somewhat with that of Rita Brara, a sociologist at Delhi University whose dissertation focused on marriage and kinship and their effects on land tenure in Malerkotla. She writes:

> The Malerkotla chapter of the *Punjab Riyasati Praja Mandal* had focused attention upon the unfair eviction of cultivators from their lands. The leaders had spearheaded the demand for relief from the exorbitant revenue dues and taxes and sought parity with the cultivators of the neighbouring tracts. As far as the State was concerned, the activities of the Praja Mandal were illegal and the activists were dealt with severely right until 1946.[7]

In spite of their illicit nature, several groups did repeatedly meet within the kingdom's borders, largely drawing from the Sikh population, who sought greater autonomy as agriculturalists, particularly in terms of land rights; lower taxes; and the right to fix their own prices.[8] They published pamphlets, held rallies, and formed networks with other Praja Mandals in the states of Patiala, Nabha, and Jind. Several newspapers were occasionally banned for publishing anti-nawab articles; these included the *Riyasati Dunya*, edited by Talib Hussain a land rights activist, and the *Muslim Outlook*.[9] According to Walia, the peasants in Malerkotla continually agitated for their land rights over and against the elite Muslim landlords, the *khawanin*—ethnic Pathans descended from the ruling clan. Although some of the agitators were Muslim agriculturalists from the Khamboj ethnic group, this was largely a Hindu and Sikh movement. In 1927 they set up a Zamindara Association and presented their case to the viceroy at Simla. This phase of the anti-*riyasat* land rights movement culminated in the village of Kothala on July 18.[10] On this day a demonstration was brutally suppressed, with fourteen people reportedly shot and killed by the nawab's forces. There were mass arrests. In the subsequent investigation, the Malerkotla ruler, Nawab Ahmad Ali Khan, attributed the deaths to overzealous police work and disciplined the superintendent. No further action was taken.[11] However, annual gatherings at the site in memory of the dead persisted. The state records occasionally noted whether or not any demonstration occurred on the anniversary of the incident, indicating that it was an ongoing point of concern for the rulers.

In addition to the Praja Mandal movement, the struggle to bring about representative democracy had an effect in Malerkotla. While most efforts to organize against the royal house were quickly subdued, and demonstrations such as the one at Kothala were violently dispersed, the polarizing religious politics that were deepening in India were also felt in Malerkotla. A number of organizations and all political parties were illegal. One of the most influential Hindu nationalist groups, the Rashtriya Swayamsevak Sangh (RSS), was eventually banned in 1948 (in response to Gandhi's murder by a former RSS member), but their activities were also curtailed during the *riyasat*.[12] Congress and the Muslim Ahrar Party were non grata as well. From the records it is clear that rallies took place from time to time within the kingdom's borders, but most political activism was quite limited. State archives also contain specific directives from the secretary of the Punjab States Agency encouraging Malerkotla state officials to observe and curtail the activities of individuals known to "work in conjunction with other Congress organizations for the purpose of undertaking anti-Government work."[13] These directives and the banning of such hard-line organizations as the RSS indicate that even in a princely state like Malerkotla, where relations between religions were most often characterized as quite positive, political mobilization along communal lines was increasingly a part of life in the quarter-century leading up to Partition in 1947.

Another conflict that complicated the period prior to Partition involved disputes within the royal family about processions during the first ten days of Muharram, when the Shi'i branch of the family would sponsor parades in honor of the martyrdom of Imam Hussain, the grandson of Prophet Muhammad, in 680 CE. In these parades, people carried *alam*s (standards) through town, and on the tenth day of the month of Muharram, the day Hussain died, a riderless horse and *taziya*s (replicas of his tomb shrine) are processed as well. Although these disputes were long-standing and seem to have been mostly within this elite group, State and British records make frequent mention of the Sunni-Shi'a tensions in the same files that deal with the *arati-namaz* issue, clearly indicating a perceived linkage. There is some speculation on the part of state government, not wholly dismissed by the British, that the Hindu-Muslim conflict was exacerbated by disgruntled members of the royal family itself who wished to create trouble for the nawab. Thus the Sunni-Shi'i quarrel related at least in part to the centuries of infighting over royal succession and in part to sensitivities about the processions themselves. Abdallah, the schoolteacher who contacted me about the riots, also spoke of the Sunni-Shi'i question, though in this case, he minimized the significance of the problem, possibly reflecting the generally pacific Sunni-Shi'i relations in contemporary Malerkotla.

> ABDALLAH: The Shi'a-Sunni quarrel was always there, whenever they had their horse procession, a quarrel was there. Efforts would be made, and then the matter would cool down.
>
> AB: But Shi'a-Sunni quarrels occur now in places, and sometimes are very serious.
>
> ABDALLAH: No, it was never serious, it just became inevitable, and communal riots might occur. So, the people, peace-loving people, easily pacify them, and there is communal harmony.

Indeed harmony between Sunni and Shi'a nowadays does seem to be more or less the status quo. During the 2001 Muharram observations, several Sunnis actively supported the Shi'i commemoration; some even made food and drink to distribute to the processors. Some Hindus joined in the parade, helping to carry the *taziyas* (replicas of Imam Hussain's tomb). I witnessed no obvious tension in the town in spite of the fact that three major local festivals coincided over the course of ten days.[14] For several days the usually crowded streets of Malerkotla were completely overwhelmed with processions and people, but this never led to any conflict. The only competition was between different Shi'i groups, and it concerned the timing of the parades or the order of procession. Local Shi'a are split between two principle communities—the sayyids and the shaykhs. The sayyids, as descendants of the Prophet, trace their heritage outside of India, whereas the shaykhs are Indian converts. There is some cooperation but also significant competition between these two groups.

The Shi'a in Malerkotla have enjoyed a fair amount of state patronage and reportedly little persecution, though their population remains small—about five hundred families today. Rulers or members of the royal family built several of the imambaras in town. Perhaps one of the most important reasons why Sunni-Shi'i relations did not escalate to a dangerous level is the generally positive relationship with the ruling family. In an example of royal patronage, at a *majlis* (memorial gathering) at the Riyasati Imambara I encountered one of the surviving wives of Malerkotla's last nawab, Mujawwar Nisa'. She believed quite strongly in the spiritual benefit of attending these gatherings. She attends this *majlis* annually, and she and her husband were major patrons (in better times) of the Riyasati Imambara. She informed me that the mother of Nawab Sikandar Ali Khan (d. 1881) built this imambara because her son was born after she had prayed to Imam Hussain for a child. In the building there is a picture of Nawab Ahmad Ali Khan and of Ayatollah Khomeini. The begum clearly appreciated the emotional dirges (*marsiya* and *noha*), though she did not herself engage in *matam* (flagellation) and, like most Sunnis, said that it is wrong to harm the body in this way.

In spite of, or more likely because of, the patronage and participation by the ruling family, state records do include reports of conflicts, particularly concerning the taking out of *taziyas* and *'alams* during the observations of Muharram. However, these appear more often than not to be conflicts between Shi'i groups or members of the nawab's family who sought preeminence in the order of procession or were refusing to allow the marchers to proceed over their territory. At several points in the mid-nineteenth century, controversies arose over the celebrations of Muharram involving the sons and grandson of Nawab Bahadur Khan (r. 1763–1766). According to Inayat Ali Khan, the author of the 1882 *Description of the Principle Kotla Afghans*, the nawab's son, Dalel Khan "had a taste for Shyaism [*sic*]" and thus

> brought out a horse imitative of Ali's charger, Duldul (Zuljenah),
> for procession which excited the religious feelings of the Sunnis so
> much that they crossed the path of it, and a *melee* ensued in which

Dalel Khan lost his two upper front teeth, and the reader of the dirges of Hassan and Hussein was severely cudgeled. Henceforth Dalel Khan never dared publicly to profess the all-revered Shaya [*sic*] rite.[15]

Dalel's son, Ghulam Mohammad Khan, however, showed no such reservations, and he resolved upon "performing openly in the town of Kotla those ceremonies which would have hurt the feelings of the Sunnis; rendering imminent an affray between the two sects. For the sake of public peace he was debarred from his intention by Mr. Barnes, the Commissioner of Ambala."[16] Although it appeared necessary to appeal to the British authorities outside the state for the directive to be heeded, the prohibition was followed up by an order from Nawab Sikandar Ali Khan to confine and regulate the procession. This order specifies the routes to be taken by the various groups bringing out *taziyas* and *'alams*, the timing of these processions, and the amount of accompanying ceremony that may occur involving recitation of *nohas* (dirges for the martyrs) along the way. The edict is at pains to reaffirm the right to process as one sees fit within one's own territory, as urban Malerkotla in those days was made up of dozens of minor *jagirs* (land grants) belonging to the various branches of the ruling clan.

An important principle of local conflict resolution was affirmed by Sikander Ali Khan in his edict which gave preference to past precedent as the determining factor in deciding the proper course of action. This clearly asserted the priority of calm over conflict, whether the grievances were valid or not. And so Ghulam Mohammad is explicitly directed "to abstain from any innovations which would wound the feelings of the Nawab and his subjects."[17] The prohibition on innovations in the observance of Muharram brought this particular controversy to a close and allowed for Ghulam Mohammad and other members of the royal family to step back from their aggressive postures without anyone feeling a loss of honor. The reliance on precedent as a problem-solving strategy would be tried again in the *arati-namaz* conflict, but with considerably less efficacy because no one agreed on what the precedent was.

The Sunni-Shi'i troubles arose again in 1935 in the middle of the *arati-namaz* affair. The *Fortnightly Report* from the political agent of the Panjab States reported that a Sunni-Shi'i dispute occurred over a Duldul (Hussain's martyred horse) procession during Muharram to be taken out by Ihsan Ali Khan, a Shi'i member of the royal family (see fig. 3.1). Although permission for the procession and its route had been duly received from the nawab the previous year, things went awry. The procession was supposed to proceed through a neighborhood known as Sherwani Kot. But the khan who possessed the *jagir* of that property, Muhammad Ali Khan, was suspected of being an Ahmadi. Ahmadis are a followers of Mirza Ghulam Ahmad (d. 1908), a religious leader who claimed ongoing revelations from Allah.[18] Anti-Ahmadi sentiment is strong among Sunnis and Shi'a in South Asia, and many regard Ahmadis as non-Muslim

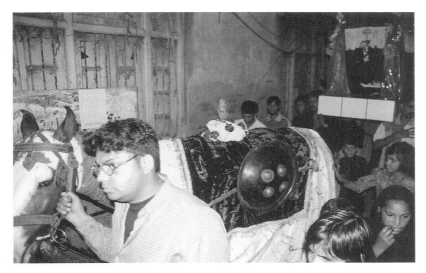

FIGURE 3.1. Procession of Imam Hussain's horse *duldul* during Muharram observations.

heretics. As Muhammad Ali Khan's house was on his prescribed procession route, Ihsan deemed it unacceptable to pass the home of a kinsman he regarded as a heretic. The route was altered with the permission of the nawab, but Ihsan Ali Khan was apparently unhappy with the new arrangement. Some in the Sunni community objected to the new route, which brought the Shiʻi procession more directly through their neighborhood. The nawab asked Ihsan Ali Khan not to take out his procession or at least to postpone it until a settlement could be reached. Angered, Ihsan did not take out either a Duldul or a *taziya*. In the estimation of the anonymous British author of the *Fortnightly Report* of June 15, 1935, the dispute was not so much a Sunni-Shiʻa problem but was really about the nawab's tense relations with his extended family. Ihsan Ali Khan's supporters asserted that the nawab was trying to stir up Sunnis to make Ihsan look bad or appear to be a troublemaker. They said that the old route was fine, requiring only a small change to avoid the Ahmadi's house. The nawab said the settlement would have been fine except that Ihsan involved a Muslim political activist, Maulvi Birjis Ahmad from Firozepore, in the matter, thus raising the stakes to an antiroyalist issue. The report's author concludes that there were "probably faults and obstinacy on both sides."

In his report on the *arati-namaz* troubles that also occurred in 1935, the investigating officer, J. C. Donaldson, observed that Nawab Ahmad Ali Khan was suspicious of his cousin Ihsan's possible role in instigating, or at least exacerbating, that conflict. Though he suggests that the nawab himself was more to blame than Ihsan Ali Khan for the Muharram difficulties, Donaldson does state, "it is a fact that Ihsan Ali Khan resents his position and dislikes the Nawab, and it may be that he has consorted with discontented Hindus in Malerkotla."[19] The matter is not pursued as it pertains to internal state matters, and meddling in that is something which Donaldson "can see nothing to be gained." Subsequent reports mostly remark simply that the Sunni-Shi'a matter remains quiet, indicating that it remained a watchful issue but not an open conflict.[20]

Although the Praja Mandal and the Sunni-Shi'a issues are not causally linked to the *arati-namaz* disputes, they are part of the broader context in which those disputes arose. After all, Malerkotla was not a large kingdom, being only 167 square miles. The town center was mostly populated by Hindus and Sikhs and was only 13 percent Muslim, according to the 1931 census. Thus anti-*riyasat* and intra-*riyasat* conflict would certainly have been well known to the players in the *arati-namaz* issue. From those other disputes it is clear that Malerkotla was a kingdom where antigovernment sentiment was held by a broad cross-section of the populace, including some within the royal family. Though it is unlikely that a majority of the residents shared these sentiments, the attitude was pervasive.

Katha-Arati-Namaz: The Malerkotla Triangle

The circumstances leading up to and following the death of a local Hindu man in a 1935 riot in Malerkotla call into question the prevailing myth of Malerkotla's pacific interreligious relations. The victim, Puran Mal, was a member of a family that had both sponsored a *katha* (Hindu devotional recitation) in a house overlooking an Ahl-e Hadith mosque and owned a local temple where the *arati*, devotional hymns, conflicted with the time for prayer at another mosque. Puran Mal was the only fatality in the riot that was sparked by the *katha* in Malerkotla's main bazaar. Indeed, Puran Mal's death, the subsequent execution of two people accused of responsibility, and the mysterious death of a Muslim girl are the products of not one but *two* lingering disputes between Hindus and Muslims over prayer timings in Malerkotla. These disputes began in 1923, climaxed in 1935, and appear to have been resolved in 1940, just a few years before the Partition of 1947. Furthermore, this conflict took place in the context of several other contentious issues in the *riyasat* (kingdom), among them the Praja Mandal movement and the Sunni-Shi'a conflicts outlined above. This wide range of issues clearly indicates that rather than eternally pacific relations, Malerkotla has experienced, and ultimately managed, serious interreligious conflicts. The drama of this particular crisis, termed the *arati-namaz* issue by the British investigators, is increased by the multiple interests and issues that converged, involving the relations between a Muslim minority elite and the Hindu and Sikh majority subjects of a small princely state under British protection during a period of accelerating anti-British and antiroyal activism and growing communal sentiment.

Ethnically, the Hindus involved in the *arati-namaz* dispute were principally Chaudhrys, members of a loose-knit, multi-caste, multireligious network of landowners. The Hindus who supported them included shopkeepers as well as the proprietors of all the local temples which ceased holding *arati* for five years. It is difficult to imagine that such a long suspension of ritual activity would not have a deleterious impact on communal relations, even if (as is likely) the strike was imperfectly kept. The Praja Mandal movement, for its part, was largely the province of tenant farmers, especially Sikhs. The Muslims involved in Praja Mandal were also tenant farmers, most likely Khamboj as this class now makes up the largest proportion of the Muslim agriculturalists in Malerkotla today. The *arati-namaz* issue involved an ideologically and ethnically wide spectrum of Muslims, from the weavers who operated the mosque near the Chaudrian temple to the Ahl-i Hadith who were proximate to the *katha*. Finally, the Sunni-Shi'i problems revealed substantial divisions within the elite Pathan ruling class. So why did the *arati-namaz* question become so inflamed at this time? It is impossible to say precisely why in May 1935 the conflict took root. But the simultaneous existence of multiple other contestations over the local distribution of power indicates that this was an attractive moment for those seeking a further realignment of authority and resources. Furthermore, the fact that the ultimate resolution was brought about by the disputing parties themselves, and *not by the state* or the British, indicates that conflict management came to be seen as the best guarantor of maximal influence and resources in the views of the disputing parties themselves. Whereas in 1935 conflict seemed expedient, by 1940 mutual accommodation emerged as the winning horse in the race.

And so it was that during the 1930s in Malerkotla there were at least two murders, two riots, three investigations by British and local officials into religious disputes, and three occasions upon which large groups left the state en masse to protest the nawab's policies on religious issues. The nawab during this time, Ahmad Ali Khan, built schools, a college, hospitals, and brought the railroad to Malerkotla. Yet British records also describe him as a weak-willed man, prone to overspending and constantly in debt. Furthermore, it is clear from both the Punjab State Archives and the British India Office Collection that Ahmad Ali Khan had a tendency to head for Simla—the British summer capital in the Himalayan foothills—at the first sign of trouble. This indicates that he felt greater security in his ties with the British than with the popular support of his subjects. Though his actions hardly seemed to curry favor with the British either. For example, in a *Fortnightly Report* chronicling the goings on throughout the region, dated September 30, 1935, the nawab's behavior is strongly criticized:

> The behavior of His Highness the Nawab of Malerkotla during the recent troubles in his state cannot be passed over without mention. He changed orders when pressed by relatives, showed abject fear of

his subjects and after releasing the arrested disturbers of the peace fled on the excuse of ill health to Simla when a Muhammadan demonstration was made at the palace at Malerkotla.[21]

Nawab Ahmad Ali Khan's cowardice in the face of protests and tension in his kingdom can only have exacerbated those situations. The disputes in question were over the coordination of timing of prayer at two different mosques with various Hindu rituals in neighboring buildings, the release of a Hindu couple believed to have killed a Muslim girl but never charged, the prosecution and execution of Muslim youths for killing a Hindu man in a riot, and the dismissal of the local mufti. The nawab and his government were accused by turns of communalism, meaning he was perceived as favoring one community or the other—the Muslims as his coreligionists or the majority Hindus, as he was afraid of them and in their financial debt.

Given his absenteeism, the nawab's management of these disputes leaves much to be desired. So it is largely to the credit of the community that these inflammatory events did not cause greater trouble and that they were eventually resolved. More important, for ongoing communal relations in Malerkotla, the ultimately successful management of those struggles added to the collective tension-wisdom, establishing a sufficiently solid basis for interreligious nego-tiation and organization that helped to stabilize the principality during the time of Partition. Though sanctioned and supported by the state, the resolution was formulated and agreed upon by leaders from the religious communities involved, rather than through government intervention. Though the role of the state is often identified as the primary factor in whether or not interreligious violence occurs, in this case we can see a far more complex web of allegiances and relationships. The nawab is accused of Hindu sympathies in part because he demoted and eventually fired the Shi'i chief judge who had dismissed charges against the Hindu couple on whose property the slain Muslim girl's body was found. The nawab's appointed mufti came to lead a "*hijra*" (exodus) out of Malerkotla in protest over perceived anti-Muslim bias. The very complexity of the disputes that are given the single label of "communal" in the records defies such simple characterization, and their autochthonous resolution defies the expectation of conflict studies.

The Conflict Begins

On May 7, 1935, one Peshawri Mal was sponsoring a Ramayan *katha* on behalf of a sick woman of his household.[22] The space chosen was a rooftop owned by a kinsman that overlooked a mosque. The mosque, called the Lohari (iron-worker's) mosque belonged to the Ahl-e Hadith sect. The situation was unfor-tunate, or perhaps deliberate, as of all Islamic sects, the puritanical Ahl-e Hadith are among the least likely to tolerate the sound of music or singing—whatever its source—during their prayers.[23] On this particular night some of the Lohari Mosque congregation objected that the *katha* was clearly audible during the 'Isha prayers, the last of the five obligatory prayers of the day. Negotiations ensued to arrange the times for the recitation or to reduce its volume during *namaz*, but the next night a large group of Muslims had gathered and claimed the sound was still invading the aural space of their prayers. A violent clash ensued. Both communities claimed that past precedent validated their religious practice. The Muslims declared that no such *katha* had taken place there previously and that there was no reason why it should have to be so loud during their prayers. The Hindus retorted that indeed *kathas* had occurred within earshot of that mosque and others and that the recitation in no way prevented Muslims from praying. The situation reached an impasse, as news began to spread to Hindus and Muslims outside Malerkotla who then sent bands of activists to join the fray. The tension persisted for several months.

Then in mid-July the situation took a turn for the worse when a nearly identical dispute cropped up between another mosque and a temple in another neighborhood in Malerkotla. The temple, perhaps not coincidentally owned by Peshawri Mal's family, performed its evening *arati* in such a way and at such a time as to be clearly audible to the Muslims praying *maghrib namaz* in an adjacent mosque. *Arati* can be a rather noisy form of devotion as the *pujari* (priest) performs rituals accompanied by hymns, bells, and other instrumentation. Both groups claimed that their own worship services had traditionally been performed either first or, at most, simultaneously. The Hindus said they always performed *arati* at sundown and that the Muslims were only making it a problem now. The Muslims declared that the *arati* had always begun sometime after their prayers and that beginning earlier was a deliberately provocative innovation. Again negotiations failed, and a large group of Muslims gathered to protest. Reports vary, but it seems that a number of people were injured, likely less than a dozen. The *arati* was shut down, and discussions began between the aggrieved parties. On July 22 the *pujari* of the temple and the *imam* (prayer leader) of the mosque were summoned to the nawab's court to settle the matter. The next day, in a sworn statement before the District Magistrate, the *pujari* and the *imam* both declared that the *arati* always began after the three audible *rakats* (prostration sequences) and continued as the Muslim congregation would typically perform two more silent *rakats*. Neither community, however, accepted the pronouncement of their leaders. The British officer who investigated the dispute gave a rather disparaging comment on the contradictions in evidence given by the *imam* and the *pujari,* saying, "It is rather distressing that it should be possible for the whole peace of the town to be disturbed by a dispute between two little hedge-priests of this type and their congregations."[24] Nonetheless, the nawab ruled that the past practice as described by the "hedge-priests" should be restored. Subsequently the entire Hindu community of Malerkotla went on a sort of spiritual strike, refusing to hold *arati* at all.

Restrictions on the performance of *kathas* resulted in a similar boycott of those ritual practices.

Although the nawab declared an end to the matter and fixed that the *arati* should begin after *maghrib namaz*, it is significant that he had solicited an outside investigation from the British government to forestall accusations of bias toward his own community. Yet having made this request, the nawab left Malerkotla for Simla. In his absence, from September 9 to 17, J. C. Donaldson of the Indian Civil Service conducted an inquiry into two matters of the *katha* and *arati* conflicts with *namaz*. The guiding focus of his inquiry was that prior to these disputes, relations between Hindus and Muslims in Malerkotla had been largely pacific. His main goal was to discover the past practice that had been in force and to endeavor to return the two communities to those principles of behavior. After questioning more than forty witnesses and expressing satisfaction with the cooperation and competence of the police, legal counsel, and other administrators who assisted the inquiry, Donaldson affirmed the nawab's decision. He stated that there was ample time for the performance of both *arati* and *namaz* within the prescribed periods of time. Although he saw no prohibition on *namaz* at the neighboring mosque being performed after the *arati*, Donaldson did assert that it would be strange, as well as unlikely to have been past practice, for this lone mosque to pray some twenty minutes later than all the others in town.

Donaldson concluded that *arati* at the Chaudrian Mandir used to and should again take place late in the twilight after *namaz* in the Masjid Bafindagan. In his assessment of the situation he also remarked that the matters under dispute were actually of minor religious significance. He further recommended that if consultation did not result in an agreement, the state should intervene and regulate fair practice. "It is deplorable that the former admirable good relations of the communities in this peaceful, well administered, and, to all appearances, prosperous State, where religious toleration and respect for the feelings of others were observed both by the authorities and public, should have been disturbed in this way."[25] Donaldson's estimation of good governance and prosperity was generous to the point of inaccuracy. By the late 1930s the British had brokered several substantial loans to Malerkotla from Bahawalpur State. Several files in the India Office Collection pertain only to the state's debt. Furthermore, whatever the past practice of religious tolerance had been, the immediate future turned out to belie his confidence. The situation in fact deteriorated.

The Conflict Continues

In October of 1935 the restrictions on *katha* were lifted, and as a result the Lohari mosque was virtually surrounded by houses holding such gatherings, a clear provocation. Large groups of Muslims took to the streets, resulting in clashes and Puran Mal's death.[26] Four Muslim youths were detained, and eventually two were executed for the crime. Not long after this shocking turn of events, a wall collapsed in the rain, unearthing the body of the young Muslim girl mentioned earlier; she was said to be clutching a copy of the Qur'an. The release of the Hindus who owned the property where the wall came down fueled accusations of bias from some in the Muslim community, particularly from the mufti of the state, Shafiq Ahmad. In 1936, in protest over the perceived leniency to the Hindus accused of murdering the girl, Shafiq Ahmad led a substantial number of Muslims in a protest march to Lahore. These *muhajirun* (meaning people on a *hijra* or migration), as they called themselves, remained out of the state for more than a month.[27] Meanwhile, the nawab left for Simla, leaving his new chief minister, Jamil Ahmad, to handle the situation.[28] Subsequently a state of relative disquiet must have persisted in Malerkotla, now known as the town where nothing bad ever happens, since *arati* appears not to have taken place for *five more years.*

The Malerkotla chief minister's records pick up about where J. C. Donaldson's report leaves off. Numerous letters to the nawab from one Mohan Lal Sharma, the secretary of the Malerkotla branch of the Hindu Sabha fill the file. Several of these were forwarded on to Major B. Woods-Ballard, then secretary to the resident for the Punjab states. The emphasis in the letters is that any and all restrictions on the timing of *arati* must be lifted immediately. In Sharma's words,

> It will not be unreasonable and out of time to submit to Your Highness that Our Grievance at this moment is purely a religious one. The petitioners have nothing to do with the politics of the State. The petitioners do not aspire for jobs nor for any other political favour to their community. The petitioner's community can tolerate and suffer for any wrong done to them but it is almost entirely impossible for them to have any legal restriction on their religious rights which they have been already enjoying from the times immemorial.
>
> Your Petitioners therefore humbly pray that the ban imposed on the performance of their Arati which has given rise to the protest continued over a period of five years, may be removed.[29]

Sharma's careful phrasing allows him to lodge the very complaints he claims not to be concerned with—anti-Hindu discrimination in the allocation of jobs and political power. Yet he also urgently requests the lifting of the enforced mandate, made by the nawab in 1935 and confirmed by Donaldson, that the *arati* should be postponed until the completion of the *maghrib namaz.* The restriction of the time for *arati* was observed by local Hindus as a ban. After five years of tension, a murder, a trial, two executions, an exodus, and accusations of bias from all parties, the chief minister was ready to deal with the situation.

The Conflict Resolved

After several rounds of suggested agreements, a proposal was floated that used as a model a previous compromise reached by the Hindus and "Mohammedans" of Agra in 1934 over a similar issue regarding prayer timing. The text of the Agra agreement reads: "We the Hindus and Moslems of Agra have composed our differences and will perform our customary worship and prayers according to our established and recognized usages in our temples and mosques with our mutual goodwill and without interference from either side."[30] The agreement simply stated that the Hindus and Muslims would revert to past practice of tolerance and goodwill in the performance of their customary worship. The accord also stipulated that the restrictions on worship in the temple in question be lifted.[31] The Agra agreement apparently provided a model for reconciliation between the parties who were exhausted by prolonged tension. A successful agreement was finally reached between the Hindus and Muslims of Malerkotla on September 20, 1940. The agreement is striking in the vagueness and banality of its wording. Indeed the most remarkable element of the document is its explicit rejection of the nawab's judgment and thus, to a certain extent, his authority.

> We the Hindus and Muslims of Malerkotla are not satisfied with the orders of the Darbar [the nawab] dated the 9th October, 1935, regarding the dispute about the coincidence of the times of Katha in Moti Bazar, Arati in Chaudhrian Temple and Namaz in Weavers' Mosque. With a view to restore our unity and cordial relations, we by mutual consideration have come to the understanding that the Hindus will not by their conduct in performing their Katha and Arati give any occasion which may be likely to create interference in the Namaz, and the Muslims in view of the above assurance, will not interfere in the performance of Arati and Katha.[32]

The thirty-one signatories to this agreement represent a range of religious and ethnic communities, not just those from the religious sites involved in the dispute.

The process leading up to the resolution appears to have wrought the necessary change in local sentiment to sustain the peace through some immediate resistance and provocation. Immediately following the agreement some disquiet resulted in the detention of three individuals, but the situation soon stabilized, indicating an increase in tension-wisdom as the town adapted to the resolution. In a letter dated February 9, 1941, to Major Woods-Ballard, Chief Minister Jamil Ahmad reports a significantly improved atmosphere. He gives an account of the actions taken against the troublemakers but says that later on when it was found that the relations between the two communities had greatly improved and religious controversy which was a standing menace to the peace and tranquility of this place was gradually disappearing, a general pardon was granted to all persons accused of offences of political or communal nature including the above persons, with a view to encouraging the above spirit of accord and harmony. Since then nothing untoward has happened and both the communities are duly performing their religious worship without causing offence to each other.[33]

This report, written a few months after the agreement was reached, indicates that the situation remained quiescent. The general pardon had the desired effect of reinforcing the reconciliation rather than releasing frustrated and angry elements into the community.

Perhaps most important, the positive resolution of the dispute seems to have had a lasting effect. In 1942 there were some disturbances over the selling of meat during a Jain festival. The Jains, devout vegetarians, had requested that the butchers, who were mostly Muslims, close shop for the day. They refused. Discussions took place over the next year, however, and in the *Fortnightly Report* of September 15, 1943, the author of the report declared that he was satisfied that

there has been no injury to Muslim religious sensibilities in the closing of the butchers' shops on the occasion of Jain processions in connection with the Samatsari festivals, these processions this year had to go out on two days, the third and fourth September. The butchers' shops were closed on both days and the butchers declined to accept compensation from the Jains for closing their shops. They sold meat from their houses as usual, however, and the festival passed off quite peacefully in spite of all apprehension to the contrary.[34]

Thus closes this dark chapter in Malerkotla's interreligious history, and just in the nick of time. Just four years later the Partition of Punjab would bring such a challenge to those relations that only a strong foundation could have withstood the storm.

It is significant that the final resolution to the *arati-namaz* disputes in Malerkotla came not from the nawab's mandate or the British officer's adjudication. Rather, the initiative to reach a final resolution seems to have been taken by leaders of the communities involved, in explicit rejection of the nawab's and the British officer's judgments. This is important, as the *riyasat* had tried repeatedly to resolve the situation. They attempted heavy-handed tactics on several occasions by deploying police and even summarily executing the Muslim youths for the death of Puran Mal. They tried leniency by relaxing restrictions on the performance of *katha*s and releasing the accused in the murder of the Muslim girl. They undertook third-party negotiations, bringing in a supposedly neutral British officer. In short, they ran the gamut of traditional approaches to conflict resolution. But it is clear from Chief Minister Jamil Ahmad's reports that buy-in from the community members was the crucial ingredient in bringing about an agreement that could effectively end the tension. Although the role of governing elites and the institutional will to effect compromise were also factors, the text of the resolution testifies to community resentment of the heavy-handed tactics of the rulers and places the onus of maintaining order in their holy places upon the people of Malerkotla.

How the British Officer and the Nawab Both Got It Wrong

One point of agreement between the people of Malerkotla and Donaldson's assessment is that prior to the summer of 1935 interreligious relations in Malerkotla were quite positive. Donaldson began his report:

> There was however neither evidence nor assertion that prior to these events the Hindus of Malerkotla State had been subject to any adverse discrimination, or had had any legitimate grounds of complaint that their religious liberties had been interfered with by the authorities. In fact, with the exception of a comparatively minor incident ... it is an admitted fact that there has been no Hindu-Muslim trouble in this State within living memory, until the present year.[35]

Donaldson also remarks favorably upon the skill with which residents and officials managed the ritual confluence of the two major festivals of Muharram and Dussehra in 1918, an event that resulted in violence in numerous other regions of India. He also dismissed one of the main complaints in the 1935 disruption in Malerkotla, that the ruling Muslims were prejudiced against the Hindus in resolving the matter. In fact, Donaldson praises not only the officials who managed the tense disputes, but, most significant, he credits the entire populace of Malerkotla with keeping the situation from spiraling out of control:

> The evidence before me has not shown that the State authorities or any official displayed any communal bias in the official acts by which they dealt with those disorders. Some difficult situations appear to have been handled with a tact and discretion which was creditable to the officers concerned. The fact that much more serious trouble was averted is a credit not only to them but to the population in general.[36]

After praising most of the participants, Donaldson goes on to seek out what the past practice had been that had so successfully managed similar problems up to 1935. It emerges that previously the means of coping with all potential coincidences or conflicts between worship services and public processions "seems to have been to arrange them with mutual forbearance and good will."[37]

As a trained bureaucrat, Donaldson mourns the fact that positive arrangements were never codified in such a way as to provide sound precedent in later cases. Certainly the developments in 1935 indicate that having had such policies and strategies ready to implement might have helped to nip tensions in the bud after the first incidents in May with the *katha* and *namaz* dispute. No doubt most political scientists and many conflict-resolution experts would also criticize the absence of clear procedures in place in the kingdom. However, Donaldson mentions that such codification can also have a negative result by preventing fluid and flexible negotiations appropriate to cases as they arise. The absence of official records on past incidents also has a double edge. While the omission on the one hand prevents small disputes from becoming enshrined in the public record and providing fuel for future tension, on the other hand it complicates efforts to comprehend the history and context of conflicts as they arise. Donaldson shows sensitivity to the situation, acknowledging a sound reason for *not* documenting and legalizing past resolutions of such issues:

> It cannot always be assumed that everybody will act in all circumstances exactly according to the correct routine. The excuses given by the officials for not having prepared a record [of past disputes and their resolutions] are by no means unlikely ones. At the first sign of a communal disturbance officers are usually anxious to minimize its importance in order to prevent the excitement spreading and not to put ideas into people's heads. When a settlement had been reached they might well have thought it best to let sleeping dogs lie and leave the parties alone.[38]

Although regrettable in light of the potential utility of such agreements to help resolve later conflicts, there is a strong argument to be made for *not* creating fixed policies whose formation would inevitably raise the stakes involved in a present dispute to the status of a legal precedent upon which future legislation would be based. The nawab's government had opted in the past to retain flexibility in conflicts and to minimize their effect by keeping them from becoming points for more enduring disputation.

Whether the nawab's government was trying to avoid creating grounds for future contestations by not codifying traditional practices of adaptation and accommodation or was more deliberately attempting to brush problems under the carpet is hard to know. Although today many locals do attribute Malerkotla's interreligious harmony in part to the nawab's sound management of the state, the archival evidence paints a more complicated picture. Not only did Nawab Ahmad Ali Khan leave town when unrest among his people became apparent, but he also on several occasions exacerbated tensions. First, in the middle of the *arati-namaz* conflict in June 1935, the nawab also meddled in the processions for Muharram, compromising the ability of his Shi'i kinsman, Ihsan Ali Khan, to take out his processions as previously arranged. As discussed previously, the British record indicates that he may have sought to thwart this rival branch of the family by inciting the Sunnis against Ihsan. Second, the Kothala firing incident in 1927, though not religiously motivated, pitted the Muslim ruling and landlord families against primarily Sikh and Hindu land tenants. Third, the state was in considerable financial debt, in part to local Hindu moneylenders, which fuelled the *hijra* of 1936 and accusations of apostasy and pro-Hindu policies. Fourth, this *arati-namaz* dispute dragged on from 1935 to 1940. Although it must be acknowledged that civic unrest was pervasive throughout India in this period, this is a long time for a dispute to remain unresolved. Given the length of the dispute, it is all the more surprising that interreligious relations did not worsen and that Malerkotla was not badly afflicted, even during the widespread riots in Punjab in 1946.

Donaldson also remarks on a matter of paramount concern to the British, the possibility that the religious agitations were merely a cover for anticolonial or antigovernment movements. He warns:

> The leaders of all communities in this State should beware of allow-
> ing themselves to be used as pawns in any struggle for power which
> may be proceeding between the communities in British India. They
> would be very wise not to sacrifice their own happiness and prosper-
> ity in order to please people who selfishly desire to make use of them
> as part of their strategy in that struggle and care nothing for the
> welfare of the residents of Malerkotla.[39]

This warning speaks of the broader political context of 1930s India. In 1929 the Indian National Congress, led by Mohandas Gandhi and Jawaharlal Nehru, called for full independence from Britain. The next year saw the first major expression of a desire for a separate Muslim state in an address by the poet and philosopher Muhammad Iqbal. In 1932 Gandhi initiated civil disobedience campaigns designed to fill the jails with non-violent resisters to the British regime. These campaigns often led to heightened tensions as authorities, both the British and the princely states, sought to suppress the freedom fighters. Although the movement was minimal in Malerkotla, it would have been impossible for such a small principality to remain wholly isolated from these activities.[40]

The tense situation in Malerkotla from 1935–40 is consistent with the dete-riorating relations elsewhere in India, such as between the Indian National

Congress and various Muslim organizations, most especially the Muslim League. The events in Malerkotla were known on a national level, as is revealed by newspaper clips about the events. In particular a partisan Hindu paper, the *National Call*, printed inflammatory reports of deaths and oppression by the nawab. In one undated but contemporary article titled "Malerkotla Riots," the paper reported, "We are further informed that Hindus are still being harassed[,] that they are panic-stricken, and lastly that no authentic information of what has actually happened has been allowed to leave the State."[41] There is also evidence of an increasing interest from national groups such as the Hindu Mahasabha in the late 1930s and early 1940s. The Hindu Mahasabha was closely affiliated and allied with the Indian National Congress, one of the many reasons the latter's alliance with the Muslim League had eroded some years earlier. Visits from Mahasabha, Congress, and Muslim League activists riddle the state records from this period, demonstrating that even in the kingdom of Malerkotla, the politics of the day were very much present. The late 1930s brought ambient issues into sharp relief and created the potential to link local problems with national politics, something the nawab and the British clearly wished to avoid.

Triggering Events and Symbolic Space

An interesting though brief document, the "Commissioned Report on Communal Disturbances," published by the British government in about 1928, identifies several of the most common problems leading to Hindu-Muslim conflict in British India. The list of proximate causes of disorder are remarkably similar to those proposed by modern scholars of communal conflict such as Paul Brass, Stanley Tambiah, and Sudhir Kakar. The report cites cow slaughter, festival coincidence, rival processions, and the playing of music near mosques as potentially inflammatory events. However, the anonymous author also notes that riots may occur with far less provocation: "If explosive material has been stored up, a spark will ignite it; if communal feelings are strained, the smallest pretext will suffice to start a conflagration which each side accuses the other of having provoked."[42] As we saw above, the timing of worship between two proximate religious spaces can easily become triggering incidents for conflict. During these moments of heightened religious significance, latent religious identities become central. These intensified religious sensibilities may converge with a range of grievances, some religious, some political, some overt, some suppressed. As Beth Roy points out in her study of communal conflict in Bengal, religiously defined communities may have appeared "all the more attractive as forces for change because other possible structures were lacking" as avenues for mobilization and activism.[43] This was certainly true in the *riyasat*, where political organizations were outlawed but religious groups were usually permitted and even supported. In the *arati-namaz* conflict, the confluence of grievances effectively combined, so that the competition for dominance of the spiritual sound and landscape was tied to perceived imbalances of control over other shared arenas of civic life, such as the political, economic, social, or religious spheres, increasing the possibility that violence could occur. Thus when triggering events come to resonate with the felt experience of the parties involved in the conflict and are interpreted in such a way as to require action, the possibility for conflict increases. Triggering events alone do not produce social conflict—they happen far too often. It is the confluence of event, experience, and opportunity that feeds the flame. In some case the confluence is evident to multiple actors across a wide swath of society. In other instances, mobilized activists must make the case for the event to be understood as relating to the frame of a larger grievance.

The fact that the troubles manifested in response to a struggle to control public aural and physical space also demonstrates in Malerkotla that these are powerfully symbolic domains for the inscription of authority. A similar dynamic is documented in Allen Feldman's book *Formations of Violence*, which explores documents the conflicts in Northern Ireland. Feldman demonstrates how public processions performed by Catholic Republicans and Protestant Loyalists allow each group to symbolically dominate the landscape of Belfast for the duration of their march. In these times the public space of Belfast becomes effectively Catholic or Protestant, anti- or pro-British. Each event serves to make physically manifest the proprietary claim over the territory made by each group and justified by radically opposed understandings of Northern Ireland's identity. Parades in Belfast by each group entail movement from the center of each community to the boundary zones between Loyalist and Republican areas and then back. The route

> transforms the adjacent community into an involuntary audience and an object of defilement through the aggressive display of political symbols and music. In periods of peaceful coexistence the Orange Order (Protestant) parades were occasions of great entertainment for Catholics, who often tactfully attended these events from the sidelines. But during periods of ethnic tension, marching at the interface was a predictable and intentional trigger of violence based on the formation of a schismed audience.[44]

Feldman describes how the involuntary audition and witness of another community's public display of an exclusionary identity may be either the object of curiosity and observation or a triggering event for violence. The difference between peaceful observation and hostile reaction is conditioned by the current state of tension between the representative communities and the availability of a framing narrative through which the experience of the event is contextualized for the participants. Locating the turning point is a difficult alchemy, often apparent only in hindsight. Although it is clear that such public displays may be provocative, especially during times of tension, it is not well understood how potentially *integrative* processions, festivals, and ceremonies may also be. As we shall see in subsequent chapters, Malerkotla's population has been particularly effective at maximizing the integrative power of public ritual and establishing links to the narrative frame of peaceful pluralism.

Pre-Partition Malerkotla clearly does not resemble the utopia described by the *Hindu* when that newspaper dubbed the town "oasis of tolerance" in 2005. These complicating histories are all the more interesting because the process of stabilizing interreligious relations appeared to have been sufficiently successful such that in 1947 the tensions of Partition never became openly violent within the kingdom's borders. The records reveal a government under considerable strain on a number of fronts. State and British efforts at reconciliation backfired, and the final agreement specifically rejects both of their conclusions in favor of reliance on the goodwill and past practice of the community. Thus even the resolution of conflict can be seen as an act of resistance to both official entities. Traditional methods of conflict resolution, especially third-party negotiation, were tried and failed. Community-based authorities, drawing on documentary evidence from a similar dispute in Agra, subverted royal and imperial power.

Remembering and Forgetting

The conflicts of the 1930s are remembered by some Malerkotla residents today but are not seen as contradicting the town's present identity. Rather the contrast between those times and these serves to highlight the community's resilience. The public memory of the past is central to the framing of past conflict as supportive of the present peace. The formation of social order based on shared knowledge about past practice hinges upon the coherence of collective memory. When collective memories are narrated, orally and in writing, and come to possess a normative force, and they represent what literary theorist Steven Knapp calls "collective authority."[45] Without knowing what the collective memory is omitting, it is impossible to understand the workings and the intentions of the collective authority. In Malerkotla, the collective authority that upholds the ongoing social order is expressed through stories told about the past that highlight the useful elements in Malerkotla's past (the peace at Partition, the guru's blessing, and the *barakat* of Haider Shaykh) and eliminate or minimize the contentious.

It is common for analysts of communalism in India to focus on civil society and formal associational levels, leaving out the everyday and the effects of the common place, the quotidian, the mundane.[46] Looking for ways in which individuals and groups resist violence in their midst, some theorists fix on seemingly unrelated, sporadic acts of kindness: a Hindu family shelters a Muslim neighbor during a riot, endangering their own safety;[47] a Muslim man prevents the rape of a Hindu girl caught by a mob; a Muslim trader pays for the repair of a temple damaged during a protest. Most analysts of ethnic conflict *acknowledge* the existence of such acts, but they are rarely placed at the center of the study. Yet these events are often key components of a collective memory that generates a community's self-perception. Ashis Nandy and his coauthors in *Creating a Nationality* claimed that they were seeking out moments of resistance to the violent communal conflict that followed the destruction by Hindu militants of the Babri Masjid in 1992, but their account emphasizes the debilitating effects on communities of the conservative Hindu Ramjanmabhumi movement. In their study, moments of mutual protection and support appear fragile and fleeting. Thus rather than understand how a community stays together in times of duress, we see how the unrelenting force of the Sangh Parivar undermines even the most integrated and interwoven community. However, Nandy and others do remind us that communities do not come apart easily; neighbors do not kill, rape, and loot each other without enormous provocation and systematic erosion of the collectivity's foundation. But what is the daily work of community maintenance that goes into healthy civic life? One interesting feature of this process is that the more the story about Malerkotla's past stays the same, the more it actually changes. It is not hard to understand why certain histories are neglected, altered, or elided. They are inconvenient and potentially inflammatory. To maintain the frame of harmony, many inconvenient truths disappear from public memory.

Changes in these accounts of Malerkotla's past are important because in spite of the prevailing portrayals in recent times of Malerkotla as an "island of peace," the actual past is clearly more complicated. The stories of these conflicts seem to have been overshadowed by time and dwarfed by the events relating to Partition. Those who did discuss this more conflictual past often misidentified the mosques and temple involved or attributed the ultimate resolution to the nawab. In the competitive arena of memory politics, the stories of past communal grievance have not made the cut. They are simply not the story that many want to hear or to tell. In an essay critiquing collective memory studies, Wulf Kansteiner makes the important observation that attention must be paid not only to the present-oriented production of cultural memories, but also to the "ingenuity of memory makers and the subversive interests of memory consumers."[48] The memory makers and consumers in Malerkotla seem largely uninterested in maintaining the Praja Mandal movement, the Sunni-Shi'a disputes, or the *arati-namaz* conflict as part of the collective memory. Such amnesia has the obvious result of providing Malerkotla with a history that resembles most closely its desired present. This is similar to the selective amnesia of interreligious violence reported by Gyan Pandey in relation to places in Punjab, where, although violence *did* occur, it is denied by the communities today. Instead the violence always took place elsewhere, and is displaced from the immediate moral and social environs.[49] It also helps to make sense of Malerkotla's anomalously pacific experience of Partition, to which we now turn.

Partition and Beyond: Peace, Politics, and the New India

Here in India Muslims and there in Pakistan Sikhs were slaughtered, but not a single person was killed in Malerkotla.
—Zulfikar, Malerkotla resident

In Malerkotla, the Partition of India and Pakistan in 1947 is remembered as the community's finest hour—a time when they rose to and met an enormous challenge. Although much of Punjab experienced serious interreligious violence during this period, no one died in Malerkotla. Instead, it became a safe haven for migrating Muslims from other parts of India, and the town remains majority Muslim today. Mostly harmonious interreligious relations continue in Malerkotla, even during times of strife in other regions, and so the town enjoys a reputation as a communal utopia. But as we have seen, this idealized identity is also highly complex. This chapter explores the process through which the peace at Partition is incorporated into the collective representations of the town and written into its public memory. Even when such representations and writings contain variant or contradictory ideas, theologies, and explanations, these variations and contradictions do not undermine the collective and occasionally collaborative project of bolstering the civic identity of communal harmony. After a brief discussion of Partition and its effect on Punjab, this chapter investigates how people explain Malerkotla's escape from the violence that swept through the region. These justifications for the town's unique experience of Partition set the groundwork for the trajectories along which Malerkotla develops in terms of its civil societal and political institutions, which by and large hold up under the strains of politicized religion and the challenges of pluralistic society.

All of the common explanations for the peace at Partition and the subsequently pacific interreligious relations in Malerkotla contribute to the collective authority of peaceful coexistence. It is a mistake to assume that one of these reasons for peace is the "right" one. Rather, it is the simultaneous availability of a variety of explanations that allows for creative adaptation and manipulation depending on audience and context. Yet each explanation is instructive, elucidating the microstrategies of accommodation and identification through which a community builds peace. Each story about Malerkotla embeds within itself the ethical values most identified with the town's collective character—justice, righteousness, anti-communalism, secularism, egalitarianism, bravery, and harmony. Through these stories, core moral principles are activated, communicated, and integrated into Malerkotla's past, present, and future. Enacted in the sacred and civic spaces of the town, Malerkotla becomes the place where Partition, in a way, didn't happen.

Partition

To understand Malerkotla's unusual experience of Partition, one must understand what was happening outside its borders. Punjab was the state most radically divided when India and Pakistan became independent nations on August 15, 1947.[1] In the aftermath of World War II, Great Britain's economy and society could no longer sustain its vast empire, especially in the face of growing independence movements. The new Labor government under Prime Minister Clement Attlee gauged the nation's mood and capacities and determined that the far-flung empire was no longer sustainable. Having so decided, Attlee moved quickly. Lord Mountbatten, the last viceroy of India, arrived in March 1947 to oversee the transfer of power that would occur in August, just a few months later. Many critics believe the haste with which the British departed forced the hands of both the Indian National Congress and the Muslim League, the two major negotiators trying to shape the successor state. For various reasons, division rather than federation became the expedient solution, and so Punjab and East Bengal were split off from India and became Muslim-majority Pakistan; in 1971 the Bengali part of Pakistan would become Bangladesh.

Punjab experienced particularly extreme violence, in no small part ascribable to the region's having been one of the British army's favorite recruiting grounds. Barbara and Thomas Metcalf write in their history of India that after World War II Punjab was

> a highly militarized society, long the recruiting ground for the Indian Army, with one-third of its eligible males having served in the war, the Punjab in 1947 contained vast numbers of demobilized soldiers. Many of these were Sikhs, who, as those who had lost the most from partition, took advantage of their military training and knowledge of modern weaponry, to organize and direct attacks in methodical and systematic fashion, on villages, trains, and refugee columns.[2]

These campaigns were directed against members of other religious communities. As the Pakistani Minister Sir Francis Mudie claimed in a letter to an Indian minister, "The Sikhs are carrying out a well organized plan to exterminate Muslims and drive them from the Province. They move about in regular gangs armed with weapons which undoubtedly come from Military stocks."[3] Similar accusations were made about Muslim assaults on Hindus and Sikhs in Pakistan. Although Partition is often framed as a division between Hindu India and Muslim Pakistan, Punjab was also the homeland and holy land of the Sikh faith. As the division approached, Sikhs became increasingly aware that the dividing line would split places like the Golden Temple in Amritsar, which would remain in India, from Guru Nanak's birthplace at Nankana Sahib, which would be in Pakistan. "As independence neared," the Metcalfs write, "the violence spread throughout the province, and caught up all communities, especially the Sikhs, who saw their community, with its lands and shrines, sliced in two by the Boundary Award."[4]

In East Punjab, Sikh kingdoms such as Patiala helped to organize and support the *jathas* (bands) of Sikhs who raided Muslim homes and villages.[5] For example, on September 23, 1947, the secretary governor of East Punjab, N. K. Mukerji, wrote to the maharaja of Patiala, Yadavindra Singh, asking him to curb the activities of Sikh gangs from Patiala.

> I understand Pandit Jawaharlal Lal Nehru has telegrammed to Your Highness about bands of Sikhs coming in Simla from Patiala State. Two days ago a Pakistan special [refugee train] was attacked by a Sikh armed band near Sirhind. It is obviously most essential in the interests of Sikhs and Hindus awaiting evacuation from West Punjab, if on no other ground, that attacks like these must not only cease forthwith but that any other unlawful activities of armed bands operating in and from Patiala State should be swiftly suppressed.[6]

The maharaja of Patiala was clearly implicated by Indian officials in the ethnic cleansing. He also strongly petitioned the Boundary Commission prior to Partition to retain Indian control of the Sikh holy places, especially Nankana Sahib. The situation in Patiala was of grave concern to the people of Malerkotla because of its proximity to the kingdom.

But Sikhs were by no means the only perpetrators of the violence. Entire trainloads of refugees heading in both directions were systematically slaughtered. Lines of refugees walking across the border could take days to pass through a village; one such column of marchers involved four hundred thousand people.[7] As they walked, they were vulnerable not only to the bands of armed "civilians," but also to the police and army, who were neutral at best and were often complicit in the violence.[8] The weather conspired against the refugees, whose move eastward picked up towards the end of August during the monsoons. The rainy season lingered into September, further intensifying the misery and adding to the risk of disease. Oral histories recorded by Urvashi Butalia, Ritu Menon, Kamila Bhasin, and others bring Partition to devastating life as people speak of the unspeakable. Seeing trainloads of the dead pass through their towns. Surviving by hiding amid the slaughter. Parents killing their daughters to prevent their being raped. Hearing a person being killed, tortured, or raped, but doing nothing because the victim was of a different religion. These are things that people witnessed, experienced, or did that challenge human resilience. Among my friends in Punjab was an elderly woman who had helped to run refugee camps for people coming from Pakistan to India. Several times she told me the story of arranging for dozens of women to have abortions, the pregnancies having resulted most likely from rapes en route to their new homeland. How does an individual, let alone a community or a nation, survive these kinds of birth pangs? In truth, these experiences have shaped the nations and the nationalisms that emerged. As Barbara and Tom Metcalf put it:

> The loss of life was immense, with estimates ranging from several hundred thousand up to a million. But even for those who survived, fear generated a widespread perception that one could be safe only among the members of one's own community; and this in turn helped consolidate loyalties towards the state, whether India or Pakistan, in which one might find a secure haven.[9]

Security came to be defined in sectarian terms; fear and mistrust characterized attitudes toward people of other religions. In this way the shared experiences and challenges of division shaped an India and a Pakistan (and, later, a Bangladesh) bonded together by such histories, which have been passed down to subsequent generations. Partition is part of the collective consciousness in South Asia, and nowhere more so than in Punjab.

There is something about Partition that leads historians and scholars, even those trying to be analytical and unbiased, to attempt in some way to convey the depth of the suffering and pain involved. They seek to account for the dead even as they abandon hope of ever actually counting the number who died. For example, in his essay "Partition Narratives," Mushirul Hasan writes:

> Nobody knows how many were killed during Partition violence. Nobody knows how many were displaced and dispossessed. What we know is that, between 1946 and 1951, nearly nine million Hindus and Sikhs came to India, and about six million Muslims went to Pakistan. Of the said nine million, five million came from what became West Pakistan, and four million from East Pakistan. In only three months, between August and October 1947, Punjab, the land

of the great five rivers, was engulfed in a civil war. Estimates of deaths vary between 200,000 and three million.[10]

And so the "land of the great five rivers" became two lands: Pakistan's territory encompasses three rivers, and two are in modern India.[11] For months before, during, and after August 15 these rivers were red with blood. An elderly gentleman who served in the Malerkotla army during the time recalled that "the main irrigation canal which crossed the Malerkotla state at Ahmedgarh, for days together was full of bloated dead bodies. But there was little we could do except watch them float by."[12] The impact on the living on all sides of the borders in the east and west continues to be felt, memorialized, mourned, and remembered. More than sixty years later, there is no end to the introspective efforts to understand how a nation could divide against itself in such a gruesome and damaging way, leaving deep scars and abiding enmities.

Though studies of Partition and its impact on Indian society proliferate, in many ways this remains one of the most incomprehensible events in the history of the region.[13] In Punjab, the complexity is increased because the state, in spite of a Muslim majority and a Muslim chief minister, did not support Mohammad Ali Jinnah and the Muslim League's Pakistan proposal until 1946. The Unionist government in Punjab, led by Sikandar Hayat Khan, was a coalition of large landlords from all religious groups who remained influential even after the Muslim League won the 1946 elections. The Muslim League, founded in 1906, saw control of Punjab as strategically essential to establishing its claim to represent the Indian Muslim population as a whole. In Punjab, where there was a slight Muslim majority but a multireligious ruling coalition, the case for the Muslim League's role as chief negotiators on behalf of Indian Muslims was jeopardized. Through a systematic campaign to undermine the rural landlord base of Unionist support by appealing to Muslim identity, the Muslim League eventually won the day—if barely. Punjabi Muslims who had been underwhelmed by the Muslim League's Lahore Resolution in 1940, when they raised the call for Pakistan as a Muslim homeland, began to see Partition as inevitable.[14]

Relations between ethnic and religious groups deteriorated as it became increasingly apparent that distribution of power in any post-British regime would be communally divided and constructed, whether in terms of confederated states or, as ultimately came to pass, in separate nations. Although the Congress leaders, especially Gandhi, had resisted a division of the subcontinent, eventually most accepted it as inevitable and preferable to the strong federation desired by the Muslim League. Mushirul Hasan writes:

> The Congress agreed to partition because, as Nehru stated at the All India Congress Committee meeting on 9 August 1947, "there is no other alternative." This was not an admission of failure but a

recognition of the ground realities that had moved inexorably towards the polarization of the Hindu, Muslim and Sikh communities.[15]

This worsened the situation in an already conflicted region. In Punjab, in addition to the narrow Muslim majority, the sizable Sikh population increasingly mobilized in pursuit of a Sikh state, imagined as Khalistan. This movement began in the early twentieth century, and a separate state remains the heart's desire of some Sikhs to this day. Following the period of heightened cultural and religious consolidation in the nineteenth century discussed in previous chapters, political organization among Sikhs accelerated in the early twentieth along with a movement to centralize and clarify control of the gurdwaras. The latter movement resulted in the formation of the Shiromani Gurdwara Prabandak Committee in 1920. Political organization accelerated after the massacre of hundreds of peaceful demonstrators by the British General Dyer at the Jallianwalla Bagh in Amritsar in 1919. This tragedy was followed in short order by the foundation of political organizations, especially the Central Sikh League (1919) and the Shiromani Akali Dal (SAD, 1920). The SAD was one of the key supporters of the Khalistan movement, gained increasing influence throughout the independence struggle, and remains a powerful political party in Punjab today. However, the Sikhs were a majority in only one district in pre-Partition Punjab, so they were defeated by the Muslim League at the state level. This put the final nail in the coffin of a unified, independent India.

Though these political parties were banned in princely states such as Malerkotla, nationalist and communalist sentiment did not stop at the borders of the kingdoms. Whereas Patiala's ruler fed the communal fire, with a result being an exodus of its Muslim population, Malerkotla's leaders and citizens sought to calm the fury. Surrounded by larger Sikh and Hindu states, Malerkotla in 1947 was only 167 square miles. This certainly helps to explain its nonaggressive stance but does not explain why it was spared from the attacks that left post-Partition Indian Punjab with a Muslim population of less than 1 percent. Many of those who remained were in Malerkotla.

Peace at Partition

Throughout the period of Partition, Malerkotla became known as a secure haven for Muslims traveling toward Pakistan. Many migrants journeying by road or train made Malerkotla their intermediate destination, knowing that they could rest here securely. The elderly nawab at the time, Ahmad Ali Khan, was unhealthy and played little role in keeping order. However, his son Iftikhar Ali Khan was extremely active in maintaining the security of the borders and the morale of the population. The ruling nawab and his son stayed in

Malerkotla throughout the crisis. They opened up their residential grounds for refugee camps and patrolled the boundaries. A local survey conducted in the early 1990s found that a plurality of people cited their allegiance to the nawab as their reason for staying in Malerkotla. Other common reasons for staying were loyalty to other local leaders, belief in the greater viability of the Indian state, the expectation of gaining land rights in independent India, faith in their personal and economic security in Malerkotla, and love for their homeland. Also frequently mentioned, both in the earlier survey and in my own interview experience, was the prevailing belief that those who stayed would be safe because of the abiding power of the blessing given by Guru Gobind Singh that preserved Malerkotla from any attack by Sikhs.[16] In interviews in 2000 and 2001, even some people who did not believe in the guru's protective power were convinced that the widespread Sikh obedience to the guru had saved Malerkotla and made it unnecessary for the Muslims to leave. Some believed that the many Sufi saints buried throughout the area formed a protective shield. Others credited the overall spirit and bravery of Malerkotlans themselves. Whatever their reasons, most of the population—both Muslim and non-Muslim—stayed.

While few Muslims left, many came. In 1947 tens of thousands of refugees descended upon the town, more than tripling the urban population.[17] Strained to the limits by this dramatic increase, the state repeatedly begged for help from the British, but was refused.[18] Of course, the humanitarian crisis in the camps at Malerkotla was nothing compared to the bloodshed elsewhere in the region, and was doubtless lower on the list of priorities. Camps for the refugees were set up all over the kingdom, including in the nawab's own palace grounds. An Indian army officer, Major Gurbax Singh Gill, who visited Malerkotla State on September 13, 1947, described the situation in Malerkotla: "Up till now there has been no trouble in the State but with the arrival of the refugees from outside the State the situation has become somewhat tense. Spears and axes are carried by both communities whom I saw moving along the road."[19] This tense but non-violent situation was re-created in the memory of Abdallah, the retired school-teacher:

> People did not migrate from here, but people from other states came here. They were kept in camps, and when the situation pacified, they were sent on. First they were staying in people's houses, and diseases spread, like diarrhea. Not much was left with people to feed them. So they started giving them porridge. Then an order was given that the people should be put in camps. They were forcibly taken out of houses, the camps were first put on the Nabha road, and then these were flooded, so the camps were shifted to Id-Gah road. Then from there the people were shifted to Pakistan.

Malerkotla is depicted as a town stretched to the breaking point by the needs of the refugees. Yet it was also a haven where hospitality was freely given, even if resources were limited.

A local imam echoed and extended this representation of Malerkotla's hospitable culture, weaving the peace of the past into his characterization of the community in the present day. In an interview he declared that any visitor to Malerkotla would be taken into somebody's house:

> Here there was peace [at Partition]. We cannot know why here there was peace and elsewhere there was not. People here are more compassionate (*rehman-wale*) than other places. You won't encounter such compassionate people in any other place. People eat together; give [each other] money. There are no beggars here. If someone doesn't have a place to stay who is traveling, here they will be taken into the house.

The imam's explanation for the lack of violence in 1947 describes, not a particular historical event or dynamic, but the quality of the community. Shifting from the past to the present tense, the imam connects the compassionate people of those days who resisted violence with the residents of today who share their wealth and welcome visitors. I had numerous such conversations in which the exemplary conduct of Malerkotla's citizenry was invoked as evidence of the uniquely peaceful character of the town. Residents claimed, "Not a single shot was fired in the kingdom during the Partition year."[20] Even those locals who reported that some Hindus and Sikhs did abandon their homes, fearing the large influx of Muslim refugees, also declared that their property was perfectly secure and that the nawab himself guaranteed their safe return to Malerkotla after the crisis. Khushi Mohammad, who served in the army in 1947, corroborated this. "Not only did we have to guard the state from outside aggression, but we had been ordered to protect non-Muslim property from local attempts at arson or looting," he said. Further testimony from Abdallah reaffirms this: "From Malerkotla Hindus migrated or ran away, leaving their houses. The Nawab posted police at their houses, but nobody did any damage to their houses or belongings." Hindu residents affirmed that there was a zero-tolerance policy for looting of Sikh and Hindu property, and that Iftikhar Ali Khan made efforts to be visible among all communities during the crisis.

The successful management of Partition in Malerkotla gave rise to a solidarity between religious groups that had not existed to the same extent previously. As illustrated in previous chapters, Malerkotla's pre-1947 history is replete with strains and difficulties between religions. Perhaps especially in the period immediately preceding Partition, tensions were at a high level in Malerkotla, as they were throughout India. After all, it was only a few years before that the town had seen a series of clashes between Hindus and Muslims over the perennial issue of timing prayers at an adjoining mosque and temple. Yet when the troubles began, the community drew together. Contrary to Abdallah's assertion, not quite all the Hindus left Malerkotla. The Hindu craftsman Balram, who told the story of Haider Shaykh and the horse, stayed and actually made weapons to sell in the neighborhood, including to Muslims.

> Everyone ran away. My mother was ill, and we needed money, so I made some weapons from a big piece of iron lying at home meant for cutting cotton. The head of the Jansangath Prasthan [a Hindu organization] called me and asked, "You are selling weapons to Muslims?" I said, "There is no difference. If a Muslim dies, then also we will die. If a Hindu dies, then still we are sitting between the Muslims [i.e., surrounded by Muslims]."[21]

Balram's decision to make and sell weapons to Muslims was called into question by local Hindu leaders, yet he still felt that all of their fates were entwined in the face of the chaos around them. In his conversation with me in 2001, Balram expressed some strongly anti-Muslim views. Nonetheless, in regard to the period of crisis in 1947, his community identity superseded his sectarian identity—a powerful testimony to the integrative influence of Partition on Malerkotla and on the self-perception of some residents.

Explaining the Peace

Residents and visitors to Malerkotla give a variety of explanations for Malerkotla's unique experience of Partition. As discussed in chapter 2, the most popular explanation given by locals and visitors relates to the blessings of the tenth Sikh guru, Gobind Singh. Though the guru and the nawab were on opposite sides in battle, Sher Muhammad Khan's protest on behalf of the boys is an important feature of Sikh and Punjabi history, symbolizing the possibility of rising above sectarian divisions. The blessing of the guru is still cited today as an explanation for why Malerkotla was not attacked by Sikhs in 1947. Yet in the 242 years that intervened between the blessing and the Partition, numerous battles occurred in which Sikh forces were not so restrained. Thus the guru's blessing is insufficient as a single explanation for the peaceful status quo, but the pervasiveness of this belief indicates how deeply linked this Sikh blessing is to the quality of Malerkotla's community. Many residents and visitors explain Malerkotla's Partition experience through the protective power of Haider Shaykh and the myriad saints who are buried in the area. As the saint's *wilayat*, or spiritual territory, Malerkotla was preserved through his spiritual power. Many pilgrims and devotees who visit the tomb shrine credit Haider Shaykh with the salvation of the town. Residents also see Malerkotla as a "Muslim *faqir*'s kingdom," a fact which protected the *riyasat* from the violence outside its borders.

Of the frequently given explanations for the peace in Malerkotla, the least credible is that Malerkotla has simply always been peaceful. As discussed in previous chapters, prior to 1947 the Muslim princely state of Malerkotla was often at war with its non-Muslim neighbors, and internal relations were not without serious disturbances. Thus the general peace during the Partition in Malerkotla is no mere extension of the pre-Partition status quo. The stark contrast of pre- and post-Partition interreligious relations in Malerkotla indicates that the watershed of 1947 also led to a cleansing of past histories that conflicted with the needs of the present. This proposition points to the more complicated question of governance and the role of the nawabs and other local elites in minimizing the tension and violence by promoting a civic identity of peaceful coexistence. Another commonly cited explanation for the placid state of affairs in Malerkotla is its post-Partition status as the only substantial Muslim community in Punjab. This demographic profile increases the town's appeal as a symbolically powerful electoral constituency. Some residents believe that Malerkotla enjoys a privileged status because of this unique demographic, and thus the harmonious reputation is merely an expression of enlightened self-interest to maintain their disproportionate influence.

Prior to 1947, united Punjab's population was 53 percent Muslim.[22] Following Partition, the percentage of Muslims on the Indian side of the border dropped below 1 percent and remains less than 2 percent today.[23] Throughout Punjab in the many months I lived there, I encountered people who looked back at the pre-Partition period as a kind of utopian time when there was a common Punjabi culture steeped in saint's shrines, redolent with good local foods, and alive with the sounds of sacred poetry and lovelorn ballads. The idealized Punjab knew no caste, creed, or communalism; it was the land of the five rivers where the voices of poets and saints echoed in the fields, along the riverbanks, and in the forests. This Punjabi jeremiad longs for the dream time of a shared life before it was broken by the British, by the Muslims, by the Hindus—in short, broken by outside forces, not by the poisonous paranoia and violence of Punjabis themselves. As Gyan Pandey puts it, this displacement of violence is part of constituting a community. "It is the denial of any violence 'in our midst,' the attribution of harmony *within* and the consignment of violence to the *outside*, that establishes 'community.' Violence and community constitute each other, as it were."[24] In Malerkotla and at the tomb shrine of the territory's founder Haider Shaykh the idealized past can, at least temporarily, seem presently real. This enables visitors and residents to reject symbolically the events of Partition, refuse to accept its consequences in terms of social, religious, and geographical divisions, and to inhabit a space that only existed before 1947.

This prominent position requires Malerkotla's citizens to maintain public personae as a community of "good" Muslims, docile and placid citizens of India with undivided loyalty and pacific natures.[25] To that end, Muslims stand for election from and belong to political parties that elsewhere would be considered

FIGURE 4.1. Malerkotla's member of the Legislative Assembly and its city council president (seated) at the *dargah* for a *mela*, 2001.

antithetical to Muslim interests, such as the SAD. This was particularly remark-able in the late 1990s and early 2000s, when the previous SAD chief minister, Prakash Singh Badal, forged an alliance with a Hindu nationalist party, the Bharatiya Janata Party (BJP).[26] Nonetheless, the member of the legislative assembly from Malerkotla during this period was Muslim (as always) and also a member of the SAD (see fig. 4.1). This was a period of considerable interreli-gious tension, as the BJP was in control of the central government, a brief war was fought in Kashmir with Pakistan in the summer of 1999, and border tensions between Indian and Pakistani Punjab and Kashmir remained at a fairly high level throughout the late 1990s and early 2000s. Thus maintaining a pacific reputation was crucial to ensure continued Muslim representation at the state level. Because Malerkotla's Muslim constituency provide an important oppor-tunity for state-level politicians to demonstrate their secular credentials, often the MLA from the town serves as a state cabinet minister.[27] This constituency certainly has greater leverage than it would otherwise have because of the nature of ethnic politics in India. Yet clearly this demographic situation alone is no guarantee of peace. A similar set of conditions and potential incentives has had no such effect on Kashmir or other Muslim majority zones in India. Although the coercive discipline of the state certainly plays a role in forming the civic identity, it is not alone a sufficient explanation.

Partition and the Shaykh

There is a marked difference between the pre- and post-Partition narratives about Haider Shaykh. As discussed in chapter 1, the textual sources on the saint's life and times from before Partition focused on two things: his link with Bahlol Lodhi and the multireligious appeal of his tomb shrine.[28] The oral and written narratives from after Partition shift to focus on the protective power of the saint and the positive influence of his tomb, cult, and the establishment of Islam in the region. They overwhelmingly emphasize the multireligious appeal of the Shaykh and the positive interreligious relations in Malerkotla. From newspaper articles to the history written by the last nawab Iftikhar Ali Khan, to scholarly dissertations, to chapbooks, the multireligious appeal of the shaykh surges to the forefront. This change reflects a need to come to terms with Malerkotla's escape from the devastation that surrounded it in 1947 and to establish a strong basis for the Muslim majority town's continued existence by depicting positive interreligious relations, fostering the goodwill of the majority, and generating Muslim pride and solidarity. It also reveals the subtle ways in which the history and hagiography of Haider Shaykh is crafted to incorporate the unfolding of current events into the constellation of narratives associated with him.

Haider Shaykh's significance to all the communities connected with him (*khalifah*s, Malerkotla residents, and pilgrims) is intensified by the frequent attribution of Malerkotla's peace during and since Partition to the saint's blessings.[29] This explanation is so pervasive among *khalifah*s, residents, and pilgrims that the popularity of Haider Shaykh clearly draws significantly from the widespread conviction that his *barakat* (spiritual power) preserved the town during the chaos of 1947 and in later periods of tension. Older residents and *khalifah*s reinforced this, reporting that in their view the popularity of Haider Shaykh has grown substantially since pre-Partition days. Yet it is not merely the blessings of the *buzurg*s (pious elders, often synonymous with saints) that guarantee peace. In the following exchange, Ahmad the *khalifah* who served as a *numbardar* (village chief) asserted that the blessing actually comes because encounters at the tomb provide environments conducive to positive exchange, thereby securing good relations. This emerged when I inquired why Malerkotla had not experienced violence during Partition.

AHMAD: It is only due to the blessings of the *buzurgs* [saints]. Here people have never fought for caste and religion. All people have lived in unity in time of joys and sorrow, marriages and death.

AB: Why?

AHMAD: The love between people is so strong that they never thought that they were Hindus, Muslims or Sikhs. At the shrines of the *buzurgs* people exchange love [*aapas me muhabbat bante*] with each other.

AB: But why is this is only possible here and other places it is not?

AHMAD: The main thing is the blessing of the *buzurgs*. On all four sides there are *buzurgs* and *buzurgs* here. All around the boundary of Malerkotla there are *buzurgs*. It is only through their blessing that all Muslims, Hindus, and Sikhs are one.[30]

Although Ahmad's explanation incorporated all of the saintly dead into the explanation, his central point was that at the tombs of the pious dead one of the manifest blessings is that at their shrines "people exchange love." In his view, because of this daily opportunity for peaceful interaction, Malerkotla was free of significant conflict.

Residents like Ahmad saw great value in such encounters and attributed the peace in town not just to the metaphysical benefits of entombed saints but to the material conditions their entombment facilitates. This pragmatic view of the value of shrine attendance was not just the view of Ahmad—a Muslim with familial connections to the shrine. In a further example, Vinod, a local Hindu leader, claimed that the peace in Malerkotla was ascribable to people's strong faith in these saints. He stated, "This place is safe because people believe deep in their hearts in these saints and through the strength of their belief they have remained peaceful." Vinod had also claimed that he himself primarily attended Haider Shaykh's *dargah* for social purposes, to show that he is not prejudiced against the Muslim community. For him, shrine attendance is less about personal faith in Haider Shaykh than about the perceived social and political value of the opportunity to encounter one's neighbors and publicly display an open and nonsectarian attitude. Thus, surrounded by *buzurgs*, Malerkotla is surrounded by venues where interreligious connections may be forged.

Ibrahim, a local Sufi guide, or *murshid*, also attributed the safety and security of Malerkotla to Haider Shaykh's spiritual power. In relation to Partition he said, "No murders were done here. No Hindu killed any Muslim, neither were Sikhs killed. No one felt it necessary. These all are his [Haider Shaykh's] blessings." These remarks reflect the centrality of Haider Shaykh to Malerkotla's Partition experience. Furthermore, the perception fuels the reality of interreligious peace. A nearly identical statement came from Fazlur, the caretaker (*mutawali*) of a very small *dargah* in Malerkotla. Asked why there was peace at

Partition, he replied: "This is a Muslim *faqir*'s kingdom. In 1947 the Muslims were murdered everywhere in Punjab but not in Malerkotla." Asked why this was the case, Fazlur responded, "Because of these *buzurgs*." In 1947 Fazlur was fourteen years old and living in Ahmadgarh, a town inside the kingdom a few miles from the main town of Malerkotla but within the kingdom's borders. He remembers the chaos, but also the relative calm. He was working at a shop run by his family at the time and recalled: "No murders were done here. No Hindu killed any Muslim, neither were Sikhs killed. No one felt it necessary. These all are his blessings." For Fazlur, the *murshid*, and many, many others like them, no other explanation for the peace in Malerkotla is really necessary. These saints, especially Haider Shaykh, as friends of God (*auliya' allah*) possess the power to protect and preserve everything within their *wilayat* or spiritual territory. In an area such as Malerkotla, where there are dozens of tomb shrines to these *buzurgs*, the belief is that the *wilayat* is well fortified against all dangers. The security of Malerkotla during Partition is seen as proof-positive of the power of the saints.

Partition and the haah da naara

The *haah da naara* is one of the most popular and widespread explanations for Malerkotla's peace during all times of crisis, especially Partition. As discussed in chapter 2, the blessing of the Guru following Nawab Sher Muhammad Khan's defense of his sons is seen by many as evidence of the possibility of rising above sectarian loyalties for the sake of justice. The general belief is that out of respect for this blessing, Sikhs never attacked Malerkotla and hold the place dear in their hearts. Though there is ample contradictory evidence of conflicts, part of the power of this explanation lies in the general conviction that it is in fact true. It appears that the last nawab, Iftikhar Ali Khan, himself gave great credence to the power of the *haah da naara* to preserve Malerkotla's safety, or at least saw it as a politically prudent position. A Christian missionary who had discussed this matter with the nawab wrote a letter to Punjab historian C. H. Loehlin in which he described the nawab's view of the matter.

> I too have been interested in the effect of Guru Gobind Singh's reactions to the concern expressed by the Nawab in his day. I talked with the present Nawab on two occasions about this very question. He told me some facts that verify the influence of Guru Gobind Singh's declarations during the Partition. I suggested that the presence of the Nawab's army lessened the attacks by Sikhs on Muslims. He stated that he can document evidence to show that the Sikhs actually responded to protect us Muslims by belief in what Gobind Singh had commanded. The Muslims *enroute* to Malerkotla via train were attacked, but when the Sikhs knew they were going to

Malerkotla, they spared them and personally escorted them to Malerkotla. Many Muslims fleeing for their lives were being pursued by Sikhs, trying to kill them, but when they crossed the border of Malerkotla State, they stopped and granted them their lives. There is no question in the Nawab's mind but that the Muslims were spared in Malerkotla State directly because of Gobind Singh's declaration that the Muslims of that State were to be protected.[31]

The missionary's letter strongly reinforces the widespread belief in the protective power of the guru's blessing. Though the missionary also brought up the role of the army, which is regarded by many who reject sentimental or superstitious reasoning as a more viable explanation for the peace, the nawab himself apparently denied that the army was the key factor. It is significant that at the time of the conversation between the nawab and the missionary, Malerkotla would no longer have had a standing army. Thus the future safety of the town could no longer depend upon such a resource, but must look elsewhere for security.

Nowadays lacking a local army to enforce peace and undergoing increasing fragmentation of power with the rise of democracy and party politics, the *haah da naara* and the Guru's blessing remains one of the key building blocks of community solidarity. For example, Vinod, the scheduled caste Hindu and local politician, also asserted that the blessing of the guru has preserved the town from violence in 1947 and during the period of Sikh terrorism in the 1980s and 1990s:

> Guru Gobind Singh's two young *sahibzadas* were killed in Sirhind. Guru Gobind Singh was in Raikot at that time, and he asked what had happened to his children. His army said that the two sons were assassinated and that no one raised a voice against the atrocity that occurred. Then one person said that Nawab Sahib Sher Mohammad Khan of Malerkotla raised a voice in favor of the *sahibzadas*. Then Guru Gobind Singh expressed the view that there will be peace in Malerkotla forever. This is the main reason that there is peace in Malerkotla now and in the past. In 1947 because of this blessing [*ashirvad*], there was no killing here. The Sikhs didn't come against here during the terrorism either.[32]

In this politician's view, the single most important factor that preserved Malerkotla from the violence at the time of Partition and again during the period of terrorism is the *haah da naara*. Vinod was not a superstitious man. As mentioned above, he claimed that he only visited Haider Shaykh's *dargah* as a public gesture to demonstrate his lack of religious prejudice. Nor is he a Sikh for whom the blessing of the guru would likely be a divine mandate. His primary focus of worship is Ravidas (d. ca 1529), an untouchable poet saint, whose compositions incidentally are included in the Guru Granth Sahib. Essentially, although it is by no means unusual for Hindus to revere and worship the Sikh gurus, the precedence given to the guru's blessing in preserving Malerkotla by this Hindu resident is an indication of how central the *haah da naara* is to all the communities in the town.

Partition: Preserving Islam and Muslims

The year 1947 marks a shift in the hagiographical project from one that sought to authorize the political and spiritual power of Haider Shaykh and his descendants to one that justifies and explains the continued, nonthreatening presence of Muslims in Indian Punjab. This shift from the hagiography of an individual saint to the hagiography of the territory and its inhabitants unites the purpose of *tazkira*, as described by Hermansen, to establish the genealogy and territory of the saint with the social imperative to survive as Muslims in the new India. This is particularly apparent in the treatment of Partition in Sufi Mohammad Ismail's *tazkira* (biographical dictionary) of Punjab's saints, called *Bagh anbiya' punjab* (The Garden of the Prophets of Punjab). The author is a religious teacher in Malerkotla.[33] This book, in the standard format of *tazkira* literature, gives brief hagiographies of 32 saints of Punjab and Haryana, including West Punjab, now in Pakistan.[34] The entry on Haider Shaykh has less to do with the saint than with why Malerkotla remained untouched during Partition. His answer is: because of Islam. God preserved Malerkotla through Haider Shaykh's miraculous power because it was through the saint's agency that Islam came to the region.

Ismail's narrative really takes off at the time of Partition, which he is old enough to remember. He goes into great detail about Malerkotla's unique status as a zone of peace and an island of Islam during the chaos of 1947. He attributes the special status of Malerkotla to God rather than to Haider Shaykh or any other cause. For Ismail, God preserved Malerkotla to maintain it as a bastion of the Islamic faith. To dramatize the importance of Malerkotla's role, Ismail describes the chaos that plagued the rest of Punjab and the dire refugee situation in Malerkotla. He depicts in gruesome detail the kind of violence that occurred as women were raped and children were killed.

> In 1947 when Pakistan was made, in that terrifying time refugees fled the murder and destruction that was going on in other kingdoms and cities. They fled to Malerkotla, when outside Malerkotla's borders the murder of Muslims was becoming a normal thing. They were being robbed, their women and young girls were disrespected and were stripped naked. They played *holi* with their blood and rolled their children's heads like balls and burned their houses. So the looted and ravaged refugees came in caravan loads filling Malerkotla. There was not a single unoccupied space.[35]

Though the perpetrators of the violence are not identified by religion, Muslims are clearly the targeted victims. Furthermore, the playing of *holi* with the blood refers to the Hindu festival of Holi, a carnivalesque holiday in which colored powder and water, usually red, is thrown on people with great abandon. Thus without directly saying who the perpetrators of the violence were, Ismail gives a clear indication of who he feels is to be blamed.

In the aftermath of these terrible times, Malerkotla took on a special responsibility to uphold the faith that Haider Shaykh had brought five centuries before. In Ismail's view, Malerkotla was preserved because

> it was His [God's] desire that the Malerkotlans protect the others, since through His sovereign power He desired that some work continue to be done for His religion. Therefore here [in Malerkotla] all of us Muslims need to work to expand the religion of Islam. And to our other brothers we must bring forth the message of God and His Prophet. In this way we Muslims must uplift this world and the next. The other [element in the preservation of Malerkotla] is Hazrat Sheikh Sadruddin Sadri Jahan's power and miracles—he whose original throne this is. It is because of him that Islam has come to this whole place and from this town of Maler the (kingdom) city of Malerkotla was made.[36]

Ismail clearly links the sequence of events—the coming of Haider Shaykh, the spread of Islam, the Partition, and the preservation of Malerkotla—in a causal chain traced back through the saint to God. Without this special friend of God, whom Ismail calls "one of the elect saintly and pious elders, a perfected dervish and beloved of God," the territory may well have suffered the fate that befell Muslims elsewhere.[37] How else to explain this anomalous situation but by identifying in it God's intention that some Muslims remain to uphold and maintain the faith, to do "some work" for Islam? In this way the moral force of the imagined past is linked through the saint to an imperative to maintain the religion, thereby preserving both Haider Shaykh's legacy and the safety of the residents of Malerkotla.

Ismail links God's merciful protection and the preservation of Malerkotla to the *barakat*, or spiritual power, of Haider Shaykh. He also credits Haider Shaykh with the Islamicization of the region and the foundation of the settlement. Yet these things too are possible only because "God bestows His grace on whom He chooses." This is a Qur'anic formula (Qur'an 3:74, 42:13) presented in Arabic, a phrase that appears in numerous places throughout both the Qur'an and Sufi Ismail's text. Such reiterated expressions evoke early Islamic history, placing the events of the recent past on a continuum with the events in the Qur'an. Because Malerkotla is the only place in East Punjab that did not suffer violence during

Partition and is also the only place in the region where there is a majority Muslim population, for Sufi Ismail, this is God's will made manifest.

Good Governance? The Last Nawab

Many people credit the peace at Partition to the good governance of the kingdom's rulers. Certainly there is ample evidence of failed leadership, internecine squabbles, and fiscal irresponsibility, but there is also nostalgia in some quarters of Malerkotla for the time of the kingdom, and the ruling family retain much charismatic appeal in local politics. Iftikhar Ali Khan (d. 1982) ruled only a few months as nawab but served numerous terms as an elected representative from the town. He was educated by European governesses and tutors. He traveled broadly and met two British kings—George V and Edward VIII. He became chief minister of Malerkotla in 1946. Even after the nawab's death in 1982, his family continued to hold authority in the town, being very influential in municipal and state politics.

Because Iftikhar Ali Khan took such a leadership role during Partition, acting as head of state on behalf of his ailing father, he is often praised by those who remember the times. People reported that he would ride through the area day and night, watching the borders, patrolling the refugee camps, visiting neighborhoods, and constantly reassuring people. Remembering those times, the Hindu *mistri* Balram described the nawab's active and evenhanded involvement in the defense of Malerkotla and the organization of resources for both the citizens and the refugees:

> At the time of the Nawab Iftikhar Ali Khan [i.e., in 1947], my duty was in a tent. We stopped him; he asked my name. I [told him], and he said, "Whose son are you?" My teacher was the nawab's carpenter, so I gave his name. He said, "I hope you do not have any problems. Do you need some weapons?" I said, no, there was no threat. He used to meet us daily.[38]

The nawab encouraged people of all religions to remain in Malerkotla, insisting it was their homeland. In his speech upon ascension to the throne, Iftikhar Ali Khan credited his father's long reign and secular policies with the preservation of peace in Malerkotla. Although residents remember Iftikhar Ali Khan's presence and behavior during the crisis as a significant reason for Malerkotla's calm, the nawab himself asserted that the roots of Malerkotla's peace lay in his father's secular practices during his reign.

> His late Highness during his long reign of forty-four years never let the sentiments of religion influence his task as Ruler. He always

considered religion as a private link between man and God and ruled the State as an Indian Prince. I am glad to say that this spirit of tolerance proved to be the inevitable, as behind it lay latent the whole hearted support and goodwill of the people as a token of their fullest cooperation with their beloved Ruler in maintaining peace and security within the state, when during the recent terrible disturbances the fire of arson pillage and murder fanned by communal hatred raged all round.[39]

This eloquent praise of his father presents Ahmad Ali Khan as an exemplary *Indian* prince, not a specifically Muslim one. Although this idealized depiction is challenged by the religious disputes that occurred in Malerkotla during Ahmad Ali Khan's rule, Iftikhar Ali Khan was speaking in 1948 in the wake of Partition. It is therefore unsurprising that he presents a utopian vision of the past to frame the possibility for the real success of interreligious relations in Malerkotla in 1947 to continue. After 1947, the popular and historical accounts of Malerkotla, its origins and history shift from a genealogical emphasis to a geographic one. Furthermore, the cult of personality centered on the Shaykh and his lineage that is authenticated by the earlier chronicles seems to segue into a more diffuse population. No longer is it merely the saint and his descendants—the rulers of Malerkotla and the keepers of Haider Shaykh's tomb shrine—who possess this authoritative charisma, but it is the people themselves who come to embody the essential qualities the saint and his family had previously represented. It is their collective ethical being that validates the continued Muslim authority in Sikh Punjab in Hindu India. The narratives about these Muslim rulers, who came both before and after Partition, are therefore put to work in constructing a "good" Muslim authority, whose governing principles are now (because they always have been) based on an ethos of peaceful pluralism. Continuing this genealogy of secular rule, those who knew Iftikhar Ali Khan describe him as a truly secular man, supportive of all religions and particularly of those traditions that draw from multiple religious affiliations such as the tomb cult of Haider Shaykh. Iftikhar Ali Khan had no children, though he had five wives. With no natural heir to this political legacy, the dominance of his clan has begun to fade. Until recently, the nawabi and *khalifah* families had a near monopoly on local power, but new developments indicate that other elements in the town's diverse population are finding their political voice.

Post-Partition Politics, Demographics, and Multiple Minorities

Malerkotla Muslims take great pains to publicly demonstrate their commitment to the state of India. For example, a study by S. K. Sharma in the early 1980s among Muslim elites in town found that most were glad that they chose to remain in India rather than depart for Pakistan. Most named Jawaharlal Nehru, Mohandas Gandhi, and Maulana Azad—all nationalist figures associated with the Congress Party—as their most admired politicians. By contrast, only four of the 30 people interviewed named Muhammad Ali Jinnah of the Muslim League.[40] Most felt that their security and freedom in India was greater than they would enjoy in Pakistan, an attitude borne out by many of my interviews twenty years later. Abdallah, the retired schoolteacher, declared:

> Even today I think our ancestors showed their intelligence that they stayed here. In spite of the possibility of going, they stayed here, this showed their intelligence. Those who went there are less safe. They cannot offer *namaz* [prayer] in the mosque together. They do not know when they will be attacked. Guards stand outside the mosque, and then only can they offer *namaz*. Thank God we are Hindustani. Even if we want to offer *namaz* at a railway station we can do that if it is the time for *namaz*. We have such freedom in India; that is why our ancestors did the right thing. We are free from the religious point of view. That is why I think that Maulana Azad's theory is right and guided us well and our ancestors accepted this theory and did the right thing. We have relatives in Pakistan, but we think we are happier than them.

In Pakistan, which is 97 percent Muslim, sectarian and ethnic clashes have sometimes targeted mosques. In fact, *muhajir*s, the Muslims who migrated from India, have been the target of resentment and are not always well integrated into Pakistani society.[41] There were anti-*muhajir* riots in the province of Sindh in the 1970s. Abdallah also praised the Congress leader Maulana Azad's opposition to the call for Pakistan. Azad served as president of the Indian National Congress and was a close associate of Nehru's during the independence movement. Azad argued forcefully against the need for a Muslim state, saying that Muslims as much as Hindus belonged to the land of India. In a speech in 1940 he declared:

> I am proud of being an Indian. I am part of the indivisible unity that is Indian nationality. . . . Islam has now as great a claim on the soil of India as Hinduism. If Hinduism has been the religion of the people here for several thousands of years, Islam has also been their religion for a thousand years. Just as a Hindu can say with pride that he is an Indian and follows Hinduism, so also can we say with equal pride that we are Indians and follow Islam.[42]

Such nationalist sentiments are commonly heard from Muslims in Maler-kotla. Residents here feel very much under scrutiny and often go to great lengths to demonstrate their loyalty to the Indian nation, as in the case when during the 1999 Kargil War between India and Pakistan the effigy of then–Prime Minister Nawaz Sharif was burned during a demonstration. These expressions should not be dismissed as "merely symbolic," since the stakes in being perceived as disloyal are extremely high. This type of overt display of patriotism is required of Muslims in India.[43] Ravaged by violence and scarred by divisive politics, Muslims were and are regarded as a potential fifth column. They are heavily scrutinized even in such matters as cricket loyalties. They must actively and constantly assert their allegiance to the Indian state.

In her dissertation about Malerkotla, Anila Sultana surveyed one hundred local residents. Asked why they remained in Malerkotla rather than leave for Pakistan, thirty of those surveyed said they stayed because they were loyal to the nawab. Twenty-six said they remained out of loyalty to some other local leaders.[44] As Sultana's survey allowed people to choose multiple reasons, it also revealed that the blessing of the Sikh Guru was the single most important reason for staying, and loyalty to the nawab was the second most popular. In addition many residents remained in India because they expected a better future, whereas Pakistan was an unknown quantity. Many lower caste Khamboj residents, most of them farmers, anticipated land reform to follow closely after independence, and they believed their economic prospects were brighter. Another common reason given was love for their homeland and hometown. Interestingly, however, in the earlier survey, Sharma writes that overwhelmingly those surveyed gave the credit for the general communal harmony in Malerkotla to the people, not the national government.[45] This estimation of the positive role of the people echoes the assessment of J. C. Donaldson, the British officer who investigated the disturbances over *arati/katha* and *namaz* in 1935. It also reflects the way in which that controversy was ultimately resolved through intracommunity negotiations in 1940. Both Sultana and Sharma's surveys indicate a combination of reasons for remaining in Malerkotla that range from the spiritual to the material to the political to the practical. Significantly, nonmaterial motivations are cited as commonly as the material are. Devotion to a religious figure, such as the guru, trust in local leadership, and love for the homeland are elements that make life in the town meaningful.

These metaphysical reasons were undergirded by a sense of security. Muslims, Sikhs, and Hindus reported, in my own research and that of others, a confidence in the ability of the state to protect them at the time of Partition. In fact, after the *haah da naara* and the blessings of the saint, the third most common reason given by residents for Malerkotla's peace at that time was the vigilance and dedication of the kingdom's army in patrolling the borders.[46] This argument is put forward perhaps most forcefully by a former officer in the nawab's army who was serving in 1947. Faujdar Khushi Mohammad disputed all of the other explanations for Malerkotla's stability during Partition. A longtime member of the Jama'at-i Islami, Khushi Mohammad was instrumental in founding the Islamiyya Girls School, one of the first of its kind to provide a high school education for girls. Like most Jama'at-i Islami members, he opposes the practice of *ziyarat*, and he unsurprisingly dismissed the notion that any saint's blessing had protected the town. Similarly, he discounted the prevalent perspective that Malerkotla is safe because it is beloved by the Sikhs because of Guru Gobind Singh's blessing. On the contrary, he said, "If these people [the Sikhs] had even an iota of the respect they now profess for Guru-Sahib's word, there would have been no need for me and my military colleagues."[47] Maulana Abdul Rauf, the head of the local Jama'at-i Islami during my research, echoed this perspective. Abdul Rauf, who has since passed away, argued that if all those places that had done some service to the guru were spared Sikh violence during Partition, then the town of Machhiwara should have been preserved, which it was not. After all, two Muslim brothers, Ghani Khan and Nabi Khan, rescued Guru Gobind Singh himself from Machhiwara after his escape from the battle of Chamkaur by dressing the Sikh leader as Uch da Pir and carrying him away on a palanquin. Whereas Abdul Rauf credits God and the people of Malerkotla with their safety, Khushi Mohammad gave a more pragmatic explanation for Malerkotla's safety. As Khushi Mohammad put it, "When the first trains came in from the West, the blood chilling stories told by the survivors sparked off violent reactions in Malwa (the region of Punjab in which Malerkotla is located). Malerkotla would have been no different but for our Nawab's firmness and maybe the fact that there were hardly any Sikhs living here at the time."[48] For Khushi Mohammad and many other residents, the key to the harmony at Partition was the nawab's conscientious behavior and the army's diligence in following his orders.

The role of the army was clearly an important factor in maintaining calm in 1947. Preventing communal violence or curbing it depends upon swift and unbiased law enforcement. Not only do most riot reports and commissions of inquiry investigating ethnic conflict cite police inaction, bias, or even assistance and complicity as a major problem, but so do most theorists of such conflicts. Human Rights Watch's inquiry into the violence in Gujarat in spring 2002, in which as many as two thousand people, mostly Muslims, were killed reports that police complicity was evident. First, as evidenced by the title of the Human Rights Watch report "We Have No Orders to Save You," the police often responded to pleas for assistance from Muslims with silence, claims of short resources, or simple refusal to protect the people in their precincts.[49] Human Rights Watch reported that one of the slogans of the Hindu attackers was *yeh andar ki bat hai, police hamare sath hain* (this is a secret matter, the police are with us).[50] Furthermore, in many cases the police refused to file first information reports on crimes committed, and many of those filed do not cite any individual persecutors, but rather a general mob, which would be impossible to prosecute. Police who did attempt to act in a conscientious manner were often transferred.[51] This is just one piece of evidence implicating the state government in Gujarat in supporting the Hindu rioters by providing material assistance and immunity from prosecution and by generating an atmosphere of distrust and alienation between religious communities in the state. All of the commissions of inquiry and reports affirm the necessity of police reform to bring about substantive change in what has become a climate of fear in Gujarat and, indeed, in many other parts of India. These events are also troubling because communal conflict in India always raises the specter of Partition. As Suvir Kaul puts it, "Each time Indians are killed in the name of religion, each time a pogrom is orchestrated in our cities, memories of Partition resurface."[52] When violence occurs elsewhere, Malerkotla residents and observers immediately mobilize their own memories of Partition to shore up their anticommunal sentiment and remind the populace of their history of peace and tolerance during times of stress.

Because of such examples of the failure or refusal of the police or military to intervene to stop interreligious violence, the example of the effective management of the chaos of Partition becomes a crucial case study. In Malerkotla, not only did the army patrol the borders of the kingdom in 1947, but also they were given explicit instructions to protect the non-Muslim minority population and their property. Even Maulana Abdul Rauf, the head of the Jama'at-i Islami in Malerkotla but no fan of the nawab, acknowledged the positive role the ruler played during Partition:

> When Pakistan was formed, at that time the role of the nawab was very good. The Muslims gathered here, and the Hindus went away due to fear. And the nawab gave the order that if you break the lock of any place that they have left, you will be shot. And in Sikh villages it was said that if there was any loss of a Muslim [life], the village will be burned. No Muslim dared to break the lock of a Hindu or steal from his house. He [the nawab] controlled the situation in a very good manner. It [i.e., the peace in Malerkotla] may be a blessing or God's power, or the power of the nawab's law, that whosoever is brutal to another person will be shot. There was no injustice, no banditry.

The sense of a shared fate expressed by these older residents is not one of sentimental, nostalgic unity. The charisma of royalty aside, it appears that the support for the last nawab and subsequently for his relations who held elective office (including the descendants of Haider Shaykh) was broad based and consistent.

The princely state of Malerkotla ended altogether in 1956 with the dissolution of the Patiala and East Panjab States Union (PEPSU). Nawab Iftikhar Ali Khan had served as the Malerkotla representative to the union, winning 70 percent of the vote in his first bid for elective office in 1952. The nawab ran as an independent, reportedly to avoid the divisive politics of the parties. President's rule, meaning rule by the central Indian government, was imposed on PEPSU in 1953

Table 4.1 Malerkotla Constituency, Punjab State Legislative Assembly Member (1977–2009)

	List of Winning Candidates		
Year	Winner Name	Party	Percentage of Valid Votes
2007	Razia Sultana	INC	51.86
2002	Razia Sultana	INC	34.78
1997	Nusrat Ali Khan	SAD	41.6
1992	Abdul Ghaffar	INC	43.03
1985	Nusrat Ali Khan	SAD	49.97
1980	Sajida Begum	INC(I)	50.31
1977	Anwar Ahmad Khan	SAD	52.03

Source: Election Commission of India, http://archive.eci.gov.in/Feb2007/pollupd/ac/states/s19/Aconst81.htm (accessed February 28, 2009).

because of political instability within the administrative unit, but the nawab came back to win by an even greater margin in the election of 1954, garnering 82 percent of the vote (see table 4.1). Once Malerkotla and the other PEPSU states were merged with Punjab in 1956, the nawab was defeated by the only non-Muslim ever to hold this position, Chanda Singh. Singh served only one term, however, and the nawab regained the office after joining the Indian National Congress—a major decision given the group's antiroyalist politics during the independence movement. His wife Yusuf Zaman was elected in 1962. She served one term, followed by the nawab's resumption of the position until 1972, when another of his wives, Sajida Begum, was elected. In 1977 a kinsman of the nawab, Hajji Anwar Ahmad Khan, won the office by a narrow margin, representing the SAD. This set the pattern for Malerkotla elections in which many parties—even sectarian groups—float Muslim candidates, many of whom then serve in some capacity in the State cabinet. Sajida Begum was reelected in 1980, followed by another nawabi clansman in 1985, Nusrat Ali Khan with the Akalis. In 1992 a non-Pathan Muslim was elected for the first time, Chaudhry Abdul Ghaffar, a local Khamboj leader with the Indian National Congress, and he also served as minister for education during his tenure. In 1997, the descendants of Haider Shaykh were back in power with Nusrat Ikram Khan representing the SAD and serving as sports minister for Punjab.

However, recently political power has shifted out of the nawabi family and the family of Haider Shaykh. A non-Pathan Muslim woman, Razia Sultana, was elected to the Legislative Assembly in 2002 and reelected in 2007. Sultana won the Congress Party ticket from Sajida Begum, the nawab's widow and a longtime Congress leader. Sajida Begum was reportedly very upset that the Congress ticket was given to someone else, and the chief minister at the time, Captain Amrinder Singh, dismissed her from the state party organization. Singh, himself a Congress Party member and the erstwhile maharaja of Patiala, appears to have shown no favoritism to fellow royalty in this case. The *Tribune* reported on January 21, 2003, that Sajida Begum was dismissed because she failed to support the Congress candidate who had defeated her: "Mrs. Sajida Begum, one of the oldest Congresswomen in Punjab, who was a confidant of the former Punjab Chief Minister and the Union Home Minister, Giani Zail Singh, had revolted against the decision of the party to give ticket to Mrs Razia Sultan, wife of a police officer, and 'outsider.'"[53] Along with the decline in Sajida Begum's popularity, two other members of Haider Shaykh's lineage have recently lost their positions. The previous MLA, Nusrat Ikram Khan, and the previous head of the Municipal Committee, Azmat Ali Khan (SAD) both lost elections. Azmat Ali Khan was vulnerable for a long time, but he finally lost his position when Nusrat Ikram Khan lost his own election. This signifies a new era in local politics as the relative monopoly on power held by Haider Shaykh's descendants comes to an end.

It also appears that the opening up of the political arena has resulted in an intensification of factional politics in Malerkotla.[54] After Azmat Ali Khan was dismissed, the committee elected a Hindu interim president, Kewal Kishan Jindal.[55] In August 2002, prior to a council vote to choose a new president, Jindal was assaulted, and MLA Razia Sultana has been accused of ordering the attack that left him hospitalized. An election was held in Jindal's absence that brought Faqir Muhammad to the leadership post, but an outcry in Malerkotla led to another election. Yet another referendum on March 23, 2003, brought M. S. Bholi, another Hindu and Congress Party member, to the position of Municipal Committee president. This is a fascinating situation that in some circumstances could be construed as an interreligious dispute. However, given the support bases of the various factions, that would be a hasty conclusion. In fact, Jindal himself acknowledged several Muslims who supported him at the time of the attack and afterward.[56] Furthermore, all local religious groups and parties universally condemned Jindal's assault, and a citywide *bandh* (strike) was held in protest. Among participants were Nusrat Ikram Khan; Abdul Ghaffar, another former MLA; the president of the local Truck Union, Ajit Singh; the president of the Sanatan Dharam Sabha, Kamlesh Garg; and K. K. Chopra, president of the local BJP. Abdul Ghaffar, who is extremely well respected, told the *Tribune* that the impression that the situation was a communal dispute was misleading and that it had much more to do with the proper functioning of democratic institutions in Malerkotla. He pointed out the broad, nonpartisan and nonsectarian support in the community for a full inquiry into the attack. Such a breakdown of law and order in which it is possible for the president of the Municipal Committee to be assaulted outside of the committee's office indicates a disturbing direction for Malerkotla politics. It is also a matter of concern that BJP leaders in Punjab got involved in the situation, publicly denouncing Razia Sultana and calling for an investigation.[57] However, in spite of all these divisive developments, it must be remembered that in March 2003 this town, 70 percent Muslim, elected a Hindu president to the Municipal Committee. This may well be a positive sign that although the recent political scene has been nasty, it has not been so because of divisive religious sentiment. Indeed the greatest efforts to calm the situation came from religious leaders acting in the interests of the whole community.

In addition to the electoral politics inside the town, state level politicians also take particular note of Malerkotla. During his tenure as the chief minister of Punjab from 1997 to 2002, Prakash Singh Badal (SAD) appointed Nusrat Ikram Khan to the position of sports minister and attended the 'Id celebrations for both Baqr 'Id and 'Id al-Fitr, (the two major Muslim festivals) at the 'Id Gah ('Id prayer grounds). Following the collective prayer, Badal promised to establish an Urdu institute in the town and to dedicate significant resources to expand the 'Id Gah. The former governor of the state, Lieutenant General J. F. R. Jacob, also visited Malerkotla, and he took particular care while there to attend the *dargah* of Haider Shaykh. The Sangrur District member of Parliament, Sardar Simranjit Singh Mann, has also taken a special interest in the town. His concern is based on his own personal devotion to Guru Gobind Singh and his commitment to the guru's blessing upon Malerkotla. Mann also feels a strong solidarity should exist among minority communities to counteract the growing power of the BJP and its allies. Captain Amrinder Singh, the former chief minister, makes frequent visits to Malerkotla. He attended an 'Id Milan and rally at Sajida Begum's in 2000 as he was running for office. There he made reference to the *haah da naara* in an effort to establish rapport with the Muslim community. Each of these politicians seeks in some fashion to demonstrate that he is worthy of Muslim trust and support and will protect and uphold the interests of the community. Manifesting a special bond with Malerkotla is thus a key strategy, even for non-Muslim politicians, to gain the electorate and prove their ability to govern a multicultural state.

In Malerkotla, although Muslims are a dominant majority with a long history of political authority, local Muslims feel strongly that because of their minority status in Punjab they cannot afford to let tension take root. If the Muslim majority fails to maintain the security and satisfaction of the non-Muslim residents, suspicions toward the Muslim community, which pervade India at large, could quickly take root in Malerkotla. The viability of Muslim custodianship would be called into question. Furthermore, they perceive the scrutiny of the state in numerous ways. Here alone in Punjab were police deployed on the streets during tensions after the Bamiyan Buddhas were destroyed by the Taliban in 2000 and again after the United States attacked Afghanistan in 2001. Here police were sent out during the crisis in Gujarat in spring of 2002. Thus the Muslim majority is highly conscious of its high-profile status as custodians of the safety and contentment of the non-Muslim minority. This is interpreted by some as a civic responsibility and others as a sacred trust.

Conclusion

Malerkotla as a shared community, much like the shared shrine at its center, contains and inverts contradictory conceptions and regimes of power, creating an idealized and critical reflection of a South Asian society in which the lines drawn between religions can be lethal. Although Punjab has not been a "laboratory of Hindutva" as has Gujarat, still the effect of "saffronization" in India has been felt here as well.[58] So in Malerkotla when people tell stories about Partition and link their comparatively quiescent experience to the core group of narratives about the place's history and character, the effect is to build a collective identity based on this shared ethos of harmony. Each explanatory narrative—the blessing of the saints, the blessing of the Guru, the blessing of God, the moral fiber of the community, the good governance of the rulers, the diverse population—makes available to the population a point of entry into a shared moral universe in which justice, integrity, harmony, secularism, pragmatism, and other values are tied to the essential nature of Malerkotla.

The hagiographical tradition that memorializes the saint and validates the ruling lineage and the tomb cult is expanded in the post-Partition context to include hagiographies of Malerkotla itself and the moral past that provides a mandate for the collective identity. Some personal narratives hail the quality of Malerkotla's citizens and leadership. Others describe the pacifying influence of the guru's blessing on Sikhs during Partition and since. Still others feel the protective power of Haider Shaykh and the many saints buried in Malerkotla. The less spiritually oriented look at material resources, such as the army or the political pragmatism of the rulers and politicians. The choice of explanatory stories reflects the needs and interests of the time and teller. Explanations draw on Malerkotla's particular history, selectively referencing certain events, such as the power of Haider Shaykh or the blessing of the Sikh Guru Gobind Singh, to construct a coherent explanation for what otherwise appears as a gross aberration from the Partition experience of most Punjabis. Taken together, the stories are sometimes contradictory, and yet the range and variety of accounts form a web of meaning that allows people with different experiences and needs to connect to the construction of a moral past that not only explains the past absence of communal violence but also supports the continued presence of Muslims in Indian Punjab. Through continual repetition and reinforcement, this metanarrative of peace becomes a hegemonic discourse, silencing opposition and dominating all accounts of Malerkotla.

These narratives are one means of symbolically reversing the process of Partition, of reweaving what was torn apart. The anxiety and destabilization of 1947 left scarred and fragmented people who were unable to account for their neighbors and their own actions during the transition. In Malerkotla the repetition of stories about Haider Shaykh, the *haah da naara*, and Partition are symbolic refusals of the division of India and the division of Punjabi culture, and they establish the frame of peaceful interreligious relations through which Malerkotla's experience is interpreted. Through stories that highlight and foreground past moments of cooperation, the community asserts that these moments are evidence of Malerkotla's ethic of harmony. By retelling such exemplary stories of the past in the present, the identity of Malerkotla as a zone of peace is consolidated and confirmed, and the present reality is extended into the past, further strengthening it. These multivocal narratives need not be uniform. Their coherence as a repertoire about the past and present reality of Malerkotla lies in their overall influence and the fact of their repetition, which strengthens this unity in multiplicity. The reiteration of these stories is evidence that Malerkotla residents and visitors value the shared aspects of their culture and history.

Dead Center: The Tomb of Haider Shaykh

Listen to me, this is a question of a *pir*'s place. Everyone believes in the same thing here. In one person's house there may be a Guru Granth Sahib, and he can believe in it. We believe in the *pir*, we also believe in Kali, we can have faith in anything. It is not a question of what we can't do.

—Mahesh, Hindu pilgrim and *chela*

THE shaping of Malerkotla's civic identity as a zone of peace is particularly observable through the tomb shrine and cult of Haider Shaykh, the Sufi saint who founded the town in 1454. As we have seen in previous chapters, the saint is commonly credited with having shielded the town from violence during Partition and at other times of stress in the town's history. Haider Shaykh's tomb shrine, or *dargah*, is also the location of a vibrant multireligious cult, among the most popular such sites in Indian Punjab. Muslims, Hindus, and Sikhs, resident and nonresident, visit the *dargah* daily and in enormous numbers at festival times, praying for the same blessings—children, health, wealth, employment, and so on—in much the same way that they have for generations. In a 1950 letter describing the operations of the *dargah*, the last nawab, Iftikhar Ali Khan, wrote, "His Shrine is held in great reverence by people of all castes and creeds and specially Sikhs and Hindus come from distant places to pay homage and offerings and *nazars* [amulets], even up to the present day."[1] Significantly, the ritual life of the tomb shrine seems largely unchanged from before the 1947 Partition. This lack of alteration in terms of ritual practice contrasts with the substantial shift in the symbolic significance of the vibrant Muslim shrine cult in a state from which Muslims had been systematically routed. Nowadays, the rituals and the testimonies of pilgrims, patrons, and owners at Haider Shaykh's *dargah* are the clearest evidence of how residents and visitors understand and enact Malerkotla's ethos of peaceful pluralism.

The *dargah* of Haider Shaykh is a site of enormous religious, economic, and political significance to the entire town of Malerkotla. The visitors to Haider Shaykh's tomb are a source of substantial income to the whole town, and the *dargah*, given its multireligious constituency, functions as the symbolic center of Malerkotla. The *dargah* is, in historian Wulf Kansteiner's terms, a spatial expression of Malerkotla's cultural memory, part of the "objectified culture, that is, the texts, rites, images, buildings, and monuments which are designed to recall fateful events in the history of the collective. As the officially sanctioned heritage of a society, they are intended for the *longue duree*."[2] Rituals, stories, testimonials, and interreligious encounter center on this spatial expression, incorporating the secular ethos into the collective representations of the town, its shared sacred sites, and its history. In this way the *dargah* and the people who interact with it contribute significantly to the civic project of bolstering Malerkotla's identity as a uniquely integrated and pacific community.

Furthermore, the *dargah* of Haider Shaykh provides a point of encounter between Sikhs, Muslims, and Hindus in present-day Punjab. As the only locale in Indian Punjab with a majority Muslim population, Malerkotla offers interreligious encounters that Sikhs and Hindus could easily avoid by visiting other *dargah*s in the state, many of which are managed nowadays by Hindus or Sikhs. Conscious of this diversity, residents and pilgrims physically and discursively situate themselves in ways that validate the simultaneous presence of multiple religions. For example, they may adopt each other's modes of prayer or exchange testimonials and personal advice (see fig. 5.1). Symbolically, this is a rejection of religious division and a denial of the communalized identities associated with Partition.

To attend the *dargah* of Haider Shaykh is almost to walk back in time. Here it is nearly possible to imagine that Partition never happened, that Muslims were never driven from East India and that Hindus and Sikhs never fled from the West. As one newspaper reporter described the town in 1997, Malerkotla "could very easily be mistaken for a township in UP [Uttar Pradesh, where there is a large Muslim population], but free of the strong regional chauvinism that sadly come to mark the rest of the state. Malerkotla is the only place where one can get the flavour of Punjab before 1947."[3] This experience is intensified at Haider Shaykh's tomb because reaching the *dargah* necessitates coming through a neighborhood that is almost wholly Muslim. For Hindus and Sikhs visiting from outside Malerkotla, this would be an unfamiliar and possibly intimidating experience. Yet having reached the *dargah*, one finds (on a non-festival day) an atmosphere of calm and welcoming serenity (see fig. 5.2). Moving through the space, pilgrims and caretakers, residents and visitors find themselves face to face with Haider Shaykh and with one another. Through these encounters, visitors of all religions inhabit the same space, necessitating physical and sometimes verbal

FIGURE 5.1. A Sikh pilgrim prays.

interactions with one another as well as the saint. Through observation and dialogue they learn the appropriate rituals and modes of address. They become acquainted with Haider Shaykh and his history, and they perforce recognize one another's common humanity as their similar purposes in making the pilgrimage become known. Maintaining the multi-confessional community of the

FIGURE 5.2. *Khalifahs* at the *dargah*.

saint requires that these exchanges be conducted so that both the devotional and social purposes of the pilgrimage are sustained. The public imagination about Malerkotla is shaped by the numerous ritual and narrative practices that subvert division and promote a hegemonic harmony. Given the variety of practices and practitioners at the *dargah*, this is an intense and interesting choreography.

The movement of multiple actors within a shared sacred space illuminates the microstrategies of attunement and accommodation that people with different beliefs, practices, and purposes employ within a single holy place. Although many scholars and journalists write that believers from different traditions attend the same sacred sites, the practical reality of that simultaneity is rarely fully addressed. In Malerkotla, where pluralism is so integral to the town's identity, it is perhaps unsurprising that the interreligious interactions that take place within the many sacred sites in town are an important part of constructing and substantiating that identity of peaceful pluralism. In this chapter I will examine what is actually shared in these encounters and experiences and how different actors with different ideas and agendas make space for themselves and others within the shrine's confines. I will outline the various beliefs held and the rituals performed by Hindus, Muslims, and Sikhs at Haider Shaykh's tomb. Then we will see how the substantial variation is accommodated and validated by pilgrims, ritual specialists, and the descendants of the saint. Through interviews and observations this chapter explores the two principle modes of interacting with the saint: through his blood descendants and through those pilgrims who are possessed by his spirit. It is my contention that the interactions and exchanges among residents and pilgrims enabled by devotion at the *dargah* are key elements in the production and perpetuation of a stable multireligious community.

Sharing Sacred Space

Interactions occurring at shrines like Haider Shaykh's *dargah* sustain Malerkotla's peaceful plural culture. The opportunities to "exchange love," as the *khalifah* Ahmad put it, at shared sacred sites are critical resources in forging positive impressions of or even relationships with people from different religious systems. Such relationships are possible at shared shrines because the shrine itself provides a common ground and a shared vocabulary of belief and practice that promotes exchange. In many ways the blending of religions, ethnicities, ages, genders, and classes is part of the nature of tomb shrines and not just in India. Writing of such sites in medieval Cairo, Christopher Taylor describes a scene of what he calls "vital social mixing." In the cemetery of al-Qarafa,

> a lot of vital social mixing took place; here the living mixed with the dead, the rich mixed with the poor, the powerful with the powerless,

men with women, the formally educated with the illiterate, believers with nonbelievers, authorities with outlaws, and the mundane mixed with the sacred.[4]

What was true of Al-Qarafa in the fourteenth century is true of Haider Shaykh's *dargah* today as the same variety of pilgrims make their way to the Punjab tomb. Some, as we saw in the example of Vinod, the scheduled caste Hindu leader, come for social purposes, publicly demonstrating a nonsectarian ethos through the performance of a ritual pilgrimage to a Muslim shrine. Others come for devotional reasons, to fulfill their vows and their personal needs. These ritual engagements often blur the lines between typically Sikh, Hindu, and Muslim practices, thereby manifesting a faith in the efficacy of prayer that is based more on the purity of intention than on the purity of tradition.

Furthermore, Taylor asserts that the vital social mixing that took place at al-Qarafa was a *liminoid phenomenon*, "an essential instrument of normative *communitas*, or social antistructure, which played its own important role in integrating the communal life of this great metropolis."[5] Although Malerkotla can hardly be described as a metropolis, having a population of just more than one hundred thousand, the ritual exchanges at the *dargah* do indeed integrate the population on both devotional and social levels. On the devotional level, in spite of the enormous variation in belief and practice, the common interests and concerns of the pilgrims facilitate the simultaneous presence of conflicting doctrines and rituals regarding the dead. If from a theological perspective the crucial element in ensuring the efficacy of rituals at the shrine is the purity of heart of the devotee, then the meaning of the practice is largely self-determined and tends at most shared shrines to minimize overt conflicts that would necessitate exclusion, definition, and segregation. The social implication of this theological perspective is the establishment of a functioning shared religious environment, proving that such intimate exchange is not only possible but desirable. This is reinforced at the tomb by the activities of *khalifah*s and residents as they promote the devotions and presence of non-residents and non-Muslims. Thus the formal and informal encounters at sites such as Haider Shaykh's *dargah* activate the motivating ideals of community and cooperation as people grapple with the mundane reality and necessity of forging relationships with each other, with the divine, and with the dead in a shifting and uncertain world.

Ritual Practice

One of the most powerful means through which sacred space, especially shared sacred space, is made meaningful is through ritual practice. Rituals may vary in formality from simple attendance and presence at a sacred site to an elaborately realized set of behaviors believed most effective in communicating with the saint and gaining his blessings. These behaviors also communicate with the other humans present, conveying much information about the intentions, interests, and identities of the actors. For example, a person enters the tomb shrine and directly sits down with the saint's descendants, the *khalifah*s, who are there just to talk and pass the time. A group arriving with large amounts of food or other offerings, dressed in special clothes (such as women wearing their wedding scarves), a quantity of oil lamps, and auspicious amounts of cash are marked as having a particular need that they hope Haider Shaykh will fulfill.

Presence at the shrine, therefore, can have multiple simultaneous purposes and interpretations. But both the casual and the formal visitations serve to validate the central role the tomb plays in the social and spiritual life of the community. As Emile Durkheim argued, ritual is a means of renewing the beliefs of a community and generating the fervor of collective feeling necessary for engendering solidarity.[6] As a *fait typique*, or total social fact, a ritual is also a representation and condensation of the social system that produced it, a kind of hypostatization through which that system is made manifest. Clifford Geertz perceived ritual as a symbolic fusion of the "world as lived and the world as imagined."[7] Ritual theorist Catherine Bell points out that whether a theorist regards ritual as a window through which the basic structures of a society can be viewed, a means of reconciling opposed social and cultural elements, or a means of displaying and reinforcing social norms depends mostly on his or her theoretical premises and interests. Bell's study attempts to move beyond such self-serving definitions in favor of a theory of *ritualization*, or ritual practice.

Bell highlights the strategic aspects of ritual practice and the potential for rituals to construct and reconstruct the power configurations in a culture. In Malerkotla, as in Bell's view, ritual practice is a strategy "for the construction of certain types of power relationships effective within particular social organizations."[8] Thus ritualization both reinforces social structure and creates the conditions possible for that structure to be changed. Through the process of ritualization, people come to master the techniques of control particular to a ritual context. Furthermore, ritualization cultivates techniques of *self*-control, leading to a condition of subjection not unlike that described by Foucault in which individuals internalize the coercive force of the power structure and both discipline themselves to conform to the system and finds ways to creatively thwart and alter the system.[9] Cognizant of the parameters of acceptable behavior, microstrategies of resistance become available to a practitioner. The constant dialectic between domination and resistance is a crucial aspect of a ritual system.

If ritual practice can bring about change then rituals may function as acts of resistance. The persistent, everyday, banal transactions at shared sacred sites may be understood as a "weapon of the weak," part of the "hidden transcript" of nondominant groups in a context in which highly divisive social and religious politics are the order of the day. In James Scott's formulation, these arts of resistance need not be formal or even effective.[10] Very often resistance to a hegemonic system is masked by acquiescence and is only intelligible in fragments of a hidden transcript.[11] This is a dimension of what Bell calls the misrecognition of ritual practice in which not only are many of the functions of ritual concealed from the consciousness of the practitioner who is enacting an internalized behavior, but also the meaning and interests of the ritual are concealed from the power structure and its regulators. Thus the performance of ritual takes on another strategic dimension, opening up the possibility that tacitly or overtly, participation in a particular ritual system may be an act of resistance to a hegemonic power structure. In the case of Haider Shaykh, both potential functions of ritual are activated inasmuch as practitioners are fully conscious of the challenges to their presence at the shrine by reformist elements in each major religious tradition and from without by the communalism of politics in the country. But the shrine is owned and managed by the Pathan descendants of the saint, an extended family deeply involved in local politics and business. Likewise, residents and visitors to Malerkotla are unavoidably aware of the town's unique demographics and its symbolic identity as a zone of peace, thereby imbuing their behavior within this space with additional layers of significance. Merely being present in Malerkotla or at Haider Shaykh's *dargah* does not necessarily mean that someone adheres to the prevailing ethic of harmony or advocates interreligious interaction or supports Islam and so on, but in a competitive spiritual marketplace, the choice to attend such a site to some extent validates the plural culture that exists there. Of course people can—and do— leave the shrine and vote for the BJP or SAD, but a shared community depends on more than political party affiliation. Indeed, in Malerkotla, some of the citizens most actively seeking to forge links and build bridges belong to organizations typically viewed as communal, such as the Jama'at-i Islami or the RSS.

Ritual practice at Haider Shaykh's *dargah* symbolically resists religious division. Two rituals in particular, pilgrimage and possession, are practiced by Hindus, Muslims, and Sikhs. Though certain notions and practices are indistinguishable, other ideas and behaviors are particular to one group or another. By paying attention to what is shared and what is not, we see how difference is sustained without conflict. At Haider Shaykh's tomb, pilgrims partake in a uniquely Punjabi pietistic identity, characterized by shared histories, aesthetics, and cultural values.[12] Thus the pilgrimage itself is a choice to seek out a living Islamic center in post-Partition Indian Punjab. In a more literal (and more controversial) blurring, religious divisions are subverted at the *dargah* through the possession of Hindu and Sikh devotees by the spirit of the Muslim saint.

Ziyarat and *Yatra*: Visiting the Holy Dead

As noted in the British ethnographic and administrative sources, Haider Shaykh's tomb has been a multi-confessional site at least since the nineteenth century. Nonetheless, there are considerable theological differences between Hindus, Sikhs, and Muslims and observable, if minor, variation in terms of daily ritual practice at Haider Shaykh's *dargah*. Most notably, Hindus and Sikhs may actually believe the saint to be God or a form of God, a concept abhorrent to Muslims. Muslims are more likely to offer only prayers and not to bow or give food or money. Anybody can, and many do, offer sweets, a green or blue cloth cover or *chadar* for the tomb, small clay horses, incense, oil lamps, money, goats, or objects for the maintenance of the shrine. Like the offerings, the ritual specialists are also multiple, as space is made for various modes of interactions with Haider Shaykh—through his descendants, the *khalifah*s and through visiting disciples, or *chela*s, whom he possesses.

For most pilgrims, the fact that most of the *khalifah*s do not pass on Sufi teachings or initiations is not an issue. Most believe that contact with the *khalifah*s transmits the saint's *baraka* wholly independently of their spiritual state.[13] At Haider Shaykh's *dargah* many of the *khalifah*s—both those who spend significant time and derive their primary income from the tomb's revenues and those who do not—are extremely pious and devout Muslims. There are many *panch namazi*s (those who perform the five times ritual prayers on a daily basis) and many men and women who incorporate a visit to the tomb or some other form of supererogatory prayer into their daily ritual lives. Nonetheless, the level of counsel and guidance required from the *khalifah*s by most devotees is not highly esoteric.

In addition to the *khalifah*s there is another group who have a significant role in the ongoing operation of the *dargah*. The *mujawwar* are the descendants of those who worked in the service of the saint. Although generally regarded by the *khalifah*s as lower in status, they also claim Pathan Afghan heritage, placing them among the ethnic elite. Typically, the *mujawwar* families do not sit at the shrine except on Thursday evenings, when people tend to visit such places, and on festival days. They do not dispense spiritual or personal guidance at the *dargah*, though several have taken on this role from their homes. At busy times they are always present at the shrine as there are several tombs of their ancestors outside the inner sanctum where Haider Shaykh and his family are buried (see fig. 5.3). During festivals, family members sit at these tombs to accept offerings. Also, one of their major sources of income is selling goats to the devotees, which are then offered (not sacrificed) and returned to the *mujawwar* to be sold again. There is a legal agreement between *khalifah*s and *mujawwar* regarding the management of the shrine, which has never fallen under the purview of the state. According to the last nawab, Iftikhar Ali Khan, in a letter to the Home Minister of Patiala in 1950, "The management of the Shrine is carried on as a private right jointly by the Khalifas and the Mujawars ever since the demise of the Shaykh without any interference whatever by the State."[14] The agreement stipulates the terms for the division of the offerings that come to the shrine. All coins under one rupee and all cotton cloths, and goats, sheep or other small animals are the

FIGURE 5.3. A *mujawwar* boy tends a tomb during a *mela*.

property of the *mujawwar*. Any money of more than one rupee goes to the *khalifahs*, as do silk cloth, gold or silver jewelry and articles, horses, camels or any large animals, and any movable property such as fans or fluorescent light fixtures. The food offerings are primarily sweets and cooked food, most of which is returned to the devotees as *tabarruk/prasad* or given to the *faqir*s and beggars who gather at busy times. On festival days when large amounts of cloth, money and goats come in, periodically several youths representing the various families will remove the excess to be divided later. The *khalifah* and *mujawwar* families then meet (separately) and divvy the offerings according to their own proportional agreements. During the chaos of the *mela*, however, a great deal of money is "lost" in the cracks and quick-fingered children from both families may bring home hundreds of rupees. However, there is no secret about this, as the kids brag throughout the neighborhood and there appears to be little animosity over the money that doesn't make it to the general pool.

In addition to the *khalifahs*, various resident *sevadar*s (shrine servants) materially assist the daily supervision of the *dargah*. These are people who have attached themselves to the shrine as a matter of faith or livelihood or both. These *sevadar*s clean the shrine area, especially on Friday mornings and after the *mela*s. They wash the marble floors, removing the residue from offerings—old clay lamps, sweet rice, wheat grains, goats and so on. Each tomb within the structure is rinsed and swept. Haider Shaykh's tomb is relieved of any excess *chadar*s (cloth covers) offered by the devotees, but is never left exposed.[15] Included among the population of *sevadar*s, there are a number of *faqir*s, mendicants and devotees who make the *dargah* their home—some permanently, some periodically. These people, mostly men but some women, sleep in the shelters around the shrine or in the homes of the *khalifah* and *mujawwar* families. They spend much of their time at the shrine itself, engaged in various activities ranging from devotions to conversations. Some are clearly less equipped than others to function in the world outside the shrine's space. Whether because of physical or mental challenges, some have taken a sort of refuge at the tomb. In order to do this work, their presence must be acceptable to the *khalifahs*. In the past, *faqirs* and *sevadars* who became unruly, abusive, or dissolute have been made to leave the *dargah*. However, the eccentricities of some regular personnel testify to the fact that these rules are not overly strict.[16]

Several of the *faqirs* are rarely if ever absent from the tomb, which I visited almost daily for more than a year. The connections between these individuals and the *dargah* were fascinating mixtures of faith, friendship, opportunity, and convenience. One regular is an elderly Muslim man whose mental acuity comes and goes. He was well educated and enjoyed reading and reciting the Qur'an and Urdu *na'ats* (devotional poems in praise of the Prophet). He also took me one day to one of the other famous burial shrines in Malerkotla, the Dera of Baba Atma Ram, the seventeenth-century shrine to the Hindu saint. At the Dera, he was greeted warmly, and his knowledge of Baba Atma Ram and his life and lore bespeaks the fluid culture of saint cults that has little regard for religious boundaries and definitions.

Another resident identified himself as a *bhagat* (a Sanskritic term for a devotee) of Haider Shaykh and claimed a family lineage of Sikh maharajas. (See fig. 5.4.) He, like the Muslim *sevadar* above, did not manifest the linear and pragmatic thinking necessary for functioning in the world outside the shrine. His mind wandered and wondered in intriguing and intricate pathways. He stayed close to the shrine, sometimes sitting in prayer in the Muslim fashion with his hands held open toward his face. He wore the green shirt of a dervish and a turban of the same color tied in the Sikh style. There was also an eccentric and flamboyant resident *sevadar* at Haider Shaykh's tomb (fig. 5.5). It was hard to know whether he was truly crazy or affected insanity for various purposes—getting money, avoiding questions, instigating conversations, or simply amusing himself. He would run small errands and do odd jobs at the *dargah*. He was almost invariably present at every religious festival in town, especially those involving *langar*—free distribution of food. He usually wore green, but for some Hindu holidays he was spotted sporting saffron (the color associated with that faith).

These *sevadars* provide several crucial services that maintain the *dargah*. First, many of them do work at the shrine, helping to keep it clean and in good repair. The less spiritually oriented may run errands for the *khalifahs* such as bringing tea or sending messages. Second, their presence is another validation of the efficacy and power of Haider Shaykh. Empty, unpopulated *dargahs* indicate a lack of vitality and possibly a lack of *baraka* (spiritual power). A healthy

FIGURE 5.4. A resident Sikh *faqir*.

number of *faqir*s and *sevadar*s in residence indicates a wealthy shrine, capable of supporting such individuals and a powerful shrine which gives spiritual benefits to those who dwell there in devotion. Third, as mentioned above, it is an act of merit in all religions to support religious renunciants.

Itinerant *faqir*s are semi-regular participants in the life of the *dargah*. Although not directly involved with the daily operations at the shrine, their presence is nonetheless crucial. As familiar figures at any Sufi site, they provide visible verification of the authenticity of the shrine. Some are simply beggars, going from shrine to shrine for the money they receive in alms. Others participate in ongoing pilgrimage circuits depending upon the festival calendar, the orders or customs of their *murshid*s, and their own inclinations. Such *faqir*s are invariably present at the '*urs* for Haider Shaykh, where they play a central role, reciting passages from the Qur'an and providing an opportunity for the *khalifah*s, *mujawwar*s, and other patrons to gain the *sawab* (merit) of supporting them.

Although Hindus and Sikhs come in larger numbers to Haider Shaykh's festivals, on an average day in the early hours visitors are few and mostly Muslim. Many locals come daily at this time to pray, and most of those typically present are *khalifah*s, members of the family descended from the saint who live in the surrounding neighborhood. Visitors at all hours have various habits of prayer, but there are some standards. Prior to entering the *dargah*, everyone removes his or her shoes. On entry most people proceed directly to the tomb. Most will bow and touch their forehead and kiss or sometimes press each eye to the marble surface. Some reach under the *chadar* (covering cloth) to contact the

FIGURE 5.5. A denizen of the *dargah*.

tomb itself or lift the cover up to their eyes and lips. Some people will walk around the tomb, and others simply sit. Some Muslims do not bow, believing this to be *shirk* or placing something on a level comparable with God. Most Muslims who stay to offer prayers will do so, if space permits, on the left side of the tomb where they sit or stand with their backs to the *qibla* (the direction of Mecca). As the dead in Islam are interred with their faces turned toward Mecca, sitting at this place means they are facing the saint, which is viewed as not only proper *adab* (etiquette) but also provides the most direct contact for communication. Hindus and Sikhs may sit anywhere, but most seem to prefer the space at the foot of the tomb. Many people bring offerings; those who do not do so are usually Muslim or are attending for social purposes. Typical offerings include money, sweets, small clay horses, uncooked wheat or rice, and goats. Many people will place incense or small oil lamps in a small structure directly behind the main tomb as the enclosure is entered (see fig. 5.6). Some devotees consult

FIGURE 5.6. Pilgrims light lamps.

with the *khalifah*s about their particular reasons for attending the shrine. Many of these encounters demonstrate the kind of basic human contact that most profoundly binds humans together.

In one such instance, two Hindu women arrived. They appeared unsure of how to proceed and came cautiously up to the tomb where two elderly *khalifah* women were sitting. They gave a few rupees and some sweets, bowed to the tomb, walked around and lit oil lamps in the area behind the grave. Returning to the foot of the tomb where these transactions take place, they received some *tabarruk* and then hesitantly asked the *khalifah*s for advice with their particular problem. The younger woman was the elder's daughter-in-law, and she had not conceived within two years of marriage. One of the *khalifah* women told them, "Pray to Hazratji, and you will surely get a son." The older woman replied that although she believed in the saint, her daughter-in-law did not. The daughter-in-law interjected that she didn't exactly *not* believe, she simply didn't know yet. She knew only that her mother-in-law had great faith in the saint. One of the *khalifah*s told her that many women had had sons as a result of praying there and that she could be sure of being blessed if she prayed from the heart. The women asked if they should make some particular prayer or offering. They were told no, they should do whatever they feel in their hearts and give according to their need and ability. The three women then started talking generally about the daughter-in-law's diet, health, and habits. The two older women continued to exchange advice while the younger mostly listened. Such exchanges are commonplace, even dull. Except that they are not. These conversations are human interactions between people of disparate religious affiliations who share a belief in a single spiritual figure. The conversation also exemplified the kind of mutual support—spiritual, personal, and financial—that occurs within the *dargah*. Though some of these experiences are momentary, even fleeting, the mundane quality of this encounter and others like it should not be taken for granted.

An important aspect of this situation from the perspective of countering the divisions that are emblematic of Partition is that most pilgrims to Haider Shaykh are well aware of theological and ritual contradictions between the various religions. This emerged slowly from numerous interviews with devotees. Many visitors initially responded to my query concerning ritual and conceptual differences with stock phrases suggesting vaguely that all religions are the same, the paths are many but the destination is one, and the like. On further discussion, people revealed knowledge of several external distinctions such as styles of prayer. In particular, pilgrims remarked that many Muslims do not bow to the tomb but that almost all Hindus and Sikhs will touch their foreheads, *mattha tekna*. Some non-Muslim visitors expanded on this by pointing out that Muslims pray *through* the saint to Allah whereas Hindus and Sikhs pray directly *to* the saint—a significant theological difference. This point of distinction is indeed of great concern to Muslims, especially those that object to tomb visitation as a kind of polytheism or *shirk*. In the confines of the shrine I never met anyone who felt that this variation was a problem or affected the efficacy of rituals, vows, or offerings. Difference for these pilgrims does not necessitate division. Since reformist and exclusivist elements within all the major religions oppose the practice on doctrinal and political grounds, visitation to such a place and tolerance of diversity is a pragmatic rejection of communalism in India. Before continuing to explore the ritualization occurring at Haider Shaykh's *dargah*, we must understand some of the theology regarding the status of the saintly dead in each religion.

Muslim Pilgrims

Pilgrimage to saints' tombs, *ziyarat*, in Islam is controversial. Reformist groups such as the Tablighi Jama'at and Jama'at-i Islami staunchly oppose such practices. Although they advocate respect and prayer for the souls of departed pious people, asking for particular blessings is viewed as tantamount to assigning a partner to God, or polytheism, known as *shirk*. Conservatives endorse only a qualified acceptance of tomb visitation and usually accept it only to recollect one's own inevitable death and the wisdom of preparing for it spiritually in advance, or for the purpose of invoking blessings upon the deceased. Many mainstream Muslims see *ziyarat* as beneficial for all worldly problems. Most Sufis advocate *ziyarat* with varying degrees of control and rules concerning the etiquette (*adab*) of proper visitation.[17] The saint, in his capacity as a *wali allah* or friend of God, is able to bring one's prayers closer to God than can a less spiritually realized human being.[18] The comparison is often drawn to the attempt to meet any powerful person, such as the prime minister. To gain an audience one must go through his entourage of familiars. Likewise, God is most easily approached through the mediating presence of the *auliya'*, those who are close to God. This is often likened to the worldly principle of *safarish*, a recommendation or influential connection without which very little in South Asia would get done. Having this inside track to God through the dead saint expedites all prayers, whatever they may be. Still some Muslims say that asking the saint for boons such as children or employment is inappropriate.

Opponents of *ziyarat* in India draw from several sources. A strong anti-*ziyarat* tradition relies heavily on the fourteenth-century scholar Ibn Taymiyya (1263–1328) whose ideological heir in South Asia is Shah Waliullah (d. 1762) and, drawing from him, Maulana Maududi and Muhammad Ilyas, founders of the influential reformist organizations Jama'at-i Islami and Tablighi Jama'at, respectively. Ibn Taymiyya wrote several tracts denouncing the practice of *ziyarat*.[19] He felt that prayer to a saint to mediate or intercede with God was tantamount to unbelief, because it presupposes that the saint is closer to the supplicant than is God, who is "nearer to him than his jugular vein" (Qur'an 50:16). Therefore presuming God has not heard our prayers is subjecting God to human limitations.[20] Although Ibn Taymiyya unequivocally condemned the building and visiting of monumental tomb shrines, he did give qualified approval to attending graves for the purpose of remembering one's own death, to pray to God on behalf of the dead, or to simply greet the dead in a gesture of respect. Shah Waliullah shared Ibn Taymiyya's reservations, denouncing the construction of monumental shrines and the practice of direct supplication to the saint for benefits or material gains. Yet, especially in the earlier period of his writings, Shah Waliullah affirmed the ongoing presence of the saintly dead, writing "when the spirits of perfect people are separated from their bodies they become like billows rooted on the spot."[21] Not only are the spirits of the saints present, indeed *rooted*, at the place of their interment, but these spirits are available and accessible to those who seek with a pure heart to commune with them.

Proponents of *ziyarat*, like its opponents, fall on a spectrum from the obviously partisan custodians of tomb shrines to those who, like Shah Waliullah, acknowledge the pious merit of such visitations, though they do not condone certain practices like prostration or taking vows. These advocates of *ziyarat* also cite hadith to justify their position, such as the following from a canonical collection, *Sahih Muslim*, in which the Prophet states, "I forbade you to visit graves, but you may now visit them."[22] At Haider Shaykh's tomb some Muslims respond directly to the challenge brought by critics of *ziyarat*. For example, a Muslim whose family is in the lineage of *mujawwars*, or servants of the saint, saw hypocrisy in the criticism.

We the *pirpanth* [community of the saint] believe in them. This is all true. The Jama'at-i Islami people do not believe in them. They say all this is *bekar* [useless]. Whosoever has gone to their grave, he is dead. . . . They say the Hindu people bow their heads. So what if they are doing that? If you do not want to bow your head, don't do it. Who is saying to do it? They have a double standard policy. *That* is worthless.

This *mujawwar* pointed out that just as there is no compulsion in religion (Qur'an 2:256), there is no compulsion in *ziyarat*. Another argument made by advocates of tomb visitation is based on the notion that the dead are not insentient at all but should be treated with the same, if not greater, respect and courtesy that one proffers to the living.[23] Therefore, to visit the dead is to encounter the same essential spirit of the person who once walked the earth, in an altered form but no less aware of the doings of the living.

For the faithful who approach the tombs of the dead, greeting is an essential element of the encounter. In an early writing, Shah Waliullah set forth an elaborate prescription of how to approach *dargahs*. One should enter the tomb in a state of ritual purity, approach the tomb and recite the *fatiha*, the first chapter of the Qur'an. Subsequently, one must perform two *rakat* (cycles of prayer), squat down facing the dead with one's back in the direction of Mecca, recite the Surat al-Mulk (Qur'an 67), the *takbir* (Allahu Akbar, God Is Great), profess the *shahada* (confession of faith), again recite the *fatiha* eleven times, approach the tomb calling out 21 times *ya rabb* (Oh Lord!) and repeat *ya ruh* (Oh Spirit!) into the ear of the dead. Finally, the visitor should relax and wait to see if he or she is welcomed and met with a response.[24] Though later he was more critical, Shah Waliullah's guide to visitation and others like it are highly detailed, justifying each prayer and practice with evidence from Qur'an and Hadith.[25]

Almost two hundred and fifty years after Shah Waliullah laid out his version of the appropriate code of conduct during *ziyarat*, visitors to the *dargah* of Haider Shaykh enact their own understanding of the *adab* (etiquette) of devotion. Though most visitors observe far less complicated rites, some do recommend similarly precise behaviors. An elderly hafiz (one who has memorized the Qur'an) explained that it is essential to approach a graveyard of any kind, whether a shrine or a common burial ground, in a state of purity (having performed *wuzu*, ritual cleansing) and with an attitude of humility and respect. Hafizji said, "Wherever you go you should do *wuzu*. A man does no wrong when he has done *wuzu*, he is pure."[26] He also affirmed the critical importance of properly greeting the denizens of the graveyard. Upon entering the grounds, first one must declare "salaam alaykum (peace be upon you)" so that those present will not be surprised or offended by one's sudden appearance in their midst:

Whenever you go to a graveyard you say, "Salaam alaykum." It means "May the mercy of God be upon you, O buried ones, upon the *muslimin* [Muslims] and the *mu'minin* [true believers, a degree above average Muslims]. You have gone to the grave before us, and we will come after you." This is the prayer for going to *qabrstans* [graveyards]. . . . You have gone before us, and we are coming after. Everybody has to go. That is our prayer. So first we *salaam* to the grave.[27]

A respectful greeting and salutation prior to any further activity is crucial because the souls of those buried remain present. After the greeting, Hafizji instructed that one should recite the *fatiha*, the *durud sharif* (a prayer litany invoking blessings on the followers of Abraham and Muhammad), and then one may make any special prayer according to one's needs or knowledge.[28]

Whereas Shah Waliullah indicated that the souls of buried saints are like rooted billows at the place of interment, Hafizji extended this by affirming the living presence of all those who die until the Day of Judgment. Until that time, all of God's sentient creations, that is humans and *jinn*, are understood to be alive in a way distinct from their previous corporeal existence, but nonetheless present and active in this plane of being. Hafizji explained it thus, "All of them are alive, no one is dead, they are all alive. Whosoever died is still alive from whatsoever community. Because the point is that he who dies is held accountable. God has placed this accountability on humans and *jinn*. On the *jinn* there is an accounting. On humans there is an accounting." Hafizji's view that physical death is not the final death is orthodox. In Islamic thought the souls of the dead are aware of the world but have entered a liminal zone between death and judgment called *barzakh*.[29] Here the soul is separate to a degree from the body. However, prior to the Day of Judgment it is fully within God's power to change the condition of the dead and alter their salvation status. Therefore, prayers on behalf of any of these deceased persons may benefit their ultimate fate. The relative efficacy of this is also debated between those who quantify the exponential rewards reaped through such prayers and those who merely suggest their advisability and general merit.

The spirit of Haider Shaykh is therefore present at the *dargah*. Furthermore, his spirit continues to communicate with the living through the ritual specialists who channel the saint for his devotees. Using the familiar moniker "Babaji" for Haider Shaykh, Ahmad, the *numbardar khalifah*, explained this possibility in the following way:

People think Haider Shaykh died, [but] his soul is there alive. When some disciple of Babaji's plays [becomes possessed by the saint] his *paun* [spirit] comes. So he is not dead. No, he is not dead. This is in the Qur'an Sharif and Hadith. He who links himself to God, he does not die. He only hides himself from the world.

Ahmad's perception that through linking oneself to God a person does not die is a clear reference to a passage in the Qur'an that is often cited as evidence of the ongoing relationship between the living and the righteous dead. Qur'an 3:169 declares, "Do not think of those killed in the way of God as dead, indeed they live with their God and are sustained." Although the apparent reference is to martyrs in battle, many Sufis prefer the interpretation that those killed while on the path of God (*qatilu fi sabil allah*) are those who die while striving in the greater *jihad*, the struggle with their *nafs*, their own base nature and worldly desires.[30] The great Bihari Sufi saint Sharafuddin b. Yahya Maneri (d. 1381) explained the same verse in the following way:

> Concerning the friends of God ... it has been said: "Those who are killed along the Way to God—do not number them among the dead, for they live through their Lord!" A person should be ready to give his life at the head of the Way and walk along it stripped of his own life, so that this special situation might arise wherein "they live through their Lord." ... Whoever sets out along this Way after having sacrificed his life, and continues to walk in love, has to pass by no other intermediary. This group consists of friends who seem to be annihilated but who really live, while the other group is comprised of strangers who are seemingly alive but actually dead.[31]

Thus, individuals who are able to supercede worldly attachments through their quest for essential spiritual knowledge do not die but remain awake in the grave, and their souls remain active in the world. Maneri specifically identifies this group as friends or *auliya'* who merely appear to be dead, but are in reality more alive than those strangers to God who only seem to live. The *dargah* is a point of exchange, a focus for ritual activity that maintains the active connection between the physically dead but spiritually alive saint and the inhabitants of his *wilayat*, or spiritual territory.

The actual form of Muslim ritual at any *dargah*, including Haider Shaykh's tomb, varies, depending upon the particular school of thought the Muslim belongs to with regard to *ziyarat*. For those of the Ibn Taymiyya/Shah Waliullah reformist mind-set, should such a visitation occur at all it would be brief and simple, involving only prayers and no prostration or offering. For travelers on the Sufi path the procedures may be quite elaborate and time consuming. But few Muslim, let alone non-Muslim, pilgrims know or follow the directives given in the elaborate manuals of etiquette described above. The essential elements for most Muslims are quite similar to the description given by the Hafiz in Malerkotla. One ought to enter in a state of ritual purity, having performed *wuzu*, the ablutions prior to prayer. Shoes are never worn, and most people, men and women, will cover their heads. Entering the tomb area it is not necessary to circumambulate or bow, but many do. Eventually one comes to face the side of the tomb that faces Mecca.[32] Standing or sitting one recites the *fatiha*, the opening chapter of the Qur'an, which is an appropriate recitation for any occasion. Afterward, any other part of the Qur'an, especially the thirty-sixth chapter *Ya Sin* or the Throne Verse (Qur'an 2:254) may be recited if desired.[33] This is followed by any formulaic or personal *du'a*, a supplicatory prayer. Many of these *du'a*s are commonly and widely known, such as the *durud sharif*, which invokes blessings on the persons and people of Abraham and Muhammad. Improvised, extemporaneous personal supplications may then be made.

While praying, Muslims typically hold their hands open in front of themselves, palms turned upward toward the face and heaven. Upon completing the prayers, the Muslim pilgrim passes her hands over her face and head, distributing whatever blessing might have been received and physically marking the completion of the formal prayers. After this the visitor departs; some retreat backward so as not to disrespect the saint by turning away, and others simply walk out. This form of visitation is the most basic. Those Muslims who choose to make offerings of money, flowers, sweets, or cloth grave covering known as *chadars* will typically do so immediately upon entering the tomb space (see fig. 5.7). At all times some members of the *khalifah* family will be present at the *dargah*.[34] The *khalifah*s in attendance sit facing the entrance and receive whatever is offered. If flowers or cloth covers are given, the *khalifah* present will place them on the tomb if asked, but most pilgrims do it themselves. After completing their prayers and offerings the visitors return to the foot of the tomb and receive back a portion of the offerings made, now blessed because of their proximity to the saint. This is known as *tabarruk*, a term for any substance which has come in

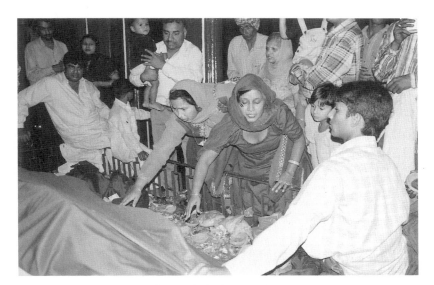

FIGURE 5.7. Contacting the tomb during a *mela*.

contact with the *baraka* laden tomb and therefore retains some portion of that spiritual power. This *tabarruk* is then brought back by the pilgrim and distributed among family and friends. If a great deal of food is offered, a small part will be left at the tomb, a small part retained by the pilgrim, and the remainder is distributed among all present, particularly *faqirs* and beggars. The numbers of these groups are small at Haider Shaykh's tomb, but at some *dargahs* like those in Ajmer Sharif or Nizamuddin in Delhi, vast numbers of poor and hungry people are fed by the visiting pilgrims.[35]

Hindu and Sikh Pilgrims

For Hindu and Sikh pilgrims at the shrine, there is less need to justify their conviction that the spirit of the saint is accessible to them at this place, but militants in both religions oppose such pilgrimages and have even attacked tomb shrines in some instances. Hindus and Sikhs perform nearly identical rituals and offerings at *dargahs*, and these practices are not unlike the Muslim rituals outlined above. Although Hindu and Sikh concepts of the status of the holy dead are fairly similar, the Hindu literature on the nature of death and transmigration is infinitely larger.[36] Hindus and Sikhs alike adhere to the notion of *samsara*, the principle of cyclic time through which souls are reincarnated. In the Hindu perspective, the soul or *atman* continues to be reborn until such a time as the whole of cosmic time ends or until the soul achieves enlightenment, known as *moksha*. At this point the cycle of *samsara* ceases, and the individual soul, or *atman*, is united with a cosmic *atman*.[37] Those who achieve *moksha* during their lifetimes are said to be *jivanmukti*—or dead while alive, existing in a state of pure consciousness no longer fettered by their gross, subtle, or cosmic body. Upon physical death, which occurs at the will of the one who has achieved *jivanmukti*, the body may be buried rather than burned. Particularly in the yogic traditions of Hinduism, physical death for those who have achieved perfect knowledge is merely another state of being.[38] The physical, or gross, body is so completely controlled by the mind of the yogic adept that death of the body merely signals a change of consciousness. Burying the body fulfills a form of yogic practice in which breath and bodily control are so complete that the practitioner is merely in a state of eternal meditation or *samadhi*, described by anthropologist Jonathan Parry as a "perpetual cataleptic condition of suspended animation."[39] Burial sites for Hindu saints are known as *samadhis* and are found throughout India. These sites often become shrines because the beneficent power of the saint remains available to devotees. In Malerkotla, the Dera of Baba Atma Ram is one such place in which Baba Atma Ram and several of his disciples are interred.

Hindus believe the Muslim saint is joined with God. Indeed many pilgrims believe Haider Shaykh to be a form of God, and they state unequivocally, *voh hamare bhagwan hai* ("He is our God"). I asked one Hindu *chela* (literally "disciple," one who is possessed by the saint) what the difference was between believing in the power of a saint and believing in God. He responded, "As I told you, he is our God. We believe in him like God. He is a form of God." Understood in this way, the saint may be prevailed upon to fulfill the needs and prayers of his devotees if he is properly worshiped. In the Hindu understanding, it is Haider Shaykh in his divine capacity who fulfils the desires of his supplicants. This is an important distinction from the Muslim perspective in which it is at least stated that it is God and God alone who grants desires, not Haider Shaykh, who is a go-between or mediator who carries the prayer of the supplicant to God. Hindus believe that the saint has united with God and so is capable of altering the physical, material, and spiritual condition of anyone, if he so desires.

The Sikh perspective on death and the dead is similar but far less elaborated than the Hindu. The Sikh faith was born from the *sant* tradition of poet-saints who dedicated themselves to seeking God and for whom religious categories and divisions were largely irrelevant. Guru Nanak, the first Sikh guru, stressed the oneness and eternality of God, the equality of humanity, and the absurdity of sectarianism. There is a strong tradition that his first declaration following his experience of God was, "There is no Hindu, there is no Muslim." Many Sikh life cycle rituals resemble Hindu rituals, but the treatment of the dead and the understanding of death in Sikh tradition are distinct. Hindu death rituals involve elaborate mechanisms to expedite and ameliorate the deceased person's transition to the next life. There are numerous ceremonies designed to propitiate the dead spirit, build for it a "body" in the afterlife, and to guarantee it a positive rebirth.[40] Furthermore, for the relatives of the deceased especially, contact with the dead or the dying process necessitates careful rituals of purification. By contrast, Sikhs, though they adhere to the notion of rebirth, have simple ceremonies, committing the dead to the pyre and disposing of the ashes in any body of water.[41] The Sikh *Rehat Maryada*, or code of conduct, then advocates a simple ceremony in which the entire Guru Granth Sahib is recited, called *akhand path*, after which mourning is completed.[42]

Yet the *Rehat Maryada*, which began to be formulated in the early to mid-nineteenth century, also emphasizes the points of distinction between the Sikh tradition and both Hinduism and Islam.[43] In particular, attendance at non-Sikh shrines is clearly opposed. The *Rehat Maryada* explicitly instructs, "Worship should be rendered only to the One Timeless Being and to no god or goddess." Furthermore, the "veneration of any graves, of monuments erected to honour the memory of a deceased person or of cremation sites, idolatry and such like superstitious observances" is strictly forbidden, as is "owning up [to] or regarding as hallowed any place other than the Guru's place—such, for instance, as sacred spots or places of pilgrimage of other faiths."[44] These formal objections stand in some tension with the actual practice of many Sikhs as it would be unusual to visit one of the major goddess temples in Punjab and find no Sikhs there. In addition, Sikhs are present in enormous numbers not only at

Haider Shaykh's *dargah*, but at other *dargah*s throughout the country. Finally, there is a strong tradition of reverence for Sikh martyrs and the places their remains are buried. This is evident from the martyr's galleries that adjoin many gurdwaras featuring paintings vividly re-creating the torture scenes of Sikh heroes such as Guru Arjan, Guru Tegh Bahadur, Baba Deep Singh, and so on.[45] There are also countless small white memorial monuments placed over places dedicated to Sikh martyrs, known as *shahids*. These monuments litter the landscape, as do Muslim graves. They too are plowed around in fields, placed within the courtyards of temples and houses and incorporated into the daily life of many people.[46] In spite of the explicit injunctions against such memorials, against the utility of pilgrimage, and against mourning beyond the death ceremonies, these places thrive and proliferate, indicating that the mass of Sikh faithful are not comfortable with the absolute cessation of relations between the living and the dead that is promulgated by official bodies such as the Shiromani Gurdwara Prabandhak Committee that oversees historic gurdwaras.

Pilgrimage to Haider Shaykh: Similarities and Differences

Although clearly there are differences between the three religions in terms of theology and doctrine regarding the saintly dead, we have also seen similarities in certain aspects of ritual practices at the shrine. One of the most common rituals involves taking vows, or making prayers for a particular desire, and then returning to make an offering in gratitude. Hindus, Sikhs, and Muslims all engage in this practice, though some Muslims are critical of it. The main difference between vows and prayers is whether the desire, say the birth of a son, is simply prayed for and an offering made in hopes of finding favor with the saint, or if a kind of bargain is made by declaring that if the desire is fulfilled, in return a certain amount of money, food, or charity will be given. Others take on obligations or practices until the desire is fulfilled such as abstention from meat or alcohol, or weekly prayers, or even fasts (though this is not supposed to be done by Muslims or Sikhs). Some devotees engage in more demanding fulfillment such as shaving the head or proceeding to the tomb from a great distance in serial prostrations, advancing only the length of one's body at each stage (see fig. 5.8). Newly married Sikh and Hindu couples frequently come to the tomb at the first festival for Haider Shaykh or, if that is not possible, at the first opportunity after their marriage. The bride wears her wedding *dupatta* (scarf), which is tied to a cloth worn by the groom. This is believed to guarantee offspring and marital happiness (see fig. 5.9). Children born through Haider Shaykh's blessing are presented at the tomb along with offerings. As it is believed that touching the child to the grave itself is auspicious, the scene at the chaotic and crowded *mela* (festival) can seem hazardous as babies are dangled near the tomb from a distance.

FIGURE 5.8. A pilgrim prostrates en route to the *dargah*.

FIGURE 5.9. A newly married couple circumambulate the tomb.

One of the most distinct ritual events at Haider Shaykh's *dargah* is the *'urs*. Though the Arabic term means "wedding," in contextual usage an *'urs* marks a saint's death day, the day upon which he was joined with God. Haider Shaykh's *'urs* falls on the fourteenth of Ramadan. The *'urs* of Haider Shaykh that I attended in December 2000 was wholly distinct from daily practice or *melas*. It was formal and markedly Islamic, involving all the local *khalifahs*, invited guests from other Sufi shrines, and dervishes and *faqirs* from all over the region. Although important Hindu and Sikh patrons of the shrine were present they mostly observed, not knowing the prayers and Qur'anic verses that are recited. However, the formality of the ceremony is impressive and conveys to these non-Muslim patrons—as well as to the Muslim ones—the power and mystery of this system of belief. A middle-aged male Sikh devotee from a nearby village declared that he came every year, though he understood little of the proceedings. Few women attended, though many watched from rooftops and windows. Being in Ramadan, the *'urs* is fairly solemn.[47] At the *'urs* in December of 2000, reportedly for the first time, one of the officiants was a *khadim* (shrine custodian) from Khwaja Muinuddin Chishti's tomb at Ajmer.[48] The *khalifahs* seemed pleased with the presence of the young representative from Ajmer and deferred to him to lead the ceremonies. He had brought an elaborate tomb covering cloth or *chadar* from Ajmer Sharif and was dressed in white silk robes and an embroidered hat. He carried himself with great poise and led the proceedings with authority and dignity, although he was only 22 years old.

In my discussion with the *khadim* about the practice of *ziyarat* he gave a spirited defense of the traditions of the saints. In his view, the emphasis on personal orthopraxy encouraged by reformist groups such as Tablighi Jama'at is arrogant and prideful to the point that it threatens to alienate not only the *pir*, but God himself:

> Muslims think they can do it themselves: say *namaz* [the five times daily prayer], read Qur'an, go on retreat. Without a doubt *namaz* is necessary for Muslims, therefore those who say *namaz* declare that from saying *namaz* your *namaz* will be accepted [by God]. But first if you are shown the way by the saints, their *namaz* has already been accepted by God. If you follow them, then God will also accept your *namaz*. If we turn our face from these *pirs*, then God will turn his face from us and he will not accept our *namaz*. *Namaz* is no doubt necessary, but we must take hold of these *pirs* also. If we don't take them, our religion is nothing. As long as you are with the saints, you will be saved at the Day of Judgment, and in this world and in the hereafter you will be happy.

The *khadim* from Ajmer invoked a number of established Islamic principles in his defense of saint veneration, in particular the veneration of worthy exemplars.

He declared that the belief that one does not need such models is evidence of the sin of pride. For the Sufi, humble piety (*taqwa*), repentance (*tauba*), and constantly seeking Allah's forgiveness (*istighfar*) for one's human failings are among the most essential states of being. Indeed in classical formulations, *tauba* is the essential first step on the Sufi path. By rejecting the help of those who have shown the way, an arrogant Muslim turns away from the *pirs* and likewise from the path of God.

In addition to the '*urs* the *khalifah*s have other particular rituals that occur at the shrine. Unlike Sikh and Hindu couples, the *khalifah* bride and groom must come to the shrine before the *nikah* (Muslim marriage service). Though much is similar, some rituals are particular to Haider Shaykh's descendants. For example, British ethnographers reported that silver equal in weight to a child's first haircut is given here, and an offering is made at the time of circumcision.[49] Some *khalifah*s assert that before they travel out of Malerkotla they come and take leave from their Haider Shaykh as they do from all their respected elders. According to a senior *khalifah*, the Malerkotla army used to come to pay obeisance prior to going to battle:

> This Malerkotla was managed by the nawab and the army of the nawab. Whenever the army of the nawab was to go for war, the forces used to first visit Haider Shaykh. They used to salute and offer *salaam* to Haider Shaykh. When these two wars broke out, the First World War and World War II, first in 1914 and second in 1939–45, the Malerkotla forces were on the side of England and America, who were called the Allies. The opponents were Germany—that is, Axis. Whenever the forces used to go for war, they used to come first to Haider Shaykh, marching all around in lines of one, two, three, four. Millions of people respect Haider Shaykh, and the forces used also to respect him. These forces used to take the blessings of Haider Shaykh, and that custom is still practiced these days. Whenever people go somewhere or the students go for their exams they come for his blessing first. Whenever there is a marriage, the bridegroom, before going to the bride's house, the groom goes for blessing from Haider Shaykh.

Many of these particular rituals are diminishing. There is no state army now, and the influence of reform movements has meant that some local Muslims no longer come to the shrine before marriage.

Hindu and Sikh pilgrims continue to observe the traditions of the tomb that their parents and grandparents passed on to them. As one male Hindu pilgrim explained, "My mother didn't have any children, she had four or five, but they died. Then a Babaji told her to come to Baba [Haider Shaykh], and she came, and I was born. Our ancestors also believed in Babaji, but after that our belief became complete." I met a number of devotees now settled abroad in Singapore, the United States, Canada, and other places who came back with their babies or their newlywed children to show their gratitude for the continued blessings of Haider Shaykh. A Sikh gentleman from Singapore said his great-grandfather had prayed here for a son and received seven. His wife, who grew up in Singapore, is now also a believer and lights candles and sings songs for Haider Shaykh every Thursday in their home.

The multireligious constituency is a point of great pride among the *khalifah*s and other local Muslims around the shrine. Non-Muslim devotees, some of them nonresident Indians living in Canada and the United States, have sponsored major capital improvement projects undertaken at the tomb, such as a large gateway, a guesthouse, and a tank. These structures and stories are integral to the experience of visiting this tomb. The obvious popularity of the shrine is evidence of the place's power and the material boons obtained by visitation. The mere presence of pilgrims from diverse religious, caste, age, gender, and socioeconomic backgrounds proves the nonsectarian sentiments of the shaykh, who clearly rewards all those who attend with a pure heart.

Ultimately it is clear that although each of the three major traditions have internal discourses challenging the practice of visiting *dargah*s, these objections or restrictions are rejected or ignored by vast numbers of people. This demonstrates that the considerable diversity of belief in terms of theological status of the dead does not undermine the unity of belief about the function of the saintly dead. To reiterate Bell's point, no uniformity of belief about ritual is necessary. And to reiterate Casey's point, places do not require uniformity of belief or practice within its environs, as long as no one is forcing exclusivity upon those present. In the perception of all three of the major religious traditions represented at the *dargah*, the saintly dead are uniquely capable of addressing the concerns of humans. Having been human themselves at one stage, the saintly dead are capable of deep empathy, compassion, and mercy for their fellow humans. All agree that the results of one's prayers depends upon the purity of one's heart as a supplicant.

It is this question of the pure heart that lies at the center of the constitution of Haider Shaykh's devotional community. The pure heart of the visitor is determined by the combined influences of the religious structures of the pilgrim's faith and those of the shaykh and his shrine. Thus there is some variation in defining this purity as most Muslims say they do not pray *to* the saint but *for* him and *through* him. Though offering reverence and respect to Haider Shaykh, there can be no question that God alone fulfills people's needs. This generates a moral code among some Muslims that is critical of those who come to the shrine to ask for material, physical, or spiritual assistance. Purity of heart means that one prays for mercy upon the deceased and upon one's self and others without attaching vows or conditions. These Muslims regard vows that stipulate some offering or devotional practice in return for a boon as a form of coercion and therefore totally inappropriate. For other Muslims purity does not preclude making the desires of one's heart known to the saint and, through him, to God, but it may mean that coercive vows are offensive. By contrast, purity of heart for most Hindus and Sikhs requires absolute faith in the shaykh's power to fulfill all desires, cure all ills, and reveal all truths. Doubt and skepticism must be abandoned, as they are a likely cause for the failure of prayers made at the shrine. Likewise, vows stipulating certain offerings or behaviors are not seen as coercion but as signs of sincerity. This is also consistent with the sacrificial model of Hindu religious practice. The classical Hindu notion of sacrifice emphasizes a reciprocal and symbiotic relationship between humans and the divine. Divine forces in this view require support and sustenance gained by the sacrificial rituals of humans. Thus rituals must be performed correctly to be efficacious and for the divine to receive the sustaining essence of the substances offered—whether animal, vegetable, mineral, or the spiritual effects of human behaviors such as fasting, asceticism, prostrations, and so on. Expecting that divine forces will therefore bless humanity by fulfilling the needs and desires of the people who support them is not coercive, it is proper. This exchange is integral to the ethical system of divine-human relations in the Hindu cosmology.

Possession

An important way in which religious divisions are ritually confounded is through the saint's ongoing presence in the bodies of certain devotees, mostly Hindus and Sikhs, who claim a special relationship to the saint and the ability to channel his spirit.[50] Inside the *dargah*, the saint's descendant *khalifah*s accept offerings, give blessings and sometimes advice, and return *tabarruk/prasad*. Inside and outside the shrine, possessed devotees called *chela*s, a Sanskritic term for disciples, enter into trance states during which they are able to communicate with Haider Shaykh. Thus the shaykh himself is present at the *dargah* in two ways. Through his lineal descendants his *baraka* is still present and is transmittable to pilgrims through physical contact. Even if the only *khalifah* present is a young child, many of Haider Shaykh's devotees, primarily Hindus and Sikhs, will seek out physical contact (by touching his or her feet, or asking the *khalifah* to lay hands on them, and so on) to obtain this residual power. The other way in which Haider Shaykh continues to be present is through his spirit (the terms *paun*, Hindi for breath and *ruh*, Arabic for spirit are both used), which becomes manifest and accessible through these *chela*s, dispensing advice, treatments, and blessings.

All around the shrine, the Sikh and Hindu *chela*s who connect to Haider Shaykh's spirit set up satellite ritual spaces. *Chela*s come to the shrine for festivals and, in lesser numbers, on Thursday nights along with groups of followers ranging from a few to a few hundred. At a given moment during the *mela* there may be hundreds of people inside and outside the tomb who are being "played" by the saint's spirit. On one occasion within the tomb enclosure itself I observed at least seven people in states of active possession and several others exhibiting all the paraphernalia of the *chela*. This may include wearing the garb of a renunciant, often green or blue (colors typically associated with Sufi saints), but almost equally often a *chela* will wear the pinkish saffron of a Hindu *sadhu*. Many *chelas* arrive in processions accompanied by at least one drummer and a retinue of disciples. They often carry with them iron rods or chains which may be used to flay themselves during the period of possession, demonstrating how completely their physical being has been overtaken by the saint. Some *chelas* approach the tomb in a state of possession, whereas others go into trance upon arrival; still others come, bow, circle, and leave with no demonstration of any altered state. Occasionally pilgrims, who do not appear to be *chelas*, lacking an entourage or any marking clothing, are possessed at the tomb (see fig. 5.10). These events are taken in stride and sometimes those in proximity will acknowledge the presence of the saint with raised hands and bowed heads, listening for any messages that might be intelligible. Usually the possession passes and the person possessed bows to the tomb and is struck firmly on the back, releasing the divine spirit from the human body.

The mode of representing a *chela*'s authority is also often reflected in the structure of the communities. Some groups are autocratic, with a single *chela* as the leader who does not allow disciples to be "played" by the saint (see fig. 5.11). These domineering *chelas* assert great control over their disciples and often manifest distinct markers of their status through their wardrobe or signage. One *chela* was nearly invisible beneath the layers of tinsel garlands that his entourage had bestowed upon him. On the other hand, some groups are rather democratic in their group structure. One particular assembly of 50 or 60 at the Haider Shaykh *mela* in June 2001 employed a bureaucratic vocabulary to describe the organization of their group, designating the primary *chela* as president and his main disciple, who also undergoes possession, as vice president (fig. 5.12). Though acknowledging the seniority of the president, the general demeanor of the group was more participatory, less obsequious, and somewhat less hierarchical than other assemblies I observed. The more controlling *chelas* tend to have many obvious markers of their identity, and the more democratic tend to be much less distinguishable from ordinary pilgrims.

Although *chelas* pay respects at the *dargah* and receive blessings from the *khalifah*s, their main foci are these satellite ritual spaces, called *chaunki*, *darbar*, or *diwan* (all these terms signify either a period or place of audience). These take place in the shelters by the tomb, in the streets under tents, in rented rooms, wherever there is space. The format of the *chaunki* is fairly consistent. The main *chela* or a senior disciple sets up a small altar, usually on the floor or ground. The altar consists of several small lamps, some sweets (usually *laddu*s, made of sugar, ghee, and chickpea flour), and maybe a few rupees. After a brief prayer in praise of Haider Shaykh, musicians play a devotional song. There is always a

FIGURE 5.10. A pilgrim going into possession at the tomb.

FIGURE 5.11. A *chela* at the tomb.

drummer (usually playing the large two sided drum called a *dhol*, or the smaller *dholak*). Sometimes also an *ektar* or *dotar* (one- or two-stringed bowed instrument) player is involved, and those gathered may also play small cymbals or other drums. After this first song, one of the congregation comes forward and bows to the altar. Depending on the size of the group this may be the principle

FIGURE 5.12. A *chela* with her entourage and a head scarf printed with "jai mata di, victory to the mother."

chela or possibly a senior disciple who also experiences possession by Haider Shaykh. If Haider Shaykh is so inclined and the *chela* is a fit vehicle, the invocation is successful, and the *chaunki* begins. The spirit of the saint is present (*parvesh*).

The presence of Haider Shaykh is signaled in a number of ways, most typically by head rolling of varying degrees of intensity accompanied by music, usually a drum. The head rolling ranges from slight nodding to whirling the entire torso. Most *chela*s have long hair, both men and women, making this an especially dramatic feature (see fig. 5.13). This practice appears to be long established at Haider Shaykh, as it is recorded in Denzil Ibbetson's 1883 ethnographic account of practices at the shrine: "At first the woman sits silent with her head lowered and then begins to roll her head with hair disheveled."[51] After some period of head rotation the *chela* stops, and so does the music. The *chela* speaks, first calling down praise on Haider Shaykh, inspiring responses from the

FIGURE 5.13. A *chela* with entourage and audience.

gathering of *jay Babaji*—victory to Haider Shaykh—from the gathering. The music resumes, and the head rolling begins again as well, usually for a shorter period. The *chela* stops, the music stops, and the question-and-answer period (*puch-batan*) commences. The *chela* usually asks what the assembly's concerns are. He or she inquires who has come with, for example, fertility issues (literally "child work," *bacche ka kam*) or job-related issues or health problems. Some audience members will rise in response, and one will be selected. The music resumes, and the *chela*'s head rolls. Then the music stops and the *chela* addresses the petitioner both telling about their situation and asking questions from the supplicant. The situation is slowly clarified, sometimes with alternating rounds of music accompanied trance and questioning until all are satisfied that the problem has been discovered and an appropriate remedy prescribed. The source of a problem, such as childlessness, may be any one of multiple causes, black magic and curses, failure to properly propitiate the Shaykh or some other divinity, bad personal habits, or negative relations. Remedies may involve prayer to Haider Shaykh, attendance at least once a year at the *dargah*, offerings of a certain kind (such as goats or a particular kind or amount of a grain or pulse), giving an amount of money, forsaking meat and alcohol, and so on. Once discussion of one person's problem has come to a close, the *chela* reenters the trance briefly and then inquires for the next person to present his or her problem. This goes on until the saint's spirit leaves. Sometimes these sessions end when a *chela* announces that the spirit has left. Other times Haider Shaykh's departure becomes apparent when a *chela* makes repeated assertions that the supplicant says are incorrect. Some *puch-batan* sessions last hours, others just a few minutes. In some cases, an uncontrolled trance indicates that the *chela* is not yet spiritually prepared to be "played" by the saint. On festival nights when there are many simultaneous gatherings, pilgrims roam the streets, going from one to another seeking true *chelas* and powerful *chaunkis* in the spiritual marketplace of Haider Shaykh's *wilayat*.

In addition to physical and material markers such as carrying iron rods, wearing garlands, traveling with an entourage, the *chelas* also authenticate their claims to represent the shaykh and their ability to mediate the needs of the devotees through their testimonials of how and when the shaykh first took hold of them. The formal and substantial features of these narratives reveal a relatively consistent pattern. Most *chelas* describe having been in a difficult circumstance from which increased faith or supplication to Haider Shaykh saved them, after which the lines of communication remained open. Some had been possessed by evil spirits. Others were lost in more human ways, drinking, acting violently, impoverished, or marginalized. One *chela* even claimed that he had been a "terrorist" with the Sikh separatist movement that ravaged Punjab through the 1980s and early 1990s until Haider Shaykh changed him. Some *chelas* report that their forebears—mother, father, grandfather, or others—had also been "played" by the shaykh. In a fairly typical narrative of his first experience of possession, Mahesh, the 62-year-old Hindu *chela* who called himself "president" of his group, explained that his first possession occurred 26 years previously (see fig. 5.14). His father had also been a vehicle for Haider Shaykh but had not instructed his son in this practice. In Mahesh's view, the ability to communicate directly with the shaykh is not something one can learn, rather it is an experience for which one can only prepare and then invite the saint. Somewhat parallel to the notion of divine grace, the saint visits whom he wills, invited or not. Mahesh recounted his own experience thus:

> I was at my brother-in-law's wedding, and the spirit of a woman had been coming into their house. My wife had had two mothers, one real and one stepmother. It was the spirit of the stepmother that was coming. They said to me, "We will show her to you, just say 'Namaste,' nothing else." Then they asked me to light *chiraghs* [oil lamps], but the spirit told me to blow them out. I slapped her, and I held on to her, and then she entered my body. She tortured me for two years until through the increasing power and blessing of Babaji she left me.

Mahesh was vulnerable to this possession by the dissatisfied spirit of his wife's stepmother because, he explained later in the interview, he had been drinking alcohol at the wedding festivities. After two years of suffering he began to attend more closely to Haider Shaykh. Through his superior spiritual strength and his mercy, the shaykh liberated Mahesh, who thereafter was able to communicate

FIGURE 5.14. The "president" *chela*.

with the shaykh at will. I asked how often he experienced the presence of Haider
Shaykh within him, and he replied, "I have never counted. He comes only when
I call. Suppose someone comes here and asked something from me while I am
talking to you. I can ask him. His spirit is in me all the time." Mahesh also
explained that although he could communicate directly with Haider Shaykh,
still he sought guidance from a guru to cultivate his ability appropriately.

The *chela*s and their followers tend to have very fluid notions of religious
identity. The vast majority of *chela*s at Haider Shaykh's tomb are Sikh and
Hindu. Their inclusive spiritual view becomes evident in the language they
use to describe their connection to Haider Shaykh. They mix traditions and
languages, stories and practices. They also insist that the absence of unitary or
exclusivist religious identities is one reason why they attend this particular tomb
of the Muslim saint they call *"hamare sanjhe pir,"* our shared saint. Furthermore, this nonsectarian cult actualizes its idealization of the true nature of
religion. For example, Mahesh used language that flows from one religious
idiom to another as he explained how his guru (typically a Hindu or Sikh term
for a teacher) initiated him into the tradition of the shaykh:

> MAHESH: We met at a *diwan* [gathering]. I expressed my desire [for
> initiation], and he said, "Okay, I will be your guru."
>
> AB: What type of instruction did you get from him?
>
> MAHESH: A way to remember the *pir* as we remember God. This is our
> *'ibadat* [devotional practice].
>
> AB: Do you have some *japa* [repetitive formula] or mantra?
>
> MAHESH: Yes, it is *japa*, or in *pir's* language it is *kalam*. In Hinduism it is
> called mantra.
>
> AB: How do you teach your disciples?
>
> MAHESH: There is no training. We say, "Just serve the *pir*, do the *japa*
> and cleave your heart to his heart."

This dialogue is an excellent example of a self-identified Hindu devotee of a
Muslim saint discursively integrating the two religions in terms that are authentic to each tradition. Having met at a *diwan* (a Persian-derived term for an
audience), the *chela* acquires a guru. The title of guru is a common Hindu and
Sikh term for a religious teacher. His guru teaches him *'ibadat*, an Islamic term
for devotional practices and habits. In my response I mistakenly assumed from
his Hindu name and use of the term "guru" that I should use a Hindu term for
recitation practices—*japa*—but Mahesh gently corrected me, explaining that in
"*pir's* language," it is *kalam*—an Arabic term for theology which in South Asian
usage usually means any Islamic writings, including devotional poetry. Finally,

in describing the discipline of *pir* worship Mahesh switched back to use the term *japa* rather than his previous insistence on *kalam* or the more specifically Islamic term for repetitive remembrance—*zikr*. This switch could imply at least two things. First it may reveal his concern to be comprehensible to me in the language and terms that I had first employed. This is the mark of an effective teacher who seeks to meet students at their level. Second it indicates that Mahesh himself regarded the concepts of *japa* and *kalam* to be more or less interchangeable means of denoting the devotional remembrance of a divine being. The discursive integration in this dialogue shows the fluidity with which Mahesh switched between the various words, practices, and beliefs appropriate to this particular religious context. The discussion also illustrates a cultural and spiritual milieu in which vocabularies linked to distinct political and religious genealogies have come to augment each other without conflict. For Mahesh the multiple terminologies enriched his meaning and gave more expansive resonance to his narrative.

In another example, Keshav, a *chela* from Sirsa, and his disciples refused altogether to take on singular religious identities. He claimed to be both Hindu and Muslim, validating this practice by saying that all are equal in the eyes of Haider Shaykh whom he described as his "guru."

AB: You are Hindu, but the Baba is Muslim?

KESHAV: I am also Muslim.

AB: Please explain . . .

KESHAV: I am explaining: he is Muslim, so I am also Muslim. If he is Hindu I am also Hindu.

AB: Then there is no difference?

KESHAV: *I* do not have any problem.

AB: So there is no difference between Hindu and Muslim religions?

KESHAV: They all are Hindu who are bowing their heads.

AB: Do they follow different rituals?

KESHAV: No.

AB: People of all religions come, but do they hold different views?

KESHAV: No.

FOLLOWER: It is like, whichever religion our hearts follow, we follow that. We see which religion has good things, and we adopt the good things of that religion. We are not concerned with whether the religion is Hindu or Muslim, we are concerned with humanity only. In whichever religion we see good points, we follow that. We find power in this *pir* so we come.

KESHAV: I also take food from Muslim houses, from Hindu houses I
take. I do not think whether he is a Muslim, Hindu, sweeper or leath-
erworker. In my guru's eyes [i.e., in the eyes of Haider Shaykh] all are
equal, so I feel this way also.

Keshav, his disciple, and many others I encountered refused to reduce their
religious beliefs, practices, and identities to a single label. The disciple did this
by explaining that religion is a matter of the heart and humanity and that "good
things" should be adopted, no matter what the sources. Keshav reinforced his
lack of distinction in relation to the shaykh by asserting that he took food from
anyone, commensality being a major indicator of the nature of interreligious
relations (or the degree of orthodoxy of those involved). Thus when Keshav says
he eats anywhere, he was also insisting that caste, ethnic, and religious distinctions do not have any ultimate meaning.

Other forms of ritualized integration also take place at the *dargah*. In addition to the possession of non-Muslims by a Muslim saint, other, more general
practices are integrated. Hindu and Sikh devotees often employ a Muslim style
of prayer, holding their hands before their faces in the typical posture of *dua'* or
supplicatory prayer. Many Sikh devotees perform service *(seva)* at the tomb,
mopping, sweeping, and cleaning it after festivals (see fig. 5.15). Though non-
Sikhs do this too, *seva* is a particularly important feature of the Sikh faith that
typifies the Sikh ethic of work as pious practice. Many Sikh groups also sponsor
langar, or communal kitchens, to feed the pilgrims—a tradition established by
the founding gurus (fig. 5.16). Such practices resonate with Sikh devotional
idioms, integrating their habits of faith into a Muslim religious space.

Within the context of the *mela*, each *chela* and his or her *chaunki* function as
miniature spiritual territories. Indeed, when posed the question of how multiple, concurrent *chaunki*s were possible—How could the spirit of a single saint be
simultaneously present in so many individuals?—the typical response was that
the spirit of Haider Shaykh is uncontainable. The shaykh surmounts this metaphysical challenge because his soul is not subject to the types of limitations
pertaining to the normal dead. One *chela* clarified this possibility by describing
the Shaykh's spirit as being like the wind: it is everywhere and nowhere at once.
*Chaunki*s taking place in the streets or in public were open to constant evalua-
tion on the part of the assembled witnesses and participants. It is a free market of
*chela*s, *chaunki*s, and devotees. Thus, the authority of the *chela*s is established in
large measure by the pilgrims' choices—that is, the devotees validate the authenticity of a *chela* and their status as competent communicators on behalf of the
shaykh and his devotees. The community of the saint signifies their recognition
of the authenticity of the *khalifah*s and *mujawwar*s by ritually, verbally, mone-
tarily, and physically engaging them. Without this crucial acknowledgment of
their authority, neither the hereditary nor the elective regulatory authorities
would have an audience.

FIGURE 5.15. A Sikh group does *seva* by cleaning the tomb after a *mela*.

Ritualizing Pluralism

Although the *khalifah*s and *chela*s work to some extent in separate spheres, there is ample potential for conflict over the distribution of resources and the boundaries of their arenas of authority. Indeed there is considerable overlap in terms of clientele, services provided, and even the location of their practices. However,

FIGURE 5.16. A group of pilgrims set up a tent for *langar*.

as noted above, rather than accentuate or manipulate these points of difference, the *khalifah*s and *chela*s seek ways to acknowledge—tacitly and overtly—each other's authority. This validation and the struggle not just to find but to create common ground is vividly illustrated by a conversation between Zulfikar, who is related to the nawab and *khalifah* families by blood and marriage and the Hindu *chela* Mahesh. The group associated with Mahesh had come to Haider Shaykh's *mela*s for many years and stayed on the grounds of Zulfikar's ice factory. There was an easy camaraderie between the descendant of the saint and the Hindu devotees who hold their *chaunki* (which Zulfikar does not attend) on his property. During a conversation between Zulfikar, Mahesh, and me, I broached the subject of apparent contradictions between Hindu and Muslim rituals and beliefs. In this context, Zulfikar broke into an extended story wherein he described an experience in which Haider Shaykh summoned him and his teacher to a conversation. He began by situating the events shortly after his return from Hajj. He was sitting with Hafizji, whose description of *ziyarat* etiquette was given above. Then a mystical invitation came from an unknown visitor to an audience with Haider Shaykh, whom he referenced by his entire name—Shaykh Sadruddin Sadri Jahan. During the interview with the saint many subjects were discussed, and Zulfikar took the opportunity to pose the question of interreligious differences and how they should be managed and understood. In particular, his question pertained to the issue most often criticized about *ziyarat* from within the Muslim community: the common belief that the saint himself is fulfilling the wishes of those who come to demand things from him. Zulfikar posed the problem thus:

> Once I was sitting in my house with Hafizji after I came back from the Hajj. An unknown person came and said, "Baba Shaykh Sadruddin Sadri Jahan is calling you." So a conversation began. The matter is long, but that which is relevant to what we are talking about is that I asked him, "Hazrat, people come here, they come for a wish. They come for a boy child, some say our business is not going well. But it is written in our book that whatever you ask, ask it from God only. But thousands of people come and ask from you. So what is the order for us, and what are the orders for them?" And so he [i.e., Haider Shaykh] responded, "This is the secret of God." He said, "Let them do their work, and you do yours." He didn't say you are right or they are right, he said these are the secrets of God. I asked, "What are those secrets?" And he said, "That only God knows." And he also said that "Whoever commits an error commits it for themselves. This is God's secret. What secret is there, He knows. He alone knows. Those whom He calls go there, and whom he does not call, will not go there. He will go there. You keep doing things your way, and they will do theirs."

Mahesh listened intently to this account, nodding and muttering affirmations to show his agreement with and deference to Zulfikar's tale. He then responded, reinforcing the special status of Haider Shaykh's descendants. He also drew several distinctions between the practices of Hindus and Muslims at the shrine. He said,

> This is a routine thing. You people go there and prostrate. You can always meet him; he will meet you. You don't have to bow your head, because he is your elder. We do his *seva*. We ask for things, you don't ask for things. We ask for things. You [merely] come and bow, [and] he will meet you. If we come he won't meet us.

This personal encounter simultaneously established Zulfikar's authority and authorized the beliefs and practices of Mahesh and his followers. It also emphasized that proper conduct in relation to Haider Shaykh, which is not universal but particular to the identity of the believer.

Having left judgment over these contradictory practices and conceptions up to God, Zulfikar established his own authority and simultaneously legitimated the beliefs and practices of the Hindu devotee. Furthermore, he asserted his credentials as an orthodox Muslim by prefacing his account with the statement that the interview occurred when he had just returned from Hajj. Finally, he concluded his narrative with Haider Shaykh's declamation "Let them do their work, and you do yours." This phrasing echoes the well known 109th *Surat al-Kafirun* of the Qur'an, which ends "to you be your religion, and to me, mine." Thus, by directly addressing the difference between Muslim, Hindu, and Sikh ritual practices, Zulfikar received a carefully worded reply asserting that Allah alone knows best why he created people to believe and act in a variety of ways. For his part, Mahesh acknowledged that Zulfikar as a descendant of the saint was able to meet the saint personally, while he and those with him had to negotiate a different sort of relationship with Haider Shaykh. This includes different rules for behavior. For example, the *chela* noted that Hindu and Sikh devotees are often instructed by Haider Shaykh during *chaunki*s to abjure the consumption of meat. Yet the Muslim descendants do eat meat, which the *chela* regarded as a special dispensation. Furthermore, some Muslims will not prostrate before the tomb, believing this practice to be akin to idolatry. Conscious of this, Mahesh referenced such divergent behavioral patterns but placed them in a category of ritual that does not require exclusive adherence to establish validity. This encounter reflected the multivocal quality of the *dargah* in which ritual variance is promoted rather than contested or prohibited. It also demonstrates that given conditions of support from both groups of religious authorities, the potentially divisive factor of a diverse religious tradition is neutralized by the leaders and validated by the constituency.

Although events like the *'urs* represent a time when the Islamic character of the saint and the shrine come to the fore, the Muslim caretakers of the shrines more often must mediate the devotions of Hindus and Sikhs. Furthermore, they do so in full consciousness of their conflicting ideas about the nature of the saint. The guardians of the shrines are well aware that in the minds of non-Muslims, prayers made to the saint are *fulfilled by the saint himself*, and not by Allah through the saint's intercession. Yet they find ways to validate these practices. The *chela*s who channel the shaykh know that the *khalifah*s and the Muslims present understand the nature of the holy dead wholly differently. Yet they operate within their own ritual idiom without changing or challenging oppositional perspectives. By marking out the space of the saint through appropriate ritual practice, pilgrims transact between these two systems of spiritual authority, validating both and creating a space that affirms the prevailing ethic of harmony.

All of the processes of exchange outlined above—dialogue, ritual interactions, mutual perceptions—enable the peaceful governance of the shrine by the authorities and the community of the saint. Both the authorities and the communities that attend regulate the appropriate conduct in the shrine through verbal directions, physical encounters, visual and expressive cues, stories, and testimonials. In this way, people attempting to wear shoes into the inner tomb space may be stopped by a *khalifah*, a *mujawwar*, a *sevadar*, or another devotee. They may notice the gaffe themselves and self-correct, or they may hear a more direct, but face-saving, corrective in the form of a story about what happened to someone who did as they did in the past. Individual pilgrims may exercise various choices in their ritual and interpersonal engagements to either maximize or minimize the possibility of interreligious exchange. The absence of a highly structured ritual process promotes ritual variation.

The potential contestation over arenas of authority of the *khalifah*s and *chela*s must be carefully managed. This management and mitigation are crucial as these dueling spaces could potentially provoke clashes between the Muslim owner-caretaker *khalifah*s and the Sikh and Hindu itinerant *chela*s. The proper functioning of this authenticating system is crucial on two levels. First, as sociologist Ron Hassner has suggested, the absence of a clear hierocratic authority at a shared sacred space is generally understood to be an exacerbating factor in terms of the tension between multiple interest groups.[52] Thus, without mutually intelligible modes of establishing their authority, the roles and purview of the various parties becomes negatively ambiguous, opening ground for contestation. Second, for many constituents, pilgrimage to the site is incomplete and ineffective if contact with certain authorities such as a *khalifah* or *chela* does not occur. Thus the absence of a single hierocratic authority at the shrine based on lineage, descent, authentic relations with the saint, or any other quality opens the regulation of the *dargah* to multiple potential contestations. Lacking a unitary narrative, ritual engagement, spatial choreography, or administrative

monopoly, the terms of engagement at the *dargah* are constantly under negotiation. Significantly, this ongoing process of negotiation—though competitive,
fragmentary, and emergent—is peaceful.[53] No significant court cases involving
the tomb's management have ever been filed, few individuals have ever been
barred from attending the shrine, and criticism concerning the regulation of the
dargah is rarely antagonistic. In this instance the competition between *chelas*
and *khalifah*s does not become antagonistic contestation. Rather, the two ritual
systems exist side by side, with devotees transacting uninhibited between them.
Furthermore, both parties tend to seek ways to validate each other, even though
they may not participate in, support, or agree with one another's perspectives or
ritual practices.

The *dargah* has also been an important locus for the display and authenti-
cation of worldly authority. State-sponsored community rituals are common at
the tomb of Haider Shaykh. Prior to Partition, at every coronation, before every
royal wedding, prior to going to battle, at 'Id al-Fitr, Baqr 'Id, and at the *'urs*, the
nawab would visit the *dargah*. In his description of the shrine of his ancestor, the
last nawab Iftikhar Ali Khan describes the site's role in important state events,
his patronage of the shrine, and the overwhelming popularity and importance of
the *dargah* to the general population. Although he acknowledges, and even
defends, the healing powers of the Shaykh's *dargah*, there is no litany of miracles
in the nawab's account. He affirms the power and efficacy of the shrine, the
veracity of miracles, and the obvious and overwhelming faith of the people, but
the significance of the shrine to the rulers as a locus of state ceremony and as a
multi-confessional site is emphasized:

> Utmost reverence is paid to the shrine of their ancestor by the Rulers
> of the State. On the occasion of accession to the throne or on the
> celebration of the two *'Ids*, offerings of horses, robes and money are
> made at the tomb on behalf of the State. Many a time the grave is
> resorted to in cases of personal differences when an oath as to truth
> or falsity of a case is to be taken. As to the extent to which the
> general public irrespective of their religion, impose a faith in the
> supernatural powers of the shrine, it is sufficient here to say that in
> month of *no-chandi* a large fair is held and the streets of Malerkotla
> are thronged with thousands of men, women and children who
> assemble and celebrate the day. Offerings of such varied nature as
> corn, cereal, sweets, rice, cloth and goats are generally made and not
> infrequently wishes are held in minds when offerings are made at
> the grave.[54]

This passage encompasses a wide range of the shrine's usage by the rulers, the
citizenry, and the devotees. Clearly state visits to the shrine acknowledged the
most significant religious events such as 'Id al-Fitr and Baqr 'Id, and the most

significant secular events such as accession to the throne.[55] Older Malerkotla residents reported that prior to departing for duty in World Wars I and II, the state army as a body filed through the *dargah* to receive Haider Shaykh's blessings before going to war. According to at least one resident, because of this blessing, "Even during the First World War and Second World War there was no personal loss in Malerkotla." This reaffirms the authority of Haider Shaykh's *wilayat* (spiritual territory) over the worldly territory, and acknowledges his role as a worldly as well as a spiritual master of Malerkotla. The authority and importance of Haider Shaykh's *dargah* was also reinforced by its role as an arbiter or honest broker in the resolution of disputes. The state, through its sponsorship of the shrine, drew authority from regular acknowledgments of the intimate link between the saint and the rulers and cultivating, by extension, the continued loyalty of the saint's devotees, who, significantly, were Hindu and Sikh as well as Muslim.[56]

After the dissolution of the princely state, the shrine continues to have a prominent role for local and regional leaders. Not only do the elected representatives from Malerkotla, many of whom share the saint's bloodline, made high-profile visits to the tomb, but so also do politicians from around the state, including the previous chief minister Captain Amrinder Singh; the present chief minister Prakash Singh Badal; and the past governor, Lieutenant General J. F. R. Jacob. Such visits both acknowledge and attempt to garner the power of the shrine as a place of universal appeal. Here the organizational force of the state and the saint become manifest to the local population. Richard Eaton describes the medieval *dargah* in relation to the constituent communities as a "mini-theater state."[57] He writes, "the shrine provided the tribes with a tiny 'theater-state' of their own; that is, it displayed throughout the ceremonies and celebrations that marked its liturgical calendar the pageantry of both the court of God and the court of Delhi, albeit on a microcosmic scale."[58] The modern *dargah* functions as a theater-state of a somewhat different order where the organizational force of the saint and the organizational force of the multiple functionaries necessary to maintain his accessibility become manifest—a theater-bureaucracy, if you will.[59]

Conclusion

Sikhs, Muslims, and Hindus all attend Haider Shaykh's tomb shrine. It is one of the most popular such sites in Indian Punjab with estimates of a hundred thousand pilgrims at the June fair. There are shared places like this throughout the region and indeed throughout India, and it is clear that the mere existence of such sites does not in itself preclude or prevent violence. Yet because saints' tombs are often beloved by those who reject unitary religious identities and loyalties, they are important indices of the quality of interreligious relations in a given locale. We have seen that elements in all three major religions target shrine worship for criticism. Places where religious militancy has been ascendant in India have seen attacks on shared sites, such as the destruction of the Babri Masjid in 1992 by Hindu extremists and that of the tomb of Wali Gujarati in the Gujarat riots of 2002. Because the opportunity for substantive interreligious interaction at shared shrines is rare in Punjab, the nature of the relationship between Sikhs, Muslims, and Hindus at Haider Shaykh's *dargah* is an important indicator of the quality and degree of relations among groups in the town.[60]

Furthermore, as a site that inverts the daily experience of most Punjabis in terms of the Muslim population in their home communities, Haider Shaykh's *dargah* is a spatial expression of the days before Partition and the idealized culture associated with pre-1947 Punjab. In the generations since, it seems that the numbers of pilgrims have only increased. As one member of the *khalifah* family who does not attend the shrine himself described, "There is a lot of difference between the *melas* of those days and the *melas* of today. There used be a lot of gathering in those days, but these days there is even more of a crowd. More of the public are coming these days. These days the offerings are greater" (see fig. 5.17). Thus the appeal and wealth of Haider Shaykh's *dargah* has grown since Partition. It is clear from the statements from devotees and *khalifah*s that this increased popularity is in part ascribable to its emblematic status as an "authentic" Muslim shrine with a living lineage of *khalifah*s. But the appeal is also because of the reputation of Malerkotla as a community much like it was in the days when Punjab was whole. For many, this is a precious, unique, and even sacred experience.

FIGURE 5.17. The crowded street outside the *dargah* during a *mela*.

Shared sacred spaces and their implications for interreligious relations become meaningful through repeated engagements within their confines and repeated accounts of their significance in and out of the shrines. Furthermore, the maximum effect is achieved when the community recognizes the site as representative of its own core values, as constitutive of those values, and as central to the collective identity. The site must resonate at the same frequency as its environs. The *dargah* of Haider Shaykh is meaningful to the people of Malerkotla because Haider Shaykh is believed to both represent and protect the ethos of communal harmony that is so integral to Malerkotla's moral character. These beliefs and the experiences that sustain these beliefs, especially the guru's blessing and the peace at Partition, are consolidated in the collective imagination through memorializing practices. Both before and after Partition Malerkotla's history and social memory have been ritualized and rooted in particular places (the *dargah*, the nawab's grave), occasions ('Id celebrations, the festivals for Haider Shaykh), and actions (pilgrimage, storytelling). These commemorative activities generate a community of memory and a ritualized pattern of harmony, regularly reestablishing and revitalizing the resources of the past to serve the interests of the present. At the *dargah* these interests are overtly devotional and personal, with a sometimes unrecognized but nonetheless effective social and political dimension that promotes religious coexistence. As we shall see in the next chapter, ritual evocations of the collective identity of peaceful pluralism in venues outside the *dargah* tend to reveal more overt social and political interests with a covert devotional and personal dimension.

Practicing Pluralism: Getting Along in Malerkotla

Our forefathers lived together, Hindu, Muslim, and Sikh. In 1947 Muslims from here did not migrate and lived here in harmony. If some small quarrels occur, later on everyone comes together. But the nature [of people] is that they easily go on the same way as before, the way of love and harmony.

—Abdullah, Malerkotla resident

W HAT sets Malerkotla apart is that in the face of potential triggering incidents—such as the unexplained death of a cow, communal riots elsewhere in India, war with neighboring Pakistan—equilibrium is quickly restored. This is the result of a great deal of work, some coordinated and deliberate, some internalized and unconscious. The work involves the repetition of identity marking features of Malerkotla's past such as the *haah da naara*, Haider Shaykh's protective powers, and the peace at Partition as part of the commemorative practices of the community that help to define the town's enduring ethos and establish the frame through which collective experiences are interpreted. Commemoration, or the making of memories—in this case collective memories—is a key element in the production of Malerkotla's tension-wisdom. This is consistent with Edward Casey's assertion that "commemoration can be considered the laying to account of perishings, the consolidating and continuing of endings. It is the creating of memorializations in the media of ritual, text, and psyche; it enables us to honor the past by carrying it intact into new and lasting forms of alliance and participation."[1] Both before and after Partition, Malerkotla's leaders and citizens have created ways to memorialize the past by emphasizing the cooperative and minimizing the conflictual. In particular, they emphasize those events that maximize the ability of all residents to identify with their collective past, such as Haider Shaykh, the guru's blessing, and the peace at

Partition. These events dominate the imaginative landscape of the community and unsurprisingly emerge as central motifs in most public affairs, particularly major religious festivals and other ceremonies involving large public gatherings.

Commemorations of the past such as the two Muslim 'Id festivals, the martyrdom observations of the Namdhari Sikhs, Independence Day, and other religious and secular holidays serve several functions. Ritual memorials are of two general types: celebration and mourning. Celebratory memorials evoke positive histories, aggregating and concentrating the values represented by those events that a community seeks to retain, reinvigorate, and perpetuate. Mourning memorials remember and reconcile past traumas, thereby maintaining memories that remind those in the present of past sacrifices, heroisms, and tribulations. Over time certain memorializations come into being and others may fall away, revealing the shifting needs and central themes of a community's process of self-identification. In the case of traumatic events, effective memorialization may contribute to the community's healing. The failure to account for past trauma to deny, repress, or reject the events may have pathological results. Sociologists Alexander and Margarete Mitsherlich term this the *inability to mourn*, and it results in a population pathologically fixated on the trauma.[2] In India, and perhaps especially in Punjab, commemorating Partition has been difficult. There are no public observations, no days of remembrance as there are for other disastrous events.[3] On the contrary, the horrors of Partition are wholly subsumed by the nationalistic pride invoked through state-sponsored Independence Day festivals. As Gyan Pandey has pointed out, the violence and trauma of Partition is erased and sublimated in the process of making of the Indian nation-state. Partition's devastation is aestheticized by the state and becomes independence: clean, free, and noble. Although "Partition *was* violence, a cataclysm, a world (or worlds) torn apart," it is treated as an unfortunate but necessary byproduct of the concomitant realization of independence, which is cast as the culmination of the historical metanarrative of India.[4] But Partition's violence must be accounted for; it cannot disappear as so many of its victims did. As Pandey argues, the legacy of the violence is very much present, even if often displaced from within a community, in the boundaries of belonging that define the community on local, regional, and national levels.[5]

In Malerkotla, this process is present, but it is also inverted as people must also account for the *non*event of violence in the town. The obvious pride in the town's emergence relatively unscathed from the horrors is tempered by residents' awareness of the violence and death that surrounded them, and their vulnerability and exposure as the sole Muslim community afterward. Therefore pride, guilt, fear, and hope intermingle in the emotions swirling around Partition's local legacy. Repeated ritualistic invocations of community pride in the way Partition did *not* happen relieves their sense of vulnerability through public demonstrations of their pacific past. The evocation of Partition memories in Malerkotla justifies, validates, and assimilates the Muslim principality into the

Indian polity through an idealized representation of the community as a model of successful interreligious integration past and present. This chapter will describe the diversity of Malerkotla's population and show how the collective ethos of peaceful pluralism is produced and perpetuated through a ritualized peace system that effectively manages conflict and stress when it does occur. The microstrategies of peace building employed by residents to handle these challenges are effective because the majority of residents see themselves as stakeholders in maintaining the essential goodwill. This process of conflict management is particularly evident when events or individuals challenge the collective authority of peaceful coexistence.

There are numerous examples of autochthonous strategies for mitigating interreligious tension in Malerkotla. But what makes these peace-building strategies effective? As in many towns, there is an ad hoc Peace Committee made up of local civic and religious leaders that is convened by the SDM at times of stress. In some places these are very effective groups, in other places they are marginalized by the civil service officials or simply regarded as useless figureheads. How is it that in Malerkotla groups such as the Peace Committee are able to work with each other and that their work is seen as legitimate and necessary by the larger community that validates their activities? It is not simply a matter of well-integrated civil societal associations or an absence of political and economic competition. The efficacy of the Peace Committee and the integrations of associations are made possible by the underlying quality of collective life in Malerkotla, as we have seen in relation to the *dargah* and the cult of Haider Shaykh. This chapter elucidates the microstrategies of peacemaking that undergird the macrolevel organizations. Central to the efficacy of local efforts at peaceful coexistence are community efforts to establish a shared idiom of pluralism and piety through memorialization practices. These memorializations are efforts to carry forward significant events and individuals from the past, and they center most especially on the multiple local explanations for the prevailing peace. So the person of Haider Shaykh, his legacy in Malerkotla, the *haah da naara*, and the peace at Partition have everything to do with the success of tried and true techniques of conflict management such as the establishment of a Peace Committee. The collective identity of Malerkotla as a place of interreligious harmony emerges from a diverse population in a variety of contexts.

Although Malerkotla has been a Muslim-dominated principality since approximately 1454, only in the post-Partition period did it become Muslim majority as Muslims from the surrounding areas moved toward the urban center. This means that ethnic and religious diversity has long been a part of life in Malerkotla. As we have seen in the preceding chapters, this situation has not always been handled with grace. But especially since Partition, Malerkotla has managed the inevitable stresses of group life extremely well and recovered equilibrium rapidly after undergoing shocks to the system. The local religious and ethnic diversity in Malerkotla makes up an economically and politically complex society in which competition for opportunity is high. Yet these groups interact locally in a wide variety of contexts ranging from the political to the social to the religious to the personal. Taken together, these multilayered relationships make the community highly resilient in times of stress. Furthermore, the Peace Committee and other established organizations swing into action, marshaling community leaders and reassuring citizens. Termed the "institutionalized peace system," by Ashutosh Varshney, the techniques of conflict management are not only institutionalized in Malerkotla, but also are ritualized. The ritualized peace system mobilizes the power of symbolic moments in Malerkotla's idealized past to promote the ethos of pluralism and harmony in the citizenry of today.[6] Reinforced through ritualized peace practices in times of stress as well as calm, Malerkotlans seem to have produced sufficient strategies of peace building at the grass-roots level to withstand the inevitable shocks to the system. Sustained by community leaders, available in the shared myths of Malerkotla's pacific past, and realized in the shrines and streets of the town, the collective ethos of peaceful pluralism is built on a structure with multiple stable foundations. Thus far this structure of peace has withstood challenges from within and without, earning Malerkotla its wide reputation as an "oasis of tolerance."

Communal Conflict: Religion, Caste, Ethnicity, and Economy

A common approach to communal conflict in South Asia treats tension or violence as not "really" religious but as misidentified or misappropriated struggles for economic and political resources. This approach presumes that where economic and electoral competition are fierce, sectarian conflict will be more likely to occur. One might expect Muslim dominance in Malerkotla's economic arena as in the political, but this is not the case. In Malerkotla, as elsewhere in India, fewer Muslims than Hindus and Sikhs are large-scale industrialists, farmers, and professionals. Although proportionally their percentages are higher in Malerkotla than in non-Muslim majority regions, the competition between communities is significant. Of the three large spinning mills in town, two are Hindu owned. Most of the metal shops and iron businesses are Muslim owned and operated. Sikhs, Hindus, and Jains run the largest and most prestigious schools. The gold and silver market is dominated by Jains, the medical field by Hindus, and agriculture by Sikh Jats and Khamboj Muslims. Potential for competition, even hostility, is significant. After all, Malerkotla is the largest industrial town in District Sangrur, with more than two thousand large and small industries operating locally. In fact the Punjab Revenue Department Web site calls Malerkotla the only industrial town "worth the name in the district."[7] This represents significant development, as prior to 1947 there was little industry locally, just two steel mills, one cotton gin, one ice factory, and three flour mills.[8] Given the post-Partition demography of Punjab, the growth of

Malerkotla is a sign that the state and local government as well as local business-people were interested in investing in the town's industry and economy. Malerkotla was and is known for a number of cottage industries, especially badge making, embroidery work, and iron goods. Malerkotla's badges are sold all over the world and purchased by the Defence Ministry and export companies. This industry alone is worth two million rupees a year (approximately $41,000) to the town, but the Delhi-based dealers who contract with local shops gain most of the profits.[9] The iron goods produced in Malerkotla are also famous. There is a widespread belief that Muslims are better metal workers and artisans than other ethnic groups, so in post-Partition Punjab, this means that people come to Malerkotla to obtain metal wares. During the festivals for Haider Shaykh that draw many thousands of visitors to the town, it is not unusual for the iron-workers from the nearby Loha Bazaar to lay out cooking utensils and containers, knives and other implements to sell near the shrine.

Land revenues are also a major source of income in the state. Late-nineteenth-century settlement and assessment reports show that 80 percent of land holdings in the kingdom were in the possession of Sikh and Hindu *jats*, with the remainder held by Muslim and tribal castes.[10] Nowadays there is a large population of Muslim Khamboj cultivators, but the outlying villages of the former kingdom are primarily Sikh and Hindu. Non-agricultural castes include the ruling Pathans and various *banias* (merchants), mostly Hindu and Jain Aggarwals. The Pathans were principally *zamindars* (landowners) or in some way related to either the nawab or the saint, and derived their livelihood through these connections. At Partition, it was this class of wealthier landlord Muslims who left in the largest numbers for Pakistan. Between out-migration and the post-independence abolition of *zamindari* land rights, the hitherto dominant Pathans experienced a radical shift in numbers and power. In the Patiala and East Punjab States Union (PEPSU) immediately after Partition, two types of landholders were acknowledged: *ala malik* and *adna malik*. The *ala malik* were the "superior owners" such as the ruling clan. *Adna malik*, or "inferior owners" were the tenants and occupants who actually worked the land. In 1954, PEPSU passed the "Abolition of Ala Malikiya Act and the Occupancy of Tenants Act" through which superior ownership was abolished, and the tenants and occupants gained proprietary rights. The Khamboj cultivators were the largest local beneficiaries of this change. Interestingly, upon ascending the throne in 1948, the last nawab of Malerkotla, Iftikhar Ali Khan, gave a speech in which he promised the imminent end of *zamindari* rights. He professed to have investigated the status of the land owned by the state and the land revenue holders *(jagirdars)* and determined that "as a matter of fact the State and Jagirdars have no title to assert this right." He further decreed that

> in the entire interests of the State, the Khawanin [ruling family] and
> Jagirdars will not have the least hesitation in sacrificing something

that will certainly contribute towards sharing greater goodwill of the people so very indispensable for the future interests of the State. I therefore have great pleasure in announcing the termination of this practice from today throughout my State.[11]

Perhaps seeing the writing on the wall, he was acting preemptively (or politically). Whatever the motivation, such reasoning and public declarations may well have contributed to his later electoral popularity.

In the 1960s, the Indian government instituted a series of agricultural reforms and development schemes that came to be known collectively as the Green Revolution. The Green Revolution subsidized fertilizers, machines, and irrigation systems and promoted numerous other initiatives that revolutionized the agricultural output of the Punjabi countryside as elsewhere in India.[12] In combination with the Green Revolution, the abolition of centralized *zamindari* rights in Malerkotla benefited the Khamboj community almost immediately. This class of tenant farmers makes up approximately 40 percent of Malerkotla's Muslim population.[13] Some Khamboj residents chafed under Pathan dominance. Several people I interviewed reported that they and their kinspeople had been prevented from learning to read and write. They claim that they were not allowed to sit in chairs when seeking audience with the nawab or one of the Khan *jagirdars*. They were not allowed to wear white clothes—this was the exclusive privilege of the nawab. Local college professor Anila Sultana, a Malerkotla native who has written several studies on Malerkotla, writes: The Khamboj "are one of the finest cultivating castes in the Punjab. . . . [Khamboj] of Malerkotla were a poor and harassed lot because they were allowed to keep only a fraction of the income of the land."[14] Khamboj and other lower castes were also historically excluded from education and government jobs, but that began to change, first under the last two Nawabs and then more radically after the dissolution of the princely states and the land reforms that took place simultaneously. With the end of *ala malik* property, the Khamboj and other lower-class Muslims, Hindus, and Sikhs became landholders and enjoyed considerable and rapid upward mobility.[15] Through government subsidies and programs they began systems of crop rotation, introduced new fertilizers, and drilled wells for irrigation, dramatically increasing farm production. With their newfound wealth the farmers opened schools, ran for local offices, and took on new civic leadership roles. The Islamiyya High School and the Islamiyya Girls High School were both founded to serve the Khamboj community in particular. Chaudhry Abdul Gaffar was elected to the Legislative Assembly and became education minister during his tenure from 1992 to 1997. Several local factories are operated by Khamboj, such as the Rashid Brothers, manufacturers of sporting equipment.

Class and ethnic diversification is also expanding in the business sector, as many enterprises in Malerkotla are either joint ventures or are highly diverse in their employee structures. For example, one local industry leader whose factories export to countries all over the world calls himself the "most secular man in Malerkotla." A Loha (ironworker) Muslim himself, he employs Hindus and Sikhs among his chief officers, but most of his employees are Muslim (reflecting the local demographics). Nonetheless, for this industrialist, secularism is a great point of pride, and he is a member of several local groups such as the Malerkotla Club, the Chamber of Commerce, and the Rotary Club, all of whose memberships are highly diverse. This local leader's multiple affiliations are in no way unusual. He represents in some ways the norm. As a Muslim he attends a particular mosque next to a Sufi *dargah* at which his brother is the imam. He is a member of the Peace Committee and well respected in the community. Indeed his ability to act effectively on the Peace Committee depends upon his solid reputation as a committed Muslim from a pious family, a wealthy industrialist, and nonsectarian in his personal relationships and business practices.

Civic Groups and Organizations

The multiple organizational affiliations of this factory owner points out the importance of civil societal integration. Social scientists have recently begun to pay more attention to the importance of such associational links both as indicators of integration and as helping to counteract conflict when it does occur. To understand how Malerkotlans negotiate the daily choreography of their interactions in the civic spaces of the town as well as the sacred spaces outlined in the previous chapter, an examination of the main organizations that make up the civil societal sphere is helpful. The dominant ethnic group is the Pathan Afghans from whom the ruling nawabi family and the heirs of Haider Shaykh's lineage are descended. As mentioned, the most populous sector of Muslims are the traditional agriculturalist Khamboj caste. The *Glossary of Tribes and Castes of the Punjab* notes that there are both Hindu and Muslim branches of this caste and that the "Kamboh is one of the finest cultivating castes in the Punjab."[16] The Khamboj and other lower-status ethnic groups have been historically discriminated against in terms of their ability to own land, educational opportunities, and social mobility. There are few Hindus, Sikhs, or Jains of the very high castes in town. As is often observed, the influence of Brahmin Hindus has always been relatively minor in Punjab in general. Hindus and Jains are mostly from mercantile castes, and Sikhs are from the agriculturalist Jat caste.

Muslim Groups and Centers

Malerkotla's Muslims are mostly Sunni. In 1908 Nawab Ahmad Ali Khan established the office of Dar ul-Ifta' and appointed a mufti for the state to supervise matters of religious law.[17] This office has gained a higher profile since 1947 in India, as the mufti of Malerkotla is now effectively the chief legal authority for the Sunni Muslim community of the whole of Punjab. In Malerkotla, he officiates at marriage, divorce, and death ceremonies, gives legal advice and decisions, declares the two 'Ids, manages the government mosques, and provides personal consultation in religious and personal matters. The mufti, Fazlur Rehman Hilal Usmani, obtained his mufti degree from Dar-al-'Ulum, Deoband in Uttar Pradesh, from whence he hails. He came to Malerkotla in 1973 as mufti. Although trained at Deoband, Usmani complicates the stereotype of extreme conservatism often associated with the school. He is a progressive man; all his daughters have sought higher degrees, and he appears on a regional television station to discuss religious issues for a largely non-Muslim audience. He runs the Dar us-Salam Islamic Center, which operates a school and other educational and outreach projects. He has published more than 60 books, including a translation and commentary on the Qur'an, a biography of the Prophet, and, most recently, a volume on Muslim personal law issues relating to marriage, divorce, and inheritance in both Urdu and English. One of his books, *Memaar-e Insaniyat* (The Architect of Humanity), addresses the importance of cultivating a society that fosters mutual tolerance and respect.[18] He serves on the All India Muslim Personal Law Board, one of the few pan-Indian Muslim organizations. On July 27, 2006, in Mumbai he issued an antiterrorism fatwa that unequivocally distinguished between jihad and terrorism: "A jihad secures for people their basic rights while terrorism snatches away these very rights and freedoms from them."[19]

Two of the most prominent conservative national Muslim groups, the Tablighi Jama'at and Jama'at-i Islami, are also active in Malerkotla. Of the two, Tablighi Jama'at is the most vigorous Sunni reformist group in town, as it is throughout South Asia and beyond.[20] This grass-roots movement began its missionary work in 1926 near Delhi under the leadership of a Sufi and scholar, Maulana Muhammad Ilyas (1885–1944). The Tablighi Jama'at is primarily intended to revitalize Islam among Muslims by fostering basic pious practices such as the five-times-daily prayers, mosque attendance for men, and training in basic knowledge such as the pronunciation of the Qur'an or the proper performance of ritual ablutions. In Punjab, especially, there is an additional mission to bring back to Islam those Muslims who became Hindu or Sikh at the time of Partition. Tablighi Jama'at requires members to go on *dawa* (missionary) tours to further their version of orthodox Islamic belief and practice.

The Tablighi Jama'at has had a profound effect on Malerkotla. Many local residents are active members, and the town provides a natural base for visiting *dawa* groups in Punjab to revive Islam in the state. Weekly meetings called *ijtima'* are held by a number of leaders, including several women. At these *ijtima'*, people recite *na'ts* or praise hymns to the Prophet, receive instruction in some basic practice or belief (such as the proper method for the prayer ablutions), ask questions about leading a religious life, testify to changes or miracles wrought by submission to Allah, offer supplicatory prayers (*du'a*) and *namaz*, if it is the appointed time. They also hear a formal exhortation from the leader. Since the time of Partition, Tablighi Jamaʿat and other conservative groups have been increasingly active locally. Their influence is noticeable to locals, who say that because of Tablighi Jamaʿat activism fewer weddings are celebrated in an elaborate fashion, music is performed less often in public, and more women wear some type of veil in public.[21] Music is also criticized, even some forms of devotional music, including *qawwali*. Sultana asserts, "In due course, partially for reasons of compulsion and partially due to conviction created in people's mind by the preachings of the Jamaʿat, the playing of music on marriages etc. has been discontinued since the early eighties."[22] Sultana also claims that the local *qawwali* singers and *mirasan*s (a hereditary group of dancing and singing entertainers) have been effectively shut down in Malerkotla. However, Malerkotla *qawwali* groups are often featured at events throughout Punjab and do perform occasionally at the *dargah* of Haider Shaykh. Furthermore, in my own experience at Muslim weddings in Malerkotla, *mirasan*s did perform at ladies singing nights leading up to the wedding and at the henna ceremony the night before the marriage itself (see fig. 6.1).[23] However, performances by *qawwali*s are indeed rare, and the *mirasan*s principally perform for the Pathan elite of the town, their hereditary patrons.

The Jamaʿat-i Islami's self-proclaimed membership is only about fifteen hundred, and the really active members are far fewer, but its local influence is considerable. The Jamaʿat-i Islami was founded in about 1938 by Maulana Abul ʿala Maududi (1903–1979) to organize the Indian Muslim community and provide a stronger foundation of Islam in the country.[24] Maududi's writings are

FIGURE 6.1. *Mirasans* performing before a wedding in Malerkotla.

extremely popular in South Asia and throughout the Muslim world, and the influence of his thought can hardly be exaggerated. One of Maududi's chief objectives was the establishment of sharia as the law of the land. Maududi opposed the Partition of India, although he moved to Pakistan after 1947 and became committed to Islamizing the constitution and the country. In Pakistan the Jama'at-i Islami became a political party. In India, the Jama'at-i Islami-e Hind stays out of politics, focusing on social service and missionary work. One of the principle activities of the Jama'at-i Islami in Punjab is the reestablishment of mosques lost in the mayhem of Partition and the restoration of Muslims who in the last 50 years either adopted Sikh and Hindu customs or simply became less observant in religious practice to get along in the new order. The leader in Malerkotla during most of my research, Maulana Abdul Rauf (d. 2003), made a point of working with non-Muslims in these efforts. For the establishment of a new mosque, for example, he sought donations, labor, materials, and other support from the entire community. At the ceremonies inaugurating these projects he invited Sikhs and Hindus, as well as Muslims, and used the opportunity to foster greater understanding of Islam.[25] In December 2000 at the celebration of the end of Ramadan, the Jama'at-i Islami, like many other organizations sponsored an 'Id Milan, a celebratory gathering in which various invited guests speak and perform in honor of the festival. Community leaders and political parties all hosted these events, including the Congress Party; the Waqf Board; and the local member of Parliament, Simranjit Singh Mann. Rather than join this parade, the Jama'at-i Islami organized an 'Id Milan in neighboring Nabha to which representatives of all religious communities were invited and gave speeches. Maulana Abdul Rauf dismissed the gatherings sponsored by political parties as mere show, attempts to garner votes or gain local prestige. The Nabha event, by contrast, was deliberately held outside of Malerkotla, he said, as a means of reaching out to non-Muslims and informing a community less familiar with Islam about the meaning of Ramadan.

During times of stress in Malerkotla, the Jama'at-i Islami leaders have been active participants in peace committees and other bridge-building efforts. Indeed, Abdul Rauf professed respect and admiration for the local Rashtriya Swayamsevak Sangh (RSS) leader.[26] The RSS is at the center of the so-called Sangh Parivar, the Hindu-right network. As both the Jama'at-i Islami and the RSS are often regarded as radical organizations, it is significant that in Malerkotla they are not oppositional groups and even work together in some endeavors. Abdul Rauf claimed to have "family relations" with local RSS leaders, and he said he visited Hindu homes for Diwali and such occasions. He extolled the importance of Muslims in Punjab, saying that though they are few in number, Muslims are like salt, you need just a little but without it there is no flavor. Abdul Rauf also declared that loyalty to one's own faith does not necessitate hostility toward any other religion. "Love with one's religion is not a bad thing, but you should not hate the other religion," he said. "As all parents love their children, likewise the religion is also loveable. But you should not have hatred for other religions." The Jama'at-i Islami has a book center next to one of the main gates of Malerkotla that distributes literature, and recently the group sponsored the production of a Punjabi translation of the Qur'an.[27] Maulana Abdul Rauf is also the imam of a small mosque that is one of the only mosques in which there is a space available for women to attend and hear the Friday *khutba* (sermon). The Sunni Jama' Masjid (congregational mosque) is in the center of town not far from the Diwan Khana palace. There are hundreds of mosques throughout the town. Some are connected to Sunni sects like the Ahl-e Hadith, whereas others are dominated by a particular clan or ethnic group. Sunni women, as in South Asia in general, do not attend mosques for prayers. The Jama'at-i Islami mosque is an exception, though most of the women who attend on Fridays are in Maulana Abdul Rauf's own family.

The Shi'a are well established in Malerkotla, thanks in no small part to patronage in the past from the nawabs and their kin. According to community leaders, most local Shi'a belong to the Isna 'Ashari (Twelver) sect. There are approximately twenty-five hundred Shi'a, comprising two groups: the sayyids, who trace their descent from the Prophet Muhammad; and the shaykhs, who descend from Indian converts. The two main Shi'i associations serve each of these populations; the Anjuman Hussaini is associated with the sayyids, and the Anjuman Haideri represents the shaykh community.[28] Many residents report that relations between sayyids and shaykhs are often tenser than those between the Shi'a and Sunni populations. There is one Shi'i Jama' Masjid and five *imambaras*, the shrines of the Shi'a that house *taziyas* (replicas of Imam Hussain's tomb) and are usually attached to mosques. The nawab's family constructed the Shi'i Jama' Masjid and two other *imambaras*. The mother of the second-to-last nawab built one as the fulfillment of a vow she made to Imam Hussain when praying for a son. It is known as either the *Sarkari* (government) or *Riyasati* (royal) *Imambara*. There is also the Imambara Ihsaniyya, constructed by a relative of the nawab, Ihsan Ali Khan. This is directly opposite the Diwan Khana (the public palace of the nawabs). In the late nineteenth century the Khojgan *biraderi* (brotherhood or clan) built an *imambara* with its own resources, independent from the government. The Khojgan are shaykhs and are a very tight knit and active group. Another small *imambara* has recently been put up directly across from Imambara Khojgan and is run by the Anjuman-e Hussaini.

In Malerkotla, though the Shi'a are few in number, during the first ten days of the Muslim month of Muharram they are suddenly ubiquitous. Shi'a from all over the state come here to celebrate Muharram, the memorial observation marking the martyrdom of Hussain, the Prophet Mohammad's grandson, along with 72 of his companions in 680 CE on the battlefield of Karbala by the Umayyad Caliph Yazid. For Shi'a all over the world this event signifies the ultimate sacrifice and victory (even in death) of Hussain for the preservation of true Islam against the oppressive, depraved, and evil Caliph Yazid. The magnitude of the sacrifice of Hussain exceeds all human capacity to acknowledge, but the rites of Muharram are an effort to do so. The rituals continue for several months, but the climax is Muharram. For the first ten days the Shi'i population holds regular *majalis* (sg. *majlis*) or gatherings in private homes and in the *imambaras*. During a *majlis* the group will together recite dirges called *noha* and *marsiya* concerning the various members of Hussain's band of followers and Hussain himself, dwelling on their pitiable state as they lay besieged by Yazid's forces and denied access to water even for the women and children.[29] After a period of recitation, one among the group, or the imam if present, will recount a *hadis*, a story about Imam Hussain or one of the heroes of Karbala. This telling should ideally be imbued with such pathos that it brings the assembly to tears.[30]

The shedding of tears in memory of the martyrs of Karbala is seen as a sign of one's deep sense of indebtedness to Hussain and his household and sorrow for their loss. This debt and anguish is further acknowledged in the custom of *matam*, or self-flagellation, which Shi'i men and women engage in as the emotion of the recited *noha*s and *marsiya*s reaches a crescendo. Most often *matam* consists solely of *hath ka matam*, breast beating with the hand of varying degrees of severity (see fig. 6.2). Indeed to have a visible mark or even to draw blood from the blows is regarded as a badge of honor. For most women and men this is the extent of *matam*. Some men and boys also engage in *matam* involving knives or swords, usually only on the tenth day of Muharram (known as *'ashura*, or the tenth, in the Arab world but simply as Muharram in India), which is the height of the observations marking the day Imam Hussain was killed. There is a procession through the town made up of mourners from all the Shi'i and some from other religious communities. Many Shi'i women take part in the procession, but they walk apart from the men and do not engage in public *matam* or recitations of *noha*s. Various groups carry *taziyas* (replicas of Imam Hussain's tomb) and *'alams* (standards) that have been carefully crafted over the preceding year for this occasion. Some *taziyas* and *'alams* are passed down from generation to generation in a family or congregation. Others are made to be disposable as the entire procession concludes with the interment of several *taziyas* in a special ground, known as Karbala, dedicated for their burial. In Malerkotla the participants recited dirges and engaged in increasingly vigorous *matam* all along the procession route until arriving at an open ground near the Ihsaniyya *imambara* at which the *zinjil ka matam* and *talwar ka matam* took place (see fig. 6.3). A huge crowd watched this as a spectacle from rooftops and around the square. After this the procession proceeded toward Karbala, stopping for an exhortation from an imam about the significance of the day and the importance of publicly demonstrating the magnitude of Hussain's sacrifice on behalf of all Muslims. By the end of the procession, many of the participants were hoarse or even voiceless from their recitations and were bruised or bloody from the *matam*. Yet every single person with whom I spoke at the completion and on the day

FIGURE 6.2. Shi'i women's *majlis* during Muharram.

after—including those who had performed *talwar ka matam*—said they wished they could do more to acknowledge their gratitude to Imam Hussain.

Although the primary participants in the procession are Shi'a, Hindus participate as well, especially young children, for whom carrying a *taziyya* is regarded as an especial blessing (see fig. 6.4). Hindus also take vows before the *taziyas* that are installed throughout the year in the various *imambaras* in town (fig. 6.5).[31] The caretakers of three of the *imambaras* informed me that this was quite common and that Imam Hussain was regarded by Hindus and Muslims alike as extremely effective in granting children to supplicants. At the completion of the procession I observed in Malerkotla in 2001, a Hindu woman left an offering of *khir* (sweet milk rice) at the ground of Karbala to acknowledge a prayer that was fulfilled through the blessing of Imam Hussain. Although many Shi'a fast on this day, others partake of tea and fruit-sweetened water and sometimes *halwa* (a sweet porridge filled with

FIGURE 6.3. *Matam* with knives during a Muharram procession.

nuts and raisins) offered along the procession route by Sikhs, Hindus, and Sunnis (see fig. 6.6). Sunnis in Malerkotla sometimes participate in other ways. At several *majalis* I encountered Sunni men and women who professed an appreciation for either the depth of devotion of the Shi'a or for Imam Hussain himself, or a respect and affection for a neighbor or friend that impelled them to attend. At one house I met a young Sunni man who was good friends with a Shi'i man whose family was hosting the *majlis*. He said that although his friendship was acceptable to his family, his mother told him not to eat in their house (a request that he ignored). In this case, whereas personal connections overrode familial sanction, it indicates that prejudices are still widely felt.

Nowadays there is considerable cooperation and coordination between sayyids and shaykhs concerning the conduct of Muharram, although competition and frustration persist. In 2001 the two communities negotiated and renegotiated with each other over the order of events, the route, and the timing of parades and *majalis*. Each group sponsored an imam to come and lead them through the ten days of nearly constant religious devotions. The *imam* based at the Khojgan *imambara*, originally from Uttar Pradesh, traveled to another Shi'i community, an exchange that is quite typical. Members of both Shi'i groups attend the public addresses of the visiting imams. During the major procession, the imam sponsored by the Anjuman Haideri gave a sermon, and everyone sat in the street to hear his discourse. Both visiting imams were dynamic speakers, bringing their audiences to tears and inciting cries of approbation from the assemblies. For the more routine *majalis*, sayyids and shaykhs do not intermix to the same degree. Nonetheless, the Shi'i community has been active in

FIGURE 6.4. Hindu children carry a *taziya* during Muharram procession.

promoting interreligious dialogue. In 1999, a group from the Khojgan community sponsored an *Ekta Sammelan* (unity program) featuring leaders from all religious communities speaking about the principles of their traditions. Although the event was not repeated in 2000 or 2001, it indicates a concern among the minority Shi'a to foster positive relations with other communities.

Sikh Groups and Centers

The Sikh population in Malerkotla is overwhelmingly Jat. Jats are a multireligious caste of farmers and pastoralists who dominate the whole of Indian Punjab. There are a few higher-caste Sikhs as well—Bedis, Sodhis, and others—but as an agricultural hub, Malerkotla's Sikhs are mostly Jat. As noted previously, there has not historically been a large Sikh population in Malerkotla.

FIGURE 6.5. The *taziya* and *alams* in one of Malerkotla's *imambaras*.

Most Sikhs are from the area because there was little out-migration and therefore not much property that could be assigned to refugees from Pakistan. There
was a small influx of refugee Sikhs from the Sindh and Punjab regions of
present-day Pakistan. Although the percentage of Sikhs in Malerkotla is considerably less than that in Punjab in general (about 11 percent), as a majority in

FIGURE 6.6. Sunnis prepare food during the Muharram procession.

the state (63 percent), their local influence is considerable. Much of the land cultivated in the outlying villages that were formerly part of the kingdom are owned and farmed by Sikhs. There are six gurdwaras in Malerkotla. As the central space of Sikh worship, the gurdwara houses the Guru Granth Sahib (the compiled poetic hymns of the Sikh gurus and other saints) as the focus of worship. Some gurdwaras contain relics of the gurus or famous Sikhs in history (usually weapons or armaments), but in Malerkotla this type of historic gurdwara does not exist. The oldest gurdwara in town, the Singh Sabha Gurd-wara, was built through the patronage of Nawab Ahmad Ali Khan in the 1920s (fig. 6.7). Another, more recently built, memorializes the *haah da naara* of Nawab Sher Mohammad Khan. The land for this gurdwara was bought from one of the widows of the last nawab and features a shellacked photocopy of the purported *haah da naara* letter and a kiosk with the letter translated from Persian into English and Punjabi. A third is inside of one of the old royal mansions and is principally patronized by a small population of refugees from Sindh who were resettled in these buildings as a few remaining members of the nawab's family left for Pakistan. The largest gurdwara is newly built but also on the site of a former palace.

In terms of other Sikh sects, there is a Nirankari Center near the Government College and a large Namdhari Martyrs Memorial on the Khanna road. Both groups practice an austere and simple form of Sikhism, focusing on the holy text and esteeming a living guru. The Nirankaris believe in a formless God and eschew all customs and practices that resonate with Hinduism, Islam, or Christianity. The Namdharis focus on the Adi Granth rather than the Guru Granth

FIGURE 6.7. Singh Sabha Gurdwara.

Sahib, and they believe in a living Satguru who is an incarnation of true God consciousness.[32] Orthodox Sikhs regard the notion of a living guru as heretical. The governing bodies of the Sikh faith, in particular the Shiromani Gurdwara Prabhandak Committee, which oversees historic gurdwaras and performs many other regulatory functions, have excluded Namdharis from participation. In Malerkotla both of these groups have little effect on the political life of the town as the Nirankaris keep to themselves, and there is only one resident Namdhari family who stays at the martyr's memorial full time. However, the Namdhari memorial is a major local landmark.

Among the Sikh organizations locally there is a Sikh Welfare Society that draws members from all the gurdwaras in the community. They engage in a variety of social programs, such as taking up a collection for the relief of a number of Sikhs who were killed in the summer of 2001 in the Kashmir Valley. Together the gurdwaras put together parades for the birthday celebrations of the gurus. Guru Nanak's *janam purb* (birthday celebration) is observed with particular fanfare involving a *nagar kirtan* parade in which in which the Guru Granth Sahib is taken throughout town on a cart as a blessing for the community (see fig. 6.8). This symbolically circumscribes the town and simultaneously incorporates the area under the protective power of the both the *guru granth* and the *guru panth*. Many Sikh holidays are observed less elaborately in Malerkotla itself, as many Sikh residents tend to travel to the places where the festivals are traditionally commemorated, such as Diwali at Amritsar or Hola Mohalla at Anandpur Sahib.[33] If unable to travel such a great distance for these holy days,

FIGURE 6.8. *Nagar kirtan*, the local Sikh community, blesses Malerkotla.

residents often travel to Patiala or Ludhiana or another city where there are larger Sikh populations, historic gurdwaras, and, therefore, bigger festivals.

The biggest Sikh festival in Malerkotla is not associated with mainstream Sikh sacred history, but marks the martyrdom of the Namdharis in 1872. As discussed in chapter 2, this was the brutal and summary execution by the British of 69 Namdharis who were accused of being among those who had attacked Malerkotla, ostensibly for cow killing. The commemoration of the execution is one of the most important annual events for the Namdharis, and the martyr-dom festival (or *shahidi mela*) is attended by thousands of people. The event is held on January 17, 18, and 19, the anniversary of the firings, which also took place over three days. There is all night *kirtan*, constant *langar*, and thousands in attendance. A smaller festival to commemorate these events occurs on the seventeenth of every month. The events take place on the grounds of the monu-ment erected by the Namdharis in the form of a gigantic sword, perforated with a hole for every martyr with smaller ones representing the children. Only one Namdhari family lives in Malerkotla full time, but these events draw Namdharis from the surrounding area, particularly from their center at Bhaini Sahib, approximately an hour distant, and even from Delhi. The fair is also an obli-gatory stop on the campaign trail. In 2001, Chief Minister Parkash Singh Badal addressed the gathering. This was interesting given the well-known support of the Namdharis for the opposition Congress Party, which they regard as the party of the freedom struggle they see themselves as having begun in the mid-nineteenth century. Namdharis view Badal's Shiromani Akali Dal Party with suspicion, as it is associated with the type of Sikh identity politics that tends to exclude non-normative Sikh groups. Orthodox Sikhs in particular object to the Namdharis' belief in a living guru. However, during a visit to the annual Namdhari gathering in 1999, Badal referred to the living guru of the Namdharis as "Satguru," meaning True Guru, during his speech, causing an enormous fracas among his party loyalists and the orthodox.[34] At the 2001 *mela*, no such mention was made, but Badal's speech in person was clearly far less compelling to the gathering than was the telephone call from the aging Satguru Jagjit Singh (b. 1920) that was piped in over the loudspeakers.

Sikh sectarian politics and the repressive Indian governmental response led to a long period of terrorism in Punjab during the 1980s and early 1990s. The violence and tension affected Sangrur District (where Malerkotla is located) significantly, but Malerkotla itself was largely left unscathed.[35] Although curfew was imposed frequently here, as it was in the rest of the region, there were no local casualties. Again many residents attribute this to the blessing of Guru Gobind Singh and the ongoing affection of the Sikhs for the town. Certainly the relatively low population of Sikhs would be another disincentive to violence. Sikhs in Malerkotla and the outlying villages engaged in acts of goodwill toward the Muslim population even during this difficult period. Many Muslim resi-dents reported that when curfew was imposed during Ramadan and it was difficult to obtain food from the countryside, Sikhs would set up places to distribute water and food for the breaking of the fast. Sikh residents claim that the separatist elements were very weak in Malerkotla.

Hindu and Jain Groups and Centers

The Hindu population in 1981 (the last census available with this breakdown) was a little more than 20 percent. There are many temples, some quite old, indicating the long history of the Hindu and Jain communities in the town. Indeed, some local Jains and Hindus claim that their families were sent to the area by Bahlol Lodhi to develop the new settlement commercially and make the region a livable place for the sophisticated daughter of a sultan. The Hindu residents in Malerkotla itself are mostly from trade and lower castes. The local Jain community, as is common in India more broadly, is also largely from this merchant class. There are three significant Jain sites and centers in town (fig. 6.9). Hindu and Jain merchants have a substantial presence in the bazaars, and own many of the buildings in the central markets.

There are several organizations representing Hindu interests. It is clear from state records that the Hindu Mahasabha was active in Malerkotla in the past, though its activities here and elsewhere in India are much diminished with the growth of other Hindu political groups. The Hindu Mahasabha was formed in 1915 to counteract the Indian National Congress and the Muslim League. They sought to activate the Hindu majority politically and revive Hinduism to combat the invidious effects of Christianity and Islam upon the integrity of the

FIGURE 6.9. Inside a Jain temple, Malerkotla.

Hindu territory of India. Along with groups such as the Arya Samaj (which does not appear to have been particularly vibrant in Malerkotla), the Hindu Mahasabha had a profound effect on religious revivalism in Punjab. After the assassination of Mahatma Gandhi by Nathuram Godse, a former member of the RSS, the organization was banned throughout India. In Malerkotla the last nawab Iftikhar Ali Khan issued a declaration rendering the RSS an "unlawful body."[36] The various organizations of the Sangh Parivar (RSS, VHP, BJP) are present but not very popular in Malerkotla. A local RSS leader said the group began locally in 1938 with 25 or so people and nowadays has about 50 members (in a town of more than one hundred thousand). He presented their activities as being *for* Hindus rather than against any community, a view that closely resembles the attitude of Maulana Abdul Rauf. Another RSS member blamed the British for the divisions that later arose between Hindus and Muslims. Both men separated their cultural, character-building efforts from the political work of the BJP. The BJP has never been particularly successful in town, although a party unit does exist. Since an alliance was formed between the BJP and the SAD in 1998, the BJP has tended to take a back seat. There is an active Sanatan Dharam Sabha in Malerkotla. Sanatan Dharam, meaning the eternal religion, usually refers to a revivalist form of Hinduism that seeks to get back to the Veda and the "essentials" of the faith, cleanse Hinduism of caste restrictions, and encourage personal piety. Various other Hindu and Jain committees form to manage the celebration of major festivals or to represent particular sections of society. There are, for example, caste-based organizations such as the Aggarwal Sabha and the Brahmin Sabha. These groups and other organizations with a broader appeal engage in advocacy for their constituency and charitable and social welfare activities (fig. 6.10).

There are three temples in Malerkotla that stand out from the crowd as especially significant to residents: the Hanuman Mandir, the Kali Mandir and the Dera of Baba Atma Ram. The largest temple (boasting also the largest idol) is the Hanuman Mandir. This is a new temple, in the heart of the commercial district. In the courtyard of the temple is a gigantic image of Hanuman that looms over the entire city and is visible from a great distance.[37] This temple also houses a large meeting hall where weddings, awards programs, religious lectures and performances, and other events take place. On Tuesdays, the day dedicated to Hanuman, large numbers of devotees come to make offerings and receive blessings. The Kali Mandir is a very active temple with a new building but an old *murti* or idol of the goddess. On Saturdays, the day of the goddess, and during the *navaratri*, the nine nights of the goddess, this temple is extremely busy.

The oldest Hindu site in town is the Dera of Baba Atma Ram, who was a Bairagi sadhu from the Neem Margi *sampraday* (lineage). A strong local tradition claims that Atma Ram and a Muslim saint, Shah Fazl, placed the foundation stone of Kotla in the mid-seventeenth century at the behest of the nawab. This gesture is seen as providing a literal foundation for Malerkotla's pluralism and open society. At the Dera, Tuesdays are especially busy as the temple boasts

FIGURE 6.10. A *havan* in Malerkotla marking the end of a reading of the *Ramcaritmanas.*

a *murti* of Hanuman carved from an unusually large piece of coral (see fig. 6.11). The Dera also hosts Dussehra, one of the largest non-Muslim religious festivals in Malerkotla, on the tenth day after the *navaratri.*[38] For the nights leading up to Dussehra, plays of the Ram story, called *Ramlila*, are put on at venues

FIGURE 6.11. A Hanuman *murti* made out of coral, Dera Baba Atma Ram, Malerkotla.

throughout town. Some Muslims also attend these dramas. On the day itself the entire town—Hindus, Sikhs, and Muslims—all turn out at the Dera where a gigantic papier-mâché effigy of Ravana, the villain of the *Ramayana*, is burned. This event is important as it, perhaps more than any other, brings together the entire community. Muslim groups sponsor booths at the Dera distributing free cold water to participants. In 2001 the person staffing one booth said that although he did not himself believe in Rama and the events being celebrated, he enjoyed the spectacle and the opportunity to serve the community. The appeal of Dussehra for Muslims, and likely for most participants, is less religious than spectacular, as the parade and celebration are enjoyed by everyone in town.[39] Throughout Malerkotla people observe the parade, which includes people dressed up as Rama and Sita, from walls and rooftops, then follow the procession to the Dera for the dramatic denouement as the Ravana effigy is burned.

The Practice of Everyday Pluralism

Muslims attend the Dera on nonfestival days as well. This is the case at other shrines in South Asia, especially those known for healing certain disorders. For example at the Dera one morning, the *pujari* (priest) and his son were both in attendance, as was the celibate *mahant*, or head of the sadhu (renunciant) lineage associated with the shrine. It was a Tuesday morning, and many people were coming through to pay their devotions to the unique Hanuman *murti* at the Dera. After the steady flow had reduced to a trickle, a man and his son came in and sat before the younger *pujari* (fig. 6.12). They presented the *pujari* with a

FIGURE 6.12. A *pujari* blesses a Muslim child at the Dera of Baba Atma Ram, Malerkotla.

bottle of water, and the Brahmin priest began to murmur Sanskrit mantras, invocations capable of focusing and channeling divine energy. After a few minutes, the *pujari* inserted a leafy twig into the bottle and, still softly uttering mantras, sprinkled the boy with the blessed water. After this the *pujari* gave the man and his son some advice about how to proceed, consuming small amounts of the water several times a day. After they had gone, the *pujari*, knowing the nature of my research, informed me that the two visitors had been Muslim. I asked the *pujari* how he felt about their coming, and he responded simply that it was a normal thing. People are people, he said, and when they are in trouble, they seek help. If he can help them, he does. The universality of human concerns such as healing, in this case for a type of skin disorder, is also a common reason for Sikh and Hindu presence at Muslim shrines. The healing process is also not dissimilar as praying and Qur'anic recitation over water, and its subsequent consumption is a traditional practice for Muslims.[40]

Such public and private engagements provide critical opportunities for residents of multiple religious orientations to engage in symbolic interactions. This opportunity is not unlike that afforded by the *dargah* discussed in the previous chapter. Public demonstrations of mutual support intensify the social effects of exchange when, for example, Hindus, Sikhs, and Sunni Muslims support the Shi'i Muharram procession by offering food and drink to the participants. According to one Muslim resident, "When 'Id comes in the hot summer, Hindu and Sikh brothers make stalls for cold water for their Muslim brothers. Similarly on their occasions, our society does this service."

This mutual support and sometime participation is echoed on a smaller scale at ritual acknowledgments of life passages. Malerkotla's integration is evident at wedding parties and funerals as people of all religious faiths are present, and provision is invariably made for dietary differences and gender separation. As Mahmud, a middle-aged schoolteacher explained, the fact that the religions do not share all of the same daily religious practices (though many may jointly participate in Sufi shrine worship) is not the correct measure of interreligious relations. There is no need for Hindus or Sikhs to pray in a mosque or for Muslims to pray in a temple. The depth of connection is manifest in the respect for difference and in the participation in one another's significant life transitions.

> I am 45 years old, and I have never seen a Hindu or Sikh offering *namaz*. But if there is some gathering—suppose somebody died—and on the third day people gathered, but the space nearby the house is not enough, so arrangements were made in some mosque, then Hindu, Sikh friends come there, and if there is some gathering in the Gurdwara or Mandir we go there. But neither they nor we say to each other to follow or perform each other's ways of worship.

Their religion is for them, ours is for us, and if we will compel them, then there will be a fight.[41]

This commonsense approach to living with religious diversity is the norm in Malerkotla, but the approach is *made* normal through practice and repetition. It is also made to resonate within the religious worldview of the speaker as the last sentence evokes two verses from the Qur'an: "To them their religion and to you yours," (109:6) and "Let there be no compulsion in religion" (2:256). Through public participation in events of ritual significance to the town, to one of its religious communities, or to a particular family or individual, the interreligious fiber of Malerkotla remains interwoven and becomes more difficult to fray.

Local commensality was also frequently cited as indicative of the positive state of social relations in Malerkotla. Countless times when I was invited for tea or for a meal in people's homes (which happened with heartwarming regularity), neighbors would come in to visit and meet the foreign guest. Quite often these neighbors were from a variety of religious backgrounds, and they ate and drank together without reserve. Weddings I attended invariably made provision for vegetarians. As indicated also by Mahmud in his statement above, people of all faiths regularly attend funeral prayers. Many people I interviewed said that they exchanged sweets and food with their neighbors and friends of all religions on festival occasions and for life cycle rituals such as births, deaths, and weddings. The ability to eat together is a key index of the level of integration in Indian society. Because of the variety of dietary and purity restrictions in the three main religions in Malerkotla, it would not be surprising if few people exchanged food or ate with members of another faith. Hindu purity laws are such that certain higher-caste individuals are understood to be barred from sharing food not only with non-Hindus but with Hindus of a lower status. In addition, some Hindus are vegetarians and will not eat from vessels that have been used for meat. Sikhs have no explicit restrictions in these terms, but any meat they eat has to be killed in a manner called *jhatka*, meaning that the head of the animal is severed in one blow. Neither Hindus nor Sikhs are supposed to eat beef. Muslims, on the other hand, eat beef but do not eat pork. They should only consume *halal* meat that is killed by slicing the jugular vein and allowing the blood to drain from the body. Muslims and Sikhs are barred from drinking alcohol, but no such restriction exists for Hindus. In addition to these religious strictures on food, there are numerous cultural prejudices. Even in ostensibly egalitarian Muslim households, servants are often not allowed to use the same vessels and utensils as the family. Or recall the Sunni youth who said that he had been told never to eat in the houses of Shiʻi friends.

This abundance of regulations and customs could certainly impede the likelihood that Muslims, Sikhs, and Hindus will eating together. And it is true that some members of all these religions will avoid such occasions. Sometimes the avoidance involves accepting but not consuming certain foods so as not to offend. Furthermore, people take care to provide food that would not be proscribed, such as sweets from a shop rather than homemade items that may cause the recipient to pause. As one local Muslim explained, "on Diwali they come and give sweets to us, on 'Id we go and give sweets." In addition, some Muslim residents report that Hindus and Sikhs who are not strict *will* take *halal* meat if it is offered. Mahmud, the schoolteacher, confirmed this point:

> Just as we don't take *jhatka* meat, the strict Sikhs do not take *halal* meat. But our Hindu and Sikh friends who come to our house, they take meat with us. That is always *halal*. They eat more than we do. But the strict ones do not take it, and we don't insist that they do. If somebody wants to eat, he can; if not, it is up to him. We don't insist they eat because if somebody insisted that we take *jhatka* meat we would feel bad.[42]

Here Mahmud points out that bad feelings may arise if the situation is one of force and it would be wrong to press someone to violate his or her sense of what is right within his or her own belief system. Symbolically, the act of eating together and on occasion transgressing normative rules regarding diet and commensality is an important index of Malerkotla's integrated society. Such seemingly small, daily exchanges are in fact integral to sustaining the level of communal harmony in Malerkotla that enables the community to rise above such crises as Partition and the terrorism.

Although theorists such as Varshney emphasize business and civil societal links as most crucial to maintaining the peace, Mahmud pointed out that business connections among people of different religions are hardly unique to Malerkotla ("I think business links are everywhere") and thus do not necessarily prevent interreligious disturbances. Rather, he said, Malerkotla's peace "has occurred naturally. In Malerkotla people don't get caught up in any quarrel." As Nandy illustrated in the case of Jaipur's gem industry, business links there did not prevent violence from occurring in the wake of the Ayodhya movement, nor did they prevent a gradual erosion of interreligious relations.[43] However, Mahmud overstated the inefficacy of business ties. Business relations are important measures of the degree of integration in a community. Alone they do not suffice, but as a part of a larger web of interconnection, joint business ventures are confidence-building measures and clear reminders of community interdependence. Many townspeople liken Malerkotla to a family, and the analogy is important. The common daily irritations of life together in a household do not in normal circumstances threaten its foundation. And in Malerkotla, disparate and opposed personalities and lifestyles coexist and sometimes clash, but the residents (like siblings) resolve their conflicts quickly upon reflection.

Marc Gopin points out the power of family terminology in his work on conflict management in the Middle East. Familial terms possess great power that can be used to heal or harm. The shared "family history" between Jews, Christians, and Muslims in his work is a source of both recognition and resentment.[44] In Malerkotla, familial terminology, especially the principle of brotherhood (*bhaichara*), is generally deployed to signify positive relations and perceptions of the other. Mahmud pursued the family metaphor to describe closeness in Malerkotla and the relative insignificance of difficulties between the various groups:

> We do not have any problem here. Maybe some small annoyances are there. These things also happen between two brothers, between father and son. The matters were never so serious that it pinched you for long or hatred was engraved on your heart. Now you might have seen an 'Id Milan at which Sikhs and Hindus were present, if they have some attachment then they come. Regarding marriages, yesterday there was a Muslim girl's marriage, and many Hindus and Sikhs were there.

Mahmud did not deny the difficulties of group life. Indeed his comments came in a conversation with him and the retired schoolteacher Abdullah in which we were discussing numerous past instances of conflict. But his statement reflected the reaction of a functional family in which the "small things" do not prevent people from attending each other's major life events—marriages, festivals, funerals, and so on.

The analogy of the family was also employed by Maulana Abdul Rauf. He described the manner in which Muslims, Sikhs, and Hindus deal with each other in familial terms. In particular he highlighted the way the nawabs treated non-Muslim subjects during times of tension:

> Sometimes people appear differently on the outside than we think inside, but we see in Malerkotla that people have stood by the other communities of people. Muslims, Hindus and Sikhs, they have helped each other. When there was Partition of India and Pakistan, at that time Malerkotla was an island, there was no facility for food, so the Sikhs brought food from outside to Malerkotla. And in a similar way, once the Sikhs attacked Malerkotla, and then Hindu people came forward. As at that time the Muslims were feeble, the Sikhs asked the Hindus, "What is the attitude of the nawab towards the Hindu girls or women?" So at that time a Hindu *buzurg* [saint] came forward and said that he treats the Hindu girls as his own daughters, and they [i.e., the Sikhs] took their army back and retreated.[45] And when there was brutality against the Sikhs,

Muslims helped them. In the Mughal times when nobody could raise his voice against the king, at that time the nawab helped the Sikhs. If they were corrupt in their hearts, they would have enjoyed the situation and said let the Hindus or the Sikhs die. But no, they came forward to help them.

In this statement Maulana Abdul Rauf expressed the commonly held belief that the townspeople rallied around one another during the chaos of Partition and at other times as well. He expresses the value of the *haah da naara* not in metaphysical but practical terms, as an example of an antisectarian solidarity that characterizes Malerkotla to this day. Rauf links these past events to the perennial ability of Malerkotla residents to respond effectively to each successive challenge to the community. It is significant that the perceived test of the honesty of the nawab was his treatment of Hindu women and girls. The role of violence against women and the rumors of such violations as features of riots and ethnic conflict is well established.[46] Here the expression of familial relations is evoked to describe the fatherly benevolence of the Muslim rulers and the intimacy of relations between religious groups.

Civil Society

Critically important to the social integration in Malerkotla is the "vital social mixing" that occurs in its neighborhoods and civic organizations. Although given the demographics it is not surprising that there are areas, such as around the tomb of Haider Shaykh, that are mostly Muslim, the newer neighborhoods and the marketplaces are not segregated or ghettoized. Associational integration in Malerkotla is quite strong. Civic associations proliferate in Malerkotla, ranging from international organizations, such as the Rotary Club, to local literary societies (Sahit Sangam), to a group of cactus lovers (Greenwood Cactus and Succulent Society). As in any vibrant community there is an organization representing every imaginable interest. It is difficult to know how many such associations are present and how many are actually active, as many are not incorporated and therefore are not listed with the municipality. Some groups last only a few meetings, and others endure with very few members and a limited mandate. The membership and leadership are often deliberately multireligious. Several associations I visited and group leaders I interviewed were explicit about their concern to have representation from all groups. People feared being labeled communal and took care to actively recruit members of various religions and sects. Thus it is common for the office holders in many organizations to represent multiple religious groups. For example, the local Bar Association, Bar Clerk Association, Chemist's Association, Journalists' Coordination Committee, Manufacturer's and Supplier's Association, Malerkotla Printer's Association, Rotract [sic] Club, Leo Club, Malerkotla Welfare Association, Malerkotla

Heritage Society, Ex-Serviceman League Committee, Punjab Pensioner's Association, and Malerkotla Improvement Trust all have or have had a mix of Hindus, Muslims, and Sikhs on their executive boards.[47]

A few groups tended to be dominated by a single religious group, but still had a plural membership such as the Rotary Club, which has tended to have Hindu and Jain leadership. Nonetheless, the Rotary Club traditionally organizes events in observation of Islamic festivals. In 2001, for example, they held an 'Id Milan, a gathering to congratulate the Muslim community at the end of Ramadan.[48] Although its agenda is nonreligious, the Rotary Club took the opportunity to publicly manifest a nonsectarian ethos. Indeed, such events are commonly organized by many groups in Malerkotla as a means of reaching out to the Muslim-majority population. In another example, the Guru Nanak Samaj Sudhar and Sports Club and the various Youth Clubs may all compete together in public contests. It is also important to highlight that representatives of multiple religious traditions oversee several of the largest occupational and professional groups, such as the Bar Association and the Manufacturers and Suppliers Association. Such integration fosters open communication, reduces competition and tension, and helps create a sound basis for interreligious interaction. The combination of interreligious and intrareligious organizations is an important aspect of Malerkotla's plural society. The existence of public spaces for both types of engagement fosters security within different religious communities and maximizes the opportunities for open exchange and the forging of shared interests between religious communities. Varshney asserted that the key indicators for whether a place is riot prone are the absence of interethnic engagements and of associational and everyday links between ethnic groups. Areas where civic life is characterized by a high degree of engagement at these two levels tend to be peaceful, whereas those where such links are absent or where *intra*ethnic groups are ascendant tend toward violence. Varshney singles out the formal associational level over the semiformal or informal everyday as the essential ingredient in maintaining social harmony.

The insight into the critical role of civil society is important and goes far to shift the discussion of ethnic conflict away from the statist and primordialist debates which have hitherto dominated the field. More problematic is Varshney's assertion that while "everyday and informal forms of civic communication may be sufficient to keep peace in villages," nonetheless "they cannot have the same effect in cities. Associational civic engagement is necessary for peace in interethnic urban settings."[49] While I agree that associational links are an important element in building what he calls the "institutionalized peace system," his account does not further our understanding of the relationship between the everyday and the associational levels of exchange.[50] One must ask whether a society with strong formal associations is possible without a vibrant community life in the streets and homes and shrines of a locale. I prefer to conceive of a spectrum of formal and informal links that bind communities publicly, privately, politically, economically, spiritually, and personally.

An interesting example of an external stressor that had a significant impact on Malerkotla neither made the news nor involved loss of life. Yet its importance in local lore as a key moment in interreligious relations indicates its centrality in the constitution of Malerkotla as a peaceful society. This event was the December 6, 1992, burning of a Jain center and damage to a Hindu temple in the aftermath of the destruction of the Babri Masjid in Ayodhya. According to many locals, after the news of the demolition spread in town, some agitated Muslims marched to a Vishvakarma Temple in the Bhumsi neighborhood of Malerkotla, not far from Haider Shaykh's tomb, and tore one of its walls down. The police came quickly, community leaders gathered, and the destruction was stopped. The youths most responsible were, reportedly, disciplined and eventually exiled. A Muslim industrialist provided money to repair the temple. Also in the aftermath, a Jain center in the Moti Bazaar burned down. Conflicting reports exist about this. Most Jains and Hindus claimed that Muslims burned the building, though no one is clearly identified. Some Muslims hedged the question, believing that the building was burned for the insurance money or because the Jains wanted to build a larger center in the historic city center. Others acknowledged that Muslims, usually identified as "angry youths," did burn the building.

These events were important not because of the burning or breakage, but the way in which the town reacted. Rather than exploding into further violence or retaliation, the Muslim community paid for the damage and disciplined those responsible. Indeed, as Maulana Abdul Rauf, the head of the local Jama'at-i Islami, explained, this is a common response among Malerkotla residents of all religions:

> Here sometimes the situation has been bad. Sometimes bad things have happened, but when the atmosphere became bad at times the Muslims themselves asked those Muslims not to do such things, and the Hindus did the same thing to Hindus, otherwise the Muslims would have helped only Muslims and the Hindus helped only Hindus. The situation would have deteriorated. Here a lot of such committees were founded of Hindus and Muslims whose main aim was to suppress the bad elements and bad things, we should not help any type of bad element. So that is why the bad people were not successful in their intentions.

Abdul Rauf makes a crucial point about the importance of self-policing on the part of the various religious communities. Externally imposed, coercive measures are less likely to be effective. A prominent Muslim businessman who contributed a substantial amount to repair the temple also makes this point. He declared that whenever a problem occurs in Malerkotla, the communities themselves discipline the perpetrators. The schoolteacher Mahmud extended the analysis:

> Muslims of Malerkotla condemned this burning. Because the Qur'an does not allow it. The Qur'an says that if you are at war, and if somebody hides himself in his religious place, you spare him. So how can the followers of Islam think of putting somebody's religious place on fire? If we will attack or burn other religion's religious places, they will burn our religious places. There will be quarrels, and living will become hard.

Mahmud clearly recognized the importance of mutual respect and the reality of mutual dependence. He finds a religious basis to justify his assertion that Muslims in Malerkotla opposed the attack by members of their own religion. Thus his position gains strength by drawing from a pragmatic understanding of community life and grounding in his religious faith.

Local RSS leaders also claimed they helped to reduce tensions during the 1992 disturbance. They called the perpetrators "misguided people," a relatively subdued response even ten years afterward. They met with those people who seemed most prone to retaliation and their neighbors, family, and friends. They also seemed to have confidence in the role of the police in stabilizing the situation and showing people "how to go right." The head of the RSS in Malerkotla, Dharamvir Gupta, said that not only was the temple wall damaged but that the attackers tried to burn the *pujari* as well. Still, they saw their role as pacifiers rather than agitators because "from conflict both communities become weak."[51]

Members of all religious communities remember the event as significant; it was a time when the fabric of Malerkotla was tested, and its integrity prevailed. Through a combination of measures, residents managed the shock of the destruction of the Babri Masjid and the unjust retaliation on local Hindu sacred sites. By refusing to harbor the guilty and making reparations for the damage the Muslim leadership preempted any backlash and created space for conciliatory Hindus to come forward. The momentum of these mutual efforts allowed the situation to defuse quickly and left little room for divisive elements or outside politicians to capitalize. In an interview, a former police superintendent in Karnataka explained that intracommunity involvement in discouraging disruptive individuals and in reporting their activities to the police is crucial to controlling interreligious tensions. Certainly considerable social and moral force was brought to bear through the variety of tactics used by local leaders and regular citizens of all religions. In a large town, this is not merely a matter of the village council or the principal actors meeting and coming to an agreement. The possibilities for multiple interpretations of the temple damage are many times increased, as is the potential for outsiders to take up the issue. That such efforts, if they even occurred, were thwarted before they could have an effect demonstrates enormous resourcefulness on the part of the local community. These strategies to reestablish equilibrium in Malerkotla are examples of what Varshney identifies as "mechanisms of peace." Although I do not agree that civil society alone "is the missing variable in available theories," as Varshney asserts, civil society is a crucial element in constituting a stable, multicultural community.[52] Supported by networks in neighborhoods, workplaces, and places of worship and by relationships at the associational, political, and official levels, the people of Malerkotla kept the peace and strengthened their shared stake in the collective ethos of harmony.

The Ritualized Peace System

The efficacy of interreligious exchanges in establishing linkages on the level of civil society is not independent of the experience of the interpersonal in the so-called "private" sphere, nor is the social wholly dependent upon the personal. For example, a person may have excellent business dealings and give political support to adherents of multiple religious communities based entirely upon self-interest and have no interreligious friendships. The reverse may also be true. However, in a region where interreligious exchanges take place in an atmosphere of congeniality and peace, it is far more likely that the civil and political societies within that region will develop, endure, and be meaningful. This repertory of engagement strategies employed by multireligious and multiethnic authorities and communities generates an institutionalized peace system. In this system, the modes of interaction and validation between religions and between authorities and those they govern are structured to promote a society capable of withstanding challenges.

The most crucial moment in conflict intervention immediately follows the initial reaction to some triggering event. Failure to take rapid and perceivable action in response to a provocative incident leaves the management of its significance up for grabs. If Malerkotla were the kind of place where individuals such as the incendiary VHP leader Praveen Togadia (who was arrested in 2003 for distributing *trishuls*, the trident-shaped weapon associated with the god Shiva, to crowds in Rajasthan) had a substantial audience, then there have been several moments when someone like him could have polarized the town. Instead, Malerkotla has responded relatively calmly to inflammatory events such as the Sikh nationalist terrorism of the 1980s and 1990s, the Ayodhya dispute and the destruction of the Babri Masjid in 1992, a rumored cow-killing, the Kargil war with Pakistan in 1999, the destruction of the Bamiyan Buddhas by Afghanistan's Taliban regime in 2000, the anti-Muslim reaction in other areas of Punjab to the Buddhas' demolition, and the horrors of the Gujarat violence in the spring of 2002. Any of these events could, and in other places did, trigger interreligious conflict and violence.

When in the mid-1980s a cow turned up dead in Malerkotla, a rumor began that it had been maltreated and then killed by some Muslim youths. Both cow and pig slaughter have been illegal in Malerkotla since the late nineteenth century, and neither beef nor pork is readily available in town to this day. When the rumor took hold, a crowd gathered, and tensions increased. The police and the deputy commissioner, the highest-ranking civil servant, arrived. Together they made efforts to resolve the problem and disperse the assembly, initially to no avail. The head of the local Jama'at-i Islami, Abdul Rauf, described the incident thus:

> There was a [Hindu] boy, he created the mischief by spreading the rumor that some Muslims had slaughtered a cow. Muslims then were determined that before they would leave, he should apologize. But he would not apologize. The DC [deputy commissioner] tried very hard but in vain. He said, "I will have to take the course of law." Something came in my mind. I suddenly stood up and said, "I swear by God that if I have made a mistake, forgive me, never ever will I do such a thing again, which can cause riots in the city." After I said this, two people from the RSS stood up and said also that "I swear to God, and say that if I have made some mistake, forgive me for that." Like this, one, two, three, people turn by turn stood up, and then that person's turn [the one who had started the rumor] came, and he also said, "I swear by God, if I have made some mistake, forgive me, I will never ever do such a thing which can spoil the peace of the city." Then everybody was happy; from all sides people said congratulations. The DC came out and said the matter is solved.

Even filtered through an individual's memory, this is a description of a functioning institutionalized peace system. The DC arrived promptly, as did community leaders from the various religious groups. Although Abdul Rauf places the responsibility for the incident on a Hindu rumormonger and emphasizes his own role in defusing the tension, he also acknowledges the RSS leaders for immediately following his initiative in asking for forgiveness.[53]

The appeal for forgiveness is an important strategy for bringing about reconciliation and managing conflict. Conflict resolution theorist and practitioner Marc Gopin places great emphasis on rituals of forgiveness. He explains that the gesture of apologizing and forgiving is not merely symbolic but opens up new possibilities for relationships between the partisans to a conflict. Though Abdul Rauf is not professionally trained in techniques of conflict management, he seemed to have a natural instinct for the kinds of gestures that can truly transform a situation. By apologizing first for something everyone knew he had not himself done, he removed the stigma and potential loss of honor associated with apologies. Furthermore, because of his position as a respected local leader, he actually gave apologizing a kind of symbolic status that increased the cultural capital of those who chose to ally with him. In recounting the incident, he shared credit for mitigating the tension with members of a Hindu partisan organization, acknowledging that peacemaking is a collective project. The willingness of the RSS leaders to put themselves on the line by asking for public witnesses to their commitment to interreligious peace created space for the Hindu who had started the rumor to ask for forgiveness. Another crucial element of the strategy's efficacy was that all sides validated the resolution and acknowledged it as sufficient reparation to bring the conflict to a close.

In more recent years local solidarity has been tested on several occasions. After the destruction of the Bamiyan Buddhas in Afghanistan in March 2001 there were several anti-Muslim attacks in Punjab and other areas of India. Rumors flew about pig meat being thrown into mosques and Qur'ans being burned. Many Muslims in Malerkotla grew angry that the actions of the Taliban were bringing such insults to Indian Muslims. They were also concerned that these relatively minor incidents would escalate and knew that if that occurred, Malerkotla would experience even more scrutiny. Several local Muslims suggested demonstrating in the streets to protest the offenses to Muslim sentiments. Simultaneously, some Hindus were agitated about the destruction of the Buddhas. National Hindu groups were vocal in their outrage at the loss of these monumental Buddha statues, and they were clear in assigning blame to Islam in general, not the Taliban in particular. This anger was also felt in Malerkotla. Some suggested a march and demonstration to protest the destruction. Clearly, the possibility that two demonstrations would take place to express outrage at perceived affronts to religious feelings could be a volatile situation. A meeting of the Peace Committee took place in response to this stress, and cooler heads prevailed. Rather than take part in protest marches, which have historically been triggers for conflict, Malerkotla residents and shopkeepers of all religions observed a one-day *hartal* or closure of shops and offices. In this way the disapprobation of the community for both the destruction of the Buddhas and the attacks on Islamic symbols was jointly expressed, and the opportunity for creating further bad feelings was avoided. Similarly, after Hindu-Muslim violence in Gujarat in spring 2002 resulted in the death of two thousand people, all eyes in Punjab turned toward Malerkotla as people wondered if the community would respond in anger or retaliate against local Hindus. Instead, Malerkotla's citizens banded together in opposition to the divisive violence, and nothing happened. The *Tribune* reported a tense, but quiet, situation.

It is significant that the public ceremonies at which key events from the past are commemorated have been and continue to be sponsored by the state, the municipality, by religious organizations, political parties, and civic groups. The strategic deployment and linkage of the *haah da naara* and the peace at Partition to a new situation as it emerges serves to remind and reinforce the collective identity of peaceful pluralism. The invocations associate those events and the ideals they represent with the power elites who articulate these values at social, political, and religious events. Such a process is also documented in a Japanese case in John Nelson's article "Social Memory as Ritual Practice" concerning post–World War II Japan. In this study, Nelson points out that everyday socio-cultural practices promoted by power elites shape the meaning of social memory, giving the practices ritual significance. In the case of Japan, the government's support of museums in which to enshrine and fix the ambivalent histories of Japan's war history was a means of coping with the realities of human loss and the ideological defeat that accompanied the military devastation. By incorporating the war dead into the realm of the spirits who guide the nation and creating a space in which memory, history, and the spirit world could be united, the government (in need of stability) and the population (in need of healing) combined to create a moral community of memory.

> At an abstract level, the spirits of the founding fathers and mothers of the nation are ever present as guides and coercive examples for present-day correct policy and behavior.... The way that they are referenced through social memory and commemorative rituals interacts not only with traditional religious values but also, as we shall see, with the nation's highest political leaders and their networks of alliance and power.[54]

This is similar to Casey's notion of memorialization, in which cultural memory and identity are constituted by and constitutive of the places in which community life takes place. As Casey writes, commemorative rites connect bodily memory with place memory, enabling us "to honor the past by carrying it intact into new and lasting forms of alliance and participation."[55] Examples from Malerkotla's past are ritualized through repetition and invocation at every opportunity, honoring the ethical models and creating opportunities for subsequent generations to identify with and appropriate the collective memories.

In Malerkotla, we have seen how the founding father Haider Shaykh is enshrined and made present as a guide and coercive example. Similarly, Nawab Sher Muhammad Khan and the *haah da naara* are constantly invoked as positive models. Furthermore, the peace at Partition is attributed to a constellation of causes ranging from Haider Shaykh's blessing, to the effective policies of Nawab Iftikhar Ali Khan, to the brave performance of the army, to the sound character of the community at large. This diffuse but interconnected network of participatory actors extends the credit and the power of the calm in 1947 to a wide circle of founding fathers and mothers. By investing every public gathering with the collective remembrance of these moments of interreligious cooperation, and the individuals who perpetrated them, Malerkotla's community identity as a zone of peace is actively produced and reinforced.

Peace Triggers

As seen in the previous chapter about the ritual life at the tomb of Haider
Shaykh, in Malerkotla, there is not only an institutionalized but also a ritualized
peace system that sustains the community through such stresses. These rituals
are not exclusive to the religious spaces of the town, but also include civil
societal and social rituals that evoke and instantiate Malerkotla's mythic past
and idealized self-perception. As Marc Gopin points out, "mythical possibility is
the midwife of cultural conflict resolution and peacemaking."[56] Communal
violence often occurs following triggering incidents such as a cow killing or
conflict over prayer timing. Too often neglected are what one might call "peace
triggers," symbolically powerful actions that help to restore or sustain a peaceful
community equilibrium. In Malerkotla people make use of several key elements
in the town's mythic history—the *haah da naara* protest over the execution
of Guru Gobind Singh's sons, the peace of Partition, the blessings of Haider
Shaykh and the other saints, the character of the townspeople, and so on. Partition and the *haah da naara* are particularly powerful condensations of the
moral authority of the past so that even the most cursory reference is sufficient
to evoke the ethical implications of the events. For example, the centrality of the
haah da naara as a peace trigger became quite evident during celebrations for
the two 'Ids. Both 'Ids are important times in Malerkotla. The chief minister of
Punjab almost always comes for the 'Id prayers, after which he makes a speech
promising the community all sorts of things. At both 'Id prayers in December
2000 and March 2001, the chief minister at the time, Prakash Singh Badal,
promised funds to expand Malerkotla's overflowing *'idgah*, the special 'Id prayer
grounds. He also professed support for an Urdu academy. During these festivals,
Malerkotla becomes the most important place in Punjab, and all the power
elites who have an interest in cultivating this Muslim-majority constituency
must come to town. 'Id, therefore, is an opportunity for Malerkotla residents
to publicly demonstrate their sense of their own importance in Punjab and
beyond.

For example, at the end of Ramadan in December 2000, the pace of life in
Malerkotla picked up sharply. The winter days had been warm enough that
people did not move around much, and there had been a perceptible slowing
of daily life during the holy month. In the evenings, as soon as the fast was
broken and prayers were said, the bazaars filled with people shopping, eating,
and going to *iftar* meals. On 'Id al-Fitr, the date marking the end of the fast, and
for several days afterward, the social and political life of Malerkotla was busy
from dawn to dark with 'Id Milans. 'Id Milans are formal gatherings, sponsored
by various organizations, for the purpose of acknowledging the end of this
important religious obligation. Many civic groups and political parties organized 'Id Milans, and there was clearly a priority on bringing the most

distinguished person available to attend as chief guest; prominent politicians from all over Punjab were more than willing to preside. In 2000 the Punjab State Waqf Board sponsored an 'Id Milan in Malerkotla at which the chief guest was Surjit Singh Barnala, then governor of the newly created neighboring state of Uttaranchal Pradesh. The Shiromani Akali Dal-Mann hosted an event at which the party's leader and the member of Parliament from Malerkotla's district, Sardar Simranjit Singh Mann, was the main attraction. The Jama'at-i Islami organized an 'Id Milan in the neighboring town of Nabha, where there are few Muslims, using the opportunity to reach out to and educate non-Muslims. Sajida Begum, who was the last nawab's youngest wife, a former MLA, and a local Congress Party leader, hosted an 'Id Milan at the Diwan Khana palace presided over by Captain Amrinder Singh, then campaigning for the position of chief minister to which he was subsequently elected. All of these events began with a Qur'an recitation and the performance of *na'ats*, liturgies in praise of the Prophet Muhammad. Poets recited their own works, which often, but not always, focused on Islamic themes. Religious leaders exhorted the gathering to greater piety. Prominent community members spoke on all manner of topics. One subject was *always* the *haah da naara*.

The heightened significance and profile of the 'Id Milan context clearly indicated the centrality of this episode in the mythmaking about Malerkotla. Nearly every speaker—Muslim and non-Muslim—mentioned the bravery of Nawab Sher Muhammad Khan when he stood up for justice and true Islam against the pressure of his Mughal superiors. The innocence of the children, the rapacity of the Sirhind chief Wazir Khan, the tenacity of Sher Muhammad Khan—all of these themes reverberate for several days through the streets of Malerkotla over crackling public address systems. The *haah da naara* is literally ubiquitous, impossible to escape, told by one speaker even when the previous speaker had described the same event. There is little variation or detail given in most speeches, and the emphasis is consistently upon the nawab's bravery in confronting his co-religionists and calling them to task for a just cause. If the nawab in such difficult conditions could put justice over loyalty to his confessional community, then what should stop people today from doing the same? The relentless repetition of the tale forces the audiences to recognize the *haah da naara* as a powerful precedent for present-day interreligious relations. The symbolic event is linked to a call for people to rise above religious sectarianism and join together to forge a united India (under the SAD, the Congress Party, on behalf of Malerkotla, etc.). For example, in 2000 the leader of Punjab's Congress Party, Captain Amrinder Singh, spoke on these themes at an 'Id Milan. As he was in the middle of campaigning for the 2001 elections, Singh was obviously concerned to garner the support of this key constituency. Furthermore, Singh was the erstwhile Maharaja of Patiala, one of the largest and most powerful of Punjab's former princely states. Throughout his speech he referenced the kinship between the two kingdoms, accentuating their similarities as royal houses and their past cooperation. And of course he opened his address with a reference to the *haah da naara*.

> First of all, on this special occasion I congratulate you. My family has an old relationship with this city. Nawab Sher Khan Sahib gave the *haah da naara* for our innocent *sahibzadas*. This is history. If the Hindu, Muslims and Sikhs maintain their unity, India can become a marvelous country. If we do something with our whole hearts, we can do anything. Punjab is like a family.

Captain Amrinder Singh, a Sikh on the campaign trail in a Muslim town at a Muslim celebration, clearly felt that he could most effectively draw in the largely Muslim assembly by reminding them that the bonds between Sikhs and the Muslims of this town go back for generations. He extended the past solidarity to the present and then asserted that India's future lies in religious unity.

I asked many locals what they thought about the ubiquity of the *haah da naara* at all public affairs. Most people responded that it was only natural that Sikh and Hindu politicians would try to find common ground with the Muslim population through such references and vice versa. Some saw it as evidence of Sikh faith and obedience to the will of their guru. Others extended the political and social invocations of the *haah da naara* to include the peace at Partition, citing it as the reason why Sikhs did not attack the principality in 1947. Overwhelmingly people felt that the references were an expected and inevitable feature of every public assembly. The very naturalness and unquestioning acceptance of the invocation indicated that the *haah da naara* is as revealing of the community's self-perception as it is of the perception of outsiders such as Captain Amrinder Singh. This was evident from the following typical exchange. I asked one of the *granthis* who officiates at the Haah da Naara Gurdwara in Malerkotla about the public use of the *haah da naara*.

> AB: In every political or religious program here in Malerkotla, at every function, people talk about the *haah da naara* and Nawab Sher Moham-mad Khan. Why is this story so important?

> GRANTHI: This is important because when the children [of Guru Gobind Singh] were being walled, their knees and feet were cut so the bricks could be set straight. The nawab said, why are you being so cruel? Why such brutality? These children are like our children. You should fight with those who are fighting you, not with these children. And he left the gathering. That is the story of the *haah da naara*. This all comes in the Dasam Granth of Guruji. It is written in the *sakhi* [i.e., the stories of his

life] and it comes in the guru's writings. That is why it is so well known. A Muslim MLA or MP can get elected here because of this. In our area in District Sangrur from here the MLA is always Muslim.

AB: Like [Nusrat Ikram Khan, the MLA at the time from the SAD]?

GRANTHI: Yes, always a Muslim from this community.

AB: Why?

GRANTHI: Because Sikh people vote for them.

Although his account adds some gruesome details, misattributes the story to the Dasam Granth of Guru Gobind Singh, and overstates Sikh electoral influence in Malerkotla, his understanding of the power of the *haah da naara* is quite typical of Malerkotla residents. This particular *granthi* was quite elderly and from a village that had been within Malerkotla state territory in 1947. He recollected those times and asserted that Malerkotla was preserved from Sikh violence because the place was beloved by Sikhs out of respect for the nawab's protest and the guru's blessing. In this telling it becomes clear how intimately bound up with one another all of these events are and how elemental to Malerkotla's collective identity the repetitious invocation of the *haah da naara* is for the residents. The repetition of the story in times of peace at public events gives the references in times of tension their force as peace triggers.

The ubiquity of the *haah da naara* during public events in Malerkotla contrasts sharply with its near absence at the Shahidi Jor Mela, the festival marking the martyrdom (*shahidi*) of the two sons of Guru Gobind Singh, Zorawar and Fateh Singh. This event goes on for three days in Sirhind, the site of their execution. The entire district in which Sirhind lies is now called Fatehgarh Sahib, the Place of Victory after the moral and spiritual victory of the *sahibzadas* over their captors. The Shahidi Jor Mela, much more than the 'Id events in Malerkotla, is the place where Punjab's political agenda is set. Every political party puts up an enormous tent in which endless speeches are made and honored guests of national prominence, such as the famous Indian actor and erstwhile politician Amitabh Bachhan, give stump speeches.[57] Yet here in Sirhind, just meters away from the gurdwara that displays a piece of the very wall in which the guru's sons were executed, here the *haah da naara* all but disappears. I only once heard mention of the nawab's protest—by a Muslim from Malerkotla speaking in the tent of the Sangrur MP Simranjit Singh Mann. One of Mann's major platform positions concerns minority religious rights, and so he is very interested in Malerkotla and supportive of Muslim issues. It is not surprising that reference to the *haah da naara* would be made in his tent. The *haah da naara* serves as a kind of talisman for the Muslim speaker. The mere reference clearly allies him with the dominant interpretation of the nawab's actions which placed justice above religious affiliation. The weight of ritually reenacted collective memories provides a structure of reinforcement for the community identity of peace. Having survived and surmounted the horrors of Partition, the key symbolic events of Malerkotla's history have become repositories for a collective desire to embody and practice the idealized identity. As with so many other major religious events, politics and religion blend at the Shahidi Jor Mela in Sirhind and at the 'Id Milans in Malerkotla. This interweaving of party platform and moral ethos is a subtle exchange, balancing deeply held conviction with politically expedient slogans.

Discord and Discourse

As in any culture, the structures of authority and the codes of conduct are often invisible, but are perceivable through the patterns of behavior or consciousness dominating in the region. At Haider Shaykh's *dargah* and in Malerkotla, the hegemony of the institutionalized peace system is manifest in the overwhelming tendency in all spheres of community life toward an engaged pluralism, which demands and defines appropriate conduct from pilgrims and citizens of all religions and perspectives. Furthermore, collective experiences are interpreted through the frame of *bhaichara* (brotherhood) as even challenging events are folded into this narrative. The efficacy of these regulatory techniques is perhaps most readily discernible in the few instances in which people expressed opposition to the prevailing ideology. For example, once as I walked through the main bazaar in Malerkotla I was beckoned into a shop owned by a middle-aged Hindu man. He warned me against blindly accepting the vision of Malerkotla as a peaceful place, saying that people are often *kapti*—deceitful, insincere, and false. He seemed unhappy, complaining that it was impossible to say anything negative about anyone without being attacked. This indicates that he felt the pressure of social censure were he to give voice to his "politically incorrect" views. Unsurprisingly, the man declined to be interviewed on the record and did not wish to be recorded.

Another vivid example of resistance to the dominant frame also serves to highlight how very dominant the ethos of harmony actually is. Balram, the Hindu *mistri* who told the story of Haider Shaykh recorded in chapter 1, changed subjects from his story of Haider Shaykh and the horse to discuss the relations between Muslims and Hindus in town. First he invoked the Hindu epic *Mahabharata*. He had earlier recounted the commonly held belief that there is a connection between the epic and Malerkotla. Many locals of all religious faiths assert that the ruler of the region prior to Haider Shaykh was a descendant of Bhima, one of the five Pandava brothers who fought for justice and the restoration of dharma against their immorally motivated kinsmen the Kauravas. However, the *mistri* uses his reference to the epic to shift the purpose of his narrative and introduce a theory about the origin of Islam. Following the

Mahabharata war, he claimed, the losing Kaurava, King Dhrtarashtra, and his wife Gandhari went to Mecca. Over time, the Kaurava clan became known as the Quraysh, the clan into which the Prophet Muhammad was born. Thus the Muslim people are descended from the people who threatened *dharmarajya*, the rule of order in India. Furthermore, their ritual practices are improperly oriented, a somatic signal of their inherent immorality. He said, "This is our belief, that the Quraysh are from the Kauravas. Those people bow their heads to this side [west]. We are *suryavanshi* [turned to the sun], we do obeisance to the sun. Now in these countries, the idols of Mahatma Buddha are broken, the idols are broken." The last remark refers to the destruction by the Taliban of the Bamiyan Buddhas in 2001. This conversation took place at the same time and clearly reflects the anti-Muslim sentiment that arose in the aftermath of the destruction. Associating the Quraysh and the Prophet Muhammad with the ruler defeated by the forces of dharma is clearly meant to demean them. This assertion also triggered an increase in anti-Muslim sentiment in the conversation as a whole.

The reference to the Bamiyan Buddhas led to a general debate over the relationship between Hindus and Muslims in the town. One man asserted vehemently that there was no love between the communities and that the Muslims oppress and shun Hindus in numerous ways: by not inviting them into their homes, complaining about noise from temples, thinking Hindus are dirty, and so on. These assertions brought on an interesting reaction from the others present.

> ARUN: If you construct one temple, these "sister fucker" Muslims get burnt. Have we ever asked them why they offer *namaz* five times a day?
>
> GOPAL: *We* feel good that they take the name of God.
>
> ARUN: If we use speakers in the temples, the whole area has a problem. All the *mian* [Muslims] of Malerkotla have a problem, they say our children are sleeping, stop it, you are doing *arati* [worship]. Sometimes I say let it go. Sometimes I reply with anger and sometimes with humbleness. Even a degraded asshole *mian* who does not know how to talk has an objection [to Hindu prayer].
>
> BALRAM: See, the thing is our Vishvakarma Mandir, a man came there and said, "Stop the [loud]speaker, it is the time of our *namaz*. I said, "Go to Pakistan if you want to offer *namaz*."
>
> CHAMAN: Leave it. Don't make jokes.
>
> BALRAM: It is not a joke. It is a matter of good manners.
>
> CHAMAN: Maybe you might have relations with the wrong or bad people. I have relations with good people.

This was a heated debate in the group, as they expressed frustration and even hostility toward the Muslim population. Arun felt strongly that Malerkotla was falsely painted as a peaceful place. Balram's feelings were mixed, and the other two, Gopal and Chaman, believed that Malerkotla's reputation as a peaceful town of communal harmony was essentially true, though not without complication. They pointed out that bad things happen everywhere but asserted that most people are good. However, no group, religious or political, is exempt from corruption. As Chaman put it:

> Only 2 [percent] or 3 percent are bad elements, only [they] spoil the whole community. Now we Jains have four hundred houses, but only a few give the right way to society. Like those that are not allowing the *munshis* [Jain mendicants] to come to Malerkotla. All the institutions have villainy, there is cheating or swindling in all temples. There is cheating, they are running their own business. All are money takers—managers, the subdivisional magistrate, and deputy commissioner are money takers.

He shifted the discussion of communal relations to a general indictment of social institutions, including the Sikh subdivisional manager and the Hindu deputy commissioner. He also expressed frustration with the political parties, all of which manipulate religion for their own advantage. Chaman characterized the political party of the BJP, for example, as "a cunning party," adding, "They take the names of Hindus, but they are against them. They have taken the veil of religion." All four men nodded in agreement with this assessment.

Ultimately, this exchange brought to the fore a counter-discourse to the dominant portrayal of Malerkotla as a zone of peace. This debate indicated that the dominant narrative of Malerkotla was by no means a comfortable fit for everyone and in so doing also demonstrated how powerful and pervasive the "myth of Malerkotla" actually is. It allowed both the airing of divisive and contradictory perspectives and created an opportunity for members of the Jain and Hindu community to find space for themselves in a town heavily dominated by Muslims and Muslim history. Though well versed in, and proud of, aspects of Malerkotla's history, their pride was tinged with some resentment of Muslim dominance. Similarly, Balram had praised the miraculous powers of Haider Shaykh and expressed devotion to the saint, but in his narrative, he positioned Haider Shaykh above the sultan, thereby critiquing Muslim rule through his praise for the saint.

The institutionalized peace system is observable on the grass-roots level in this exchange. Arun, who voiced the greatest distrust and dislike for Muslims, was quieted by his friends, who attempted to remind him that corruption is not exclusive to any religion and that most people are goodhearted. Such exchanges show how communities within Malerkotla manage their own identities within the framework of Pathan Muslim dominance and power. Frustration and resentment are certainly present in some individuals and groups. But even as the frustration and hostility were articulated, the men's concerted efforts to pacify Arun clearly signaled it to be inappropriate. This echoes the perspective taken by Abdul Rauf, who asserted that the key to peace is the practice of self-policing within each religious community. This microstrategy of peace building constrains hostile, extremist, or combative elements within each group and compels them toward the normative moral order through methods most appropriate and resonant to that individual or group. By internalizing this ethos of harmony, the coercive power of the entire community reinforces the dominant identity of Malerkotla and the *dargah* of Haider Shaykh as places of peace.

Conclusion

In Malerkotla, in spite of local, regional, and national situations that test the fabric of the community, the collective ethos of harmony retains its integrity, and the community remains bound together. In fact, the focalization and trans-valuation tend to work in the opposite way they do in the situations of conflict studied by Tambiah. Triggering events set in motion the institutionalized peace system. Furthermore, among the key resources mobilized as a microstrategy of peace building is the repertory of explanations for the town's pacific nature. Frequent public references to Haider Shaykh, the *haah da naara*, the peace at Partition, or the collective ethos of harmony help to establish and sustain an accommodative equilibrium. These stories are repeated in times of peace as well, allowing them to resonate among residents as authentic representations of their collective identity. Certain past events are understood as emblematic of the essential nature of the place. Even though everyone knows counterexamples and can cite grievances, the power of the dominant narrative of peace eventually orients the community toward the organizing myth of Malerkotla. The narratives and rituals, as cultural practices, both express and construct the nature of collective self-imagining in Malerkotla. Dipankar Gupta explains the role of cultural practices in generating a shared understanding of what it means to belong to a particular community.

> Cultural practices, therefore, create specific cultural spaces where interactions are governed by the ability to read metaphors which have multiple interpretations (or vocalities). To belong to a culture is to belong to a space where there is an awareness of the accepted interpretation, enlivened by particular metaphors. Though metaphors are open to many vocalities, only a few gain salience and can be called their regnant set of interpretations.[58]

The many vocalities in Malerkotla are clearly dominated by a hegemonic interpretation of the past. People do not repeatedly invoke the Kothala firings or the *arti-namaz* disputes from the early twentieth century. They do replay over and over the *haah da naara* and the peace at Partition and laud the power and appeal of Haider Shaykh. The accepted interpretation of the past validates the present reputation of peaceful coexistence.

Malerkotla contains a diverse population and all their complex histories. Although these histories are by no means only peaceful up until the Partition of India, the virulence of past conflict is not allowed to poison the present. Instead, people expect and enforce respect and tolerance. One resident explained how the core value of respect is central to the collective tension-wisdom of Malerkotla. He said, "In reality, from this we come to know that everybody respects each other's religion. They do not say to each other to adopt this religion. They follow their own religion, and this has maintained the brotherhood. This is what is special about Malerkotla." The efficacy of conflict management in Malerkotla since Partition is ascribable in part to the self-regulation of the populace and a general acceptance of the hegemony of a pluralistic ideal on the political and civil societal levels. The coercive force of the community's idealized image of itself is brought to bear on those who sow dissent, and as a result the organizations often blamed for divisiveness, such as the Jama'at-i Islami and the RSS, sit down together to further shared interests. These mostly positive relationships penetrate every level of society, from politics and civil society to neighborhoods and religious shrines.

Conclusion

Hatred increases due to hatred. Love kills hatred.
—Maulana Abdul Rauf (d. 2003)

U NDERSTANDING Malerkotla and the dynamics of pluralism in this town helps us to understand how functioning multireligious communities work. Although it is essential to research places where conflict is endemic, it is equally important to see the day-to-day life of a place where tension and conflicts are managed productively. Much work remains to be done to discover if some of the lessons of life in Malerkotla are applicable and replicable elsewhere. But inasmuch as Malerkotla is a typical town full of all the normal vicissitudes of group life, it provides an object lesson in coexistence. It is also an important corrective to the notion that Muslims are engaged in a clash of civilizations with non-Muslim cultures. Here we have seen centuries of events and characters that defy such simplistic labels and demand closer examination.

Exploring the alleyways of Malerkotla and the files of the dusty archives has revealed a rich tapestry of personalities that has shaped the place into its current form. But Malerkotla is not frozen in time. Recently I returned for a wedding to a rapidly changing landscape. The roads are still terrible, but old buildings are giving way to new structures. Some of the buildings demolished were historic, such as some that made up the façade of the Moti Bazaar that Nawab Ahmad Ali Khan had built, reportedly on the model of Jaipur's pink city, though far less grand. Still, the imprint of the past is still discernible in the present, not least in terms of the shared investment in the collective identity of peaceful pluralism. As we have seen, in Malerkotla this collective identity is produced and perpetuated through memories, ritual practices, stories, and other efforts of people seeking ways to live in a diverse and often challenging world. Caught between national Hindu hegemony and the challenges of sustaining a community of minorities, Malerkotla residents and visitors explain the past in ways that help them to coexist in the present. The experiences of conflicts and conflict management provide the basis for the tension-wisdom of today, as Malerkotla's resilience during times of stress has repeatedly been tested. The grassroots strategies of peacemaking are not abstract principles taught in seminars. The institutionalized peace system that responds to triggering incidents relies on the availability of multiple explanations for the quality of the Malerkotla community. Because no one justification for the peace during and since Partition dominates, everyone in town is able to locate themselves within the frame of peace that has come to characterize the collective identity.

Three key narratives are at the root of the peace-building practices and pragmatics of coexistence that emerge in the post-Partition period. First, tales of the settlement's founder, Haider Shaykh, describe his arrival and activities in the region and his protective powers. These stories ground the ethos of secularism and harmony in the ongoing popularity of the saint's multireligious cult. The beliefs, practices, and narratives centered on Haider Shaykh are observable evidence of the possibility for people of all religions, genders, ages, castes, and classes to be simultaneously and peacefully invested in a shared space. Second, Nawab Sher Muhammad Khan's protest and Guru Gobind Singh's subsequent blessing exemplify the possibility of rising above sectarian loyalties in defense of a moral principle rooted in a religious tradition. After all, many believe that the nawab protested the execution of the guru's sons on Islamic grounds. Third, these stories and others are linked to the success of the community in surviving and transcending the trauma of Partition that took such a horrific toll on the rest of Punjab. The peace during Partition emerges as the pivotal moment in Malerkotla's history, marking a shift in the collective representations of the town, its history, and its heroes. This establishes the dominant frame through which the experiences of the past and present are filtered and made sense of, allowing peace-building efforts to resonate with the lived experience of the community.

These important individuals and events in Malerkotla's past have come to shape collective representations of the community's identity as a place of peace. The shared shrine to Haider Shaykh and the shared history of the *haah da naara* together play powerful roles in sustaining a peaceful multireligious civil society. They are not competing explanations; on the contrary, some people point to both as reasons for Malerkotla's reputation as an "island of peace." Indeed, some people link the two together, crediting Haider Shaykh with Sher Muhammad Khan's protest or claiming that the guru blessed the shaykh, rather than his descendant Sher Muhammad Khan. These beliefs lie outside the realm of historical evidence, but the force of faith in the guru, the shaykh, the miraculous preservation of Malerkotla during Partition, and so on turns the perception into historical reality. And the mythology of these events stabilizes the framing discourse about the town's essentially pacific nature. After rising above the bloodshed of Partition in 1947, these individuals and events became symbols of Malerkotla's identity, appeared in the media, memorialized in collective rituals, and idealized as models of good governance—whether they merited such accolades or not. In this way they have become powerful resources in the molding of a peaceful plural society in a region. These figures and events blend into the collective imagination of Malerkotla's residents and visitors, intermingling with later happenings such as the peace at Partition. The coercive force of this collective representation constrains residents to act in accordance with the ideal and gives force to the corrections that bring dissonant voices into line.

It is worth emphasizing that, though rarely publicly acknowledged, Malerkotla's pre-Partition history is full of interreligious conflicts. Yet from Partition forward, the perception takes root that Malerkotla is a place free of interreligious contention. The collective authority of the normative version of Malerkotla's history also conceals complicating histories and experiences. These hidden transcripts and potential memories emerge on certain occasions—when triggering incidents spur conflict, when personal grievances and experiences are at odds with the dominant culture—releasing tension and preventing a buildup of resentment. As a collectivity, residents walk the careful line between adhering to a particular view of why Malerkotla has managed to maintain its peace and allowing for a variety of other perspectives on that peace. This is reflected in a statement from Abdullah, the retired schoolteacher. Abdullah acknowledged the multiple popular explanations—the blessings of Haider Shaykh and the blessing of Guru Gobind Singh—and yet maintains his own opinion that the ultimate credit belongs with God. By acknowledging the significance of the other accounts for those who believe in them, Abdullah makes a critical space for variation on the theme of peace.

> See, about Guru Gobind Singh it is said that his blessings are on this kingdom. And it is also said this is a land of *buzurgs* [saints], on all sides are *buzurgs*. Both are the reasons [for the peace]. Sikh people say that because of the guru's blessing, Malerkotla is safe. Muslims say it is because of these *pirs* that Malerkotla is safe. My views are these, whether it is the blessing of the guru or the blessing of the *buzurgs*, God wanted to preserve this place. It *is* safe. The reason may be any of these. For some people, one idea is more prevalent. For the Sikhs it is more prevalent that to keep good relations with the Muslims they say that our gurus had relations with these people. The nawab of this place saved the children of our guru, and our guru gave a blessing to this city, and this city was saved. With this comes brotherhood, and we can say there is unity.[1]

Abdullah recognized that his Muslim and Sikh neighbors may have different explanations from his own for the peace in Malerkotla, but the essential point is that they all agree there *is* peace. Whether attributed to the guru, to the saints such as Haider Shaykh, to God, or some other reason, everyone has a claim to the peace and a stake in it.

In the case of Haider Shaykh, this is possible because the saint, his history, his hagiography, his *dargah*, and his territory can be made to fit into most everyone's grand narrative of peace, no matter their religion. For some the saint is one example of a pan-Indian process of Islamicization. For others he is their progenitor whose arrival here marks the origin of their own life, livelihood, and faith. For some the shaykh is a powerful, miracle-working saint whose intercessory powers have brought health, wealth, and children as well as peace. And for yet others he is an important man whose marriage to an emperor's daughter led to the settlement of the region, and whose legacy of peace and justice must be respected but not worshiped. The shaykh is a chameleon to his interlocutors. He morphs in each account, conforming to each person's idea of citizenship, devotion, domination, mediation, or heritage. Furthermore, it is not merely through narratives that these ideals are realized. The rituals performed at the tomb also represent a range of ideas and behaviors available to the adherents of multiple religions, facilitating mutual attunement for visitors of all faiths. From the highly Islamic formality of the Ramadan '*urs* to the efflorescence of people, practices, and possessions at the *mela* to the mundane social exchanges at the shrine, the space is not only the stage upon which an ideal of openness and pluralism is publicly performed. The site itself, its structure, situation, and the ways in which its built environment is imagined, engaged, and maintained are also resources in generating an atmosphere of expansiveness rather than exclusivity.

The tomb shrine of Haider Shaykh functions as a center for the concentration and redistribution of the constitutive elements of authority. The rich ritual and narrative repertoires of the site enable residents and devotees to assume multiple subject positions in relation to the shrine. The multiplicity activates and validates the *dargah* as a collective representation of a place in which an idealized plural society actually exists. This process does not require personal belief in the power of Haider Shaykh. Vinod, the low-caste Hindu politician, attended the shrine primarily to demonstrate publicly that he is a secular man without prejudice toward Muslims. He and others saw it as politically and socially advisable to participate openly in the tomb cult. Others expressed the spiritualized view that at the shrine pilgrims "exchange love" between one another as they commune with the shaykh. The belief in the ongoing presence and accessibility of the saint's spirit makes the continuation of worship a critical element for residents and devotees. Proper *adab* (etiquette) must be observed in relation to the saint, but the variant interpretations of what constitutes appropriate behavior or belief rarely come into conflict as pilgrims, and others are ritually and spatially attuned to one another and tend toward accommodation and interaction rather than exclusion. In this way, the complex ritual and narrative repertoire of devotion and exchange at Haider Shaykh's *dargah* activates the site as a resource in making Malerkotla a *wilayat* of peace.

Partition's effect upon Malerkotla was very different from its effects else-where. The ability of the community to rise above religious divisions and defend the integrity of the collective makes Partition a moment of shared success, which has had an integrating influence on the local population. Motivated by their status as religious minorities, all the local religious groups have an interest in maximizing the efficacy of this idealized identity. As a suspect national minority, Muslims must manifest publicly and constantly that they are loyal citizens and above suspicion. Hindus as a numerical minority locally must also perpetuate the dominant identity for their own continued comfort. Sikhs, caught in the middle as a local and national minority but a regional majority, also have interest in maintaining the identity of peace. By maintaining an active repertoire of tales concerning the *haah da naara* and Partition, in addition to the complex of narratives associated with Haider Shaykh and the other local saints, Mal-erkotla residents and visitors create the conditions necessary for the type of coalition building, trust, and nonsectarian political economy that sustains the multireligious community. In this way the abstract ideal is made practical, supporting the imagined reality with the lived experiences of residents and visitors.

The dominant narrative is not uncontested, however. Peace, it turns out, is just as multicausal as conflict, and Malerkotla's placid public image masks multiple contributing and challenging factors. Tension-wisdom is not about the elimination of conflict, it is the ability to manage tension in a fundamentally prosocial manner. In the dispute over the public performance of *arati* and *namaz* in the 1930s a very serious division in Malerkotla's community fabric could have taken root. Likewise, the virulent sentiments expressed by some within the community today could, if allowed, escalate into much more perva-sive and poisonous sentiments. These potential triggers of conflict do initiate disputes and clashes, such as the buildings burned after Ayodhya. But these incidents can also function as peace triggers, mobilizing local leaders, govern-ment officials, neighborhoods, friends, and enemies to counteract the conflict, setting the institutionalized peace system into motion. As we saw in the account of Maulana Abdul Rauf, a key element of this system is the self-management of each group and sect within the community: " . . . when the atmosphere became bad at times the Muslims themselves asked those Muslims not to do such things, and the Hindus did the same thing to Hindus. . . ." This automatic response to "bad elements," as Rauf termed them, speaks to a sense of responsibility for supporting congenial collective life rather than blaming the other for everything. What is more, such efforts do not cease after a crisis, but continue. As Rauf pointed out, "such a lot of committees were founded." Potential conflicts are obviated through active outreach efforts by community leaders, residents, and visitors from outside. The proper functioning of these shared ritual and civic spaces is assured by cooperation among potentially competing interest groups and by the coercive force of Malerkotla's dominant ethic of harmony.

The making of this collective ethos is both voluntary and coercive. On the one hand, residents buy in to the utopian vision of the town because they are fully conscious of the benefits this idealized perception brings in terms of increased political cache and generally quiescent social relations. On the other hand, dissent is discouraged, narratives are disciplined, and acceptable speech and behavior are constrained by the institutions and ideologies that dominate in Malerkotla. Those who do not attune themselves to the prevailing theme of harmony are "attuned" by others through a variety of techniques, including conversational corrections, group dialogues, or interventions. Produced at the shrine and in the streets, the hegemonic identity is authenticated and perpetuated in the interest of sustaining this Muslim-majority town and maximizing its regional power. There is undeniably a historical, political, and social process in Malerkotla that suppresses divisiveness and rewards conviviality. Peace, pluralism, and a unified conception of community, therefore, are the products of the convergence of spiritual, political, and cultural interest.

The institutionalized peace system that makes up this process is observable in the civic and sacred spaces of the town during public events like the 'Id Milans and other religious observations, poetry readings, sports events, and the Ekta Sammelan. It is also evident in memorializing practices like pilgrimage or the formulaic invocation of past events like the *haah da naara*. Daily interactions between residents and visitors within these sacred and civic spaces allow the ideal of pacific pluralism to resonate with mundane experience. Some of these elements of the peace are operationalized concretely, such as peace committees, municipal committees, community welfare societies, and the other organized civil societal groups. Others methods are semiformal, such as the procedures employed by Hindu and Sikh *chela*s in encouraging their clientele to support and patronize the Muslim *khalifah*s. Their conversational tactics are given strength and a degree of formality, as they temporally and temporarily become vehicles for the voice of the saint. Informal inter- and intrapersonal exchanges also reinforce the positive value on bridge building, conciliation, and interreligious harmony. As evidenced in the conversation in which several Hindus and Jains expressed frustration, even anger, the opportunity to voice opposition is critical, but is actively countered and suppressed. And as Lakoff argues, even the resistance to a dominant frame serves to reinforce the cognitive structures of the frame itself. The peace of Malerkotla is by no means devoid of pressure, social control, and enforcement, but this does not undermine the high level of community participation in telling the dominant story of Malerkotla and participating in the supporting institutions ranging from electoral contests to associational memberships to pilgrimages. The symbolic power of this identity is an important resource for the entire community as it has heightened the civic profile on the state level, maximizing Malerkotla's ability to compete for finite resources in terms of government support and political power. The personal value of the community identity is perhaps best expressed by one resident who said, "Our forefathers lived together, Hindu, Muslim, and Sikh. In 1947 Muslims from here did not migrate and lived here in harmony. If some small quarrels occur, later on all become one. Our nature is that we easily go on the same way as earlier, the way of love and harmony."

This book is an effort to expose the daily activities and microstrategies of engagement that contribute to Malerkotla's peace. These are typically taken for granted, both by social theorists and by communities themselves. But such conscious and unconscious efforts at inclusion and participation are good indicators of the depth of engaged pluralism in a multicultural society. The role of shared spaces, both sacred and civic, in supporting multiconfessional communities is a crucial part of the practice of pluralism. In Malerkotla these spaces are numerous, and they are *cultivated*. At the level of governance, political and civil society, and in everyday contexts, people of all religious affiliations engage in a variety of exchanges from the economic to the interpersonal. They do so not by bracketing their religious identities but by using their religious beliefs as a basis for such exchange. As in the example of Abdul Rauf, the Jama'at-i Islami leader, who actively sought to build bridges with other faiths, it is clear that one does not have to forsake a strong commitment to one's own religion to engage in interreligious dialogue. Nor, as in the conversation between Zulfikar and the *chela* is it necessary to determine proper belief and practice for others. In Malerkotla, the tendency is to validate and accept the legitimacy of contradictory or distinct ideas and behaviors even as people affirm their own convictions.

Malerkotla may not be an earthly paradise, but it has gained a reputation as a communal utopia. In this town where "brotherhood is handed down as tradition" (*Times of India*, March 2, 2002) residents and visitors are aware of the mythology that has developed to account for the unique features of the community—the peace at Partition, the Muslim majority, and the pacific interreligious relations. By articulating, reiterating, enacting, and memorializing Malerkotla's idealized identity both at the shrine and in the streets, Malerkotla's residents collectively forge a conception of their community that rejects divisive and antagonistic communal identities. Divisiveness is countered with an identity of inclusion that serves the majority of townspeople's spiritual, political, social, and cultural needs. Inclusiveness and unity are observable at the shrine of Haider Shaykh, in the everyday interactions in Malerkotla's neighborhoods, and in the institutions of civil society. This quality of life also resonates with a romanticized memory of pre-Partition Punjabi culture in which the lines separating Sikh, Hindu, and Muslim traditions and practices were often blurry. In this idealized form, Punjabi culture superceded religious affiliation, and the memory of this *punjabiyyat*, or "Punjabiness," further authenticates the idealized identity of Malerkotla as a multireligious zone of peace. The post-Partition role of Malerkotla as the only Muslim-majority principality in Indian Punjab has heightened the town's political profile. Therefore, under close scrutiny and with a great deal at stake, the residents of Malerkotla enforce an ethos of harmony and order discernible in the dominance of narratives that sustain the status quo and practices that reinforce integration and inclusion.

It is impossible to know what will happen in Malerkotla's future. The town is growing quickly, with a 20-percent population growth rate between the 1991 and 2001 censuses. It is one of the major industrial and agricultural centers in the district and the state. Old power bases are shifting as new groups and leaders emerge. Malerkotla does remain a bastion of Punjabi Muslim culture. Muslims in Indian Punjab today are often émigrés from Uttar Pradesh and Bihar seeking work in this comparatively wealthy state. As one Punjabi Muslim living outside Malerkotla recently expressed, he often feels closer to his Sikh and Hindu Punjabi neighbors and colleagues than to the non-Punjabi Muslims who dominate his local mosque. The cultural affinities of Punjabis in terms of food, literature, music, and so on remain strong, though globalization and mass media are having a homogenizing effect here as elsewhere. Sometimes the past and present do not coexist comfortably: local landmarks are swallowed up by larger structures and traditional leaders are sidelined by new social dynamics. Still, in terms of Indian Punjab's Muslim history and culture, Malerkotla is also an extremely important place, and local pride in this heritage is evident. The extent to which the past is prologue remains to be seen, but it is a rich resource for those who choose to continue the traditions of peaceful pluralism.

Appendix A: Malerkotla Ruling Family

Ruler	Years Ruled
Ruler	*Years Ruled*
Shaykh Sadruddin Sadari Jahan	1454–1509
Shaykh 'Isa	1508–1538
Khan Muhammad Shah	1538–1545
Khwaja Madud Khan	1545–1566
Fateh Muhammad Khan	1566–1600
Muhammad Bayzid Khan	1600–1659
Feroz Khan	1659–1672
Sher Muhammad Khan	1672–1712
Ghulam Hussain Khan	1712–1717
Jamal Khan	1717–1755
Bhikan Khan	1755–1763
Bahadur Khan	1763–1766
'Umar Khan	1766–1780
Asadullah Khan	1780–1784
Ataullah Khan	1784–1810
Wazir Ali Khan	1810–1821
Amir Ali Khan	1821–1846
Mehboob Ali Khan	1846–1857
Sikander Ali Khan	1858–1871
Ibrahim Ali Khan	1871–1908
Ahmad Ali Khan	1908–1947
Iftikhar Ali Khan	1947–1948

Appendix B: The Call for Justice, *haah da naara*

Iftikhar Ali Khan gives this translation in his *History of the Ruling Family of Sheikh Sadruddin Sadar-i-Jahan of Malerkotla* of the letter ostensibly written by Nawab Sher Muhammad Khan to Aurangzeb in protest over the 1705 execution of Guru Gobind Singh's two youngest sons, Zorawar and Fateh. Though the historical validity of this letter is questioned by Punjab historians, it is widely accepted in the popular culture.

"O mighty king of the world who on account of thy justice has placed thy throne on the azure vault; may the dappled horse of the skies be ever under thy control because thou hast eclipsed the brilliance of Sun and Moon by the splendour of thy innumerable victories.

"The humble and devoted petitioner with all respect due to the grandeur of the shadow of God and to the might of the saviour of the world, most respectfully begs to lay his humble appeal before your most Gracious majesty and hopes from Your Imperial majesty's unfathomable kindness and illimitable magnanimity that the August person of the shadow of God, vice regent of the holy Prophet (Peace [page 36] be on him) in this world, the incarnation of God's mercy over his creatures by sheer magnificence, be pleased to bestow his compassion and forgiveness on the young sons of Gobind Singh the 10th Guru of the Sikh nation. The Viceroy of Sirhind province with a view of avenging the disobedience and disloyal activities of the Guru which might have been committed by him, has without any fault or crime of the guiltless and innocent children simply on the basis of their being the scions of Guru Gobind Singh, condemned these minor sons liable to execution and has proposed to wall them up alive till they die. Although no one dare to raise an objection against the order of the Viceroy whose order is as inevitable as death, yet the faithful servants and well-wishers of Your August majesty's empire deem it most advisable to humbly appeal and bring to Your Majesty's benign notice. May it be said that if in view of certain important political considerations Your Majesty is disposed to inflict suitable punishment on the Sikh Nation for their undesirable activities in the past, it would be quite compatible with justice but your Majesty's humble and devoted servant thinks that it would, in no way be consistent with the principles of sovereignty and supreme power to wreak the vengeance of the misdeeds of a whole nation on two innocent children who, on account of their tender age [are] quite innocent and unable to take a stand against the all powerful Viceroy. This sort of action obviously appears to be absolutely against the dictates of Islam and the laws propounded by the founder of Islam (May God's blessings be showered on him) and Your Majesty's humble servant is afraid that the enactment of such an atrocious Act would perpetually remain an ugly blot on the face of Your Majesty's renowned justice and righteousness. It may graciously be considered that the mode of inflicting the punishment and torture as contemplated by the Viceroy of Sirhind can by no means be considered compatible with the principles of Supreme rule, equity and justice.

"In view of above considerations Your Majesty's humble and devoted servant most respectfully takes the liberty of suggesting that if your Majesty considers it expedient that the sons of Shri Guru Gobind Singh may be kept under restraint from indulging in disloyal activities, it would be more appropriate, if they could be interned in the Royal capital at Delhi, till they are duly reformed, so as to willingly acknowledge allegiance and loyalty to the throne. In the alternative both the boys may be placed under my care so as to keep a check on their actions and movements and not to allow them to entertain any kind of ideas of sedition or disloyalty in their minds. Although the humble petitioner fears that this humble appeal which is prompted exclusively by the sense of veracity and loyalty to the throne may be deemed as transgressing the limits of propriety, yet the fear of God [page 37] and the urge of faith does not allow the undue suppression of truths. If this humble appeal has the honour of meeting the Royal acceptance, it shall be most fortunate. If however unfortunately it is deprived of the honour of acceptance, still Your Majesty's humble and devoted servant shall have the consolation of having performed the sacred duty of expressing what was right and just and not having allowed his pen to deviate in the expression of truth."

Source: Khan, Iftikhar Ali. *History of the Ruling Family of Sheikh Sadruddin Sadar-i-Jahan of Malerkotla (1449 A.D. to 1948 A.D.).* Edited by R. K. Ghai. Patiala: Punjabi University Press, 2000 [1948], pp. 35–37.

Notes

INTRODUCTION

1. "Oasis of Tolerance" (*Hindu*, April 1, 2005), "Where Peace Reigns Supreme" (*The Tribune*, August 19, 2006), and "Muhabbat aur man ki ghavarah Malerkotla" (*Hind Samachar*, 2000). Other headlines include: "Malerkotla Muslims Feel Safer in India" (*Indian Express*, August 13, 1997) and "Where Brotherhood Is Handed Down as Tradition" (*Times of India*, March 2, 2002).

2. Throughout the book, names have been changed except in the case of public figures speaking on the record.

3. James A. Aho, *This Thing of Darkness: A Sociology of the Enemy* (Seattle: University of Washington Press, 1994), p. 104.

4. Jawaharlal Nehru quoted in Shashi Tharoor, *Nehru: The Invention of India* (New York: Arcade Publishing, 2004), p. 226.

5. For more discussion of the nature of Indian secularism, see Mushirul Hasan, *Legacy of a Divided Nation: India's Muslims Since Partition* (Boulder, CO: Westview Press, 1997), esp. chap. 5: "Secularism: The Post-colonial Predicament"; and Rajeev Dhavan, "The Road to Xanadu: India's Quest for Secularism," in *Religion and Personal Law in Secular India: A Call to Action*, ed. Gerald Larson (Bloomington: Indiana University Press, 2001).

6. Talal Asad, *Formations of the Secular: Christianity, Islam, Modernity* (Palo Alto, CA: Stanford University Press, 2003), p. 16.

7. Ashis Nandy, "The Twilight of Certitudes: Secularism, Hindu Nationalism, and Other Masks of Deculturation," *Postcolonial Studies* 1, 3, 1998: 289.

8. Partha Chatterjee, "Fasting for Bin Laden: The Politics of Secularization in Contemporary India," in *Powers of the Secular Modern: Talal Asad and His Interlocutors*, ed. David Scott and Charles Hirschkind (Stanford, CA: Stanford University Press, 2006), p. 57.

9. Constitution of India, Articles 15, 25, 26, 29, and 30. http://lawmin.nic.in/coi/contents.htm (accessed December 20, 2007).

10. Chatterjee, "Fasting for Bin Laden," p. 57.

11. The quotations are references to newspaper headlines about Malerkotla: Asit Jolly, "The Myth of Malerkotla," *Asian Age*, May 11, 1997; "Oasis of Tolerance" (*Hindu*, April 1,

2005), "Where Brotherhood Is Handed Down as Tradition" (*Times of India*, March 2, 2002). The documentary "The Legend of Malerkotla" was directed by Iqbal Malhotra.

12. There is one other town in the northwest of the state, Qadian, where there is a significant population of Muslims. Qadian is the spiritual center of the Ahmadiyya movement that recognizes Mirza Ghulam Ahmad (d. 1908) as a prophet of God, a claim that is vigorously disputed by mainline Muslims. For example, Ahmadis are not recognized as Muslims in Pakistan, though they self-identify as such. For more on the Ahmadiyya, see: Spencer Lavan, *The Ahmadiyah Movement* (Delhi: Manohar, 1974); and Yohanan Friedmann, *Prophecy Continuous: Aspects of Ahmadi Religious Thought and Its Medieval Background* (Berkeley: University of California Press, 1989). For a critical analysis of the movement see Abulhasan 'Ali Nadwi, *Qadianism: A Critical Study*, a translation of *al-Qadiayani wa al-Qadiyaniyah* (1962) by Zafar Ishaq Ansari (Lucknow: Academy of Islamic Research and Publications, 1967). For a view from within the faith, see Bashiruddin Mahmud Ahmad, *Ahmadiyyat, or the True Islam* (Qadian, Punjab: Talif-o-Isha'at, 1924) or www.alislam.org.

13. Stanley Wolpert estimates one million dead, but this is certainly on the high end of the estimates, which range from two hundred thousand up to a million. In part because of the enormous population shift of around fifteen million people, the true number of casualties will never be known. See Stanley Wolpert, *A New History of India* (New York: Oxford University Press, 1993). See also G. D. Khosla, *Stern Reckoning: A Survey of Events Leading Up to and Following the Partition of India* (Delhi: Oxford University Press, 1989).

14. Interview, October 8, 2000.

15. J. S. Grewal and S. S. Bal, *Guru Gobind Singh: A Biographical Study* (Chandigarh: Punjab University Publication Bureau, 1967), pp. 127–142.

16. Ibid, p. 233 n. 25.

17. Ishtiaq Ahmed, "Punjab Holocaust of 1947," *News* (Lahore), January 5, 2008. http://www.thenews.com.pk/editorial_detail.asp?id=71390 (accessed January 8, 2008).

18. These sources will be discussed in detail in chapter 2.

19. Interview, January 30, 2001.

20. Mian Muhammad Sadullah, ed., *The Partition of the Punjab, 1947: A Compilation of Official Documents*, Vols. 1–4 (Lahore: National Documentation Centre, 1983); Kirpal Singh, ed., *Select Documents on Partition of Punjab, 1947—India and Pakistan: Punjab, Haryana, and Himachal-India and Punjab-Pakistan* (Delhi: National Book Shop, 1991); Rukhsana Zafar, *Disturbances in the Punjab: 1947—A Compilation of Official Documents* (Islamabad: National Documentation Centre, 1995).

21. Census of India, 2001. Data available at: http://www.censusindia.gov.in/Census_Data_2001/Census_Data_Online/Social_and_cultural/Religion.aspx (accessed December 14, 2007).

22. The information on religion from Malerkotla's 2001 census was obtained by appeal to the Census of India in a Right to Information request by my research assistant—an Indian citizen. The letter also stated that 1991 data by religion is not available because in that year such data for towns with populations under 100,000 was not taken. In that year Malerkotla's population was 88,600. S. L. Jain, Deputy Director and CPIO (SS Div.), Census of India, to Rachana Rao Umashankar, June 23, 2009.

23. Census of India, 2001, lists 106,802 citizens, of whom 56,872 are male and 49,930 are female, 59,101 are literate (34,583 male literates and 24,518 females). Sir Denzil Ibbetson, *Panjab Castes (reprint of The Races, Castes, and Tribes of the People)* (Lahore:

Superintendent, Government Printing, Punjab, 1916 [1883]), pp. 104–106; and Gopal Krishan, "Demographic Change," in *Punjab in Prosperity and Violence: Administration, Politics and Social Change, 1947–1997*, ed. J. S. Grewal and Indu Banga (Chandigarh: Institute of Punjab Studies, 1998), pp. 156–176; Peter Hardy, *The Muslims of British India* (Cambridge: Cambridge University Press, 1972).

24. Quoted in Wulf Kansteiner, "Finding Meaning in Memory: A Methodological Critique of Collective Memory Studies," *History and Theory* 41, 2 (2002): 182.

25. Hayden White, "Narrativity in the Representation of Reality," in *The Content of the Form: Narrative Discourse and Historical Representation* (Baltimore: Johns Hopkins University Press, 1987), p. 6.

26. Jan Assmann, *Religion and Cultural Memory* (Stanford, CA: Stanford University Press, 2006), p. 94

27. In his book *Don't Think of an Elephant* (White River Junction, VT: Chelsea Green Publishing, 2004), Lakoff calls frames "mental structures that shape the way we see the world" (p. xv). Similarly, in an article in the *American Prospect* ("Framing the Dems: How Conservatives Control Political Debate and How Progressives Can Take It Back"), he defines a frame as "a mental structure that we use in thinking" (September 2003: 32). Framing as a social communicative practice is also central in the work of Erving Goffmann. See *Frame Analysis: An Essay on the Organization of Experience*, (NY; Harper and Row, 1974).

28. Lakoff, *Don't Think of an Elephant*, p. xv.

29. Thapar goes on to say, "Attempts are also made to see the reality of Indian politics in terms of such religious communities. Politics is seen as the interaction of religious communities, and political allegiance relates to the same identity. Political action is designed to further the interests of a particular religious community. The notion of the religious community claims a historical basis and takes the identity of the community as far back in time as possible, so as to add to the legitimacy of the identity" ("Communalism and the Historical Legacy: Some Facets," *Social Scientist* 18, 6/7 [1990]: 5).

30. Neither communalism nor its study are new phenomena. See Sandria Freitag, *Collective Action and Community: Public Arenas and the Emergence of Communalism in North India* (Berkeley: University of California Press, 1989); Cynthia Kepley Mahmood, "Rethinking Indian Communalism: Culture and Counter-Culture," *Asian Survey* 33, 7 (1993); Ashis Nandy, "The Twilight of Certitudes: Secularism, Hindu Nationalism, and Other Masks of Deculturation," *Postcolonial Studies* 1, 3 (1998); Gyan Pandey, *The Construction of Communalism in Colonial North India* (New Delhi: Oxford University Press, 1990).

31. There are many, many polemical books that argue one side or the other for the existence of a temple or the restoration of a mosque. For a pro-temple example, see Koenraad Elst, *Ayodhya: the Case against the Temple* (New Delhi: Voice of India, 2002). For more scholarly works, see Mushirul Hasan, "Ayodhya and Its Consequences: Reappraising Minority Identity," in Mushirul Hasan, ed., *Legacy of a Divided Nation: India's Muslims since Independence* (Boulder, CO: Westview Press, 1997); David Ludden, ed., *Making India Hindu: Religion, Community, and the Politics of Democracy in India* (New York: Oxford University Press, 2005); Gerald Larson, *India's Agony over Religion* (Albany: State University of New York Press, 1995);

Arvind Sharma, ed., *Hinduism and Secularism: After Ayodhya* (New York: Palgrave, 2001); Peter van der Veer, *Gods on Earth: The Management of Religious Experience and Identity in a North Indian Pilgrimage Center* (London: Athlone Press, 1988).

32. See Amrita Basu, ed., *Community Conflicts and the State in India* (Delhi: Oxford University Press, 1998); Praful Bidwai, Harbans Mukhia, and Achin Vanaik, eds., *Religion, Religiosity, and Communalism* (Delhi: Manohar, 1996); Partha Chatterjee, *The Nation and Its Fragments: Colonial and Postcolonial Histories* (Princeton, NJ: Princeton University Press, 1993); Gyanendra Pandey, *The Construction of Communalism in Colonial North India* (New Delhi: Oxford University Press, 1990); and Peter van der Veer, *Religious Nationalism: Hindus and Muslims in India* (Berkeley: University of California Press, 1994).

33. An excellent example of this sort of thinking is an undated report, likely from the early 1930s, prepared by the British government in India on communal disturbances. It cites numerous common causes of Hindu-Muslim conflicts, frequently attributing them to heightened sensitivities and religious fervor around certain practices, particularly the confluence of public processions, the sacrifice of cattle by Muslims, and the playing of music near one another's holy sites. See Oriental and India Office Collection, L/P&J/7/132, *Commissioned Report on Communal Disturbances*. For an interesting study of the role of public performance in exacerbating tensions, see Freitag, *Collective Action and Community*.

34. See Pandey, *Construction*.

35. See Ayesha Jalal, *The Sole Spokesman: Jinnah, the Muslim League, and the Demand for Pakistan* (New York: Cambridge University Press, 1985).

36. Prime Minister's High Level Committee, "Social, Economic, and Educational Status of the Muslim Community of India" (New Delhi: Cabinet Secretariat), November 2006. Hereafter referred to as the Sachar Report.

37. Ibid., p. 11.

38. There are many excellent works on the Sangh Parivar and Hindu nationalism, including Christophe Jaffrelot, *The Hindu Nationalist Movement in India* (New York: Columbia University Press, 1996); and Christophe Jaffrelot, ed., *The Sangh Parivar: A Reader* (New York: Oxford University Press, 2005).

39. The most virulent groups include the Shiv Sena and the Bajrang Dal. For more on these groups see Thomas Blom Hansen, *Wages of Violence: Naming and Identity in Postcolonial Bombay* (Princeton: Princeton University Press, 2001). There is also a women's wing of the RSS called the Rashtriya Sevika Samiti; see Tanika Sarkar, "The Woman as Communal Subject: Rashtrasevika Samiti and Ram Janmabhoomi Movement," *Economic and Political Weekly*, August 31, 1991.

40. "RSS Stands by Resolution," *Hindu*, March 23, 2002. The context of the resolution was a meeting in Bangalore, the sixth in a series of dialogues with Christian groups. http://www.hinduonnet.com/2002/03/23/stories/2002032303680100.htm.

41. In perhaps the most famous case, a female witness was one of thirty-seven of seventy-three witnesses to recant, turning "hostile" on the stand in a trial that took place more than a year after the events of spring 2002. Zahira Sheikh was an eyewitness to the death of her father and thirteen others who were burned alive inside the family's bakery business during the violence. Speaking out after the trial, she told of systematic harassment that led her and her relatives and other witnesses to believe that the

government itself would destroy their lives if she continued to press charges. http://www.rediff.com/news/2003/oct/09best1.htm (accessed November 14, 2003).

42. United States Commission on International Religious Freedom Annual Report 2003 (Washington, D.C.: U.S. Department of State, 2003), p. 17. Available at http://www.uscirf.gov/countries/region/south_asia/india/india.html (accessed December 20, 2007).

43. USCIRF Countries of Particular Concern: India. http://www.uscirf.gov/countries/countriesconcerns/Countries/India.html (accessed December 20, 2007).

44. Gyanendra Pandey, "Can a Muslim Be an Indian?" *Comparative Studies in Society and History* 41, 4 (1999).

45. "Muslims Burn Sharif's Effigy," *Tribune*, July 9, 1999. http://www.tribuneindia.com/1999/99jul10/punjab.htm#9 (accessed January 20, 2008).

46. The lyrics of the song are explicitly religious, homologizing "Mother India" to the Hindu goddess Durga. The voice of the singer also repeatedly asserts, "I bow to you Mother," an act that would be impossible for most Muslims. Tribune News Service, "Malerkotla Muslims Sing Vande Mataram," *Tribune* (Chandigarh), September 6, 2006.

47. The *Vande Mataram* controversy was of concern to Muslims all over India. At least one Sunni group issued a *fatwa* (legal opinion) that it was acceptable for Muslims to sing the first two verses, which more abstractly invoke "Mother India." See "Now a *fatwa* to sing *Vande Mataram*," in the *Times of India*, September 7, 2006. http://timesofindia.indiatimes.com/articleshow/1964371.cms. For an overview of the *Vande Mataram* from a Muslim perspective, see "*Vande Mataram*—A Historical Perspective," in the *Islamic Voice*, December 1998. http://www.islamicvoice.com/december.98/community.htm#VAN

48. In 2008, these two members were Asaddudin Owaisi from the All-India Majlis-e Ittehadul Muslimeen from Hyderabad and E. Ahmed from the Muslim League Kerala State Committee. Lok Sabha Web site, http://164.100.24.209/newls/partywise-list.aspx (accessed January 19, 2008).

49. Interview, July 16, 2004.

50. Paul Brass, *Theft of an Idol: Text and Context in the Representation of Collective Violence* (Princeton, NJ: Princeton University Press, 1997), p. 9.

51. Sudhir Kakar, *The Colors of Violence: Cultural Identities, Religion, and Conflict* (Chicago: University of Chicago Press, 1996); Gyanendra Pandey, "The Long Life of Rumor," *Alternatives* 27, 2 (2002); and Stanley J. Tambiah, *Leveling Crowds: Ethnonationalist Conflicts and Collective Violence in South Asia* (New Delhi: Vistaar Publications, 1996).

52. Tambiah, *Leveling Crowds*, p. 81.

53. See Brass, *Theft of an Idol*; and Tambiah, *Leveling Crowds*.

54. Gustave Le Bon, *The Crowd: A Study of the Popular Mind* (Mineola, NY: Dover Publications, 2002).

55. Varshney, *Ethnic Conflict*; and Ashutosh Varshney, "Ethnic Conflict and Civil Society: India and Beyond," *World Politics* 53 (April 2001): 362–98.

56. Varshney *Ethnic Conflict*, p. 10.

57. Aho, *This Thing of Darkness*, p. 104.

58. Varshney, *Ethnic Conflict*, p. 25.

59. An additional criticism of Varshney's study centers on the data he uses to establish which communities are violence prone. He relied on violent incidents that had appeared in the national English-language press. Numerous studies—ranging from the Human Rights Watch report on Gujarat to colonial-era riot reports and the work of Ashis Nandy et al. in the aftermath of the Ayodhya events in 1992—pay close attention to the potentially deleterious role of the vernacular press in communal conflicts. Certainly the less sensational newspaper of record would not report such rumors or fear mongering. Furthermore, a fight or demonstration that does not result in fatalities can have a powerfully deleterious effect on some social networks and never make the news or be misreported.

60. The riots in the mid-1980s and early 1990s that accompanied L. K. Advani's pilgrimage procession exceed a thousand, approximately three thousand were killed subsequent to the destruction of the Masjid in 1992, and as recently as 2002 two thousand were killed in Gujarat in riots related to the Ramjanmabhumi movement. See Ashis Nandy, Shikha Trivedy, Shail Mayaram, and Achyut Yagnik, *Creating a Nationality: The Ramjanmabhumi Movement and Fear of the Self* (New Delhi: Oxford University Press, 1995).

61. For a few of these studies, see: Simon Digby, "Encounters with Jogis in Indian Sufi Hagiography," unpublished paper, School for Oriental and African Studies, 1970, and "Medieval Sufi Tales of Jogis and Tales from the Afghan Sultanates in India," in *Wonder Tales of South Asia* (New Delhi: Manohar, 2000); Richard M. Eaton, "Sufi Folk Literature and the Expansion of Indian Islam," *History of Religions* 14, 2 (1974); and Tony K. Stewart, "In Search of Equivalence: Conceiving the Muslim-Hindu Encounter through Translation Theory," *History of Religions* 40, 3 (2001). See also David Gilmartin and Bruce Lawrence, eds., *Beyond Turk and Hindu: Rethinking Religious Identities in Islamicate South Asia* (Gainesville: University Press of Florida, 2000).

62. See Farina Mir, "Genre and Devotion in Punjab's Popular Narratives: Rethinking Cultural and Religious Syncretism," *Comparative Studies in Society and History* Sufia Uddin, *Constructing Bangladesh: Religion, Ethnicity, and Language in an Islamic Nation* (Chapel Hill: University of North Carolina Press, 2006), and Tony Stewart 2001.

63. This is a small but expanding field. In India, the studies of Gottschalk and Assayag are particularly valuable: Peter Gottschalk, *Beyond Hindu and Muslim* (New York: Oxford University Press, 2001) and Jackie Assayag, *At the Confluence of Two Rivers: Muslims and Hindus in South India* (Delhi: Manohar, 2004). In the Mediterranean world, scholars such as Glenn Bowman and Maria Couroucli are paying close attention to the practice of shared sacred space. See Glenn Bowman, editor, *Sharing the Sacra: the Politics and Pragmatics of Inter-communal Relations around Holy Places* (New York: Bergahn Books, forthcoming). In the holy land there is an expanding network of scholars working across the Israeli-Palestinian border. Some of their work is represented by the organization PUSH (Promoting Dialogue and Cultural Understanding of our Shared Heritage) http://pushproject.org/ (accessed February 26, 2009). Some of the scholars working in this arena are Yitzhak Reiter, Ora Limor, and Yusuf Natsheh.

64. Roger Friedland and Richard Hecht, "The Bodies of Nations: A Comparative Study of Religious Violence in Jerusalem and Ayodhya," *History of Religions* 38, 2 (1998).

65. The notion of attunement first came to my attention in the conversational analyses of Frances Trix in her book about her conversations over many years with her Sufi

teacher. She coined the term "conversational attunement" following after a study of a classical music quartet's practice of attunement, through which they learn to hear and respond musically to one another in improvisational contexts. See Frances Trix, *Spiritual Discourses: Learning with an Islamic Master* (Philadelphia: University of Pennsylvania Press, 1993), pp. 18–19.

66. Ibid, p. 112.

67. This is addressed by Richard Hecht in his article, "The Construction and Management of Sacred Time and Space: The *Sabta Nur* at the Church of the Holy Sepulchre," in *Nowhere: Space, Time, and Modernity*, ed. Roger Friedland and D. Bowen (Berkeley: University of California Press, 1994).

68. Casey's reference to "gathering" evokes a Heideggerian concept about the nature of space as having a kind of centripetal quality to pull meaning into itself. Edward S. Casey, "How to Get from Space to Place in a Fairly Short Stretch of Time: Phenomenological Prolegomena," in *Senses of Place*, ed. Steven Feld and Keith Basso (Santa Fe, NM: School of American Research Press, 1996), p. 26.

69. Robert Hayden, "Antagonistic Tolerance: Competitive Sharing of Religious Sites in South Asia and the Balkans," *Current Anthropology* 43, 2 (2002), p. 206.

70. Ibid, p. 207.

71. Georg Simmel, *Conflict* (New York: Free Press, 1955 [1908]).

72. Anthony Gill, *Render unto Caesar: The Catholic Church and the State in Latin America*, (Chicago: University of Chicago Press, 1998).

73. John R. Hall, "Religion and Violence: Social Processes in Comparative Perspective," in *Handbook for the Sociology of Religion*, ed. Michele Dillon (New York; Cambridge University Press, 2002), p. 15.

74. Ron E. Hassner, "Understanding and Resolving Disputes over Sacred Space," *Stanford Center on Conflict and Negotiation Working Paper*, 62 (2002), p. 11.

75. See especially chapter 5, "Religious Identities at the Crossroads," in Joyce Burkalter Flueckiger, *In Amma's Healing Room: Gender and Vernacular Islam in India* (Bloomington: Indiana University Press, 2006). Quotation is on pp. 168–69.

76. For several focused approaches to this question, see Gilmartin and Lawrence, eds., *Beyond Turk and Hindu*. On the subject of the construction of religious identities in India, see Paul R. Brass, "Elite Groups, Symbol Manipulation and Ethnic Identity among the Muslims of South Asia," in *Nationalism: Critical Concepts in Political Science*, ed. John Hutchison and Anthony D. Smith (London: Routledge, 2000); Mushirul Hasan, ed., *Islam, Communities and the Nation: Muslim Identities in South Asia and Beyond* (Delhi: Manohar, 1998); Mushirul Hasan, "Minority Identity and Its Discontents: Ayodhya and Its Aftermath," in *Religion, Religiosity and Communalism*, ed. Harbans Mukhia, Praful Bidwai, and Achin Vanaik (Delhi: Manohar, 1996); and Francis Robinson, *Islam and Muslim History in South Asia* (New Delhi: Oxford University Press, 2000).

77. Jackie Assayag, p. 251.

78. Ibid.

79. I attempted on several occasions to count these shrines, at one point reaching fifty-three. However, this is by no means reliable as behind many walls, in the middle of fields, and in other less readily accessed areas there are burial sites of

Muslim saints, Hindu yogis, and Sikh martyrs, all of which may receive ongoing attention and propitiation from people on a semi-regular or daily basis. Furthermore, residents have their own accountings, reflecting the places that are significant to them.

80. The *dargah* of Shaykh Ahmad Sirhindi (d. 1624) is also in Indian Punjab. Sirhindi is one of the most prominent Muslims of his period, but in contemporary Punjab his shrine is not well attended. In part this is because of the general exodus of Muslims from Indian Punjab in 1947, but this is compounded by the *dargah*'s proximity to the massive historic gurdwara, Fatehgarh Sahib, which marks the spot where the two young sons of Guru Gobind Singh were martyred. Though more famous and significant in terms of his influence on South Asian Islam, among non-Muslims Sirhindi is far less popular.

81. D. Ibbetson, E. D. MacLagan, and H. A. Rose, *A Glossary of the Tribes and Castes of the Punjab and North-West Frontier Province* (Lahore: Government Printing House, 1919 [1883]), p. 645.

82. *Punjab State Gazetteers*, Vol. 15: *A Malerkotla State 1904* (Lahore: Civil and Military Gazette Press, 1908), p. 44.

83. Ibid, p. 44.

84. Glenn Bowman, "Response to Robert Hayden," cited in Hayden, "Antagonistic Tolerance," p. 220.

85. Glenn Bowman, "Nationalizing the Sacred: Shrines and Shifting Identities in the Israeli-Occupied Territories," *Man* 28 (1993): 442–448.

86. In an introduction, Ian Talbot warns that pre-Partition Punjabi culture should not be idealized as free of religious communalism. He remarks, "It was only in the celebrations of the Sufi shrines that 'distance' was broken down between communities who were otherwise near neighbours, but living in separate worlds." Although I disagree with his pessimistic view of the level of integration in community life, his singling out of *dargahs* as idealized places of exchange is significant. Ian Talbot, introduction to Anders Bjørn Hansen, *Partition and Genocide: Manifestation of Violence in Punjab, 1937–1947* (New Delhi: India Research Press, 2002), p. x.

CHAPTER 1

1. This is also an uncited quotation from the 1904 *Gazetteer* of Malerkotla State produced by the British government. Iftikhar Ali Khan, *History of the Ruling Family of Sheikh Sadruddin Sadar-i-Jahan of Malerkotla (1449 A.D. to 1948 A.D.)*, edited by R. K. Ghai (Patiala: Punjabi University Press, 2000 [1948]), p. 2.

2. Although he is widely described as a Suhrawardi, there is no active *khanqah* or center of Sufi training at this *dargah*. His descendants maintain the tomb, but few of them are very knowledgeable about Sufi practice.

3. Shaykh Baha-ul Din Zakariyya (d. 1262) and Shaykh Ruknu'd-Din Abu'l Fath (d. 1335) were grandfather and grandson and among the most famous saints of the Suhrawardi lineage in the subcontinent. However, their dates are clearly inconsistent with Haider Shaykh's, who died in 1515. Still, it is certainly not uncommon to link later Sufis to the most renowned, popular, and powerful saints in their lineages. For those who attend the shrine who are aware of the variety of Sufi lineages, Haider

Shaykh is universally identified as Suhrawardi. Multan, now in Pakistan, was a great center for Sufism, particularly the Suhrawardi *silsila* (lineage).

4. The date for Bahlol Lodhi's conquest of Delhi is typically given as 1451 when the Sayyid dynasty, which ruled briefly in the first half of the fifteenth century, fell. See Romila Thapar, *A History of India*, Vol. 1 (Delhi: Penguin Books, 1966), p. 280.

5. Although there are no contemporary records of this marriage, it is reported that on at least one other occasion Lodhi married one of his daughters to a saint. According to Punjab historian Fauja Singh, "During the period of his reign, Bahlol got a large stone-tomb constructed commemorating the death of his son-in-law, Mir-i-Miran, a great saint of the place. The saint had received a *jagir* in dowry in the neighborhood of Sirhind and at this place a tank, *bibisar*, was constructed by the princess or by her brother, Sikander Lodhi." Fauja Singh, "Sirhind during the Sultanate Period," in *Sirhind through the Ages* ed. Fauja Singh, (Patiala: Punjabi University Press, 1984), p. 18.

6. The 1904 *Gazetteer* lists the original grant as 12 large and 56 small villages. The 12 large villages are Maler, Hadiaya, Barnala, Phul, Mahraj, Langowal, Sanghera, Pail, Ghamkaur, Amrgarh, Balian, and Amloh. This arrangement seems typical of the types of land grants given in the pre-Mughal period. Iqtidar Husain Siddiqi, "Wajh-i-ma'ash Grants under the Afghan Kings (1451–1555)," *Medieval India: A Miscellany* (London: Asia Publishing House, 1972).

7. The parentage of these children is given in accordance with Iftikhar Ali Khan's *History of the Ruling Family*, p. 6; and Inayat Ali Khan's *A Description of the Principal Kotla Afghans* (Lahore: Civil and Military Gazette Press, 1882), p. 7.

8. Her *dargah* is on the outskirts of Malerkotla by the 'Id Gah. There is the stump of the tree said to have sprung from a piece of her palanquin. Some, but not many, devotees of Haider Shaykh come to pay their respects here.

9. The death date of the Shaykh is typically given as 1515, but the *hijri* date actually converts to 11 October 1516. Iftikhar Ali Khan's *History* gives Haider Shaykh's ruling dates as 1449–1508. *The Gazetteer of Native States* (1908) gives 1466 as the date of foundation of Maler. Denzil Ibbetson, E. D. MacLagan, and H. A. Rose, in *A Glossary of the Tribes and Castes of the Punjab and North-West Frontier Province* (Lahore: Government Printing House, 1919 [1883]) lists 1454. In all cases, the source for these dates is not given.

10. Officially the land was a *jagir*, not an independent kingdom. In return for the right to derive income from the property, the authority was expected to return a portion of his receipts to the overlord at Delhi and to depute a certain number of troops upon demand. Furthermore, upon the death of a *jagirdar*, the rights over the land would have to be conferred by the central powers to his descendants. If the ruler was uncertain of the landlord's loyalty or in need of land to give as a reward to some other retainer, the property could change hands.

11. Sufi Muhammad Ismail, *Bagh anbiya' punjab* (Maler Kotla: Janab Publishing, 1995), p. 165.

12. The Arabic term *wali* signifies closeness, and its cognates encompass meanings ranging from physical proximity, to friendship, to governance. *Wilayat* in its temporal sense refers merely to sovereign power and governance. A *wali* can signify both a worldly governor or guardian as well as a holy person or saint. A related term

mutawalli denotes a manager of a property, and is often applied to the caretakers of Muslim shrines. J. M. Cowan, ed., *Hans Wehr Dictionary of Modern Written Arabic* (Ithaca, NY: Spoken Language Services, Inc., 1994).

13. Shaykh 'Abd al-Haqq Muhaddith Dihlawi, *Akhbar al-akhyar* (Karachi: Dar al Isha,' 1963) and Hamid ibn Fazl Allah Jamali, *Siyar Al-Arifin* (Lahore: Markazi Urdu Board, 1976).

14. When the Punjabi town of Malerkotla appears in the news nowadays, it is often with headlines such as "Malerkotla: An Island of Peace" (*India Today*, July 15, 1998), or "Malerkotla Muslims Feel Safer in India," (*Indian Express*, August 13, 1997), or "Where Brotherhood Is Handed Down as Tradition" (*Times of India*, March 2, 2002).

15. Charles Briggs, *Competence in Performance: The Creativity of Tradition in Mexicano Verbal Art*, (Philadelphia: University of Pennsylvania Press, 1987), p. 1.

16. Ibid.

17. Ibid., p. 99.

18. Catherine Cubitt, " Memory and Narrative in the Cult of Early Anglo-Saxon Saints," in *The Uses of the Past in the Early Middle Ages*, ed. Yitzhak Hen and Matthew Innes (New York: Cambridge University Press, 2000), p. 36.

19. Ibid.

20. Henry Glassie, "The Practice and Purpose of History," *Journal of American History* 81, 3 (1994): 962.

21. Steven Knapp, "Collective Memory and the Actual Past," *Representations* 26 (Spring 1989): 123.

22. Marcia Hermansen, "Religious Literature and the Inscription of Identity: The Sufi Tazkira Tradition in Muslim South Asia," *Muslim World* 87, 3–4 (1997): 322.

23. Inayat Ali Khan, *Description*. Khan devotes the last third of this work to his dispute with his brother and the British for land rights to the nawab's share of the land they inherited from their father. As Ibrahim Ali Khan was adopted by his uncle Nawab Sikander Ali Khan (d. 1871), Inayat argues that he forfeits his inheritance from his father as he obtained all the land and revenue from the throne upon his ascension.

24. A. C. Arora, "Malerkotla Succession 1871–72: Its Reflections on the British Policy," *Punjab History Conference* 16 (1982): 252–59. See also the India Office Collection files: R/1/1/220, "Marriage of Ahmad Ali Khan to Cousin Disapproved" (London: OIOC); R/1/1/696, "Mental Incapacity of Nawab; R/1/1/707, "Arrangements for Administration of Malerkotla" (London: OIOC, August 1885).

25. Inayat Ali Khan, *Description*, pp. 5–6.

26. Ibid., p. 7.

27. The edited version that came out in 2000 is based on a manuscript likely written just after Partition in 1947 since the last item in the book is Iftikhar's speech on ascending to the throne in 1948. Iftikhar Ali Khan, *History of the Ruling Family*, pp. 144–147.

28. Ibid., p. 8.

29. On the nature of land settlements and the rulers and authorities in India, see Rita Brara, "Marriage and Kinship" (PhD diss., Delhi University, 1989); Robert Frykenberg, ed., *Land Control and Social Structure in Indian History* (Madison: University of Wisconsin Press, 1969); and Siddiqi, "Wajh-i-ma'ash Grants."

30. The great Chishti Sufi saint Nizamuddin Auliya was said to have refused to call upon the seven rulers at Delhi during his lifetime who tried to contact him and draw him

into their affairs. Indeed, he is reported to have said that his *khanqah* had two doors; if the ruler came in one, he would leave through the other. The Suhrawardiyya lineage, on the other hand, was much more inclined toward the worldly and did not repudiate those in authority. From the origins of the lineage in Baghdad to its arrival in India, the Suhrawardiyya were criticized for maintaining palaces and lifestyles that rivaled or exceeded the rulers. See Simon Digby, "The Sufi Shaykh as a Source of Authority in Mediaeval India," *Purusartha* 9 (1986).

31. Iftikhar Ali Khan, *History of the Ruling Family*, p. 6
32. Ibid., p. 8.
33. Ibid.
34. The copy of this work that I had access to did not include any biographical statement about the author. The text was in the possession of a local historian in Malerkotla who lent me his copy.
35. The Kotla part of the name is clear, as the term signifies a small fortification (*kot* = fort). There is general agreement that this portion of the name came when the first nawab, Bayazid Khan, was permitted to build the fortifying wall that encircled the settlement but was separate from the area known as Maler near the tomb of Haider Shaykh.
36. Israr Afghani, *Hayat Lodhi*, (Saweem, Pakistan: Tarikh Jamiat, 1907), pp. 31–33.
37. "Brief Historical Sketch of the Malerkotla State and Ruling Family," p. 1.
38. M. I. Hussain, *A Brief War History of the Malerkotla State (1914–1919)* (Lahore: Civil and Military Press, 1920), p. 2.
39. *Malerkotla State Gazetteer* (Lahore: Civil and Military Gazette Press, 1904), p. 2.
40. Denzil Ibbetson, E. D. MacLagan, and H. A. Rose, *A Glossary of the Tribes and Castes of the Punjab and North-West Frontier Province* (Lahore: Government Printing House, 1919 [1883]), p. 644.
41. *Maler Kotla State Gazetteer* (1904), p. 44.
42. See Bernard S. Cohn, *Colonialism and Its Forms of Knowledge: The British in India* (Princeton, NJ: Princeton University Press, 1996); Nicholas Dirks, *Castes of Mind: Colonialism and the Making of Modern India* (Princeton, NJ: Princeton University Press, 2001); Harald Fischer-Tine and Michael Mann, eds., *Colonialism as Civilizing Mission: Cultural Ideology in British India* (London: Anthem Press, 2004).
43. L/P&J/170, *Puran Mal Murder* (London: OIOC); R/1/1/2687, *Hindu Muslim, Arti-Namaz* (London; OIOC, 1935); R/1/1/2860, *Muslim Agitation in Malerkotla* (London; OIOC); R/1/1/2936, *Muslim Agitation at Malerkotla* (London: OIOC); "Miscellaneous Papers Relating to Communal Problems in Malerkotla," 206, (Maler Kotla: Office of the Revenue and Finance Minister, 1935–1946).
44. November 14, 2001.
45. To command the jinn, as Haider Shaykh does in this example, is evidence of a high degree of spiritual power. Several people in Malerkotla reported to me that they were capable of perceiving the jinn and controlling them. One man said that as an experiment he had recited the *Surat al-Jinn* (Qur'an 72) a number of times, which is said to give one power over the jinn. At the end of his recitation a jinn appeared and asked what was his command. The man responded, "Go, you are free." The man further said that no one should be enslaved and that he was wrong to have attempted to bring anything, even a jinn, under his power.

46. January 28, 2001.

47. Richard M. Eaton, *The Rise of Islam and the Bengal Frontier: 1204–1760*, (Berkeley; University of California Press, 1993), pp. 207–8.

48. This harmonizes quite well with the process that Eaton describes, in which the career of a saint is "made a metaphor for historical changes experienced by people." The story of Haider Shaykh, like that of Shaykh Jalal al-Din Tabrizi, recounted in Eaton's work, "seeks to make sense of the gradual cultural shift," as the area transitioned into Islam and into the structure of centralized Muslim power. The multiple stories of this transition reveal the multiple experiences of that change, and thus some narrators assert a pre-Muslim settlement in the area.

49. Richard Eaton, "Approaches to the Study of Conversion to Islam In India," in *Approaches to Islam in Religious Studies*, ed. Richard C. Martin (New York: One World Press, 1987), pp. 113–116.

50. October 5, 2000.

51. For more on the relationship between *wilayat* (territory, in the Sufi context spiritual authority) and *walayat* (sainthood or the state of being close to God), see Vincent J. Cornell, *Realm of the Saint: Power and Authority in Moroccan Sufism* (Austin: University of Texas Press, 1998); Pnina Werbner, *Pilgrims of Love: The Anthropology of a Global Sufi Cult* (Bloomington: Indiana University Press, 2003), especially chapter 5, "Wilayat."

52. May 31, 2001.

53. March 8, 2001.

54. May 30, 2001.

55. Khalifah Anwar Ahmad Khan, *Hazrat Sadr Udin Sadare Jahan (Rehmat) urf Baba Hazrat Shaykh Ji Malerkotla di Puri Jivani* (Malerkotla: Jivan Glass House, n.d.), p. 9.

56. November 12, 2000.

57. This inside-outside quality in which the storyteller in a sense appears in his own story is very similar to a process described by Dwight Reynolds in his book *Heroic Poets, Poetic Heroes: The Ethnography of Performance in an Arabic Oral Epic Tradition* (Ithaca, NY: Cornell University Press, 1995).

58. Cubitt, "Memory and Narrative," p. 36.

59. "Shaykh Sadruddin Sadr-i Jahan" is written above the entrance to the tomb, but it is written in Urdu script, making it difficult for the mostly Punjabi- and Hindi-speaking visitors to read.

60. Alessandro Portelli, *The Death of Luigi Trastulli and Other Stories* (Albany: State University of New York Press, 2001), p. 1.

61. Iftikhar Ali Khan, *History of the Ruling Family*, p. 3.

62. March 10, 2001.

63. In the *Ramayana*, one of Ram's stepmothers (i.e., one of his father's other wives) insisted that her husband place her son on the throne instead of Ram, the eldest son and rightful heir.

64. Actually, Birbal was the minister to the emperor Akbar, not Babur. He was a very wise Hindu advisor, and the stories of his discussions with the ruler are among the best-loved and most popular fables and morality tale cycles in India.

65. The first nawab to actually be given that title was Bayzid Khan (r. 1600–1659), not Sher Mohammad Khan (r. 1672–1712).

66. Cubitt, "Memory and Narrative," p. 31.

67. I never received a clear response clarifying the date of publication, but it was likely printed sometime in the early 1980s.

68. Another story included here is widely known in town. In this tale, the shaykh, while performing *wuzu* [ablutions before prayer], somehow lost his shoe in the river. Although his disciples were alarmed, Haider Shaykh simply told the river to return the shoe, and the river shifted its course toward Ludhiana. Still today there is no river flowing through the town, but residents explain that the *dargah* is in a high place because in the time of the shaykh there had been water there. Indeed British accounts also reference an ancient waterway that is still apparent because it is a flood zone in the monsoon. In this tale, Haider Shaykh's presence in the area has left an indelible impression on the natural environment of Malerkotla.

69. Anwar Ahmad Khan, *Hazrat*, p. 3.

70. Ibid., p. 4.

71. November 8, 2001.

72. Anwar Ahmad Khan, *Hazrat*, p. 6.

73. This is the paradigm of Sufi penetration outlined by Richard Eaton, in which he describes the progression of warrior Sufis into the frontier areas of Muslim authority to be followed by Sufi reformers, literati, and landed elites. Eaton, *Sufis of Bijapur 1300–1700: Social Roles of Sufis in Medieval India* (Delhi: Munshiram Manoharlal, 1996 [1978]), p. 36.

74. Tony K. Stewart, "In Search of Equivalence: Conceiving the Muslim-Hindu Encounter through Translation Theory," *History of Religions* 40, 3 (2001): 260–87.

75. Ismail, *Bagh Anbiya'*, p. 164.

76. Ibid., p. 167.

77. Ismail goes no further with this commentary, but the mention of it, so completely out of context cannot be accidental. It is certainly consistent with his overall emphasis on the spread of Islam.

78. Ismail, *Bagh Anbiya'*, p. 167.

79. Khalid Zubairy, *Malerkotla Itihas ke Darpan Me* (Malerkotla: Tarkash Publications, 2000).

80. Nur Faruqi, "Maler Kotla: Maudi Aur Hal Ki Ekni Hai," *Felicitation Volume* (2000), p. 1.

81. Safia Haleem, "Study of the Pathan Communities in Four States of India," http://www.khyber.org/articles/2007/StudyofthePathanCommunitiesinF.shtml (accessed April 25, 2008).

CHAPTER 2

1. Copland argues that the authoritarian nature of princely states reduced the incidence of violence. See Ian Copland, "The Political Geography of Religious Conflict: towards an Explanation of the Relative Infrequency of Communal Riots in the Indian Princely States," *International Journal of Punjab Studies* 7, no. 1 (2000).

2. Abdali also defeated the Marathas in the second Battle of Panipat in 1761. The Marathas were a central- and western-Indian-based dynasty who, like Abdali and the Rohilla Afghans, took advantage of the power vacuum at Delhi.

3. Iftikhar Ali Khan had five wives, though only four at any one time, in accordance with Islamic law. Two of his wives, Sajida Begum and Yusuf Zaman, served as members of the Legislative Assembly, as did the former nawab himself. During the time of my research (1999–2004), only Sajida Begum and one other wife, Mujawwar Nisa', were alive.

4. 'Isa's share went to his son Muhammad Shah, who lost it as a punishment for his involvement in a murder plot. However, he subsequently increased his land holdings through some skillful maneuvers during the unsettled period of the Mughal emperor Humayun's exile at the hands of Sher Shah. This also served the purpose of cutting off the *khalifah* cousins from any claim to the property, as it was now his by purchase rather than through hereditary claim. The Hassan branch became wholly dependent on the shrine for their livelihood after this. Iftikhar Ali Khan, *History of the Ruling Family*, pp. 13–14.

5. A *suba* was a territorial administrative unit used by the Mughals. Under Akbar there were twelve. Within each *suba* were numerous smaller units known as *sarkar* (territory of a governor). During this period Maler encompassed 103,444 *bighas* of land and possessed an army of one hundred cavalry and five hundred infantry. Abu 1-Fazl Allami, *Ain-i Akbari*, translated by Colonel H. S. Jarrett (New Delhi: Crown Publication, 1988), Vol. 2, p. 301.

6. Throughout Iftikhar Ali Khan's history, he repeatedly expresses bitterness about the degree of control exerted over the territory by the Mughal authorities. "The Emperors of Delhi were at that time sole owners of landed property in India. Therefore whosoever possessed a State like Malerkotla was to all intents and purposes a tenant and not the virtual owner of the land over which he ruled. An unfavorable report by the Governor of that province or the whim and fancy of the king was all that was required to deprive the ruler of his State." Iftikhar Ali Khan, *History of the Ruling Family*, pp. 15–16. Central authoritarianism on the part of the Mughals is documented in the work of modern historians such as Muzaffar Alam, Percival Spear, and K. A. Nizami, as well as the contemporary chroniclers including Badauni, Abu Fazl, Ferishta, and others. See Muzaffar Alam, *The Crisis of Empire in Mughal North India: Awadh and Punjab, 1707–1748* (New Delhi: Oxford University Press, 1986); Percival Spear, *The History of India* (New York: Penguin, 1965); Khaliq Ahmad Nizami, "The Suhrawardi Silsilah and Its Influence on Medieval Indian Politics," *Medieval Indian Quarterly* 2 (October 1950); and Iqtidar Husain Siddiqi, "Wajh-i-Ma'ash Grants under the Afghan Kings (1451–1555)."

7. In 1757 the British East India Company defeated the nawab of Calcutta, Siraj-ad-Daula, in the Battle of Plassey. This marked the shift from a trading outfit that merely meddled in government affairs to an administrative body. From 1757 onward, British power expanded throughout the subcontinent. It was consolidated after an 1857 rebellion of army troops was crushed, the East India Company was dissolved, the British Empire declared India to be a colony, and the last Mughal emperor was dethroned.

8. Iftikhar Ali Khan devotes more of his *History of the Ruling Family* to Sher Muhammad Khan than to any other ruler in the kingdom's history. See *History*, pp. 28–41.

9. The number of references in various sources to these events are simply too many to mention. Some of the older Sikh chronicles that give accounts include Bhai Kahn

Singh Nabha, *Gurshabad Ratnakar Mahan Kosh* (1926); Ratan Singh Bhangu, *Panth Prakash* (New Delhi: Bhai Vir Singh Sahit Sadan, 1998 [1841]); Sainapat, *Sri Gur Sobha*, edited by Ganda Singh (Patiala: Punjabi University Press, 1967); Giani Gian Singh, *Panth Prakash* (Amritsar: Bhai Catar Singh Jiwana Singh, 1923); *Tawarikh Guru Khalsa* (Amritsar: Khalsa Naishanala Ijamsi, 1923 [1892]). Most modern descriptions of these events includes Sher Muhammad Khan's *haah da naara*.

10. Bairagis are a sect of Vaishnava yogis, renunciant Hindus devoted to Vishnu.

11. Under Shivaji Bhonsle (1627–1680) the Marathas established a sizable kingdom in the region of western India now identified as Maharashtra. Shivaji fought constantly with Aurangzeb and eventually was awarded the right to call himself raja (king). He was crowned chhatrapati (lord of the universe). After Shivaji, the Marathas continued to be a force in North and West India until Ahmad Shah Abdali and his army of Afghans defeated them at the second Battle of Panipat in 1761. Shivaji still holds a very high position among Hindu nationalists who regard him as a successful resistor to Muslim rule. Indeed in early 2004 there was an outcry over a book by James Laine, *Shivaji: Hindu King in Islamic India* (New York: Oxford University Press, 2003), which offended the sentiments of enough Hindus to result in an attack on one of the archives where Laine did research. During the attack numerous irreplaceable Sanskrit and Tibetan manuscripts were destroyed.

12. Nawab Bhikam Khan (r. 1755–1763), Nawab Bahadur Khan (r. 1763–1766), Nawab Umar Khan (r. 1766–1780), Nawab Asadullah Khan (r. 1780–1784), Nawab Ataullah Khan (r. 1784–1810). See also Appendix A, Malerkotla Ruling Family.

13. Iftikhar Ali Khan, *History of the Ruling Family*, p. 61.

14. The *missal* period runs roughly from the 1715 death of Banda Bahadur until the rise of Maharaja Ranjit Singh in 1780. Indu Banga, "Formation of the Sikh State: 1765–1845," in *Five Punjabi Centuries*, ed. Indu Banga (New Delhi: Manohar, 1997), pp. 84–88.

15. This family remains a powerful charismatic presence in the Sikh community. The current scion, Sarabjot Singh Bedi, lives at Una in Himachal Pradesh. His home and the tombs of several of his progenitors are pilgrimage destinations.

16. Gursharan Singh, *History of Pepsu: Patiala and East Punjab States Union, 1948–1956* (Delhi: Konark Publishers, 1991), p. 9. A slightly different account is given in Mian Bashir Ahmed Farooqi, *British Relations with the Cis-Sutlej States (1809–1823)* (Patiala Languages Department, 1971 [1942]). In this study, after Maharaja Ranjit Singh had taken Faridkot, he "then forced the Muslim Chief of Malerkotla to undertake to pay a lakh of rupees for which the Rajas of Patiala and Jind agreed to stand surety. [fn Metcalfe to Government, October 25, 1808, Bk. 5, Lt. 26, Copy] Metcalfe accompanied the Raja of Lahore up to Malerkotla but refused to 'follow the army in campaign' any further and strongly remonstrated against Ranjit's encroachments towards the east of the Sutlej" (p. 6). As Colonel David Ochterlony, then agent to the governor general (later Resident at Delhi) pursued negotiations with the Cis-Sutlej chiefs for their accession to British protection, he arrived at Malerkotla. Having reached agreements with the rajas of Patiala and Nabha, "He then proceeded to Malerkotla, where the 'much respected and venerable' Pathan Chief, Ataullah Khan, was the ruler from whom the Raja of Lahore had demanded a large sum of money. The Colonel reinstated the Chief in power who, 'but a few months since anticipated another visit from the Raja of Lahore which would doubtlessly have terminated in his absolute

expulsion and ruin.' [fn Ochterlony to Edmonstone, February 9, 1809, Bk. 10, Lt. 6, Original]." Thus having propped up the Malerkotla State and achieved satisfactory control of all the kingdoms of the Cis-Sutlej region, the British were firmly ensconced in the region and well positioned to mount their eventual assault on Maharaja Ranjit Singh.

17. Suraj Narain Rau, "Cis-Sutluj Sikh States, 1800–1849" (PhD diss., Panjab University, n.d.), pp. 107–108.

18. For more on the Mughal period see Irfan Habib, *An Atlas of the Mughal Empire* (Aligarh: Centre of Advanced Studies, 1982); and John F. Richards, *The Mughal Empire* (New York: Cambridge University Press, 1993).

19. See Rita Brara, "Marriage and Kinship" (PhD diss., Delhi University, 1989), pp. 63–69.

20. The entry "Malerkotla" in the 1881 *Imperial Gazetteer of India* (ed. W. W. Hunter [London: Trübner and Co., 1881]), p. 267, says it was a nine-gun salute. However, according to the 1886 and 1904 *Gazetteers*, it was an eleven-gun salute. See "Malerkotla," in *Imperial Gazetteer of India* (London: Trübner and Co., 1886), p. 255; and "Malerkotla," in *Imperial Gazetteer of India* (London; Trübner and Co., 1908), p. 400.

21. L/P&S/13/877, *Indian States, General Questions. Debts: Maler Kotla* (London: OIOC); R/1/1/1418, *Debt of Malerkotla to Calcutta Firms* (London: OIOC); R/1/1/2023, *Irregularities of Nawab Re: Payment of Debt* (London: OIOC, 1930); and R/1/1/4156, *Malerkotla Finance* (London: OIOC, 1944).

22. Cited in Indra Krishen, "An Historical Interpretation of the Correspondence (1831–1843) of Sir George Russell Clerk, Political Agent Ambala and Ludhiana" (PhD diss., Panjab University, 1952), p. 64.

23. R/1/1/3832, *Malerkotla Affairs: Appointment of Successor, Administrative Scheme* (London: OIOC, 1942).

24. Krishen, "Historical Interpretation," p. 65.

25. During my research in Malerkotla, I visited numerous times with Mujawwar Nisa', known locally as the "Tonk-walli Begum," since she hails from the Rajasthani kingdom of Tonk. In a vivid example of the disputes over property now, this begum lives in one of the old palaces, the Mubarak Mahal, which is literally crumbling around her. Furthermore, different members of the family, in various stages of dissolution, live in sections of the building, never talking with one another if at all possible. Some of these people are accused by locals of stealing from her and selling things, and others of being drug addicts. The sister lived with her and a couple servants, though it was unclear how they sustained themselves if not by occasionally selling heirlooms.

26. Ibrahim's brother was Inayat Ali Khan, the author of the *Description of the Principal Kotla Afghans*. Inayat argued that when their uncle (who, he claimed, was a hermaphrodite and a homosexual and had no children of his own) adopted his brother, Ibrahim's property should have devolved entirely to him, as he was now the heir to the throne and all the state territories and assets. Inayat Ali Khan, *Description*, p. 60.

27. For example, www.namdhari.org claims that the goal of the attack on Malerkotla was to put the British on notice about the growing resistance to their rule. The page presents the perspective of the Namdharis on the events by claiming one of the Namdhari leaders had addressed his party of attackers after the assault and before their arrest. Hira Singh is made to say to his compatriots, "We had achieved our

target. We had conveyed our feelings to the British Government that now the Indians had woken up. They would neither tolerate foreign rule nor hurt to their religious sentiments and self respect." (Accessed December 14, 2003).

28. *Malerkotla Gazetteer*, 1904, p. 7.

29. These festivals also occur on the eighteenth of every month on a much smaller scale, and still draw Namdharis from all over the region.

30. Some of these sources are: Ratan Singh Bhangu, *Panth Prakash*; J. S. Grewal and S. S. Bal, *Guru Gobind Singh*; Sainapat, *Sri Gur Sobha*; Bachan Singh, *Fatehgarh Sahib Di Darshan*; Ganda Singh, "The Boy Martyrs of Sirhind," *Sikh Review*, December 1957; Giani Gian Singh, *Panth Prakash*, and *Tawarikh Guru Khalsa*; Guru Gobind Singh, *Zafarnama*, translated by Darshan Singh (New Delhi: ABC Publishing House, 2000); Puran Singh, *The Victory of Faith or the Story of the Martyrdom* (Amritsar: Khalsa Agency, 1908); Ranbir Singh, *Glimpses of the Divine Masters* (New Delhi: International Traders Corp., 1965); Sahib Singh, *Guru Gobind Singh* (Jullundur: Raj Publications, 1967).

31. On the invitation of two rival rulers in Garwhal and Sirmur, Guru Gobind Singh set up a base at Paonta in 1685. The increasing population and power drew the attention of both the Mughal *subedars*, or military governors, on the plains and the Hindu kings in the mountains. He spent three years here in relative peace, regrouping his armies, recruiting from the Afghans no longer at war and the *mahants* (heads) of temples in the region whose considerable landholdings often made them military leaders as well. However, the rival interests of these parties and their fear of his growing power resulted in several battles in 1688 and the guru's return to Anandpur, which he had had to abandon three years previously. Grewal and Bal, *Guru Gobind Singh*, pp. 127–142.

32. As each sign begins with the Punjabi letter *kaka*, they have come to be known as the five *k*'s.

33. Subsequently this code of conduct, known as *rehat*, has been codified by one of the central Sikh oversight groups, the Shiromani Gurdwara Prabhandak Committee. http://www.sgpc.net/sikhism/sikh-dharma-manual.html (accessed September 22, 2009).

34. Grewal and Bal, *Guru Gobind Singh*, p. 127. Some sources call the Sirhind ruler Bazid.

35. Gobind Singh and his retinue went on to Chamkaur, where the two elder sons were killed in battle. The guru himself escaped and stayed on the move until in 1706 he traveled to the Deccan with the intention of meeting with Aurangzeb. While he was en route, however, the emperor died. Gobind Singh then traveled to Delhi to meet with the heir apparent, Bahadur Shah, who kept him attached to the court as he traveled south to pursue the missions in the Deccan begun by Aurangzeb. The guru was killed at a place called Nanded on October 18, 1708.

36. Ironically, since Partition the lineage *has* failed, in a sense, as the last nawab had no children and most of his immediate family have either died or gone to Pakistan.

37. The Begum Mujawwar Nisa', one of Nawab Iftikhar Ali Khan's wives, had in her possession a sword she claimed was a gift from the guru. The guru is also believed to have given a pitcher to the ruler of Raikot in 1704. This blessing is reported to have saved the town from the violence of Partition, just as the guru's blessing preserved Malerkotla. See Ian Copland, "The Master and the Maharajas: The Sikh Princes and the East Punjab Massacres of 1947," *Modern Asian Studies* 36, 3 (2002): 694 n. 98.

38. Satinder Kaur asserts that many people believe that it is Sher Muhammad Khan's brother Khizr Khan who is referenced as Khwaja Mahdud in Guru Gobind Singh's famous epistle to Aurangzeb the *Zafarnama*. In this text he mentions one Khwaja Mahdud who stood behind a wall and jumped into the fray along with the army and is killed. The guru mourns, "Alas had I seen his face, I would have, in spite of myself blessed him." Cited in Kaur "History of Malerkotla State," p. 48.

39. Louis Fenech discusses the central role of martyrdom in the making of the Sikh tradition in his book *Martyrdom in the Sikh Tradition* (New Delhi: Oxford University Press, 2000).

40. Harjot Oberoi argues that one of the driving events that led to the establishment of the Singh Sabha was the Kuka massacre in Malerkotla in 1872. He remarks that this incident led to fears that "this would sour the Sikh romance with the Raj." Oberoi, *The Construction of Religious Boundaries: Culture, Identity, and Diversity in the Sikh Tradition* (Chicago: University of Chicago Press, 1994), p. 235.

41. Ikram Ali Malik, "Muslim Anjumans and Communitarian Consciousness," in *Five Punjabi Centuries*, ed. Indu Banga (New Delhi: Manohar, 1999), p. 113. On the Anjumans and other Muslim organizations in Punjab, see Edward D. Churchill Jr., "Muslim Societies of the Punjab, 1860–1890," *Panjab Past and Present* 8, 1 (1974); David Gilmartin, "Religious Leadership and the Pakistan Movement in the Punjab," *Modern Asian Studies* 13, 3 (1979); Iftikhar H. Malik, "Identity Formation and Muslim Party Politics in Punjab, 1897–1936: A Retrospective Analysis," *Modern Asian Studies* 29, 2 (1995); and Iftikhar H. Malik, "Muslim Nationalism and Ethno-Regional Postulations: Sir Fazl-i-Husain and Party Politics in the Punjab," in *Punjabi Identity in a Global Context*, ed. Pritam Singh and Shinder Singh Thandi (New Delhi: Oxford University Press, 1999).

42. Malik, "Muslim Anjumans," p. 122. There are also references to various anjuman's activities in the Malerkotla State Archives, "6/Anjuman-I-Hidayat Agitation" [82/6/1/1937—100/6/124/1939] and "71/Z(B)/10/1938—Anjuman-I-Muhajirin." 1938.

43. N. Gerald Barrier, "The Punjab Government and Communal Politics, 1870–1908," *Journal of Asian Studies* 27, 3 (1968); Dietrich Reetz, "In Search of the Collective Self: How Ethnic Group Concepts Were Cast through Conflict in Colonial India," *Modern Asian Studies* 31, 2 (1997); K. L. Tuteja, "The Punjab Hindu Sabha and Communal Politics, 1906–1923," in *Five Punjabi Centuries*, ed. Indu Banga (New Delhi: Manohar, 1997).

44. Giani Gian Singh, *Tawarikh Guru Khalsa*, p. 778.

45. Oberoi, *Construction*, pp. 410–416.

46. Puran Singh, *The Victory of Faith*, p. 29.

47. Although the Congress did not officially call for full *swaraj* until 1930, leaders like Bal Gangadar Tilak in the early twentieth century did appeal for Indian independence.

48. Ganda Singh, "The Boy Martyrs of Sirhind," *Sikh Review*, December 1957, p. 40.

49. Bachan Singh, *Fatehgarh Sahib di darshan* (unknown publisher and date), p. 23. This Punjabi chapbook appears recent because of its print and production quality.

50. Bhai Kahan Singh Nabha (1861–1936) was one of the major ideologues of the Singh Sabha movement. He is also the author of the *Mahan Kosh* (Great Dictionary), an encyclopedic dictionary of Punjab. In the *Mahan Kosh* entry for Malerkotla, Nabha references the guru's blessing: "It is from here that the ruler Sher Mohammad Khan

having heard of the order to kill the small Sahibzadas at the fort in Sirhind raised a protest and told the Suba that to behead the children would be a sin, for this reason the Sikhs regard this kingdom with reverence (*sanman*). In the Gurpratap surya it is also written that the tenth guru declared, 'Let this Malerian's roots be green.'" Bhai Kahan Singh Nabha, *Gurushabad Ratnakara Mahan Kosh* (Chandigarh: Bhasha Vibhag Punjab, 1999).

51. Operation Blue Star, authorized by Gandhi in 1984, was designed to rout out Sikh militants who had taken over the Golden Temple at Amritsar. However, the fire-bombing and artillery barrage resulted in a massacre of hundreds, the wounding of many more, and the destruction of many priceless artifacts of the Sikh faith.

52. Dr. Manmohan Singh, "Nikian Jindan-Vada Saka: Story of Child Martyrs," December 2000, http://www.sikhreview.org/december2000/moral.htm (Accessed April 19, 2002).

53. "Sikh Sacrifice: Supreme Sacrifice of Young Souls," http://www.sikhworld.co.uk/page5.html (accessed June 19, 2002)

54. This account is clearly polemical, inflammatory, and inconsistent with the dominant version. Nonetheless, that this event is singled out by the author (who has issued postings on "Women in Islam", "Gay Sex in Muslim Paradise," and other provocative topics) as the crucial moment to prove the truth of Islam to a Sikh audience demonstrates how central this moment is in Sikh-Muslim relations. Seemingly driven by a desire to undermine any positive portrayal of the Muslim faith, the author directly attacks the central feature of the narrative—Sher Muhammad Khan's courage to oppose the boys' execution. Sukha Singh, "In the Name of Islam," April 17, 2000, http://www.gillit.com/_disc2/000004b5.htm (accessed May 10, 2003).

55. Some accounts assert that she died from exposure in the Thanda Burj. The *Tawarikh Guru Khalsa* asserts that she was martyred by falling to her death. "Hearing of their murder, Mata Gujri fainted and fell from the tower in which she was imprisoned and gave up her breath." Giani Gian Singh, *Tawarikh*, p. 778.

56. Copland, "The Master and the Maharajas," p. 696.

57. Iftikhar Ali Khan's father, Ahmad Ali Khan, died in 1947. Iftikhar Ali Khan ruled for less than a year before Malerkotla's accession to India in the independent period took force. There was then a transitional period when Malerkotla and the other kingdoms were governed by the Patiala and East Punjab States Union (PEPSU). Khan's service as a representative to PEPSU is not mentioned in the history, nor is his service as a member of the Legislative Assembly after PEPSU's demise in 1954. Iftikhar Ali Khan died in 1982.

58. This assertion must be balanced against a contemporary account of Sher Muhammad Khan's presence and valor in battle against Banda Bahadur. Muhammad Qasim authored the *Ibratnama* in about 1723, an account of the campaigns of Banda Bahadur. He specifically references Malerkotla and Sher Muhammad Khan's active defense of Wazir Khan in a battle against the Sikhs. Although Iftikhar Ali Khan is claiming only that Sher Muhammad Khan did not attack Guru Gobind Singh, still the fact of Sher Muhammad Khan's ongoing loyalty to the Mughal powers is undeniable. Qasim writes, "A great battle occurred twelve *kurohs* from Sahrind [sic]. The young men of the army of Islam, showing exemplary bravery, tasted martyrdom, after obtaining repute in the field of valour. Especially was heroism displayed in this

battle by Sher Muhammad and Khwaja 'Ali, Afghans of Kotla Maler, who in this *sarkar* [district] were masters of a host and commanded trust. After much fighting, they stood firm like the Pole Star within that very circle and surrendered their lives to the Creator. You may say, they attained goodness and good name in that field of valour." It is also worth noting that Qasim makes no mention of the *haah da naara*. J. S. Grewal and Irfan Habib, eds. *Sikh History from Persian Sources* (New Delhi: Tulika, 2001), p. 116.

59. Iftikhar Ali Khan, *History of the Ruling Family*, p. 37.

60. Ibid.

61. Ibid., pp. 34–35.

62. Ibid., p. 35.

63. There is ample evidence from the Qur'an and the Hadith that the killing of noncombatants, especially women and children, is expressly forbidden in the waging of war (usually called *harb* or *qatl*, rather than *jihad*). For example, Qur'an 5:32 states, "Whosoever kills an innocent human being, it shall be as if he has killed all mankind, and whosoever saves the life of one, it shall be as if he had saved the life of all mankind."

64. Iftikhar Ali Khan, *History of the Ruling Family*, p. 34.

65. Ibid., p. 36.

66. The complete text of the purported letter as reproduced in the nawab's history is attached as an appendix.

67. *Proceedings of the Punjab History Conference* (Eighteenth Session, 1983), p. 201.

68. My suspicion is that it appeared during the height of the Praja Mandal movement against the princely states. As the preponderance of these freedom fighters were Sikhs, it is plausible that Nawab Ahmad Ali Khan may have sought to shore up his support from this group by reviving this historical moment of Sikh-Muslim cooperation. However, no evidence exists to confirm or deny this speculation.

69. The phrase *haah da naara* does not specifically indicate either an oral or a written objection. The verb it is usually paired with *marna*, which means "to strike." As a compound, *haah da naara mariya*, "He gave a cry for justice," is emphatic and indicates a force and conviction that the English translation does not fully indicate.

70. Iftikhar Ali Khan, *History of the Ruling Family*, p. 36.

71. Ibid., p. 37.

72. Ibid., p. 35. This may well be an unattributed translation from Bhai Kahan Singh Nabha's *Mahankosh* entry for Malerkotla. See note 50.

73. Inayat Ali Khan, *Description*, pp. 13–14.

74. Ismail, *Bagh Anbiya'*, p. 173.

75. Khan, *History*, p. 39.

76. Sohan Singh, *Life and Exploits of Banda Singh Bahadur* (Patiala: Punjabi University Press, 2000).

77. See also Kaur, "History of Malerkotla State," pp. 56–67. Kaur further asserts that a "Shahukar sadhu, Atma Ram Bairagi gave Banda Bahadur rs. 4,000 not to destroy Malerkotla." She reports that "a fair is held at the site of this confrontation at Nimani Kadsi, a village one mile from Malerkotla." I was unable to confirm or deny this. Kaur also identifies the main reason for Banda's not damaging Malerkotla, in spite of passing through the Muslim principality many times, as the blessing of Guru Gobind Singh.

78. Varinder Singh Bhatia, "Banda Singh's Attitude towards the Muslims," *Proceedings of the Punjab History Conference* (Twenty-Eighth Session, 1996), p. 74.

79. Ganda Singh and Teja Singh, *A Short History of the Sikhs* (Bombay: Orient Longman, 1950), p. 73 n. 2.

80. Sohan Singh, Banda Bahadur's biographer, claimed that although he came seeking to recover the body of Anup Kaur, Banda encountered a former patron, rather than a *guru-bhai*, who entreated him not to attack. Singh describes the events in the following way:

> But fortunately for the man and the place, there was a *sahukar* [wealthy man] at whose house Banda, in his days of asceticism had sojourned—a kindness which he gratefully remembered. That *sahukar* implored him to spare the town as well as the life of the Nawab, and to accept from him a present of rs. 5000 besides homage as over-lord. Thus it was that Malerkotla escaped pillage which, but for the intercession of a friend of Banda's, was quite inevitable.

Banda then demanded Anup Kaur's bones and had them properly cremated. Even with such provocation, it is said he did not attack. Although this is an interesting story, it is unsubstantiated, and some historians simply assert that Banda's route from Nabha on the campaign following Sirhind did not lead through Malerkotla. For whatever reason, Banda Bahadur did spare Malerkotla the wrath he visited upon Sirhind. Sohan Singh, *Life and Exploits*, pp. 66–67.

81. Ramesh Walia, *Praja Mandal Movement in East Punjab States* (Patiala: Punjabi University Press, 1972), p. 30.

82. September 21, 2001.

83. June 4, 2001.

84. Alessandro Portelli, *The Death of Luigi Trastulli* (Albany: State University of New York Press, 2001), p. 2.

85. Ibid., p. 15.

86. March 29, 2001.

87. May 31, 2001.

88. May 31, 2001.

89. Grewal and Bal refer to Wazir Khan of Sirhind as a *faujdar*, that is, an army commander, as opposed to a *subedar*, the governor of a province, or *subah*. Grewal and Bal, *Guru Gobind Singh*, p. 138.

90. W. L. McGregor took note of this practice of removing the bricks in his *History of the Sikhs* (1846); cf. Grewal and Bal, p. 234 n. 25. It also appears as a direct order from the guru as depicted in the *Tawarikh* of Giani Gian Singh (1841). Singh writes, "The order was given that that city [Sirhind] should not dwell in peace. 'From such a great sin, my Sikhs will plunder and loot and devastate the place and every Sikh will take its bricks and throw them into the Sutlej.'" Giani Gian Singh, *Tawarikh*, p. 778.

CHAPTER 3

1. Anna Bigelow, "Malerkotla: A Heritage Going to Seed," *Tribune* (Chandigarh), December 12, 2000. The unfortunate title is not mine. The article is also available online: http://www.tribuneindia.com/2000/20001202/windows/main1.htm

2. Jan Assmann distinguishes between potential and actual cultural memories. Potential cultural memories may have left a historical record, but they do not feature in the active repertoire of public memory. Jan Assmann, "Collective Memory and Cultural Identity," *New German Critique* 65 (1995): 132, cited in Wulf Kansteiner, "Finding Meaning in Memory: A Methodological Critique of Collective Memory Studies," *History and Theory* 41, 2 (2002): 182.

3. Nowadays, according to the local RSS leaders, the Hanuman Mandir is the center of their activities.

4. Indeed there are several files in the India Office Collection of the British Library devoted to Malerkotla's debt and the various measures undertaken by the British to manage the situation. See R/1/1/4156, *Malerkotla Finance* (London: OIOC, 1944); L/P&S/13/877, *Indian States, Gen'l Questions. Debts: Maler Kotla*: IOR; R/1/1/1418, *Debt of Malerkotla to Calcutta Firms* (London: OIOC); R/1/1/2023, *Irregularities of Nawab Re: Payment of Debt* (London: OIOC, 1930).

5. Ramesh Walia, *Praja Mandal Movement in East Punjab States* (Patiala: Punjabi University Press, 1972).

6. Ibid, p. 171.

7. Rita Brara, "Marriage and Kinship" (PhD diss., Delhi University, 1989), pp. 149–50.

8. Giani Kehar Singh, *Praja Malerkotla di Dard-Kahani* (Desh: Dardi Press, n.d.), p. 67.

9. IOC, L/P&S/13/1345, Malerkotla Affairs.

10. Another report lists the secretary of the Panjab Riyasti Parja Mandal as S. Ranjit Singh of Malerkotla. According to this account, the main complaint against the nawab was that he was obsessed with grandeur and had legalized *satta* gambling, a kind of numbers game. In Malerkotla the movement was multireligious, and it unified wide sectors of society. Both Sikhs and Muslims were among the first officeholders. Giani Kehar Singh, Sewa Singh, and Talib Hussain were the main Malerkotla activists. B. S. Nijjar, *Punjab under the British Rule, 1849–1947* (New Delhi: K B Publications, 1974), pp. 32–47. Brara, "Marriage and Kinship," p. 149; Ramesh Walia, *Praja Mandal*, pp. 49–50; S. K. Sharma, "Political Beliefs and Attitudes of a Religious Minority: An Exploratory Study of the Muslim Elite in Malerkotla," in *Political Dynamics of Punjab*, ed. S. C. Wallace (Amritsar: Guru Nanak Dev University, 1981).

11. For more, see L/R/5, *Vernacular Press Reports—Kothala* (London: OIOC, 1927) and R/1/1/1685, *Malerkotla Affairs: Zamindari Association* (London: OIOC, 1927).

12. Malerkotla State Archives, File 1-C/47-A, 1948, "Declaration of RSS as Unlawful Body."

13. Chief Minister's Office, File 4 of 1937, "Confidential D.O. letter No: F-1-Misc/37, dated 23rd March 1937, from the Secretary, Punjab States Agency," Punjab States Archives.

14. First was the Hindu celebration of *navaratri*, or the nine nights of the goddess. During this time several local Hindu groups sponsored *kathas* and *bhajan* (devotional song) singing sessions. These gatherings were often in public and often at night, as were many of the Shi'i *majalis*. The eighth day of *navaratri* is Ramnaumi, for which a local temple had sponsored a reading of the *Ramcaritmanas* of Tulsidas (a medieval Hindi version of the Sanskrit epic *Ramayana*) and a parade through town.

The Ramnaumi celebrations were broken up not because of any communal trouble but because the *homa* (fire ritual) that marked the completion of the reading resulted in a truly terrifying bee swarm due to the smoke rising into an old tree at the temple. The ensuing chaos ended after an hour with several people hospitalized and more than 50 given shots to reduce their reactions to the multiple stings they had received. Later the organizers blamed the events on having begun the *homa* prior to the absolute completion of the recitation to keep the procession on schedule. This disrespect was remedied, and the festival proceeded.

Several days prior to the tenth day there was a large gathering for Haider Shaykh, as is typical of the first Thursday of the lunar month, which always draws substantial numbers of devotees, five thousand to ten thousand. Easter and the birthday celebration for Guru Hargobind also fell during this period but did not involve any significant gatherings.

15. Inayat Ali Khan, *A Description of the Principal Kotla Afghans* (Lahore: Civil and Military Gazette Press, 1882), pp. 21–22.

16. Ibid., pp. 23–24.

17. Ibid., p. 27.

18. The Ahmadiyya are a sect regarded by most other Muslims as non-Muslim because of their belief that Mirza Ghulam Ahmad communicated directly with God, challenging the orthodox position that Muhammad was the last prophet. Their base in India is in Qadian in north central Punjab. The group has been banned from numerous religious activities in Pakistan, including building their mosques in such a way that a non-Muslim might mistake them for orthodox mosques.

19. IOC, L/P&S/1345, Malerkotla file, p. 30.

20. IOC, L/P&S/1345, Malerkotla file.

21. IOC, L/P&S/13/1345 Malerkotla affairs.

22. A *katha* is the public performance of a holy Hindu text. The term literally means story or telling, but in a religious context it applies specifically to sacred texts. One of the most common *kathas* is the recitation of the *Ramayana*, the epic story of the god-king Rama's activities restoring righteous rule on earth. A *katha* would typically be chanted, but there may also be some instrumentation and the occasional interjection of songs, often based on the poetry of the text.

23. Termed the "piety people" by historian of Islam Marshall Hodgson, the Ahl-e Hadith reject the binding authority of the four canonical schools of Sunni law as they do not give reliable credence to the principles of *qiyas*, analogical reasoning, or *ijma'*, consensus of the community. Rather they are textual literalists who strive to base every decision and all lifestyle practices solely on the Qur'an and the Sunnah of the Prophet.

24. IOC, L/P&S/13/1345 Malerkotla affairs, file p. 93 (report p. 29).

25. Ibid., p. 101 (report p. 37).

26. IOC, L/P&J/170, *Puran Mal Murder*.

27. IOC, R/1/2860, Report on Muslim Agitation in Malerkotla State and Proposals for Future Administration of the State and IOC, R/1/2936, Muslim Agitation at Malerkotla.

28. Ultimately they returned, Mufti Shafiq Ahmad was dismissed, and a new mufti was appointed. I heard a fascinating story about this *hijra* from a resident whose father had been a supporter of the mufti's. According to the story, as the people left on the

road toward Ludhiana, a great storm arose. The mufti and the *muhajirun* stopped and recited the *fatiha* and *durud sharif*, and the rain fell on either side of the road, allowing the party to pass comfortably.

29. Letter from Mohan Lal Sharma, Secretary Hindu Sabha, Malerkotla, to H. H. the Nawab, Malerkotla, dated June 8, 1940, Punjab State Archives, Malerkotla Chief Minster File 10 of 1936.

30. Reprinted in Punjab State Archives, Malerkotla Chief Minister's file 10, pp. 55–6.

31. Section 144 of the Criminal Procedures Code allowed for the unilateral imposition of curfews and restrictions to preserve public safety. The same section of code was applied to the temple in the *arati-namaz* dispute and to the performance of *kathas*. *Maghrib namaz* was also prohibited in the Masjid Bafindagan. Text of the Agra agreement is on page 55 of the Punjab State Archives, Malerkotla Chief Minister File 10, 1936.

32. Chief Minister File 10, 1936, pp. 63–66.

33. Ibid., p. 73.

34. IOC, L/P&S/13/1345 Malerkotla affairs.

35. IOC, L/P&S/1345, Malerkotla file, file p. 68 (report p. 4).

36. Ibid., file pp. 69–70 (report pp. 5–6).

37. Ibid., file p. 73 (report p. 9).

38. Ibid., file p. 86 (report p. 22).

39. Ibid., file p. 101 (report p. 37).

40. IOC, R/1/1/3006, *Congress Activities in Malerkotla.*

41. "Malerkotla Riots," in *The National Call.* Photocopy of article included in India Office Collection file IOC, L/P&S/1345, Malerkotla file.

42. L/P&J/7/132, *Commissioned Report on Communal Disturbances*: IOR, no date. The report includes a list of communal conflicts and stops in 1928.

43. Beth Roy, *Some Trouble with Cows: Making Sense of Social Conflict* (Berkeley: University of California Press, 1994), p. 165.

44. Allen Feldman, *Formations of Violence: The Narrative of the Body and Political Terror in Northern Ireland* (Chicago: University of Chicago Press, 1991), p. 29.

45. Steven Knapp, "Collective Memory and the Actual Past," *Representations* 26 (Spring 1989): 123.

46. Ashutosh Varshney, *Ethnic Conflict and Civic Life: Hindus and Muslims in India* (New Haven, Conn.: Yale University Press, 2002).

47. Ashis Nandy, Shikha Trivedy, Shail Mayaram and Achyut Yagnik. *Creating a Nationality: The Ramjanmabhumi Movement and Fear of the Self* (New Delhi: Oxford University Press, 1995); and Sudhir Kakar, *Colors of Violence: Cultural Identities, Religion, Conflict* (Chicago: University of Chicago Press, 1996).

48. Kansteiner, "Finding Meaning," p. 179.

49. Gyan Pandey, *Remembering Partition* (New York: Cambridge University Press, 2001), esp. chap. 10.

CHAPTER 4

1. There are many excellent studies of the 1947 Partition and independence of India and Pakistan. A good place to begin is with Yasmin Khan's *The Great Partition: The Making of India and Pakistan* (New Haven, Conn.: Yale University Press, 2007).

2. Barbara D. Metcalf and Thomas Metcalf, *A Concise History of India* (New York: Cambridge University Press, 2002), p. 217.

3. Sir Francis Mudie to Sir Chandu Lal Trivedi, September 17, 1947, in Kirpal Singh, ed., *Select Documents on Partition of Punjab-1947: India and Pakistan: Punjab, Haryana, and Himachal-India and Punjab-Pakistan* (Delhi: National Book Shop, 1991), p. 525.

4. Metcalf and Metcalf, *Concise History*, p. 217.

5. Mian Muhammad Sadullah, *The Partition of the Punjab, 1947: A Compilation of Official Documents* (Lahore: National Documentation Centre, 1983). See also Kirpal Singh, *Select Documents on Partition of Punjab, 1947: India and Pakistan* (Delhi: National Book Shop, 2006), and *Disturbances in the Punjab, 1947: A Compilation of Official Documents* (Islamabad: National Documentation Centre, 1995).

6. Secretary Governor of East Punjab N. K. Mukerji to Maharaja of Patiala Yadavindra Singh, September 23, 1947, in Kirpal Singh, *Select Documents*, p. 533.

7. Urvashi Butalia, *The Other Side of Silence: Voices from the Partition of India* (Durham, NC: Duke University Press, 2000), p. 61.

8. Ibid., pp. 61–62; Stanley Wolpert, *A New History of India* (New York: Oxford University Press, 1997), p. 348.

9. Metcalf and Metcalf, *Concise History*, p. 218.

10. Mushirul Hasan, "Partition Narratives," *Social Scientist* 30, 7/8 (2002): 36.

11. The word "Punjab" comes from the Persian *panj aab*, meaning five waters.

12. Khushi Mohammad, quoted in Asit Jolly, "Myth of Malerkotla," *Asian Age*, May 11, 1997. I interviewed Faujdar Khushi Mohammad at great length and spent a lot of time with him and his family. However, the audiocassettes with these interviews have been lost.

13. Many valuable studies of Partition are available. Some recent titles include Ritu Menon and Kamla Bhasin, *Borders and Boundaries: Women in India's Partition* (New Delhi: Kali for Women, 1998); Butalia, *Other Side*; Mushirul Hasan, ed., *Inventing Boundaries: Gender, Politics, and the Partition of India* (New Delhi: Oxford University Press, 2000); Suvir Kaul, ed., *The Partitions of Memory: The Afterlife of the Division of India* (Bloomington: Indiana University Press, 2002); Gyanendra Pandey, *Remembering Partition* (New York: Cambridge University Press, 2001).

14. In a compelling article about the role of Muslim religious leaders in the eventual support of the Muslim League, David Gilmartin argues that the Unionist Government, caught between the interests of the rural landlords and the urban elite had tended for years to cultivate the landlords' support. For this reason the *sajjida nishins* who controlled the tomb shrines of the Punjab as well as large tracts of land that had been granted to those tomb shrines, tended to support the Unionist Party. But with the aggressive campaigning of the Muslim League, whose appeal superceded the question of rural and urban interests focused on the question of religious identity, these leaders began to see a real possibility for gaining authority as landlords *and* as religious leaders within the party's structure and within any future Pakistani state. See David Gilmartin, "Religious Leadership and the Pakistan Movement in the Punjab," *Modern Asian Studies* 13, 3 (1979).

15. Mushirul Hasan, "Partition Narratives," p. 33.

16. This cannot be regarded with any certainty as a scientific survey, but the findings certainly coincide with my own perceptions and communications. This survey was

included in the doctoral dissertation by Anila Sultana, "Muslims of Malerkotla: A Study of Change" (Punjabi University, Patiala, 1993), p. 78.

17. Punjab State Archives, "Disturbances and Refugees," File 1/1-C/47-a/1947.

18. Ibid. See also "Refugee and Evacuee Information," Malerkotla File, 1947. File no. 2(19) PR/47; L/P&S/13/1345. *Malerkotla* (London: Oriental and India Office Collection).

19. Visit to Malerkotla State by Major Gurbax Singh Gill HQ5 Inf. Bde. Malerkotla File, 1947. File no. 2(19) PR/47.

20. Khushi Mohammad, quoted in Jolly, "Myth of Malerkotla."

21. March 10, 2001.

22. According to the 1941 Census of India, Punjab was 53 percent Muslim, 31 percent Hindu, and 15 percent Sikh.

23. According to the Census of India, 2001 the Muslim population of Punjab was 1.6 percent, or 382,045. http://www.censusindia.net/religiondata/index.html (accessed February 3, 2004).

24. Pandey, *Remembering Partition*, p. 188.

25. The paradox of the Indian Muslim (or Muslim Indian) is the subject of Gyan Pandey's compelling article, "Can a Muslim Be an Indian?" in *Comparative Studies in Society and History* 41, 4 (1999): 608–29.

26. The BJP at this point was in power in the central government of India. The BJP is closely linked with Hindu extremist organizations such as the Vishwa Hindu Parishad (VHP) and the Rashtriya Swayamsevak Sangh (RSS). This so-called "family" of organizations forward an ideology of Hindu pride known as "Hindutva" (i.e., "Hindu-ness").

27. From 1998–2001 the MLA was Nusrat Ikram Khan, who also served as sports minister in the cabinet of Prakash Singh Badal. Past MLA's have also been cabinet ministers, demonstrating the somewhat disproportionate prominence this Muslim constituency has had.

28. Lepel Griffin, *Rajas of the Punjab* (Delhi: Low Price Publications, 2000 [1870]); D. Ibbetson, E. D. MacLagan, and H. A. Rose, *A Glossary of the Tribes and Castes of the Punjab and North-West Frontier Province* (Lahore: Government Printing House, 1919 [1883]); *Maler Kotla State Gazetteer* (Lahore: Civil and Military Gazette Press, 1904); "Malerkotla," in *Imperial Gazetteer of India*, edited by W. W. Hunter (London: Trübner and Co., 1881); "Malerkotla," in *Imperial Gazetteer of India* (London: Trübner and Co., 1886); "Malerkotla," in *Imperial Gazetteer of India* (London: Trübner and Co., 1908); "Malerkotla State," in Muhammad Din, *Yadgar-i darbar-i tajposh* (Lahore: Yadgar Press, 1911).

29. The other most common explanation for Malerkotla's peace is the blessing of the Sikh Guru Gobind Singh after hearing of the Malerkotla Nawab Sher Muhammad Khan's objections to his sons' execution at Sirhind in 1705.

30. January 28, 2001.

31. C. H. Loehlin, "Guru Gobind Singh and Islam," *Proceedings of the Punjab History Conference*, Vol. 2, 1966, p. 95.

32. February 21, 2001.

33. Sufi Ismail has written several books on Islamic and Sufi subjects, focusing on death, preparation for death and the life to come, and collections of praise liturgies to the prophet. Ismail is a sober man and rather intimidating. I met with him, but he was terse and unforthcoming, and the interview quickly ended. Sufi Muhammad Ismail, *Bagh Anbiya' Punjab* (Malerkotla: Janab Doctor Muhammad Nizamuddin Sahib,

1995); *Kabr Ki Pahali Rat* (Malerkotla: Kutub Khana Ibrahimiya, 1996); *Kabr Kya Kahti Hai* (Malerkotla: Maktaba Rahimiyan, 1971); and *Na'atun Ka Bagh* (Malerkotla: Kutub Khana Ibrahimiya, 1965).

34. On Sufi *tazkira* see Carl W. Ernst and Bruce B. Lawrence, *Sufi Martyrs of Love* (New York: Palgrave Macmillan, 2002); and Marcia Hermanson, "Religious Literature and the Inscription of Identity: The Sufi Tazkira Tradition in Muslim South Asia," *Muslim World* 87, nos. 3–4 (1997).

35. Ismail, *Bagh Anbiya'*, p. 176.

36. Ibid., pp. 176–77.

37. Ibid., p. 171.

38. March 10, 2001.

39. Iftikhar Ali Khan, *History of the Ruling Family*, p. 145.

40. S. K. Sharma, "Political Beliefs and Attitudes of a Religious Minority: An Exploratory Study of the Muslim Elite in Malerkotla," in *Political Dynamics of Punjab*, edited by S. C. Wallace (Amritsar: Guru Nanak Dev University, 1981), p. 83.

41. Stanley Tambiah addresses the riots between Sindhis and *muhajir*s (migrants) in Karachi in chapter 6, "Ethnic Conflict in Pakistan," of his *Leveling Crowds: Ethnonationalist Conflicts and Collective Violence in South Asia* (New Delhi: Vistaar Publications, 1996), pp. 163–210.

42. Quoted in Stephen Hay, ed., *Sources of Indian Tradition*, Vol. 2 (New York: Columbia University Press, 1988), p. 240.

43. As Gyan Pandey describes in his article, "Can a Muslim Be an Indian?" in the aftermath of Partition, the consolidation of the nation is a project that necessitated drawing distinctions between who is a legitimate member of the nation and who is not.

44. Sultana, "Muslims of Malerkotla," p. 80.

45. Sharma, "Political Beliefs," p. 67.

46. Ian Copland, "The Political Geography of Religious Conflict: Towards an Explanation of the Relative Infrequency of Communal Riots in the Indian Princely States," *International Journal of Punjab Studies* 7, 1 (1999).

47. Asit Jolly, "Myth of Maler Kotla," *Asian Age*, May 11, 1997.

48. Ibid.

49. For more on such reports, see Concerned Citizens Tribunal (Justice V. R. Krishna Iyer, Justice P. B. Sawant, Justice Hosbet Suresh, K. G. Kannabiran, Aruna Roy, K.S. Subramanian, Ghanshyam Shah, Tanika Sarkar), "Crime against Humanity: An Inquiry into the Carnage in Gujarat" (Mumbai: Citizens for Justice and Peace, 2002); Kamal Mitra Chenoy, S. P. Shukla, K. S. Subramanian, and Achin Vanaik, "Gujarat Carnage 2002," *Outlook*, April 4, 2002; Human Rights Watch, "'We Have No Orders to Save You': State Participation and Complicity in Communal Violence in Gujarat," *Human Rights Watch* 14, 3(C) (2002).

50. Human Rights Watch, "We Have No Orders," p. 22.

51. Ibid., p. 49.

52. Suvir Kaul, *The Partitions of Memory: The Afterlife of the Division of India* (Bloomington: Indiana University Press, 2001), p. 3.

53. "Veterans Resign, Sultana Unfazed," *Tribune*, January 22, 2003.

54. This is an argument made by both Paul Brass and Stanley Tambiah. Mass politics opens up an arena for competition in which political leaders seek to garner power

and support by activating divisive religious identities. See Paul R. Brass, *Language, Religion and Politics in North India* (New York: Cambridge University Press, 1974), and *Theft of an Idol*; Tambiah, *Leveling Crowds*; and van der Veer, *Religious Nationalism*.

55. Recent developments indicate that Jindal was replaced in August of 2002 by one Faqir Muhammad (not to my knowledge linked to the nawab or *khalifah* families). Confusing and contradictory reports appear in the *Tribune* from July through August of 2002. See, for example, August 30, 2002, http://www.tribuneindia.com/2002/20020830/punjab1.htm'14.

56. *Tribune*, August 29, 2002, quotes Jindal saying, "'I passed out and regained consciousness half an hour later. Some friends—Mr Haleem Farooqui, Mr Des Raj Verma, both councillors, and Mr M. Jamil-ur-Rehman—brought some clothes for me. I pulled myself inside the hall where the meeting was still on and brought the matter to the notice of the SDM [Sub-Divisional Magistrate], who commented that he was 'following his orders.'"

57. *Tribune*, August 20, 2002.

58. The notion of Gujarat, where thousands of Muslims were killed in pogroms in the Spring of 2002, as Hindutva's laboratory comes from a comment by Praveen Togadia, the general secretary of the Vishwa Hindu Parishad (VHP). Togadia reportedly announced that the events in Gujarat and the subsequent reelection of the Gujarat Chief Minister Narendra Modi, who administered the state during this period, testified to the success of an experiment in the laboratory of Hindutva. This was widely reported in the Indian press.

CHAPTER 5

1. Iftikhar Ali Khan, "Letter from Iftikhar Ali Khan to M. R. Bhide, Esq. the Regional Commissioner and Home Minister of the PEPSU (Patiala and East Punjab States Union)" dated January 11, 1950, Punjab State Archives, Dharam Arth, 464/103.

2. Wulf Kansteiner, "Finding Meaning in Memory: A Methodological Critique of Collective Memory Studies," *History and Theory* 41, 2 (2002): 191.

3. Jolly, "The Myth of Malerkotla," *Asian Age*, 1997.

4. Christopher Taylor, *In the Vicinity of the Righteous: Ziyara and the Veneration of Muslim Saints in Late Medieval Egypt* (Leiden: Brill, 1999), p. 224.

5. Ibid.

6. Emile Durkheim, *Elementary Forms of Religious Life*, translated by Karen E. Fields (New York: Free Press, 1995), esp. chaps. 5 and 6: "The Origins of these Beliefs."

7. Clifford Geertz, *The Interpretation of Cultures* (New York: Basic Books, 1973), esp. chap. 6, "Ritual and Social Change," and chap. 15, "Deep Play: Notes on a Balinese Cockfight."

8. Catherine Bell, *Ritual Theory, Ritual Practice*, (New York: Oxford University Press, 1992), p. 197.

9. See Graham Burchell, Colin Gordon, and Peter Miller, eds., *The Foucault Effect: Studies in Governmentality* (Chicago: University of Chicago Press, 1991); Michel Foucault, *Discipline and Punish* (New York: Vintage, 1977); and *Power/Knowledge* (New York: Pantheon, 1972).

10. James C. Scott, *Weapons of the Weak: Everyday Forms of Peasant Resistance* (New Haven, CT: Yale University Press, 1985).

11. James C. Scott, *Domination and the Arts of Resistance: Hidden Transcripts* (New Haven, CT: Yale University Press, 1990).

12. The notion of a shared piety observable in Punjabi cultural formations is an important contribution from the work of Farina Mir on the *qissa* ballad tradition. See Farina Mir, "The Social Space of Language: Punjabi Popular Narrative in Colonial India, 1850–1900" (PhD diss., Columbia University, 2002).

13. *Khandan* is the term most frequently deployed by members of the Nawabi and *khalifah* families to designate that they are from the "Khan" Pathan Afghan lineage. All of these people use the surname Khan, and many are quick to note the difference between "real" Khans and those Muslims of native Indian descent who adopt the name as a means of upward mobility.

14. Iftikhar Ali Khan, "Letter to Mr. Bhide."

15. At most *dargahs* of any size, there are few times when the tomb itself is wholly denuded of *chadar* or flowers. At monumental *dargah*s such as those at Ajmer and Gulbarga, the rituals involved in cleaning the tomb are elaborate and often the exclusive privilege of the descendants or hereditary caretakers.

16. However, another local shrine to an apocryphal *pir* is managed by a *faqir* who used to attend the *dargah* of Haider Shaykh. When he was accused of possibly assaulting a woman at the *dargah*, he was forced out. Now he claims that Haider Shaykh's spirit visits the shrine he supervises every Thursday night to avoid the crowds.

17. For more on the *adab* of *ziyarat*, see Carl Ernst, "An Indo-Persian Guide to Sufi Shrine Pilgrimage," in *Manifestations of Sainthood in Islam*, ed. Grace Martin Smith and Carl W. Ernst (Istanbul: Isis Press, 1993); and Robert Rozehnal, *Islamic Sufism Unbound: Politics and Piety in Twenty-First Century Pakistan* (New York: Palgrave Macmillan, 2007).

18. The literal meaning of the word *wali* (pl. *auliya'*) designates one who is close to God.

19. See especially Ibn Taymiyya, "*ziyarat al-qubur*," in *Majmu'at al-Risa'il w'al-masa'il* (Cairo: Lajnat al-Tuath al-Arab). In his study of *ziyarat* in medieval Cairo, Christopher Taylor (*In the Vicinity of the Righteous*, p. 172) points out that even in his own time Ibn Taymiyya's view was not shared by the majority of scholars, *ulama.'* Indeed, he died while imprisoned in Damascus for publishing a polemical tract against *ziyarat*.

20. Ibn Taymiyya dismisses the justifications for tomb visitation as unlawful innovation (*bida'*) by focusing on hadith that indicate Muhammad's disapproval of the practice. For example, a tradition from the canonical collection *Sahih Bukhari* references the habit of Christians of building tomb shrines to their holy dead: "If any religious man dies amongst those people they would build a place of worship at his grave and make these pictures in it. They will be the worst creature in the sight of Allah on the Day of Resurrection" (*Sahih Bukhari*, 8:419).

21. J. M. S. Baljon, "Shah Waliullah and the Dargah," in *Muslim Shrines in India: Their Character, History and Significance*, ed. Christian W. Troll (Delhi: Oxford University Press, 1989), p. 191.

22. *Sahih Muslim*, 4:2131.

23. The renowned Sufi scholar Abu Hamid al-Ghazali (d. 1111) makes this point in book 4 of his classic work *Ihya 'Ulum al-Din* (The Revivification of the Religious Sciences), explaining the eternity of the soul thus:

Death cannot destroy the soul, which is the place of Allah's *ma'rifat* (gnosis), because it is something spiritual. Death causes the change of the condition of the soul, and relieves it from the prison of its bodily cage. It does not end as Allah says: "Think not of those who are slain in Allah's way as dead. Nay, they live, finding their sustenance in the presence of their Lord; they rejoice in the bounty provided by Allah. And with regard to those left behind, who have not yet joined them (in their bliss), the (Martyrs) glory in the fact that on them is no fear, nor have they (cause to) grieve. They glory in the Grace and the bounty from Allah, and in the fact that Allah suffers not the reward of the Faithful to be lost (in the least)." One should not think that this position is acquired only by those that are martyred on the battlefield, because every breath of an *'arif* [one who possesses spiritual knowledge] is a martyr.

Although al-Ghazali is primarily describing the souls of the righteous dead, his understanding of the nature of death is that it merely causes a "change of the condition of the soul, and relieves it from the prison of its bodily cage."

24. Baljon, "Shah Waliullah," pp. 189–190.
25. For studies of these manuals *kitab adab al- ziyarat*, see: Averil Cameron, "On Defining the Holy Man," in *The Cult of Saints in Late Antiquity and the Middle Ages: Essays on the Contribution of Peter Brown*, ed. James Howard-Johnston and Paul Antony Hayward (New York: Oxford University Press, 1999); Tewfik Canaan, *Mohammedan Saints and Sanctuaries in Palestine* (Jerusalem: Ariel Publishing House, 1927); Carl W. Ernst, "An Indo-Persian Guide to Sufi Shrine Pilgrimage," in *Manifestations of Sainthood in Islam*, ed. Grace Martin Smith and Carl W. Ernst (Istanbul: Isis Press, 1993); Josef W. Meri, "The Etiquette of Devotion in the Islamic Cult of Saints," in *The Cult of Saints in Late Antiquity and the Middle Ages: Essays on the Contribution of Peter Brown*, ed. James Howard-Johnston and Paul Antony Hayward (New York: Oxford University Press, 1999); C. Taylor, *Vicinity of the Righteous*.
26. August 2, 2001.
27. January 28, 2001.
28. The *durud sharif*, also called the *durud-e Ibrahim* is one of several blessings recorded in the Hadith of the Prophet that are therefore seen as particularly powerful and beneficial. *Durud* is the Urdu, in Arabic they are called *salawat*.

    allahuma salli 'ala muhammadin wa 'ala illi muhammadin kama sallayta 'ala ibrahima wa 'ala illi ibrahima innaka hamidun majid, allahuma barika 'ala muhammadin wa 'ala illi muhammadin kama barakta 'ala ibrahima wa 'ala illi ibrahima innaka hamidun majid

    [Allah shower blessings upon Muhammad and his family as you showered blessings upon Ibrahim and his family, indeed You are Praiseworthy, Glorious.

    Allah bless Muhammad and his family as you blessed Ibrahim and his family, indeed You are Praiseworthy, Glorious.]
29. One of the few scholarly works on death in Islam is Jane Idleman Smith and Yvonne Yazbeck Haddad, *The Islamic Understanding of Death and Resurrection* (Albany: State University of New York Press, 1981).
30. In Islam, there are two degrees of what is usually termed the "soul" in English. The *nafs* is the baser level of spirit, which animates our material selves. *Nafs* is also

possessed by other sentient beings such as animals, and humans are believed to be constantly struggling against their *nafs* to curb instincts and impulses that lead us away from God. The higher degree of spirit, termed *ruh*, is a more subtle essence. The goal of much spiritual practice is to separate the *ruh* from the *nafs*, thereby freeing it to unite with God. Until the last day, the *ruh* remains "alive" in the sense that it is still possible to pray on behalf of the departed and hope that they will receive the rewards of that prayer. For those, such as the saints, who were perfected in life, the *ruh* of the saint is able to perform intercessory prayers on behalf of the living. This last point is an issue of some dispute among Muslims.

31. Sharafuddin Maneri, "Letter 86: Coming to Terms with Oneself," in Paul Jackson, *Sharafuddin Maneri: The Hundred Letters* (New York: Paulist Press, 1980).

32. In Islam corpses are always buried facing Mecca. Thus to address the deceased properly one must approach the head of the tomb on the *qibla* side.

33. Ya Sin, the thirty-sixth *sura* of the Qur'an is often recited as a memorial for the dead. See Juan E. Campo, "Burial," in Jane Macauliffe, editor, *Encyclopedia of the Qur'an* (Leiden: Brill, 2001), pp. 263–65.

34. There is a schedule, more or less formal, which determines the branch of the family that is responsible for officiating at the site during specified hours of the day. On Thursdays and for festivals, when attendance at the shrine is greater, typically representatives of all the *khalifah* families are there.

35. For more on Sufi shrines in South Asia, see: P. M. Currie, *The Shrine and Cult of Mu'in Al-Din Chishti of Ajmer* (Delhi: Oxford University Press, 1989); Richard M. Eaton, *Sufis of Bijapur, 1300–1700: Social Roles of Sufis in Medieval India* (Delhi: Munshiram Manoharlal, 1996 [1978]); Carl W. Ernst, *Eternal Garden: Mysticism, History and Politics at a South Asian Sufi Center* (Albany: State University of New York Press, 1992); Carl W. Ernst and Bruce B. Lawrence, *Sufi Martyrs of Love* (New York: Palgrave Macmillan, 2002); Miles Irving, *"The Shrine of Baba Farid Shakarganj at Pakpattan,"* in *Notes on Punjab and Mughal India: Selections from Journal of the Punjab Historical Society*, ed. Zulfiqar Ahmed (Lahore: Sang-e-Meel Publications, 1988); Claudia Liebskind, *Piety on Its Knees: Three Sufi Traditions in South Asia in Modern Times* (Delhi: Oxford University Press, 1998); Desiderio Pinto, *Piri-Muridi Relationship: A Study of the Nizamuddin dargah* (Delhi: Manohar, 1995); John A. Subhan, *Sufism: Its Shrines and Saints* (New York: Samuel A. Weiser, 1970 [1938]); Christian W. Troll, ed., *Muslim Shrines in India: Their Character, History and Significance* (Delhi: Oxford University Press, 1989); Peter van der Veer, "Playing or Praying: A Sufi Saint's Day in Surat," *Journal of Asian Studies* 51, 3 (1992); Kerrin Von Schwerin, "Saint Worship in Indian Islam: The Legend of the Martyr Salar Masud Ghazi," in *Ritual and Religion among Muslims of the Subcontinent*, ed. Imtiaz Ahmad (Lahore: Vanguard, 1985); Pnina Werbner and Helene Basu, eds., *Embodying Charisma: Modernity, Locality and the Performance of Emotion in Sufi Cults* (London: Routledge, 1998).

36. Hindu death rituals and understandings of the nature of the soul are highly elaborated in countless sources. The Sikh tradition, on the other hand, has paid little attention to this matter. Beyond a general belief in reincarnation and a priority upon cremation of the dead, there seems to be little material indicating a concern with the status of the dead. There is, however, a highly active cult of the powerful dead, particularly of martyrs of the faith. See Stuart Blackburn, "Death and Deification:

Folk Cults in Hinduism," *History of Religions* 24, 3 (1985); Louis Fenech, *Martyrdom in the Sikh Tradition* (New Delhi: Oxford University Press, 2000); Victor Turner, "Death and the Dead in the Pilgrimage Process," in *Religious Encounters with Death: Insights from the History and Anthropology of Religions*, ed. Frank Reynolds (University Park: Pennsylvania State University Press, 1977).

37. This is the Vendantin perspective, only one of several schools of thought about the nature of human life and death and the status of the soul in the Hindu traditions. Other conceptions maintain there will always be a distinction between the soul of a human and the divine soul, and that the state of perfect enlightenment is a state of pure devotion to the divine principle—a relationship of reciprocity that requires that distinction to remain.

38. Jonathan Parry has done particularly interesting studies of death in Hindu traditions. See "Death and Digestion: The Symbolism of Food and Eating in North Indian Mortuary Rites," *Man* 20 (1985); *Death in Banaras* (Cambridge: Cambridge University Press, 1994); "The End of the Body," in *Fragments for a History of the Human Body*, ed. Michel Feher (New York: Zone, 1989); "Ghost, Greed and Sin: The Occupational Identity of Benares Funeral Priests," *Man* 15 (1980); "Sacrificial Death and the Necrophagous Ascetic," in *Death and the Regeneration of Life*, ed. M. Bloch and J. Parry (Cambridge: Cambridge University Press, 1982).

39. Both Hindus and Muslims believe that the bodies of the saintly dead do not corrupt in the grave. Jonathan Parry, "Sacrificial Death and the Necrophagous Ascetic," p. 96.

40. David Knipe, "Sapindikarana," in *Religious Encounters with Death: Insights from the History and Anthropology of Religions*, ed. Frank Reynolds (University Park: Pennsylvania State University Press, 1977).

41. Many Sikhs do prefer to bring their dead to the gurdwara at Kiratpur at the foot of the Himalayas, but this is not regarded as prescriptive to the same degree that immersion in the Ganges is the optimal end of life for Hindus.

42. On the *rehat* see W. H. Mcleod, *The Chaupa Singh Rahit-Nama* (Dunedin, New Zealand: University of Otago Press, 1987).

43. An excellent assessment of the process of formulating the *rehat* and the process of creating unique rituals in order to foster a sense of religious identity can be found in Oberoi.

44. "Sikh Reht Maryada, Chapter X, Article XVId," Shiromani Gurdwara Prabhandak Committee, http://www.sgpc.net/rehat_maryada/section_four.html (accessed May 17, 2008).

45. See Louis Fenech, *Martyrdom in the Sikh Tradition.*

46. In some cases these shrines also become more substantial places of worship, as do the sites where revered Sikh leaders died or were killed, such as the Gurdwara Rakab Ganj in Delhi marking the place where Guru Tegh Bahadur's body was burned after his head was cut off and taken by a faithful disciple to Anandpur in Punjab.

47. During this month Muslims are supposed to rededicate themselves to their religion. Any superogatory prayer, practice, charity, or good deed reaps additional spiritual benefit (*sawab*), which may be dedicated to others, including the saintly dead such as

Haider Shaykh. Far more people than usual perform the five daily prayers, and an atmosphere of mixed piety and celebration prevails for the duration.

48. It is common for there to be an exchange of *khalifahs* at the time of an *'urs*, especially within a lineage (*silsila*) and it is not uncommon for Sufis affiliated with other lineages to attend the *'urs* of a saint from another *silsila*. For the *'urs* of a major figure such as Khwaja Muinuddin Chishti or his disciple Khwaja Niza-muddin Auliya, representatives from Chishti shrines will arrive to reaffirm their spiritual allegiance and reverence for the founding Shaykhs. These events can be somewhat fraught with tension as the shaykhs of these centers must both dem-onstrate and be given the appropriate amount of respect and honor according to their status within the *silsila* and the acknowledged level of their spiritual attain-ment. It is sometimes visibly awkward when a shaykh arrives at an *'urs* to ensure that he is placed properly in relation to the tomb and the head of the host *dargah*. Not showing or being shown the proper deference, giving inadequate offerings, or failing to observe the etiquette of the hierarchy may result in all kinds of difficulties, even fractures within the communities. For more, see Robert Rozehnal, *Islamic Sufism Unbound: Politics and Piety in Twenty-First Century Pakistan* (New York: Palgrave Macmillan, 2007).

49. These practices and others are recorded in D. Ibbetson, E. D. MacLagan, and H. A. Rose, *A Glossary of the Tribes and Castes of the Punjab and North-West Frontier Province* (Lahore: Government Printing House, 1919 [1883]), p. 644.

50. In a year and a half I never witnessed or heard of a Muslim who was "played" by the spirit of the saint at this shrine. A common term for being possessed by the saint is *khelna*, or playing.

51. Ibbetson et al., *Glossary*, pp. 644–645.

52. Ron E. Hassner, "Understanding and Resolving Disputes over Sacred Space," *Stanford Center on Conflict and Negotiation Working Paper* 62 (2002).

53. This notion of the incomplete and emergent quality of history is a methodological and theoretical intervention put forward by many in the subaltern studies and post-colonial historiography schools of thought. Excellent examples of such works include: Partha Chatterjee *The Nation and Its Fragments: Colonial and Postcolonial Histories* (Princeton, NJ: Princeton University Press, 1993); and Gyan Pandey, "In Defense of the Fragment: Writing about Hindu-Muslim Riots in India Today," *Representations* 37 (1992), and *The Construction of Communalism in Colonial North India* (New Delhi: Oxford University Press, 1990).

54. Iftikhar Ali Khan, *History of the Ruling Family*, p. 9.

55. These are the two major festivals of Islam: 'Id al-Adha or Baqr 'Id marking Ibrahim's willingness to sacrifice his son Ismail, and 'Id al-Fitr marking the end of the fasting month of Ramadan.

56. Remember that Inayat Ali Khan in his book *A Description of the Principal Kotla Afghans* had lamented the absence of Sufi followers to provide a reliable support base for Haider Shaykh and his household. As it emerges, the clientele of the shrine are loyal to the saint's descendants.

57. Here Eaton is extending Clifford Geertz's notion of the Balinese temple as a theater-state. See Clifford Geertz, *Negara: The Theatre State in Nineteenth-Century Bali* (Princeton, NJ: Princeton University Press, 1980).

58. Richard M. Eaton, "The Political and Religious Authority of the Shrine of Baba Farid," in *Moral Conduct and Authority: The Place of Adab in South Asian Islam*, ed. Barbara Metcalf (Berkeley: University of California Press, 1984), p. 347.

59. David Gilmartin explores the ways in which this authority was negotiated and validated through the courts during the colonial period. He argues that whereas prior to the advent of the British there was a close link between the temporal and spiritual authorities at the *dargahs* in his study, once the worldly power was wholly subsumed by the colonial regime, only the spiritual dimension remained as a means of verifying authority at the shrine. Whereas before the British the symbiosis was more complete, now the political authority was based entirely upon the relations with local landowners and tribal leaders. These relations being complicated by marriage bonds and other allegiances, the only other negotiable source of authority lay in the role of the *dargah* as an Islamic educational institution. Thus the ability of the *sajjida nishin* to effectively disseminate Islamic values and provide spiritual guidance becomes the only real variable in the equation of power at the *dargah*. David Gilmartin, "Shrines, Succession and Sources of Moral Authority," in *Moral Conduct and Authority: The Place of Adab in South Asian Islam*, ed. Barbara Metcalf (Berkeley: University of California Press, 1984).

60. Ian Talbot cautions that pre-Partition Punjabi culture should not be idealized as free of religious separatism. He observes, "It was only in the celebrations of the Sufi shrines that 'distance' was broken down between communities who were otherwise near neighbours, but living in separate worlds." Although I disagree with his pessimistic view of the level of integration in community life, his singling out of *dargahs* as idealized places of exchange is significant. See Ian Talbot, introduction to *Partition and Genocide: Manifestation of Violence in Punjab, 1937–1947*, by Anders Bjørn Hansen (New Delhi: India Research Press, 2002), p. x.

CHAPTER 6

1. Edward S. Casey, *Remembering: A Phenomenological Study* (Bloomington: Indiana University Press, 1987), p. 257.

2. Alexander and Margarete Mitscherlich first put this concept forward in the context of coping with the violence committed and experienced by Germans in WWII in their book *The Inability to Mourn: Principles of Collective Behavior* (New York: Grove Press, 1975).

3. The events of Operation Bluestar are often marked by events in gurdwaras throughout the region. A closer parallel would be the Jewish observance of Yom Hashoa, the day of mourning for the victims of the Nazi program of extermination. Memorialization of the trauma of mass death is often a key element in community healing. Conversely, the failure to find a collective means of reconciling such trauma, particularly when accompanied by denial of the events themselves, as often happens in South Asia, can result in a pathological "inability to mourn."

4. Gyanendra Pandey, *Remembering Partition* (New York: Cambridge University Press, 2001), p. 7.

5. See Pandey, *Remembering Partition*, esp. chap. 8, "Constructing Community."

6. Ashutosh Varshney, *Ethnic Conflict and Civic Life: Hindus and Muslims in India* (New Haven, CT: Yale University Press, 2002), p. 11.

7. Department of Revenue, Government of Punjab, http://punjabrevenue.nic.in/gaz_sang19.htm (accessed May 20, 2008).

8. According to Sultana, in 1975 the region was declared "industrially backward" by the Punjab government and received subsidies for development. The situation has certainly changed today. See Anila Sultana, "Muslims of Malerkotla: A Study in Social and Cultural Change 1947–91" (PhD diss., Punjabi University, 1993).

9. Vikrant Jindal, "This Town Makes Badges Too," *Tribune*, April 5, 2001. http://www.tribuneindia.com/2001/20010405/punjab1.htm (accessed November 28, 2001).

10. "Orders Passed on the Assessment Report of the Maler Kotla State by Col. L.J.H. Grey, C.S.I. Commissioner and Superintendent, Delhi Division, on the 13th October, 1891."

11. Iftikhar Ali Khan, *History of the Ruling Family*, p. 146.

12. Punjab's population is overwhelmingly rural (70 percent), but the state represents only 2.9 percent of India's land under cultivation. Nonetheless, by 1970, the state supplied 24 percent of the nation's wheat crop. Nowadays, Punjab produces almost 60 percent of India's wheat crop and 40 percent of the rice. However, the Green Revolution is not an uncontested success story. Rather, the introduction of crop rotations, fertilizers, genetically engineered seeds, and especially irrigation have resulted in a high yield, but these methods are exhausting the environment. The water tables have dropped to alarming depths, the nutritional content of the produce has been measurably reduced, and the resulting overproduction leads to biannual procurement crises. Much grain goes bad for lack of markets and adequate storage. Many farmers go broke and in some cases have committed suicide, weighed down by debt incurred to acquire the foreign seeds, fertilizers, and to drill deeper wells for irrigation.

13. In terms of the caste and class makeup of Malerkotla, the Muslims are roughly divided into six large groupings. The elites are the Pathan Afghans linked to the founder Haider Shaykh and his lineage and associates. These include Yusufzais, Lodhis, Kakkars, and Sherwani clans. There are also a few families of Mughal descent. After these are the Rajputs, a class of higher-caste converts from Hinduism. Among these are the Khanzadas, Rangar, Bhatti, Chauhan, and Rathore *gotras* or subgroups. The professional castes include the Khamboj, Gujjar, Marasi, Lohar, Kumhar, Nai, Dhobi, Dhunia, Julaha, Ansari, and Faqiri groups. Among these the Khamboj represent nearly 40 percent of the total Muslim population. As previously mentioned, this caste is the primary cultivating class among the Muslim population and continues to dominate local farming. There are two large groups of Shi'i Muslims: sayyids and shaykhs. The sayyids claim direct descent from the house of the Prophet (Hussaini, Hassani, Bokhari, Zaidi, Jilani, Jafri). The shaykh community represents Hindu converts to Shi'i Islam (Ansari, Faruqi, Qureishi, Siddiqui, Usmani). Many of these family names are shared by Sunni Muslims, and cannot be seen as a clear indicator of Shi'i identity. However, in Malerkotla only Shi'a use "Shaykh" as a surname or second name.

14. Anila Sultana, "Hierarchical Change in the Muslim Society of Malerkotla in the Post-Independence Period," *Punjab History Conference* 27 (1995): 206–7.

15. Ibid, p. 210.

16. D. Ibbetson, Ibbetson, E. D. MacLagan, and H. A. Rose,. *A Glossary of the Tribes and Castes of the Punjab and North-West Frontier Province* (Lahore: Government Printing House, 1919 [1883]), p. 444.

17. Since independence the Punjab state government has managed the office. The government appoints the mufti, pays his salary, and maintains several local Muslim properties and institutions including three local mosques and the 'Id Gah, where the Muslim community gathers for prayers on the two 'Ids.

18. Mufti Fazl-ur-Rehman Hilal Usmani, *Memaar-e-Insaniyat* (Malerkotla: Jamia' Dar-us-Salam, 1991) and *The Islamic Law: Marriage, Divorce, Inheritance* (Malerkotla: Darus Salam Islamic Centre, 2000). Also see Vikrant Jindal, "A Codifier of Islamic Laws," *Tribune*, December 5, 2000.

19. The fatwa was issued at a meeting sponsored by two activist groups based in Mumbai, Citizens for Justice and Peace and Muslims for Secular Democracy. The full statement of it can be found at http://www.cjponline.org/muftifatwa.htm (accessed February 19, 2008).

20. See Mumtaz Ahmad, "Islamic Fundamentalism: The Jama'at-i Islami and Tablighi Jama'at of South Asia," in *Fundamentalisms Observed*, ed. Martin Marty and Scott Appleby (Chicago: University of Chicago Press, 1991); and Barbara Metcalf, "Living Hadith in the Tablighi Jama'at," *Journal of Asian Studies* 52, 3 (1993), and "New Medinas: The Tablighi Jama'at in America and Europe," in *Making Muslim Space*, ed. Barbara Metcalf (Berkeley: University of California Press, 1996).

21. Anila Sultana, "Muslim Institutions and Organisations in Malerkotla and Their Impact on the Muslim Community," *Punjab History Conference* 28 (1996).

22. Ibid., p. 266.

23. It is worth pointing out that the *mirasans* tend to complain about reduced employment and low income, and several Pathan families said they hired them less frequently and would more often use recorded film music for wedding parties.

24. Although the U.S. State Department's "Patterns of Global Terrorism" for 2002 (http://www.state.gov/s/ct/rls/pgtrpt/2002) does not include Jama'at-i Islami among its listed groups, it does identify Hizbul Mujahideen as the "militant wing" of Jama'at-i Islami. Indian politicians have often sought to link Jama'at-i Islami with Hizbul Mujahideen and other Islamic organizations they view as antistate. The Students Islamic Movement in India has been so linked and has been banned by the Indian Government under the Prevention of Terrorism Ordinance (2001). Typically journalists and authors will lump Jama'at-i Islami in with a range of radical Islamic groups. See, for example, B. Raman, "Jama'at-e-Islami, Hizbul Mujahideen, and Al-Qaeda." South Asia Analysis Group (http://www.saag.org/papers7/paper699.html, 2003).

25. Yoginder Sikand, "An Islamist Approach to Inter-Faith Dialogue: The Jama'at-i Islami of India," *Qalandar* (2003). www.islaminterfaith.org

26. There is a small RSS chapter in the Malerkotla area, smaller BJP appeal, and no discernible activity from any other Hindu extremists.

27. The Punjabi translation is of the Yusuf Ali edition, which is probably the most widely disseminated Qur'an in the world as it is subsidized by the Saudi Arabian government. The Qur'an, translated by Yusuf Ali (Elmhurst: New York; Tahrike Tarsile Qur'an).

28. For more on the Shi'a in South Asia, see especially Syed Akbar Hyder, *Reliving Karbala: Martyrdom in South Asian Memory* (New York: Oxford University Press, 2006). See also Juan Cole, *Roots of North Indian Shi'ism in Iran and Iraq* and *Sacred Space and Holy War*. See also the work of David Pinault: *Horse of Karbala*, "Shi'ism in

South Asia," *Muslim World* 87, 3/4 (1997): 235–57, and *The Shiites: Ritual and Popular Piety in a Muslim Community* (New York: St. Martin's Press, 1993).

29. These dirges, called *noha* and *marsiya*, are chanted rhythmically but, like all Muslim recitations, are never referred to as music or singing. For an excellent study of Shi'i women's *majalis* and *marsiya* traditions, see Amy Bard, "Desolate Victory: Shi'i Women and the Mar'siyah Texts of Lucknow" (PhD diss., Columbia University, 2002).

30. For more on the workings of a *majlis* see Bard, "Desolate Victory"; and Hyder, *Reliving Karbala*, 2006.

31. In addition, H. A. Rose notes that Hindu women make vows for children and dedicate their sons to Islam until a certain age as water bearers in the *taziya* procession of Muharram, after which they return to the Hindu fold. See Rose's *Rites and Ceremonies of Hindus and Muslims* (New Delhi: Amar Prakashan, 1983 [1908]), p. 16.

32. The Adi Granth is an earlier compilation of hymns.

33. Diwali, typically the Hindu festival of lights in honor of Lakshmi, goddess of wealth, is observed by the Sikh community for another reason. On this day it is believed that the sixth guru, Hargobind, was released from prison by the Mughal ruler. It is celebrated at Amritsar with great fanfare as the entire Golden Temple is lit with lamps and candles, and an enormous fireworks display is held. The next day is the first of the lunar month, a day upon which it is auspicious to bathe during the earliest part of the day. Thus many thousands of people throng the Golden Temple to see the Diwali spectacle and bathe. Hola Mohalla was instituted by Guru Gobind Singh to be a martial festival beginning the day after Holi, a Hindu spring festival of colors when people douse one another with colored water and powder. Large crowds gather at Anandpur, the scene of the birth of the Khalsa (the pure followers of the guru), and observe martial arts displays and other amazing feats.

34. Satguru can also be a name used for God. Badal also declared Satguru Ram Singh's birthday, January 29, a permanent holiday in Punjab. See the *Tribune*, January 18, 2001. This move was also regarded as deeply troubling by elements of the Sikh orthodoxy.

35. According to the "Punjab Backgrounder," prepared by the South Asia Terrorism Portal, 70 percent of the violence during the terrorism was confined to three districts—Gurdaspur, Amritsar, and Ferozepur—but Sangrur experienced 227 killings in 43 separate incidents. See www.satp.org.

36. Punjab State Archives, Malerkotla File No. 1-C/1948.

37. This is typical of a recent rash of Hanuman temple building described by Philip Lutgendorf in his article "My Hanuman Is Bigger Than Yours," *History of Religions* 33 (Fall 1994).

38. In North and Northwest India Dussehra is associated with Ram, but in eastern India it is a day of the goddess.

39. There are only 50 or so Christian families in Malerkotla itself. It is a small but close-knit group. There is one church associated with the Protestant Church of North India. It does not always have a pastor in residence, but at least once a month a minister comes from Ludhiana to lead services. The local Christians reported excellent relations with the Muslim majority and other religions in Malerkotla. Indeed some Muslims observed the Christmas and Easter celebrations at the church and

participated in the feast and festival atmosphere. In the outlying countryside Christianity has a firmer hold and is increasing in popularity, especially among low caste and outcaste groups.

40. For more on healing traditions in the Muslim context, see Joyce Flueckiger, *In Amma's Healing Room: Gender and Vernacular Islam in South India* (Bloomington: Indiana University Press, 2006).

41. January 22, 2001.

42. January 22, 2001.

43. Ashis Nandy et al., *Creating a Nationality: The Ramjanmabhumi Movement and Fear of the Self.* (New Delhi: Oxford University Press, 1995), pp. 123–55.

44. See Marc Gopin, *Holy War, Holy Peace* (New York: Oxford University Press, 2002), especially chapter 2, "Family Myths and Cultural Conflicts," pp. 7–36.

45. This may be a reference to when Banda Bahadur attacked Malerkotla, ostensibly to recover the body of Anup Kaur, as discussed in chapter 2.

46. Brass, *Theft of an Idol*; Kakar, *Colors of Violence*; Pandey "Fragment"; Tambiah, *Leveling Crowds*; Van der Veer, *Religious Nationalism*; Veena Das *Life and Words: Violence and the Descent into the Ordinary* (Berkeley: University of California Press, 2007).

47. Source is the *Tribune* from articles published from 1998 to 2003.

48. 'Id al- fasting month of Ramadan and 'Id al-Adha, known in India as Baqr 'Id, is the festival of sacrifice, marking Ibrahim's willingness to sacrifice his son Ismail in accordance with God's command. 'Id Milans are a major part of civic life in Malerkotla and are sponsored and attended by multiple religious, social, and political groups.

49. Varshney, *Ethnic Conflict*, p. 52.

50. The institutionalized peace system is something of an homage to Varshney's sometime debating partner Paul Brass, who developed the notion of an institutionalized riot system, undermining the theory that riots were spontaneous eruptions.

51. July 16, 2004.

52. Varshney, *Ethnic Conflict*, p. 52.

53. I did look for media reports of the incident and found none. Other locals remembered the incident vaguely but were not present at the meeting Rauf described.

54. John Nelson, "Social Memory as Ritual Practice." *Journal of Asian Studies* 62, no. 2 (2003), p. 445.

55. Edward S. Casey, *Remembering: A Phenomenological Study* (Bloomington: Indiana University Press, 1987), p. 257.

56. Marc Gopin, *Holy War, Holy Peace*, p. 8.

57. Bachhan was elected to Parliament in 1984 as a Congress representative for the Allahabad District in Uttar Pradesh. He resigned before completing the five-year term.

58. Dipankar Gupta, *Learning to Forget: The Anti-Memoirs of Modernity* (New York: Oxford University Press, 2005), p. 33.

CONCLUSION

1. January 22, 2001.

Bibliography

Afghani, Israr. *Hayat Lodhi*. Saweem, Pakistan: Tarikh Jamiat, *hijri* 1325 (1907).

Ahmad, Imtiaz, ed. *Caste and Social Stratification among Muslims in India*. New Delhi: Manohar, 1973.

———. *Ritual and Religion among Muslims of the Subcontinent*. Lahore: Vanguard, 1985.

Ahmad, Mumtaz. "Islamic Fundamentalism: The Jama'at-i Islami and Tablighi Jama'at of South Asia." In *Fundamentalisms Observed*, edited by Martin Marty and Scott Appleby. Chicago: University of Chicago Press, 1991.

Alam, Muzaffar. *The Crisis of Empire in Mughal North India: Awadh and Punjab, 1707–1748*. New Delhi: Oxford University Press, 1986.

Allami, Abu l-Fazl. *Ain-i Akbari*. Translated by Colonel H. S. Jarrett. New Delhi: Crown Publications, 1988.

Appleby, R. Scott. *The Ambivalence of the Sacred: Religion, Violence, and Reconciliation*. Lanham, MD: Rowman & Littlefield Publishers, 2000.

Arora, A. C. "Malerkotla Succession 1871–72: Its Reflections on the British Policy." *Punjab History Conference* 16 (1982): 252–59.

Asad, Talal. *Formations of the Secular: Christianity, Islam, Modernity*. Stanford, CA: Stanford University Press, 2003.

———. "Religion, Nation-State, Secularism." In *Nation and Religion: Perspectives on Europe and Asia*, edited by Peter van der Veer and Hartmut Lehmann. Princeton, NJ: Princeton University Press, 1999.

Ashk, Gur Kirpal Singh. "Where Brotherhood Is Handed Down as Tradition." *Times of India*, March 2, 2002.

Assayag, Jackie. *At the Confluence of Two Rivers: Muslims and Hindus in South India*. Delhi: Manohar, 2004.

Assmann, Jan. *Religion and Cultural Memory*. Stanford, CA: Stanford University Press, 2006.

Bakshi, S. R. *The Making of India and Pakistan: Select Documents*. Vol. 6. New Delhi: Deep and Deep Publications, 1997.

Baljon, J. M. S. "Shah Waliullah and the Dargah." In *Muslim Shrines in India: Their Character, History, and Significance*, edited by Christian W. Troll. Delhi: Oxford University Press, 1989.

Banga, Indu, ed. *Five Punjabi Centuries: Polity, Economy, Society and Culture C.* 1500–1990. New Delhi: Manohar, 1997.

———. "Formation of the Sikh State: 1765–1845." In *Five Punjabi Centuries*, edited by Indu Banga and J. S. Grewal. New Delhi: Manohar, 1997.

Bard, Amy. " Desolate Victory: Shi'i Women and the Mar'siyah Texts of Lucknow." PhD diss. Columbia University, 2002.

Barrier, N. Gerald. "The Punjab Government and Communal Politics, 1870–1908." *Journal of Asian Studies* 27, no. 3 (1968).

———. "Sikh Politics and Religion: The Bhasaur Singh Sabha." In *Five Punjabi Centuries*, edited by J. S. Grewal and Indu Banga. New Delhi: Manohar, 1997.

Basso, Keith. *Wisdom Sits in Places*. Santa Fe: University of New Mexico Press, 1996.

Basu, Amrita, ed. *Community Conflicts and the State in India*. Delhi: Oxford University Press, 1998.

Bayly, C. A. *Origins of Nationality in South Asia: Patriotism and Ethical Government in the Making of Modern India*. Delhi: Oxford University Press, 1998.

Bell, Catherine. *Ritual Theory, Ritual Practice*. New York: Oxford University Press, 1992.

Bhangu, Ratan Singh. *Panth Prakash*. New Delhi: Bhai Vir Singh Sahit Sadan, 1998 [1841].

Bhasin, Kamla, and Ritu Menon. *Borders and Boundaries: Women in India's Partition*. New Delhi: Kali for Women, 1998.

Bhatia, Varinder Singh. "Banda Singh's Attitude towards the Muslims." *Proceedings of the Punjab History Conference* 28 (1996).

Bhullar, Dalbir Singh Dhillon, and Shangana Singh. *Battles of Guru Gobind Singh*. New Delhi: Deep and Deep Publications, 1990.

Bidwai, Praful, Harbans Mukhia, and Achin Vanaik, eds. *Religion, Religiosity, and Communalism*. Delhi: Manohar, 1996.

Birch, Captain G. *Selections from the Notebooks Kept by Captain G. Birch Assistant to Agent to the Governor General, Karnal Agency,* 1818–1821. Lahore: Government Printing Office, 1921.

Blackburn, Stuart. "Death and Deification: Folk Cults in Hinduism." *History of Religions* 24, no. 3 (1985).

Bowman, Glenn. "Nationalizing the Sacred: Shrines and Shifting Identities in the Israeli-Occupied Territories." *Man*, Volume 28, 1993.

———, ed. *Sharing the Sacra: the Politics and Pragmatics of Inter-communal Relations around Holy Places*. New York: Bergahn Books, forthcoming.

Brara, Rita. "Kinship and the Political Order: The Afghan Sherwani Chiefs of Malerkotla (1454–1947)." *Contributions to Indian Sociology* 28, no. 2 (1994): 203–41.

———. "Marriage and Kinship." PhD diss., Delhi University, 1989.

Brass, Paul. "Elite Groups, Symbol Manipulation and Ethnic Identity among the Muslims of South Asia." In *Nationalism: Critical Concepts in Political Science*, edited by John Hutchison and Anthony D. Smith, 879–911. London: Routledge, 2000.

———. *The Production of Hindu-Muslim Violence in Contemporary India*. Seattle: University of Washington Press, 2003.

———, ed. *Riots and Pogroms*. New York: New York University Press, 1996.

———. "Secularism out of Its Place." In *Tradition, Pluralism, and Identity*, edited by Veena Das, Dipankar Gupta, and Patricia Uberoi. New Delhi: Sage, 1999.

———. *Theft of an Idol: Text and Context in the Representation of Collective Violence*. Princeton, NJ: Princeton University Press, 1997.

———. *Language, Religion and Politics in North India*. New York: Cambridge University Press, 1974.

Briggs, Charles. *Competence in Performance: The Creativity of Tradition in Mexicano Verbal Art*. Philadelphia: University of Pennsylvania Press, 1987.

Brown, Peter. *The Body and Society*. New York: Columbia University Press, 1988.

———. *The Cult of the Saints*. Chicago: University of Chicago Press, 1981.

Buehler, Arthur F. "Currents of Sufism in Nineteenth and Twentieth Century Indo-Pakistan: An Overview." *Muslim World* 87, nos. 3–4 (1997): 299–314.

Burchell, Graham, Colin Gordon, and Peter Miller, eds. *The Foucault Effect: Studies in Governmentality*. Chicago: University of Chicago Press, 1991.

Butalia, Urvashi. *The Other Side of Silence: Voices from the Partition of India*. Durham, NC: Duke University Press, 2000.

Bynum, Caroline Walker. *Metamorphosis and Identity*. New York: Zone Books, 2001.

———. "Shape and Story: Metamorphosis in the Western Tradition." Jefferson Lecture, National Endowment for the Humanities, 1999 http://wwneh.gov/news/archive/19990322b.html [accessed March 22, 1999].

Cameron, Averil. "On Defining the Holy Man." In *The Cult of Saints in Late Antiquity and the Middle Ages: Essays on the Contribution of Peter Brown*, edited by James Howard-Johnston and Paul Antony Hayward. New York: Oxford University Press, 1999.

Casey, Edward S. "How to Get from Space to Place in a Fairly Short Stretch of Time: Phenomenological Prolegomena." In *Senses of Place*, edited by Steven Feld and Keith Basso. Santa Fe, NM: School of American Research Press, 1996.

———. *Remembering: A Phenomenological Study*. Bloomington: Indiana University Press, 1987.

Chanda, S. N. *Saints in Indian Folklore: Tales of Saints Known in Various Parts of India*. Delhi: Konark Publishers, 1998.

Chatterjee, Partha. "Beyond the Nation? Or Within?" *Social Text* 16, no. 3 (1998).

———. "Fasting for Bin Laden: The Politics of Secularization in Contemporary India." In *Powers of the Secular Modern: Talal Asad and His Interlocutors*, edited by David Scott and Charles Hirschkind. Stanford, CA: Stanford University Press, 2006.

———. *The Nation and Its Fragments: Colonial and Postcolonial Histories*. Princeton, NJ: Princeton University Press, 1993.

Chenoy, Dr. Kamal Mitra, S. P. Shukla, K. S. Subramanian, and Achin Vanaik. "Gujarat Carnage 2002." *Outlook*, April 4, 2002.

Churchill, Edward D., Jr. "Muslim Societies of the Punjab, 1860–1890." *The Panjab Past and Present* 8, no. 1 (1974): 69–91.

Cohn, Bernard S. *Colonialism and Its Forms of Knowledge: The British in India*. Princeton, N.J.: Princeton University Press, 1996.

Cole, Juan R. *Roots of North Indian Shi'ism in Iran and Iraq: Religion and State in Awadh, 1722–1859*. Berkeley: University of California Press, 1988.

———. *Sacred Space and Holy War*. New York: Palgrave Macmillan, 2002.

Communalism Combat. *Dateline Gujarat: Inside Hindutva's Laboratory* 2002. Available from http://www.sabrang.com/cc/archive/2002/marapril/dateline.htm.

Concerned Citizens Tribunal (Justice V. R. Krishna Iyer, Justice P. B. Sawant, Justice Hosbet Suresh, K. G. Kannabiran, Aruna Roy, K. S. Subramanian, Ghanshyam Shah,

Tanika Sarkar). "Crime against Humanity: An Inquiry into the Carnage in Gujarat." Mumbai: Citizens for Justice and Peace, 2002.

Copland, Ian. "The Master and the Maharajas: The Sikh Princes and the East Punjab Massacres of 1947." *Modern Asian Studies* 36, no. 3 (2002).

———. "The Political Geography of Religious Conflict: Towards an Explanation of the Relative Infrequency of Communal Riots in the Indian Princely States." *International Journal of Punjab Studies* 7, no. 1 (2000).

———. *The Princes of India in the Endgame of Empire:* 1917–1947. New Delhi: Cambridge University Press, 1999.

Crooke, William. *Religion and Folklore in Northern India*. London: Oxford University Press, 1926.

Cunningham, Alexander. *Archaeological Survey of India: Report of a Tour in the Central Provinces and Lower Gangetic Doab in* 1881–82. Vol. 17. Delhi: Indological Book House, 1969 (1882).

Currie, P. M. *The Shrine and Cult of Mu'in Al-Din Chishti of Ajmer*. Delhi: Oxford University Press, 1989.

Dalmia, Vasudha, Angelika Malinar, Martin Christof, eds. *Charisma and Canon: Essays on the Religious History of the Indian Subcontinent*. New Delhi: Oxford University Press, 2001.

Daniel, E. Valentine. *Charred Lullabies: Chapters in an Anthropology of Violence*. Princeton, NJ: Princeton University Press, 1997.

Das, Veena. *Life and Words: Violence and the Descent into the Ordinary*. Berkeley: University of California Press, 2007.

Davis, Richard H. "The Iconography of Rama's Chariot." In *Contesting the Nation*, edited by David Ludden. Philadelphia: University of Pennsylvania, 1996.

De Certeau, Michel. *The Practice of Everyday Life*. Berkeley: University of California Press, 1984.

De Tassy, Garcin. *Muslim Festivals in India and Other Essays*. Translated by M. Waseem. Delhi: Oxford University Press, 1995 (1831).

Deol, Harnik. *Religion and Nationalism in India: The Case of the Punjab*. London: Routledge, 2000.

Dhavan, Rajeev, and Fali S. Nariman. "The Supreme Court and Group Life: Religious Freedom, Minority Groups, and Disadvantaged Communities." In *Supreme but Not Infallible*, edited by Ashok H. Desai B.N. Kirpal, Gopal Subramanium, Rajeev Dhavan, and Raju Ramachandran. Delhi: Oxford University Press, 2000.

Digby, Simon. "Encounters with Jogis in Indian Sufi Hagiography." Unpublished lecture, School for Oriental and African Studies, London 1970.

———. "Medieval Sufi Tales of Jogis and Tales from the Afghan Sultanates in India." In *Wonder Tales of South Asia*, 221–40. New Delhi: Manohar, 2000.

———. "The Sufi Shaikh as a Source of Authority in Mediaeval India." *Purusartha* 9 (1986).

Dihlavi, Mirza Muhammad Akhtar. "Tazkirahi Auliya Hindo Pakistan." (1972).

Din, Muhammad. *Yadgar-i darbar-i tajposh*. Lahore: Yadgar Press, 1911.

Dirks, Nicholas B. *Castes of Mind: Colonialism and the Making of Modern India*. Princeton, NJ: Princeton University Press, 2001.

———. "Ritual and Resistance: Subversion as a Social Fact." In *Culture/Power/History*, edited by Geoff Eley, Nicholas B. Dirks, and Sherry B. Ortner. Princeton, NJ: Princeton University Press, 1994.

Disturbances in the Punjab, 1947: A Compilation of Official Documents. Islamabad: Government of Pakistan, Cabinet Division, National Documentation Centre, 1995.

Dumont, Louis. *Homo Hierarchicus: The Caste System and Its Implications.* London: Weidenfeld & Nicholson, 1970.

Durkheim, Emile. *The Elementary Forms of Religious Life.* Translated by Karen E. Fields. New York: Free Press, 1995.

Eaton, Richard M. "Approaches to the Study of Conversion to Islam in India." In *Approaches to Islam in Religious Studies,* edited by Richard C. Martin, 106–23. New York: One World Press, 1987.

———. "The Political and Religious Authority of the Shrine of Baba Farid." In *Moral Conduct and Authority: The Place of Adab in South Asian Islam,* edited by Barbara Metcalf. Berkeley: University of California Press, 1984.

———. *The Rise of Islam and the Bengal Frontier: 1204–1760.* Berkeley: University of California Press, 1993.

———. "Sufi Folk Literature and the Expansion of Indian Islam." *History of Religions* 14, no. 2 (1974).

———. *Sufis of Bijapur, 1300–1700: Social Roles of Sufis in Medieval India.* Delhi: Munshiram Manoharlal, 1996 (1978).

———. "Temple Desecration and Indo-Muslim States." In *Essays on Islam and Indian History,* 94–132. New Delhi: Oxford University Press, 2000.

Eck, Diana. "The Challenge of Pluralism." *Nieman Reports* 47, no. 2 (1993).

Eliade, Mircea. *The Sacred and the Profane.* New York: Harper & Row, 1961.

Elias, Jamal. "A Second Ali: The Making of Sayyid Ali Hamadani in Popular Imagination." *Muslim World* 90, nos. 3–4 (2000): 395–419.

Embree, Ainslee. *Utopias in Conflict: Religion and Nationalism in Modern India.* Berkeley: University of California Press, 1990.

Engineer, Asghar Ali. *Lifting the Veil: Communal Violence and Communal Harmony in Contemporary India.* Hyderabad: Sangam Books, 1995.

Ernst, Carl W. *Eternal Garden: Mysticism, History, and Politics at a South Asian Sufi Center.* Albany: State University of New York Press, 1992.

———. "An Indo-Persian Guide to Sufi Shrine Pilgrimage." In *Manifestations of Sainthood in Islam,* edited by Grace Martin Smith and Carl W. Ernst. Istanbul: Isis Press, 1993.

———, and Bruce B. Lawrence. *Sufi Martyrs of Love.* New York: Palgrave Macmillan, 2002.

Ewing, Katherine Pratt. *Arguing Sainthood: Modernity, Psychoanalysis, and Islam.* Durham, NC: Duke University, 1997.

Farooqi, Mian Bashir Ahmed. *British Relations with the Cis-Sutlej States (1809–1823).* Patiala: Languages Department, 1971 [1942].

Faruki, Kemal A. "Pakistan: Islamic Government and Society." In *Islam in Asia: Religion, Politics, and Society,* edited by John L. Esposito. New York: Oxford University Press, 1987.

Faruqi, Nur. "Maler Kotla: Maudi Aur Hal Ki Ekni Hai." *Felicitation Volume,* 2000.

Feld, Steven, and Keith Basso, eds. *Senses of Place.* Santa Fe, NM: School of American Research Press, 1996.

Feldman, Allen. *Formations of Violence: The Narrative of the Body and Political Terror in Northern Ireland.* Chicago: University of Chicago Press, 1991.

Fenech, Louis. *Martyrdom in the Sikh Tradition*. New Delhi: Oxford University Press, 2000.

Firozuddin. *Yadgar-i Darbar*. Lahore: Sada'e Hind Press, 1903.

Fischer-Tine, Harald, and Michael Mann, eds. *Colonialism as Civilizing Mission: Cultural Ideology in British India*. London: Anthem Press, 2004.

Flueckiger, Joyce Burkhalter. *Gender and Genre in the Folklore of Middle India*. Ithaca, NY: Cornell University Press, 1996.

———. *In Amma's Healing Room: Gender and Vernacular Islam in South India*. Bloomington, IN: Indiana University Press, 2006.

Foucault, Michel. *Discipline and Punish*. New York: Vintage, 1977.

———. "The Ethic of Care for the Self as the Practice of Freedom." In *The Final Foucault*, edited by J. Bernauer and D. Rasmussen. Boston, MA: MIT Press, 1988.

———. "Of Other Spaces." *Diacritics* (Spring 1986).

———. *Power/Knowledge*. New York: Pantheon, 1972.

Fowden, Elizabeth Key. "Sharing Holy Places." *Common Knowledge* 8, no. 1 (2002).

Freitag, Sandria. *Collective Action and Community: Public Arenas and the Emergence of Communalism in North India*. Berkeley: University of California Press, 1989.

Friedland, Roger, and Richard Hecht. "The Bodies of Nations: A Comparative Study of Religious Violence in Jerusalem and Ayodhya." *History of Religions* 38, no. 2 (1998).

———. *To Rule Jerusalem*. New York: Cambridge University Press, 1996.

Friedmann, Y. "Medieval Muslim Views of Indian Religions." *Journal of the American Oriental Society* 95, no. 2 (1975).

Friedmann, Yohanan. *Shaykh Ahmad Sirhindi: An Outline of His Thought and a Study of Hs Image in the Eyes of Posterity*. Delhi: Oxford University Press, 2000 [1971].

Frykenberg, Robert, ed. *Land Control and Social Structure in Indian History*. Madison: University of Wisconsin Press, 1969.

Geertz, Clifford. *The Interpretation of Cultures*. New York: Basic Books, 1973.

Giddens, Anthony. *Modernity and Self-Identity: Self and Society in the Late Modern Age*. Cambridge: Polity Press, 1991.

Gill, Sam. "Territory." In *Critical Terms for Religious Studies*, edited by Mark C. Taylor. Chicago: University of Chicago Press, 1998.

Gilmartin, David. "A Magnificent Gift: Muslim Nationalism and the Election Process in Colonial Punjab." *Comparative Studies in Society and History* 40, no. 3 (1998).

———. "Religious Leadership and the Pakistan Movement in the Punjab." *Modern Asian Studies* 13, no. 3 (1979).

———. "Shrines, Succession, and Sources of Moral Authority." In *Moral Conduct and Authority: The Place of Adab in South Asian Islam*, edited by Barbara Metcalf. Berkeley: University of California Press, 1984.

———, and Bruce Lawrence, eds. *Beyond Turk and Hindu: Rethinking Religious Identities in Islamicate South Asia*. Gainesville: University Press of Florida, 2000.

Glassie, Henry. "On Identity." *Journal of American Folklore*, 107, 1994.

———. *Passing the Time in Ballymenone: Culture and History of an Ulster Community*. Philadelphia: University of Pennsylvania Press, 1982.

———. "The Practice and Purpose of History." *Journal of American History* 81, no. 3 (1994).

Goel, Sita Ram. *Hindu Temples: What Happened to Them*. Vols. 1 and 2. New Delhi: Voice of India, 1998.

Goffman, Erving. *The Presentation of Self in Everyday Life*. Garden City, NY: Doubleday, 1959.

———. *Frame Analysis: An Essay on the Organization of Experience*. NY: Harper and Row, 1974.

Gold, Ann Grodzins. *Fruitful Journeys: The Ways of Rajasthani Pilgrims*. Berkeley: University of California Press, 1988.

———. "Grains of Truth." *History of Religions* 38, no. 2, 1998.

Goldziher, Ignaz. "On the Veneration of the Dead in Paganism and Islam." In *Muslim Studies*, edited by S. M Stern. London: George Allen & Unwin, 1967.

Gopin, Marc. *Holy War, Holy Peace: How Religion Can Bring Peace to the Middle East*. New York: Oxford University Press, 2002.

———. "Jewish-Islamic Negotiations in Israel and Palestine: A Participant Observer's Critical Analysis." In *Promise and Peril*, edited by Anna Lannstrom. Notre Dame, IN: University of Notre Dame Press, 2003.

Gottschalk, Peter. *Beyond Hindu and Muslim*. New Delhi: Oxford University Press, 2001.

Grewal, J. S. *Miscellaneous Articles*. Amritsar: Guru Nanak Dev University, 1971.

———. *The Sikhs of the Punjab*. Cambridge: Cambridge University Press, 1994.

———, and Indu Banga, eds. *Punjab in Prosperity and Violence: Administration, Politics and Social Change, 1947–1997*. Chandigarh: Institute of Punjab Studies, 1998.

———, and S. S. Bal. *Guru Gobind Singh: A Biographical Study*. Chandigarh: Panjab University Publication Bureau, 1967.

———, and Irfan Habib, ed. *Sikh History from Persian Sources*. New Delhi: Tulika, 2001.

Grey, C. L. J. H. "Orders Passed on the Assessment Report of the Maler Kotla State." 1891.

Griffin, Lepel. *The History of the Principles State of the Punjab and Their Political Relations with the British Government (the Rajas of the Punjab)*. Lahore: Panco Press, 1976 [1870].

———. *Rajas of the Punjab*. Delhi: Low Price Publications, 2000 [1870].

Gupta, Dipankar. "Civil Society in the Indian Context: Letting the State Off the Hook." *Contemporary Sociology*, 26, no. 3, 1997.

———. *Learning to Forget: The Anti-Memoirs of Modernity*. New York: Oxford University Press, 2005.

Habermas, Jürgen. *The Structural Transformation of the Public Sphere: An Inquiry into a Category of Bourgeois Society*. Cambridge, MA: MIT Press, 1989.

Habib, Irfan. *An Atlas of the Mughal Empire*. Aligarh: Centre of Advanced Studies, 1982.

Hall, John R. "Religion and Violence: Social Processes in Comparative Perspective." In *Handbook for the Sociology of Religion*, edited by Michele Dillon. New York: Cambridge University Press, 2002.

Hamid, Farooq. "The Hagiographic Process: The Case of Medieval Chishti Sufi Farid Al-Din Mas'ud Ganj-i Shakar (D. 664/1265)." *Muslim World* 90, nos. 3–4 (2000): 421–37.

Hansen, Anders Bjorn. *Partition and Genocide: Manifestation of Violence in Punjab, 1937–1947*. New Delhi: India Research Press, 2002.

Hansen, Thomas Blom. *Wages of Violence: Naming and Identity in Postcolonial Bombay*. Princeton, NJ: Princeton University Press, 2001.

Hardy, Peter. "The Foundations of Islam in India." In *Sources of Indian Tradition*, edited by Ainslie Embree, 383–407. New York: Columbia University Press, 1988 (1958).

———. *The Muslims of British India*. Cambridge: Cambridge University Press, 1972.

Hasan, Mushirul. *India Partitioned: The Other Face of Freedom*. New Delhi: Roli Books, 1997.

———, ed. *Inventing Boundaries: Gender, Politics and the Partition of India*. New Delhi: Oxford University Press, 2000.

———, ed. *Islam, Communities and the Nation: Muslim Identities in South Asia and Beyond*. Delhi: Manohar, 1998.

———. "Minority Identity and Its Discontents: Ayodhya and Its Aftermath." In *Religion, Religiosity and Communalism*, edited by Harbans Mukhia Praful Bidwai, and Achin Vanaik, 167–204. Delhi: Manohar, 1996.

Hassner, Ron E. "Understanding and Resolving Disputes over Sacred Space." *Stanford Center on Conflict and Negotiation Working Paper* 62 (2002).

Hayden, Robert. "Antagonistic Tolerance: Competitive Sharing of Religious Sites in South Asia and the Balkans." *Current Anthropology* 43, no. 2 (2002): 205–31.

Hecht, Richard. "The Construction and Management of Sacred Time and Space: The *Sabta Nur* at the Church of the Holy Sepulchre." In *Nowhere: Space, Time and Modernity*, edited by Roger Friedland and D. Bowen. Berkeley: University of California Press, 1994.

Hecht, Richard, and Roger Friedland. "The Bodies of Nations: A Comparative Study of Religious Violence in Jerusalem and Ayodhya." *History of Religions* 38, no. 2 (1998).

Heidegger, Martin. "Building, Dwelling, Thinking." In *Rethinking Architecture: A Reader in Cultural Theory*, edited by Neil Leach. London: Routledge, 1997 (1971).

Hermanson, Marcia. "Religious Literature and the Inscription of Identity: The Sufi Tazkira Tradition in Muslim South Asia." *Muslim World* 87, nos. 3–4 (1997).

Howard-Johnston, James, and Paul Antony Hayward, eds. *The Cult of Saints in Late Antiquity and the Middle Ages: Essays on the Contribution of Peter Brown*. New York: Oxford University Press, 1999.

Human, Rights Watch. "'We Have No Orders to Save You': State Participation and Complicity in Communal Violence in Gujarat." *Human Rights Watch* 14, no. 3(C) (2002).

Hussain, M. I. *A Brief War History of the Maler Kotla State (1914–1919)*. Lahore: Civil and Military Gazette Press, 1920.

Hymes, Dell. "Breakthrough into Performance." In *"In Vain I Tried to Tell You": Essays in Native American Ethnopoetics*, edited by Dell Hymes. Philadelphia: University of Pennsylvania Press, 1981.

Ibbetson, D. *Panjab Castes*. Reprint of *The Races, Castes, and Tribes of the People*. Lahore: Superintendent, Government Printing, Punjab, 1916 (1883).

Ibbetson, D., E. D. MacLagan, and H. A. Rose,. *A Glossary of the Tribes and Castes of the Punjab and North-West Frontier Province,*. Lahore: Government Printing House, 1919 (1883).

Imperial Gazetteer of India. London: Trübner & Co, 1881, 1886, 1908.

India, Census of. *Census of India* [WWW]. Census of India, 1999 1999 [cited May 8, 2000].

India Office Collection L/P&J/7. *Communal Riots*. London: OIOC.

———. L/P&J/7/132. *Commissioned Report on Communal Disturbances:* OIOC, no date.

———. L/P&J/65. *Hindu Muslim Riot—Halol*. London: OIOC.

———. L/P&J/132. *Report*. London: OIOC.

———. L/P&J/170. *Puran Mal Murder.* London: OIOC.

———. L/P&J/171. *Communal Riot Sikander.* London: OIOC.

———. L/P&J/751. *Ahmadiyya.* London: OIOC.

———. L/P&J/931. *Shahidganj.* London: OIOC.

———. L/P&S/13/837. *Internal Collection 13: Fortnightly Resumes of Events in Indian States Jan 1933–April 1935:* IOR.

———. L/P&S/13/877. *Indian States, Gen'l Questions. Debts: Maler Kotla:* IOR.

———. L/P&S/13/1345. *Malerkotla.* London: OIOC.

———. L/P&S/13/1345. *Punjab States: Maler Kotla Affairs:* IOR.

———. L/R/5. *Vernacular Press Reports—Disturbance.* London: OIOC, 1943.

———. L/R/5. "Vernacular Press Reports—H/M Dispute." 1936.

———. L/R/5. *Vernacular Press Reports—Hijra.* London: OIOC, 1939.

———. L/R/5. *Vernacular Press Reports—Kothala.* London: OIOC, 1927.

———. P/Y/2731/1939. London: OIOC, 1939.

———. R/1/1/220. *Marriage of Ahmad Ali Khan to Cousin Disapproved.* London: OIOC.

———. R/1/1/696. *Mental Incapacity of Nawab.*

———. R/1/1/707. *Arrangements for Administration of Malerkotla.* London: OIOC, 1885 (August).

———. R/1/1/934. *Question of Making Permanent Return Visit of Nawab of Malerkotla.* London: OIOC, 1919.

———. R/1/1/1418. *Debt of Malerkotla to Calcutta Firms.* London: OIOC.

———. R/1/1/1685. *Malerkotla Affairs: Zamindari Association.* London: OIOC, 1927.

———. R/1/1/2023. *Irregularities of Nawab Re: Payment of Debt.* London: OIOC, 1930.

———. R/1/1/2150. *Confirm Finance Minister: Jamil Ahmad.* London: OIOC, 1931.

———. R/1/1/2687. *Hindu Muslim, Arti-Namaz.* London: OIOC, 1935.

———. R/1/1/2860. *Muslim Agitation in Malerkotla.* London: OIOC.

———. R/1/1/2936. *Muslim Agitation at Malerkotla.* London: OIOC.

———. R/1/1/3006. *Congress Activities in Malerkotla.* London: OIOC.

———. R/1/1/3758. *Petition from Sikh States Association, Malerkotla Re: Land and Tenant Rights.* London: OIOC, 1941.

———. R/1/1/3832. *Malerkotla Affairs: Appointment of Successor, Administrative Scheme.* London: OIOC, 1942.

———. R/1/1/3946. *Malerkotla: Restrictions on Nawab's Powers.* London: OIOC, 1943.

———. R/1/1/4156. *Malerkotla Finance.* London: OIOC, 1944.

———. R/1/1/4440. *Abrogation of Phulkian Pat by Patiala, Nabha, Jind and Malerkotla.* London: OIOC, 1946.

———. R/1/2860. *Report on Muslim Agitation in Malerkotla State and Proposals for Future Administration of the State.* London: OIOC.

"International Religious Freedom Report." Washington, DC: United States Commission on International Religious Freedom, 2002.

Irving, Miles. *"The Shrine of Baba Farid Shakarganj at Pakpattan."* In *Notes on Punjab and Mughal India: Selections from Journal of the Punjab Historical Society*, edited by Zulfiqar Ahmed. Lahore: Sang-e-Meel Publications, 1988.

Ismail, Sufi Muhammad. *Bagh anbiya' punjab.* Malerkotla: Janab Doctor Muhammad Nizamuddin Sahib, 1995.

———. *Kabr ki pahali rat.* Malerkotla: Kutub Khana Ibrahimiya, 1996.

————. *Kabr kya kahti hai.* Malerkotla: Maktaba Rahimiyan, 1971.

————. *Na'atun ka bagh.* Malerkotla: Kutub Khana Ibrahimiya, 1965.

Jackson, Paul. *Sharafuddin Maneri: The Hundred Letters.* New York: Paulist Press, 1980.

Jaffrelot, Christophe. *The Hindu Nationalist Movement in India.* New York: Columbia University Press, 1996.

————, ed. *The Sangh Parivar: A Reader.* New York: Oxford University Press, 2005.

Jain, Parsuram. "Haqiqat." 34. Malerkotla, 1940.

Jain, S. P. *The Social Structure of Hindu-Muslim Community.* Delhi: National Publishing House, 1975.

Jamali, Hamid ibn Fazl Allah. *Siyar Al-Arifin.* Lahore: Markazi Urdu Board, 1976.

Jindal, Vikrant. "A Codifier of Islamic Laws." *Tribune,* December 5, 2000.

————. "This Town Makes Badges Too." *Tribune,* April 5, 2001.

Jolly, Asit. "Myth of Maler Kotla." *Asian Age,* May 11, 1997.

Jones, Kenneth W. "Ham Hindu Nahin: Arya-Sikh Relations, 1877–1905." *Journal of Asian Studies,* 32, no. 3, 1973.

Juergensmeyer, Mark. *The New Cold War?: Religious Nationalism Confronts the Secular State.* Berkeley: University of California Press, 1993.

————. *Terror in the Mind of God: The Global Rise of Religious Violence.* Berkeley: University of California Press, 2000.

Kakar, Sudhir. *The Colors of Violence: Cultural Identities, Religion, and Conflict.* Chicago: University of Chicago Press, 1996.

————. *Shamans, Mystics, and Doctors: A Psychological Inquiry into India and Its Healing Traditions.* Chicago: University of Chicago Press, 1991.

Kansteiner, Wulf. "Finding Meaning in Memory: A Methodological Critique of Collective Memory Studies," *History and Theory* 41, 2 (2002).

Kaul, Suvir, ed. *The Partitions of Memory: The Afterlife of the Division of India.* Bloomington: Indiana University Press, 2002.

Kaur, Satinder. "History of Malerkotla State." Master's thesis, Punjabi University, 1977.

Kaviraj, Sudipta. "Modernity and Politics in India." *Daedalus* 128, no. 1 (2000).

Kenny, Michael G. "A Place for Memory: The Interface between Individual and Collective History." *Comparative Studies in Society and History* 41, no. 3 (1999).

Khan, Dominique-Sila. *Conversions and Shifting Identities: Ramdev Pir and the Ismailis in Rajasthan.* New Delhi: Manohar, 1997.

Khan, Iftikhar Ali. *History of the Ruling Family of Sheikh Sadruddin Sadar-i-Jahan of Malerkotla (1449 A.D. to 1948 A.D.).* Edited by R. K. Ghai. Patiala: Punjabi University Press, 2000 [1948].

————. "Letter Re: Management of Hazrat Shaikh Sadrud Din Sadar-i-Jahan." In *Home Department: Ecclesiastical.* Malerkotla, 1950.

Khan, Inayat Ali. *A Description of the Principal Kotla Afghans.* Lahore: Civil And Military Gazette Press, 1882.

Khan, Khalifah Anwar Ahmad. *Hazrat Sadr Udin Sadare Jahan (Rehmat) Urf Baba Hazrat Shekh Ji Malerkotla Di Puri Jivani.* Malerkotla: Jivan Glass House, n.d.

Khan, Yasmin. *The Great Partition: the Making of India and Pakistan.* New Haven, Conn: Yale University Press, 2007.

Khan, Zia ur-Rehman. "Municipal Politics in Punjab: A Case Study of Malerkotla Municipal Committee (1972–1982)." Master's thesis. Guru Nanak Dev University, 1988.

Khan, Zulfikar Ali. *A Voice from the East*. Lahore: Iqbal Academy Pakistan, 1982 [1922].

Khurd, Muhammad ibn Mubarak Kirmani Amir. *Siyar Al-Auliya Fi Muhabbat Al Haq*. Lahore: Markazi Urdu Board, 1980.

Kitabul Jana-iz: Death and Burial. New Delhi: Idara Isha'at-e-Diniyat, 2000.

Kozlowski, Gregory. "Islamic Law in Contemporary South Asia." *Muslim World* 87, nos. 3–4 (1997): 221–34.

———. *Muslim Endowments and Society in British India*. Cambridge: Cambridge University Press, 1985.

Krishan, Gopal. "Demographic Change." In *Punjab in Prosperity and Violence: Administration, Politics and Social Change, 1947–1997*, edited by J. S. Grewal and Indu Banga. Chandigarh: Institute of Punjab Studies, 1998.

Krishen, Indra. "An Historical Interpretation of the Correspondence (1831–1843) of Sir George Russell Clerk, Political Agent Ambala and Ludhiana." PhD diss., Panjab University, 1952.

Kular, Kulvinder. "Malerkotla Muslims Feel Safer in India." *Indian Express*, August 14, 1997.

Kumar, Krishan. "Civil Society: An Inquiry into the Usefulness of an Historical Term." *British Journal of Sociology* 44, no. 3 (1993).

Laine, James. *Shivaji: Hindu King in Islamic India*. New York: Oxford University Press, 2003.

Lakoff, George. *Don't Think of an Elephant: Know Your Values and Frame the Debate*. White River Junction, VT: Chelsea Green Publishing, 2004.

———. "Framing the Dems: How Conservatives Control Political Debate and How Progressives Can Take It Back." *American Prospect*, September 2003, pp. 32–35.

Lapidus, Ira. "The Indian Subcontinent: The Delhi Sultanates and the Mughal Empire." In *A History of Islamic Societies*. Cambridge: Cambridge University Press.

Lederach, John Paul. *The Moral Imagination: The Art and Soul of Building Peace*. New York: Oxford University Press, 2005.

Lefebvre, Henri. "The Production of Space." In *Rethinking Architecture: A Reader in Cultural Theory*, edited by Neil Leach. London: Routledge, 1997 (1971).

Lemke, Thomas. "Foucault, Governmentality, and Critique." Paper presented at the Rethinking Marxism conference, University of Massachusetts, Amherst 2000.

Liebskind, Claudia. *Piety on Its Knees: Three Sufi Traditions in South Asia in Modern Times*. Delhi: Oxford University Press, 1998.

Lindholm, Charles. "Caste in Islam and the Problem of Deviant Systems: A Critique of Recent Theory." In *Muslim Communities of South Asia: Culture, Society and Power*, edited by T. N. Madan. New Delhi: Manohar, 1995.

———. "Prophets and Pirs: Charismatic Islam in the Middle East and South Asia." In *Embodying Charisma: Modernity, Locality and the Performance of Emotion in Sufi*, edited by Pnina and Helene Basu Werbner. London: Routledge, 1998.

Loehlin, C. H. "Guru Gobind Singh and Islam." *Proceedings of the Punjab History Conference* 2 (1966).

Lutgendorf, Philip. "My Hanuman Is Bigger Than Yours." *History of Religions* 33 (Fall 1994).

Mahmood, Cynthia Keppley. "Sikh Rebellion and the Hindu Concept of Order." *Asian Survey* 29, no. 3 (1989).

Mahmood, Tahir. "The Dargah of Sayyid Salar Mas'Ud Ghazi in Bahraich: Legend, Tradition and Reality." In *Muslim Shrines in India: Their Character, History and Significance*, edited by Christian W. Troll. Delhi: Oxford University Press, 1989.

Major, Andrew. "From Moderates to Secessionists: A Who's Who of the Punjab Crisis." *Pacific Affairs*, 60, no. 1 (1987).

Malamud, Margaret. "Sufi Organizations and Structures of Authority in Medieval Nishapur." *Journal of Middle East Studies* 26 (1994).

Maler Kotla State Gazetteer. Lahore: Civil and Military Gazette Press, 1904.

Maleri, Abdullah. *Safinat Abdullah Maleri*. Lahore: Dar Matba' Siddiqi, 1992.

"Malerkotla." In *Imperial Gazetteer of India*, edited by W.W. Hunter. London: Trübner & Co, 1881.

"Malerkotla." In *Imperial Gazetteer of India*. London: Trübner & Co, 1886.

"Malerkotla." In *Imperial Gazetteer of India*. London: Trübner & Co, 1908.

"Malerkotla Bandh Today." *Tribune*, March 23, 2001.

Malerkotla Only Muslim Dominated Constituency in Punjab. February 2, 2002. Available from http://in.news.yahoo.com/020202/42/1fcyo.html. [accessed May 15, 2002]

Malerkotla State Archives. "1/1-C/47-a/1947—Disturbances and Refugees." 1947.

———. "3/9/1939—Kothala Demonstration." 1939.

———. "6/Anjuman-I-Hidayat Agitation" [82/6/1/1937—100/6/124/1939].

———. "16/Panjab Riasti Praja Mandal Conference."

———. "71/Z(B)/10/1938—Anjuman-I-Muhajirin." 1938.

———. "75/Z(B)/17/1938—Trouble at Chhapar Fair." 1938.

———. "B3/F4/1937—Inquiries into Characters." 1937.

———. "B3/F5/1937—Letters from Various Petitioners for Jobs Professing Loyalty to Nawab." 1937.

———. "B3/F8/1937—Hindu Mahasabha." 1937.

———. "B3/F8/1938—Arrests of Demonstrators at Chhapar Fair." 1938.

———. "B3/F9/1938—Copy Resignation of State Superintendent of Police." 1938.

———. "B3/F9/1938—Punjab Riasti Praja Mandal Conference, Mahmadpur, Mk." 1937.

———. "B3/F16/1939—Refusal to Allow Visitation of Prisoners, Hijra." 1939.

———. "File #1-C/47-A." 1947.

———. "Miscellaneous Papers Relating to Communal Problems in Malerkotla." 206. Maler Kotla: Office of the Revenue and Finance Minister, 1935–1946.

———. PSA, B2(a)/F10/1936. "Arti-Namaz Issue."

———. "X/Confidential Reports on Congress Movement." In *Punjab State Archives*. Patiala, 1942 (August).

———. "Y/50/Y/14/1945—Shia Affairs." 1945.

———. "Y/Reports of the Activities of Congress." 1945.

———. "Z/Shahidi Conference at Village Kothala." 1939.

Malik, Iftikhar H. "Identity Formation and Muslim Party Politics in Punjab, 1897–1936: A Retrospective Analysis." *Modern Asian Studies* 29, no. 2 (1995).

———. "Muslim Nationalism and Ethno-Regional Postulations: Sir Fazl-I-Husain and Party Politics in the Punjab." In *Punjabi Identity in a Global Context*, edited by Pritam Singh and Shinder Singh Thandi. New Delhi: Oxford University Press, 1999.

Malik, Ikram Ali. "Muslim Anjumans and Communitarian Consciousness." In *Five Punjabi Centuries*, edited by J. S. and Indu Banga Grewal. New Delhi: Manohar, 1999.

———. *Hindu-Muslim Riots in the British Punjab (1849–1900)*. Lahore: Gosha-i-Adab, 1984.

Malik, Jamal. "Dynamics among Traditional Religious Scholars and Their Institutions in Contemporary South Asia." *Muslim World* 87, nos. 3–4 (1997): 199–219.

Mandal, D. *Ayodhya: Archaeology after Demolition, Tracts for the Times*. Delhi: Orient Longman, 1993.

Mann, Gurinder Singh. *The Making of Sikh Scripture*. New Delhi: Oxford University Press, 2001.

Manshardt, Clifford. *The Hindu-Muslim Problem in India*. London: G. Allen & Unwin, 1936.

Massey, C. F., and Sir Lepel H. Griffin. *Chiefs and Families of Note in the Punjab*. Lahore: Civil and Military Press, 1940.

Mcleod, W. H. *The Chaupa Singh Rahit-Nama*. Dunedin, New Zealand: University of Otago Press, 1987.

———. *Exploring Sikhism: Aspects of Sikh Identity, Culture and Thought*. New Delhi: Oxford University Press, 2000.

———. *Who Is a Sikh?* New York: Oxford University Press, 1989.

Mehboob, M. A. "Maler Kotla Shehr Mein Talim Ki Tarqi." *Hind Samachar* 2000, 7.

———. "Muhabbat Aur Aman Ka Ghavarah Maler Kotla." *Hind Samachar* 2000, 6.

Meri, Josef W. "The Etiquette of Devotion in the Islamic Cult of Saints." In *The Cult of Saints in Late Antiquity and the Middle Ages: Essays on the Contribution of Peter Brown*, edited by James Howard-Johnston and Paul Antony Hayward. New York: Oxford University Press, 1999.

Metcalf, Barbara. *Islamic Revival in British India: Deoband 1860–1900*. Princeton, NJ: Princeton University Press, 1982.

———. "Living Hadith in the Tablighi Jama'at." *Journal of Asian Studies* 52, no. 3 (1993).

———. "The Madrasa at Deoband: A Model for Religious Education in Modern India." *Modern Asian Studies* 12, no. 1 (1978).

———. *Moral Conduct and Authority: The Place of Adab in South Asian Islam*. Berkeley: University of California Press, 1984.

———. "New Medinas: The Tablighi Jama'at in America and Europe." In *Making Muslim Space*, edited by Barbara Metcalf. Berkeley: University of California Press, 1996.

———. "Too Little and Too Much: Reflections on Muslims in the History of India." *Journal of Asian Studies* 54, no. 4 (1995): 951–67.

Metcalf, Barbara D., and Thomas R. *A Concise History of India*. Cambridge: Cambridge University Press, 2002.

Mills, Margaret. "Critical Theory and the Folklorists: Performance, Interpretive Authority, and Gender." *Southern Folklore* 47, no. 1 (1990): 5–15.

———. *Rhetoric and Politics in Afghan Traditional Storytelling*. Philadelphia: University of Pennsylvania Press, 1991.

Mir, Farina. "Genre and Devotion in Punjab's Popular Narratives: Rethinking Cultural and Religious Syncretism." *Comparative Studies in Society and History* 48, 3 (July 2006): 727–758.

Mitscherlich, Alexander, and Margarete Mitscherlich. *The Inability to Mourn: Principles of Collective Behavior*. New York: Grove Press, 1975.

Mohammad, Salim. "Role of Malerkotla State During the First World War (1914–1919)." *Punjab History Conference* 25 (1992): 172–76.

Nabha, Bhai Kahan Singh. *Gurushabad Ratnakara Mahan Kosh.* Chandigarh: Bhasha Vibhag Punjab, 1999 (1926).

Nandy, Ashis. "The Twilight of Certitudes: Secularism, Hindu Nationalism, and Other Masks of Deculturation." *Postcolonial Studies* 1, no. 3 (1998).

Nandy, Ashis, Shikha Trivedy, Shail Mayaram, and Achyut Yagnik. *Creating a Nationality: The Ramjanmabhumi Movement and Fear of the Self.* New Delhi: Oxford University Press, 1995.

Narang, A. S. "Movement for the Punjabi-Speaking State." In *Five Punjabi Centuries,* edited by Indu Banga. Delhi: Manohar, 1997.

Narang, Dr. Sir Gokul Chand. *The Plight of Punjab Minorities under the So-Called Unionist Govt.* Edited by Ram lal Tara. Lahore: Sunday Times Press, 1941.

Narayan, Kirin. "Banana Republics and V.I. Degrees: Rethinking Indian Folklore in a Postcolonial World." *Asian Folklore Studies* 52 (1993): 177–204.

Nelson, John. "Social Memory as Ritual Practice." *Journal of Asian Studies* 62, no. 2 (2003).

Neocleous, Mark. "From Civil Society to the Social." *British Journal of Sociology* 46, no. 3 (1995).

Nijjar, B. S. *Punjab under the British Rule (1849–1947).* New Delhi: K B Publications, 1974.

Nizami, Khaliq Ahmad. "The Suhrawardi Silsilah and Its Influence on Medieval Indian Politics." *Medieval Indian Quarterly* 2 (October 1950).

Oberoi, Harjot. "Brotherhood of the Pure: The Poetics and Politics of Cultural Transgression." *Modern Asian Studies* 26, no. 1 (1992).

———. *The Construction of Religious Boundaries: Culture, Identity, and Diversity in the Sikh Tradition.* Chicago: University of Chicago Press, 1994.

———. " 'From Punjab to 'Khalistan': Territoriality and Metacommentary." *Pacific Affairs* 60, no. 1 (1987).

O'Brien, Major Aubrey. "The Mohammedan Saints of the Western Punjab." *Journal of the Royal Anthropological Institute of Great Britain and Ireland* 41 (1911).

O'Connell, Joseph T., Milton Israel, and Willard Oxtoby, eds. *Sikh History and Religion in the Twentieth Century.* Toronto: University of Toronto Press, 1988.

Oring, Elliott. "The Arts, Artifacts, and Artifices of Identity." *Journal of American Folklore* 107 (1994).

———. "The Interests of Identity." *Journal of American Folklore* 107 (1994).

Pandey, Gyanendra. "Can a Muslim Be an Indian?" *Comparative Studies in Society and History* 41, no. 4 (1999): 608–29.

———. *The Construction of Communalism in Colonial North India.* New Delhi: Oxford University Press, 1990.

———. "In Defense of the Fragment: Writing About Hindu-Muslim Riots in India Today." *Representations* 37 (Winter 1992).

———. "The Long Life of Rumor." *Alternatives* 27, no. 2 (2002).

———. *Remembering Partition.* New York: Cambridge University Press, 2001.

Parry, Jonathan. "Death and Digestion: The Symbolism of Food and Eating in North Indian Mortuary Rites." *Man* 20 (1985).

———. *Death in Banaras.* Cambridge: Cambridge University Press, 1994.

———. "The End of the Body." In *Fragments for a History of the Human Body,* edited by Michel Feher. New York: UrZone, 1989.

————. "Ghost, Greed, and Sin: The Occupational Identity of Benares Funeral Priests." *Man* 15 (1980).

————. "Sacrificial Death and the Necrophagous Ascetic." In *Death and the Regeneration of Life*, edited by Maurice Bloch and Jonathan Parry. Cambridge: Cambridge University Press, 1982.

Passy, Kirin. "Malerkotla State and the First World War." *Punjab History Conference* 19 (1985): 377–81.

Pinault, David. *Horse of Karbala: Muslim Devotional Life in India*. Basingstoke: Palgrave, 2001.

————. "Shi'ism in South Asia." *Muslim World* 87, nos. 3–4 (1997): 235–57.

————. *The Shiites: Ritual and Popular Piety in a Muslim Community*. New York: St. Martin's Press, 1993.

Pinto, Desiderio. *Piri-Muridi Relationship: A Study of the Nizamuddin Dargah*. Delhi: Manohar, 1995.

Portelli, Alessandro. *The Death of Luigi Trastulli and Other Stories*. Albany: State University of New York, 2001.

Primiano, Leonard Norman. "Vernacular Religion and the Search for Method in Religious Folklife." *Western Folklore* 54, no. 1 (1995).

Qalb-i-Abid, S. *Muslim Politics in the Punjab, 1921–1947*. Lahore: Vanguard, 1992.

Quddus, Syed Abdul. *Punjab: The Land of Beauty, Love, and Mysticism*. Karachi: Royal Book Company, 1992.

Rai, Baljit. *Explosion of Muslim Population in India, Stop Islamisation of India*. Chandigarh: B.S. Publisher, 2001.

Ram, Bhai Sobha. *Gur Bilas Baba Sahib Singh Bedi*. Edited by Gurmukh Singh. Patiala: Punjabi University Press, 1988 [1810].

Ram, Jaishi. *The Punjab Civil Law Manual: Notes on the Punjab Laws' Act and Enactments Extended to the Punjab by That Act, and Also on the Customary Hindu and Muhammedan Law as Applicable to the Punjab*. Lahore: Tribune & Victoria Press, 1892.

Rau, Suraj Narain. "Cis-Sutluj Sikh States, 1800–1849." PhD diss., Panjab University, no date.

Reetz, Dietrich. "In Search of the Collective Self: How Ethnic Group Concepts Were Cast through Conflict in Colonial India." *Modern Asian Studies* 31, no. 2 (1997).

Reynolds, Dwight Fletcher. *Heroic Poets, Poetic Heroes: The Ethnography of Performance in an Arabic Oral Epic Tradition*. Ithaca, NY: Cornell University Press, 1995.

Reynolds, Frank, ed. *Religious Encounters with Death: Insights from the History and Anthropology of Religions*. University Park: Pennsylvania State University Press, 1977.

Richards, John F. *The Mughal Empire*. New York: Cambridge University Press, 1993.

Ring, Laura A. *Zenana: Everyday Peace in a Karachi Apartment Building*. Bloomington: Indiana University Press, 2006.

Robinson, Chase. "Prophecy and Holy Men in Early Islam." In *The Cult of Saints in Late Antiquity and the Middle Ages: Essays on the Contribution of Peter Brown*, edited by James Howard-Johnston and Paul Antony Hayward. New York: Oxford University Press, 1999.

Robinson, Francis. "Islam and Muslim Separatism." In *Nationalism: Critical Concepts in Political Science*, edited by John Hutchison and Anthony D. Smith, 912–37. London: Routledge, 2000.

————. "Islam and Muslim Society in South Asia." In *Islam and Muslim History in South Asia*, 44–65. New Delhi: Oxford University Press, 2000.

Rose, H. A. *Rites and Ceremonies of Hindus and Muslims*. New Delhi: Amar Prakashan, 1983 (1908).

Roy, Beth. *Some Trouble with Cows: Making Sense of Social Conflict*. Berkeley: University of California Press, 1994.

Rozehnal, Robert. *Islamic Sufism Unbound: Politics and Piety in Twenty-First Century Pakistan*. New York: Palgrave Macmillan, 2007.

Sachdeva, Veena. "The Non-Sikh Chiefs of the Punjab Plains and Maharaja Ranjit Singh." *Journal of Regional History* 2, no. 1 (1981): 1–11.

Sadullah, Mian Muhammad, ed. *The Partition of the Punjab, 1947: A Compilation of Official Documents*. Vols. 1–4. Lahore: National Documentation Centre, 1983.

Saheb, S. A. A. "A 'Festival of Flags': Hindu-Muslim Devotionalism and the Sacralising of Localism at the Shrine of Nagore-e-Sharif in Tamil Nadu." In *Embodying Charisma: Modernity, Locality, and the Performance of Emotion in Sufi Cults*, edited by Pnina Werbner and Helene Basu. London: Routledge, 1998.

Said Abdul Aziz, Nathan C. Funk, and Ayse S. Kadayifci, eds. *Peace and Conflict Resolution in Islam: Precept and Practice*. Lanham, MD: University Press of America, 2001.

Sainapat. *Sri Gur Sobha*. Edited by Ganda Singh. Patiala: Punjabi University Press, 1967.

Saini, Pritam. "Malerkotla: Past and Present." *Tribune*, 1976.

Sanyal, Usha. *Devotional Islam and Politics in British India: Ahmad Riza Khan Barelwi and His Movement, 1870–1920*. Delhi: Oxford University Press, 1996.

Sarkar, Tanika. "The Woman as Communal Subject: Rashtrasevika Samiti and Ram Janmabhoomi Movement." *Economic and Political Weekly*, August 31, 1991.

Schimmel, Annemarie. *And Muhammad Is His Messenger: The Veneration of the Prophet in Islamic Piety*. Chapel Hill: University of North Carolina Press, 1985.

———. *Islam in the Indian Subcontinent*. Leiden: E. J. Brill, 1980.

———. *Mystical Dimensions of Islam*. Chapel Hill: University of North Carolina Press, 1985.

———. "Sufism." In *Encyclopaedia Britannica*.

Scott, James C. *Domination and the Arts of Resistance: Hidden Transcripts*. New Haven, CT: Yale University Press, 1990.

———. *Weapons of the Weak: Everyday Forms of Peasant Resistance*. New Haven, CT: Yale University Press, 1985.

Sharma, S. K. "Political Beliefs and Attitudes of a Religious Minority: An Exploratory Study of the Muslim Elite in Malerkotla." In *Political Dynamics of Punjab*, edited by S. C. Wallace. Amritsar: Guru Nanak Dev University, 1981.

Sharp, Gene. *The Politics of Nonviolent Action*. Boston: P. Sargent, 1973.

Siddiqi, Iqtidar Husain. "Rise of the Afghan Nobility under the Lodi Sultans (1451–1526)." *Medieval Indian Quarterly* 4 (1961): 114–36.

———. "Wajh-i-Ma'ash Grants under the Afghan Kings (1451–1555)." In *Medieval India: A Miscellany*. London: Asia Publishing House, 1972.

Sikand, Yoginder. *Bastions of the Believers: Madrasas and Islamic Education in India*. New Delhi: Penguin Books, 2005.

———. "An Islamist Approach to Inter-Faith Dialogue: The Jama'at-i Islami of India." *Qalandar* (2003).

———. *Sacred Spaces: Exploring Traditions of Shared Faith in India*. New Delhi: Penguin India, 2003.

Simmel, Georg. *Conflict*. New York: Free Press, 1955 (1908).

Singer, Wendy. *Creating Histories: Oral Narratives and the Politics of History-Making*. Delhi: Oxford University Press, 1997.

Singh, Amarjit. *Punjab Divided: Politics of the Muslim League and Partition, 1935–1947*. New Delhi: Kanishka Publishers, 2001.

Singh, Attar, ed. *Socio-Cultural Impact of Islam on India*. Chandigarh: Panjab University Publication Bureau, 1976.

Singh, Bachan. *Fatehgarh Sahib Di Darshan*, ca. 1985.

Singh, Fauja. *History of the Punjab*. Patiala: Punjabi University Press, 1972.

———, ed. *Sirhind through the Ages*. Patiala: Punjabi University Press, 1984.

Singh, Ganda. "The Boy Martyrs of Sirhind." *Sikh Review*, December 1957.

Singh, Giani Gian. *Panth Prakash*. Amritsar: Bhai Catar Singh Jiwana Singh, 1923.

———. *Tawarikh Guru Khalsa*. Amritsar: Khalsa Naishanala Ijamsi, 1923 (1892).

Singh, Giani Kehar. *Maler Kotla Di Dard Kahani*. Ludhiana: Daftar Sandaurh, n.d.

Singh, Gurharpal. *Ethnic Conflict in India: A Case Study of Punjab*. New York: St. Martin's Press, 2000.

———. "India's Akali-Bjp Alliance." *Asian Survey* 38, no. 4 (1998).

———. "Punjab since 1984: Disorder, Order, and Legitimacy." *Asian Survey* 36, no. 4 (1996).

Singh, Gursharan. *History of Pepsu: Patiala and East Punjab States Union, 1948–1956*. Delhi: Konark Publishers, 1991.

Singh, Guru Gobind. *Zafarnama*. Translated by Darshan Singh. New Delhi: ABC Publishing House, 2000.

Singh, Harbans, and N. Gerald Barrier, ed. *Punjab Past and Present: Essays in Honor of Dr. Ganda Singh*. Patiala: Punjabi University Press, 1976.

Singh, Khushwant. *A History of the Sikhs*. Vols. 1 and 2. New Delhi: Oxford University Press, 1999.

———. *Train to Pakistan*. New York: Grove Press, 1990.

Singh, Kirpal, ed. *Select Documents on Partition of Punjab-1947: India and Pakistan: Punjab, Haryana, and Himachal-India and Punjab-Pakistan*. Delhi: National Book Shop, 1991.

Singh, Kuldip. "Baba Ram Singh and the Namdhari Movement." Master's thesis, Guru Nanak Dev University, 1987.

Singh, Mohinder. "Akalis and the Nationalist Politics." In *Five Punjabi Centuries*, edited by Indu Banga. Delhi: Manohar, 1997.

Singh, Nikky-Guninder Kaur. *The Name of My Beloved*. New Delhi: Penguin Books, 1995.

Singh, Pashaura, and N. Gerald Barrier, ed. *Sikh Identity: Continuity and Change*. New Delhi: Manohar, 1999.

Singh, Pritam, and Shinder Singh Thandi, ed. *Punjabi Identity in Global Context*. New Delhi: Oxford University Press, 1999.

Singh, Puran. *The Victory of Faith or the Story of the Martyrdom of the Four Sons of Shri Guru Gobind Singh*. Amritsar: Khalsa Agency, 1908.

Singh, Ranbir. *Glimpses of the Divine Masters*. New Delhi: International Traders Corporation, 1965.

Singh, Sahib. *Guru Gobind Singh*. Jullundur: Raj Publications, 1967.

Singh, Sohan. *Life and Exploits of Banda Singh Bahadur*. Patiala: Punjabi University Press, 2000.

Singh, Teja, and Ganda Singh. *A Short History of the Sikhs*. Bombay: Orient Longman, 1950.

Sinha-Kerkhoff, Kathinka. *The Dangers of Memory and Endangered Memory: Partition Memory and Memory of Muslims in Jharkhand, India*. Jharkhand: Asian Development Research Institute, 2002.

Smith, Grace Martin, and Carl W. Ernst, ed. *Manifestations of Sainthood in Islam*. Istanbul: Isis Press, 1993.

Smith, Jane Idleman, and Yvonne Yazbeck Haddad. *The Islamic Understanding of Death and Resurrection*. Albany: State University of New York Press, 1981.

Smith, Jonathan Z. *To Take Place: Toward Theory in Ritual*. Chicago: University of Chicago Press, 1987.

Srivastava, Sushil. *The Disputed Mosque: A Historical Inquiry*. New Delhi: Vistaar Publications, 1991.

Stewart, Kathleen. "On the Politics of Cultural Theory: A Case for 'Contaminated' Cultural Critique." *Social Research* 58, no. 2 (1991).

Stewart, Tony. "In Search of Equivalence: Conceiving the Muslim-Hindu Encounter through Translation Theory." *History of Religions* 40, no. 3 (2001): 260–87.

———. "Satya Pir." In *Religions of India in Practice*, edited by Donald Lopez. Princeton: Princeton University Press.

Subhan, John A. *Sufism: Its Shrines and Saints*. New York: Samuel A. Weiser, 1970 (1938).

Suhrawardi, Abu al-Najib. *A Sufi Rule for Novices: Kitab Adab Al-Muridin*. Edited by Menahem Milson. Cambridge, MA: Harvard University Press, 1975.

Suhrawardi, 'Umar ibn Muhammad. *The Awarif Ul-Ma'arif*. Translated by H. Wilberforce Clark. Lahore: Sh. Muhammad Ashraf, 1973.

Sultana, Anila. "The Agrarian Structure and the Muslims of Malerkotla." *Punjab History Conference* 25 (1992): 258–62.

———. "Hierarchical Change in the Muslim Society of Malerkotla in the Post-Independence Period." *Punjab History Conference* 27 (1995): 206–11.

———. "Muslim Institutions and Organisations in Malerkotla and Their Impact on the Muslim Community." *Punjab History Conference* 28 (1996): 263–70.

———. "Muslims of Malerkotla: A Study in Social and Cultural Change 1947–91." PhD diss., Punjabi University, 1993.

———. "Status of Women in Muslim Society of Malerkotla." *Punjab History Conference* 26 (1994): 266–73.

Suri, Anand Mohan, and Hari Das Suri, eds. *An Exhaustive and up-to-Date Punjab Digest: Civil, Criminal and Revenue, 1931–38*. 3 vols. Lahore: P.L.R. Office, 1938.

Talbot, I. A. Introduction to *Partition and Genocide: Manifestation of Violence in Punjab, 1937–1947*, by Anders Bjørn Hansen (New Delhi: India Research Press, 2002).

———. "The 1946 Punjab Elections." *Modern Asian Studies* 14, no. 1 (1980).

Tambiah, Stanley J. *Leveling Crowds: Ethnonationalist Conflicts and Collective Violence in South Asia*. New Delhi: Vistaar Publications, 1996.

Taussig, Michael. "Viscerality, Faith, and Skepticism: Another Theory of Magic." In *In Near Ruins: Cultural Theory at the End of the Century*, edited by Nicholas B. Dirks. Minneapolis: University of Minnesota Press, 1998.

Taylor, Charles. *The Ethics of Authenticity*. Cambridge, MA: Harvard University Press, 1991.

———. *Multiculturalism and "the Politics of Recognition."* Princeton, NJ: Princeton University Press, 1992.

———. *The Secular Age.* Cambridge, MA: Belknap Press, 2007.

———. *Sources of the Self: The Making of Modern Identity.* Cambridge, MA: Harvard University Press, 1989.

Taylor, Christopher. *In the Vicinity of the Righteous: Ziyara and the Veneration of Muslim Saints in Late Medieval Egypt.* Leiden: Brill, 1999.

Telford, Hamish. "The Political Economy of Punjab: Creating Space for Sikh Militancy." *Asian Survey* 32, no. 11 (1992).

Temple, Richard Carmac. *Legends of the Punjab.* Vols. 1–3. Patiala: Languages Department.

Thapar, Romila. "Communalism and the Historical Legacy: Some Facets." *Social Scientist* 18, nos. 6/7, 1990.

———. *Narratives and the Making of History.* New Delhi: Oxford University Press, 2000.

Trimingham, J. Spencer. *The Sufi Orders in Islam.* Oxford: Oxford University Press, 1998 (1971).

Trix, Frances. *Spiritual Discourses: Learning with an Islamic Master.* Philadelphia: University of Pennsylvania Press, 1993.

Troll, Christian W., ed. *Muslim Shrines in India: Their Character, History and Significance.* Delhi: Oxford University Press, 1989.

Turner, Victor. "Death and the Dead in the Pilgrimage Process." In *Religious Encounters with Death: Insights from the History and Anthropology of Religions*, edited by Frank Reynolds. University Park: Pennsylvania State University Press, 1977.

Tuteja, K.L. "The Punjab Hindu Sabha and Communal Politics, 1906–1923." In *Five Punjabi Centuries*, edited by Indu Banga. New Delhi: Manohar, 1997.

Uddin, Sufia. *Constructing Bangladesh: Religion, Ethnicity, and Language in an Islamic Nation.* Chapel Hill: University of North Carolina Press, 2006.

Ury, William. *The Third Side: Why We Fight and How We Can Stop.* New York: Penguin, 1999.

Usmani, Mufti Fazl-ur-Rehman Hilal. *The Islamic Law: Marriage, Divorce, Inheritance.* Malerkotla: Darus Salam Islamic Centre, 2000.

———. *Memaar-E-Insaniyat.* Malerkotla: Jamia' Dar-us-Salam, 1991.

van der Veer, Peter. "God Must Be Liberated." *Modern Asian Studies* 21, no. 2 (1987): 283–301.

———. *Gods on Earth: The Management of Religious Experience and Identity in a North Indian Pilgrimage Center.* London: Athlone Press, 1988.

———. "Playing or Praying: A Sufi Saint's Day in Surat." *Journal of Asian Studies* 51, no. 3 (1992): 545–64.

———. *Religious Nationalism: Hindus and Muslims in India.* Berkeley: University of California Press, 1994.

———, and Hartmut Lehmann, ed. *Nation and Religion: Perspectives on Europe and Asia.* Princeton, NJ: Princeton University Press, 1999.

Varshney, Ashutosh. *Ethnic Conflict and Civic Life: Hindus and Muslims in India.* New Haven, CT: Yale University Press, 2002.

———. "Ethnic Conflict and Civil Society: India and Beyond." *World Politics* 53 (April 2001): 362–98.

Vauchez, André, ed. *Lieux Sacrés, Lieux De Culte, Sanctuaires: Approches Terminologiques, Méthodologiques, Historiques Et Monographiques*. Rome: Ecole française de Rome, 2000.

Virdee, Pippa. "Partition and Locality: The Differential Impact of Violence in British-Administered India and Princely India: The Cases of Malerkotla and Ahmedgarh." Paper presented at the European Conference on Modern South Asian Studies, Heidelberg University, September 2002.

Walia, Ramesh. *Praja Mandal Movement in East Punjab States*. Patiala: Punjabi University Press, 1972.

Werbner, Pnina, and Helene Basu, ed. *Embodying Charisma: Modernity, Locality and the Performance of Emotion in Sufi Cults*. London: Routledge, 1998.

White, Hayden. *The Content of the Form: Narrative Discourse and Historical Representation*. Baltimore. Johns Hopkins University Press, 1987.

Wikeley, J. M. *Punjabi Musalmans*. Delhi: Manohar, 1991 (1915).

Wilkinson, Steven. "Consociation Theory and Ethnic Violence." *Asian Survey* 40, no. 5 (2000).

———. *Votes and Violence: Electoral Competition and Ethnic Riots in India*. New York: Cambridge University Press, 2004.

Wink, Andre. *Al-Hind: The Making of the Indo-Islamic World*. Vol. 1: *Early Medieval India and the Expansion of Islam, Seventh to Eleventh Centuries*. Leiden: E. J. Brill, 1990.

———. *Al-Hind: The Making of the Indo-Islamic World*. Vol. 2: *The Slave Kings and the Islamic Conquest, Eleventh to Thirteenth Centuries*. Leiden: E. J. Brill, 1990.

Zafar, Rukhsana. *Disturbances in the Punjab: 1947—A Compilation of Official Documents*. Islamabad: National Documentation Centre, 1995.

Zafar, Shoaib. "Muslim Perceptions of the Ayodhya Incident." Master's thesis, Punjabi University, 1994.

Zaman, Muhammad Qasim. *The Ulama in Contemporary Islam: Custodians of Change*. Princeton, NJ: Princeton University Press, 2002.

Zubairy, Mohammad Khalid. *Malerkotla itihas ke darpan me*. Malerkotla: Tarkash Publications, 2000.

Index